DIGITAL
DISCIPLINES

The Wiley CIO series provides information, tools, and insights to IT executives and managers. The products in this series cover a wide range of topics that supply strategic and implementation guidance on the latest technology trends, leadership, and emerging best practices.

Titles in the Wiley CIO series include:

Leading the Epic Revolution: How CIOs Drive Innovation and Create Value Across the Enterprise by Hunter Muller

Managing Electronic Records: Methods, Best Practices, and Technologies by Robert F. Smallwood

On Top of the Cloud: How CIOs Leverage New Technologies to Drive Change and Build Value Across the Enterprise by Hunter Muller

Straight to the Top: CIO Leadership in a Mobile, Social, and Cloud-based World (Second Edition) by Gregory S. Smith

Strategic IT: Best Practices for Managers and Executives by Arthur M. Langer and Lyle Yorks

Trust and Partnership: Strategic IT Management for Turbulent Times by Robert Benson, Piet Ribbers, and Ronald Billstein

Transforming IT Culture: How to Use Social Intelligence, Human Factors, and Collaboration to Create an IT Department That Outperforms by Frank Wander

Unleashing the Power of IT: Bringing People, Business, and Technology Together, Second Edition by Dan Roberts

The U.S. Technology Skills Gap: What Every Technology Executive Must Know to Save America's Future by Gary J. Beach

Founded in 1807, John Wiley & Sons is the oldest independent publishing company in the United States. With offices in North America, Europe, Asia, and Australia, Wiley is globally committed to developing and marketing print and electronic products and services for our customers' professional and personal knowledge and understanding.

DIGITAL DISCIPLINES

ATTAINING MARKET LEADERSHIP VIA THE CLOUD, BIG DATA, SOCIAL, MOBILE, AND THE INTERNET OF THINGS

Joe Weinman

Mike,

Marina thought you would enjoy this book. Happy to autograph it for her for you - hope you like it!

All the best,
Joe Weinman

WILEY

Published by John Wiley & Sons, Inc., Hoboken, New Jersey.
Published simultaneously in Canada.

For general information on our other products and services or for technical support, please contact our Customer Care Department within the United States at (800) 762-2974, outside the United States at (317) 572-3993 or fax (317) 572-4002.

Wiley publishes in a variety of print and electronic formats and by print-on-demand. Some material included with standard print versions of this book may not be included in e-books or in print-on-demand. If this book refers to media such as a CD or DVD that is not included in the version you purchased, you may download this material at http://booksupport.wiley.com. For more information about Wiley products, visit www.wiley.com.

Library of Congress Cataloging-in-Publication Data

Weinman, Joe, 1958-
  Digital disciplines : attaining market leadership via the cloud, big data, social, mobile, and the internet of things / Joe Weinman.
        pages cm. – (Wiley CIO series)
  Includes index.
    ISBN 978-1-118-99539-6 (hardback) – ISBN 978-1-119-03988-4 (ePDF) – ISBN 978-1-119-03987-7 (ePub) 1. Internet marketing. 2. Leadership. 3. Customer services. I. Title.
  HF5415.1265W4525 2015
  658.8' 72–dc23
                                        2015018222

COVER DESIGN: WILEY
COVER IMAGE: ©ISTOCK.COM/PETAR CHERNAEV

Printed in the United States of America

10 9 8 7 6 5 4 3 2 1

"Dedicated to Mom and Dad"

CONTENTS

CHAPTER **4** Digital Technologies 51

PART TWO—Information Excellence

CHAPTER **5** Operations and Information 65

CHAPTER **6** The Discipline of Information Excellence 83

PART THREE—Solution Leadership

PART FIVE—Accelerated Innovation

PART SIX—Successful Execution

PART SEVEN—What's Next?

CHAPTER 21 Looking Forward   329

FOREWORD

Marketplace success is much sought after, but hard to achieve. In most industries, only a handful of firms manage to outperform the majority of their contenders. Their shining results make them stand out—in terms of customer appeal, financial results, or growth prospects. Yet even they are subject to decline in a turbulent world where customer power and buyers' demands are mounting relentlessly.

Attaining market leadership is no sinecure. This was already evident some 20 years ago in the research that led to my coauthored book *The Discipline of Market Leaders*, a #1 bestseller that was published in 18 languages. The fundamental and lasting truth exemplified by the market-leading companies featured in that work, as well as the many outperformers I have studied since, is that they succeeded by not being all things to all people. Instead, they developed and honed the discipline to deliver unsurpassed value to particular customer segments on just those dimensions most pertinent to these customers—such as best total cost, best solutions, or best products. On top of that, they recognized the imperative to provide better value year after year in order to sustain their appeal to ravenous and switch-prone customers—whether through faster, cheaper, and better offerings, special treatment, or otherwise.

Then as well as now, customers want more—and they want to be delighted and surprised. Today nothing has more power to surprise than the digital juggernaut that is transforming marketplaces around the world.

In my research 20 years ago, the Internet barely registered as a crucial component of market leadership. The word *internetworking* appeared just once in my book, and the term *digital* did not come up at all. How things have changed. Today, technology is a pervasive strategic force in any market-leading company that I know, and is getting recognized as such in a rapidly growing number of other firms. In light of that, it is no surprise that as of April 2015, the world's highest-ranking companies by stock market capitalization were Apple and Google, with Microsoft, Facebook, Oracle, and Amazon not far behind, and that most of the fastest-growing enterprises can be found in the digital field.

Considering the rampant growth and importance of digital capabilities, Joe Weinman's *Digital Disciplines* could not be more timely. The immense merit of his work lies in illuminating how the dizzying array of current and emerging digital technologies are shaping and transforming the ways that companies create better customer value and, hence, attain market leadership. His insights and case studies provide a blueprint for companies of all sizes in all industries to upgrade their strategies so as to compete effectively in the digital era. The connection of his four digital disciplines with the enduring disciplines of market leaders that were outlined in my earlier book is uncanny. To me, *Digital Disciplines* shows how technology is super-charging the way customer value gets created. Weinman, in effect, is putting my original disciplines on steroids.

Digital Disciplines provides rich and interesting detail as to technology's potential and impact on customer strategy. Even with a pretty good grasp of the subject matter, I found the book eye-opening, especially in terms of the multitude of possibilities it covers that are worth exploring, and the dangers that could befall those who do not fully appreciate the necessities of the digital era.

Fred Wiersema
Customer Strategist, Chair of the B2B Leadership Board,
Institute for the Study of Business Markets at Penn State, and
coauthor of the top-selling *The Discipline of Market Leaders*

PREFACE

In 1993, two management consultants named Michael Treacy and Fred Wiersema wrote a popular *Harvard Business Review* article titled "Customer Intimacy and Other Value Disciplines." They further detailed their insights in the best-selling *The Discipline of Market Leaders*. Based on a multiyear study of dozens of companies, they argued that to be successful, firms needed to create unique value for customers through operational excellence, product leadership, or customer intimacy.

Operational excellence focuses on developing differentiated processes, for example, those that offer lower prices or greater convenience. For example, Dell had rethought the PC business, replacing store-based channels that pushed standard make-to-stock configurations with a direct-to-consumer model for assemble-to-order products, increasing convenience while lowering price-points.

Product leadership involves leading-edge products and services. Treacy and Wiersema highlighted Johnson & Johnson's Vistakon unit, which rapidly acquired the rights to and scaled up production of an innovative disposable contact lens technology branded Acuvue.

Customer intimacy entails better relationships, driven by a deep understanding of customer problems and a willingness to solve them, enabled by flexible processes, systems, people, and culture. Treacy and Wiersema pointed out that Home Depot clerks are happy to spend whatever time a customer needs to solve a home repair problem; the same for IBM sales teams.

The insights of the value disciplines approach are as true today as they were then, but the implementation details have changed—significantly. Treacy and Wiersema were well aware of the opportunities inherent in information technology, highlighting, for example, how General Electric used a system called "Direct Connect" to enable independent dealers to utilize a stockless distribution model and sell from virtual inventory, simultaneously giving GE better visibility into customer orders, dealers higher profits, and customers better service.

However, the IT of that era largely involved enterprise systems. The web was in its infancy and mobile data was nonexistent. Now we live in an era where even three-year-olds play with smartphones and tablets more powerful than the mightiest supercomputers of those bygone times. Today, the Internet permeates our lives, with massive bandwidth increases enabling new services, such as home movie streaming and mobile social networking. Sensors can detect heartbeats and tremors, GPS can track vehicles, the cloud can apply sophisticated algorithms against enormous sets of not just numerical data, but videos, speech, and images.

This book attempts to answer a simple question: How should the Treacy and Wiersema value disciplines framework be updated for this new world of cloud computing, big data and analytics, social networks, broadband wireless and wireline connections, and smart, connected things ranging from thermostats to jet planes? In other words, how do digital technologies impact value disciplines to become digital disciplines?

Simply put: Everything stays the same, yet everything changes.

Better processes can still drive a competitive edge, but mere (physical) operational excellence is no longer sufficient. It must be enabled, complemented, and extended through *information excellence*, including real-time dynamic optimization algorithms and the seamless fusion of physical and virtual worlds.

Better products and services are still desirable, but it is no longer sufficient to improve a standalone product. Today, products are not just digital and smart but connect to back-end cloud services, and from there onward to social networks and infinitely extensible ecosystems. The same goes for the physical embodiment of services—for example, healthcare services increasingly involve pills, pacemakers, and equipment connected to patient data repositories, diagnostic systems, and hospital asset management systems.

Better customer relationships are no longer just about caring, empathetic customer service employees or dedicated account teams willing to spend time on the golf course to get to know the customer. They are also about better meeting each individual customer's needs, by deriving subtle insights based on big data from all customers collectively. Examples include upsell /cross-sell in retail, more targeted recommendations in entertainment, and personalized medicine.

Finally, in today's hypercompetitive world, innovation is a critical imperative: delivering higher-quality results, faster, and more cost-effectively. Innovation encompasses not just products and services but also processes and relationships, and can benefit from new cloud-enabled constructs such as idea markets and challenges, which extend the innovation team beyond the company to the entire world.

After researching dozens of firms, the successful ones all seem to have exploited one or more of these themes; the fallen ones have largely failed to do so. Amazon.com versus Borders, Netflix versus Blockbuster, Wikipedia versus *Encyclopedia Brittanica*, WhatsApp versus telco-based texting, and dozens of other cautionary tales offer object lessons in harnessing information technology to disrupt and reimagine industries and outmaneuver competitors, or be overtaken by those who can.

This book offers what I hope will be valuable insights to boards and senior executives such as CEOs, CIOs, CDOs, CFOs, and CMOs (chief executive, information, innovation, digital, financial, and marketing officers), middle management, and line personnel in and outside of information technology. It is a book squarely at the intersection of business and technology, yet largely nontechnical. In a world where virtually all consumers are digital natives or digital immigrants, IT is no longer the province of the glass-house datacenter but an important weapon that virtually any enterprise—in business or government—must wield to be successful.

An implicit theme of the book is that winners win, not just due to random luck, but due to repeatable, structured principles. These principles align with and complement each other. For example, a focus on customer outcomes requires a continuous relationship with the customer, one that is hard to achieve with a standalone product, but one that can be enabled through a connected solution.

The book is structured to be readable from cover to cover, yet each chapter is also self-contained. As a by-product, this necessitates a bit of repetition. The book provides an introduction to some key technologies for those who are more business oriented, and an introduction to some key business strategy concepts for those who are more technology oriented.

The first few chapters provide an overview of the key insights in the book, background on Treacy and Wiersema's value disciplines framework and related strategy models, a more detailed overview of the digital disciplines, and an overview of the five key technologies—cloud, data, social, networks, and things—which, together, are the enabling platform for this new wave of competitive strategies.

Following the introductory and overview matter, there are four main sections, one to address each of the four digital disciplines: information excellence, solution leadership, collective intimacy, and accelerated innovation. Each section has three chapters: an introduction or refresher on essential background ideas such as Porter's Five Forces model or the elements of innovation, the key themes and trends defining the discipline, and a specific case study. Case studies for Burberry, Nike, Netflix, Procter & Gamble, and General Electric provide real examples of how companies are applying the disciplines.

Because successful execution and customer adoption happen largely through people, two chapters focus on human behavior and gamification; one addresses general principles, the other provides a case study on Opower, a company that is heavily leveraging principles of human motivation in conjunction with information technology to simultaneously achieve customer, business, and societal objectives.

Finally, as with any initiative, there can be challenges and caveats in successful implementation. These range from strategic alignment and project management to concerns over privacy and security.

Technology marches forward. Twitter, Facebook, Instagram, WhatsApp, Snapchat, iPads, iPhones, and many of the other elements of the modern digital age didn't exist a few years ago, and change is speeding up, not slowing down. The last chapter addresses technologies on the horizon, and offers thoughts on how to apply the book's insights.

I have attempted to capture the intent of what Treacy and Wiersema eloquently and insightfully articulated, but it's hard to interpret one's own thoughts two decades later, much less someone else's. Any errors or misinterpretations are, of course, my fault.

It is a standing curse on books like these that companies that are held up as paragons can succumb to market turbulence, which has done nothing but increase, in no small part due to information technologies. In fact, during the time it took to write this book, the companies highlighted have adjusted strategies, divested brands, made acquisitions, discontinued products and initiatives, and faced new global competitors. However, the case studies represent a point-in-time snapshot of the issues, approaches, and successes of real companies facing turbulent markets, applying the strategies herein.

A number of books covering strategy and information technology oriented toward a leadership audience provide principles and detail themes such as empowerment and transparency. I'm sure these are well reasoned, but they don't seem to provide clear direction to leaders in industries facing increasing competition and the threat of digital disruption. It's my hope that the insights in the following pages can provide you with a framework with which to pursue a focused digital strategy and attain market leadership in your industry.

Joe Weinman
June 2015

ACKNOWLEDGMENTS

The most important acknowledgment is surely to Michael Treacy and Fred Wiersema, who created a clear yet powerful framework for attaining competitive advantage while driving customer value. Without their original and compelling insights, this book wouldn't exist.

The next major acknowledgment is to all of the global innovators at companies large and small, old and new, who, in leading their organizations, have created such a rich set of case studies from which I could elicit points to illustrate and expand my thesis. As detailed in the book, this includes CEOs and key executives such as Angela Ahrendts (now at Apple), Christopher Bailey, and John Douglas at Burberry, Jeffrey Immelt, Bill Ruh, and Darin DiTommaso at General Electric, Reed Hastings and Todd Yellin at Netflix, Mark Parker and Stefan Olander at Nike, A.G. Lafley at Procter & Gamble, and Dan Yates and Alex Kinnier at Opower, as well as the leaders and innovators at the dozens of companies mentioned in the book ranging from Amazon.com to Zappos.

I'd also like to acknowledge helpful fact checks and support for interviewing executives from the companies highlighted in the case study chapters. This includes support from Joris Evers at Netflix, Holly Gilthorpe and Jennifer Villarreal at GE, Carly Llewellyn, Margot Littlehale, and Melissa Roberts at Opower, and their counterparts at Burberry, Nike, and P&G. I'd also like to thank the peer reviewers who provided helpful feedback and sanity checks on clarity and content: Tim Horan, Dawn Leaf, Jonathan Murray, Steve Sims, and especially Marla Bradstock. Needless to say, I am responsible for any remaining errors or inaccuracies.

A project like this can't come to fruition without a publisher able to appreciate the potential of a concept and demonstrate great flexibility. I have been fortunate to work again with the editorial and production team at John Wiley & Sons, including Sheck Cho, Stacey Rivera, Maria Sunny Zacharias, and Brandon Dust.

PART ONE

Overview and Background

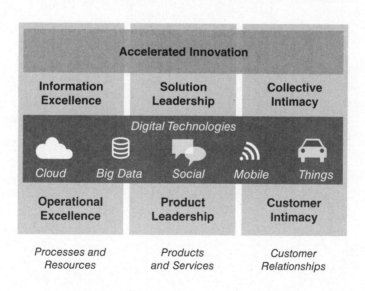

CHAPTER 1

Digital Disciplines, Strategic Supremacy

On January 24, 1848, James W. Marshall, a carpenter from New Jersey, was helping to build a lumber mill on the American River near Sacramento when he noticed a twinkle in the water. It was the gold nugget that launched the Gold Rush, which, in turn, led to a population explosion and rapid statehood for California as fortune hunters and their suppliers—selling picks, shovels, food, libations, and more—descended on the territory from around the globe. The nonnative population of California grew from under 1,000 at the time of Marshall's discovery to over 100,000 by the end of the next year, thanks to the influx of Forty-Niners—mostly men who left their families behind to find riches. Even when the Gold Rush ended, much of the population remained, and so did a need for business associates, families, and friends to communicate with each other across the emerging nation.

To help meet this need, the Pony Express was launched on April 3, 1860. It could deliver letters and small packages between St. Joseph, Missouri, and Sacramento in only 10 days, a breakthrough for that era. The Pony Express accomplished this feat by using a cleverly engineered system of over 150 stations, hundreds of specially selected horses, lightweight riders, specially designed lightweight saddles, and clever "hacks" such as a horn to alert an upcoming station to ready the next horse. The stations were spaced about 10 miles apart, the distance a horse could go at top speed before tiring. In what was a forerunner to today's packet-switched networks such as the Internet, a lightweight pouch containing the mail was handed off from rider to rider, each rider exchanging horses several times before being replaced himself.

On October 24, 1861—a year and a half after the Pony Express began deliveries—the first transcontinental telegraph network was completed, and in less than 48 hours the Pony Express ceased operations. Thus was a miracle of *operational excellence* supplanted by early information technology (IT) and what might be called *information excellence*. It foreshadowed the critical need to exploit IT—or be trampled and left in the dust.

From Value Disciplines to Digital Disciplines

To help companies avoid a fate like that of the Pony Express, this book delineates four *digital disciplines*—information excellence, solution leadership, collective intimacy, and accelerated innovation—by which IT can galvanize strategy, drive customer value, maximize competitive differentiation, help attain market leadership, and create wealth. The current darlings of Silicon Valley, such as Uber, Nest, Netflix, and Apple, utilize one or more of these strategies, but so can companies in other verticals and with century-old legacies.

Information excellence, as signaled by the transcontinental telegraph, exploits information technology, sophisticated algorithms, and the synthesis of digital and physical worlds to drive better asset utilization, better physical operational excellence, and better business processes: processes that are faster, more cost effective, higher quality, more flexible, more sustainable, or otherwise create differentiated value. Assets can be optimized with information through techniques such as better operations planning to reduce idle time and through predictive maintenance to reduce unplanned downtime.

Uber is a good example of information excellence: It rethought transportation processes by using mobile devices and matching algorithms, and improved asset utilization by using on-demand drivers and their vehicles. Other companies use similar approaches: Airbnb for living spaces; Topcoder for developers. Other examples of information excellence include optimized operations for package delivery firms such as UPS and at ports such as the Hamburg Port Authority and integrated online-offline omni-channel experiences at retailers such as Burberry, featured in Chapter 7.

Solution leadership represents the evolution of standalone products and services to smart, cloud-enabled product-service systems and ecosystems, where firms focus on customer outcomes, one-time sales become ongoing relationships, and competitive advantage evolves from mere product features to ecosystems, communities, and future potential. Products such as cars, thermostats, and dishwashers are being connected to the cloud, but so are services. For example, healthcare services are becoming delivered in part by medical equipment such as connected pills, pacemakers, and CT (computed tomography) scanners.

The Nest Learning Thermostat is a smart device that connects across Wi-Fi to the cloud. From there, it can be remotely controlled by a smartphone, and perhaps someday through smart electric grid demand response and dynamic-pricing based algorithms. Other examples include jet engines from GE that tie to cloud-based analytics and wearables from Nike and its partners that link to cloud services and social networks. Nike's digital strategy is covered in Chapter 10.

Collective intimacy is where independent anonymous transactions become intimate, long-term relationships thanks to "big data" analytics run on detailed customer characteristics and behavior. Relationships become win-win, and products and services become predictive, contextual, and personal.

Examples include upsell and cross-sell of products at etailers such as Amazon.com, improved retention and customer lifetime value at entertainment services such as Netflix, reviewed in Chapter 13, and improved health outcomes through personalized medicine leveraging repositories of genomic data such as at the Mayo Clinic.

Accelerated innovation enables companies to innovate products, processes, and relationships faster, cheaper, and better than their competition by complementing internal resources with ad hoc external ones, through open, external innovation, published big data sets, crowdfunding, open source, platforms and agile development, and crowdsourced challenges exploiting contest economics. Accelerated innovation may be viewed as a meta-discipline, since it can be applied to improve operations and information, products, services, and solutions and customer relationships.

Uber, Nest, and Apple are certainly innovators, but so are Netflix with its Prizes; Procter & Gamble, highlighted in Chapter 16, developing its next billion-dollar blockbuster brand through a combination of internal and external innovation; and GE with its Quests, featured in Chapter 17.

Most of these companies are doing something in each discipline, but GE is applying all four disciplines across its numerous businesses. Opower, a company that is also arguably pursuing all the disciplines, is an interesting case of a company whose strategy is based on applying gamification—leveraging behavioral economics and human cognitive biases—to the business of reducing energy consumption, and is overviewed in Chapter 19.

Immense wealth is being created through the strategic, disruptive application of information technologies in these ways, or lost through the failure to do so successfully: consider Netflix vs. Blockbuster, Wikipedia vs. *Encyclopedia Britannica*, Amazon.com vs. Borders, Yelp vs. Zagat, Facebook's WhatsApp vs. cellular service providers' text messaging services, Uber vs. taxis, or Google vs. any number of newspapers. Upstart startups have overtaken established brands, seemingly overnight. The digital disciplines offer a blueprint for new companies to disrupt current ways of doing business as well as for established firms to reinvent themselves via compelling, digitally enabled value propositions.

Digital disciplines are the latest incarnation of a popular strategy framework—called *value disciplines*—originally developed by Michael Treacy and Fred Wiersema 20 years ago in their seminal article for the *Harvard*

Business Review titled "Customer Intimacy and Other Value Disciplines"[1] and their bestselling book *The Discipline of Market Leaders*.[2] They proposed three value disciplines: *operational excellence* (i.e., better processes), *product leadership* (i.e., better products and services), and *customer intimacy* (i.e., better customer relationships).

Treacy and Wiersema argued that companies should ideally pursue one discipline, and that different companies can dominate different niches in the same industry by pursuing different value disciplines. Consider retailing: Wal-Mart offers convenience and low cost through operational excellence, including a global store footprint and optimized logistics; Tiffany offers product leadership by selling high quality objects of desire in elegant settings; Amazon's Zappos unit competes on customer service and relationships.

Treacy and Wiersema's insights are timeless, but the ascendance of information technologies—including the cloud, big data, social, mobile, and the Internet of Things—enables disruptive applications of the value disciplines approach which couldn't have been anticipated at the dawn of the Internet era, when the cloud was an atmospheric phenomenon, a social was a mixer, cell phones were bricks, and online meant dial-up.

Fortunately, the Treacy and Wiersema framework permits digital extension, evolution, and elaboration. As just one example, customer intimacy implied dedicated, onsite account teams in business markets and a personal touch in consumer markets: think avuncular corner butchers or personable sales clerks. In other words, customer intimacy required an organizational, people-based, cultural approach. Today, it is just as likely to entail applying sophisticated algorithms to customer transaction or other data to provide offers that maximize customer satisfaction, consumer and business customer outcomes, retention, and profitability through upsell/cross-sell and reduced churn. IT is increasingly, inexorably, inextricably intertwined with the creation and delivery of customer value. And we are just at the beginning of this digitally enabled journey.

Market leadership based on implementing these strategies can be measured in terms of traditional business metrics such as market share, revenue, profitability, labor productivity, and return on invested capital. One study[3] showed that a dollar invested in IT returned almost two, mostly through revenue growth rather than cost reduction. Moreover, this return was substantially higher than investments in R&D (research and development) or marketing, making it somewhat ironic that marketing budgets are currently[4] three times larger and growing twice as fast as IT budgets, although the CMO (chief marketing officer) is increasingly funding digital initiatives due to their strategic importance.

However, the benefits of the digital disciplines can also be measured in terms of environmental, community, and societal benefits. For example,

IT can reduce carbon footprints through substitution, such as when videoconferences replace physical travel; synchronization, as with electricity demand response; and reuse, as with collaborative consumption, sometimes called the *sharing economy*.

Or consider Ushahidi CrowdMap, a cloud-based application that has helped increase the transparency of Kenyan elections and the effectiveness of Haitian earthquake relief. The Arab Spring reached critical mass largely due to Twitter and Facebook. Basic mobile phones have increased the transparency and efficiency of fish markets in Kerala, India, increasing the availability of fish to consumers, and of incomes to fisherman.[5] While success for most businesses might be defined by profitability or market share, for a nonprofit or enlightened corporation it can (also) be measured through the achievement of social goals and alignment with values. Rather than—or in addition to—being profit-maximizing, author Dan Pink calls these organizations "purpose-maximizing."[6]

Information Excellence

Although implementation details of the four digital disciplines of necessity vary in their application across industry verticals and by firm, as generic competitive strategies, they are easy to understand.

Information excellence is not shorthand for data quality, but the employment of comprehensive real-time information, predictive analytics, dynamic optimization, and integrated virtual and physical operations to implement better business processes and to better use assets.

"Better" as perceived by customers in terms of quality and performance. "Better" in terms of financial metrics, such as returns on invested capital through better asset utilization. "Better" in seamlessly integrating the virtual and physical worlds of information and operations. "Better" in terms of activities, process design, and rightsizing assets—doing things right—and outcomes—doing the right things. "Better" as in faster, cheaper, more flexible, higher quality, more reliable, more convenient, easier to use, more available, or more sustainable. "Better" as in making better decisions; executing those decisions with higher likelihood of success; and doing it all faster than the competition. Business processes are not limited to internal back-office constructs, but extend to customers, customers' customers, and end-users, as well as to supply chain partners and other stakeholders.

Businesses can exploit information throughout virtually all processes. Which customers should be targeted with promotions? Which services are most profitable and should receive incremental marketing investments? Which direct mail layout results in the greatest response rate? Which products will sell the most this season and thus should be inventoried to minimize stock-outs? Those are obvious kinds of questions that big data and predictive analytics can help answer. But it isn't just sales, marketing, or supply chain optimization. How about whose air conditioner should be lowered or shut off to avoid brown-outs? Which of the candidates is best for this job? How fast should this train go? Which potholes should be fixed first? Is this melanoma? The essence of information excellence is acquiring data, analyzing it, synthesizing information and insight, and then making decisions and optimizing virtual and physical processes, customer experiences, and relationships.

For example, UPS plans its routes via ORION (On-Road Integrated Optimization and Navigation), which implements state-of-the-art algorithms to minimize driving distance and fuel consumption while minimizing late deliveries.[7] If an average truck needs to make 120 stops, there are 6,689,502,913,449,135,000,000,000,000,000,000,000,000,000,000,000,000, 000,000,000,000,000,000,000,000,000,000,000,000,000,000,000,000,000, 000,000,000,000,000,000,000,000,000,000,000,000,000,000,000,000,000, 000,000,000,000,000,000,000,000,000,000,000,000,000,000,000,000,000 different possible sequences of stops, not including additional options to get from one stop to the next.[8] UPS has 55,000 such routes in the United States alone, and therefore 55,000 such calculations to perform. Every day. This type of problem is obviously not amenable to human solution, and to make things even more complex, ORION needs to balance out an optimal solution with a degree of delivery consistency. UPS expects to save several hundred million dollars annually when ORION is fully deployed.

Kroger's QueVision system uses infrared cameras to track shopper arrivals, feeding a proprietary algorithm that then predicts the number of cashiers needed, reducing average wait time eightfold. And Kroger isn't just focusing on its own processes; it's also aiding consumers with theirs: a mobile app will plot out optimal paths through the store based on grocery lists.[9]

Chapter 7 will delve into Burberry, which has leveraged information excellence to achieve dramatic growth in the luxury goods industry, by offering streamed fashion shows live at stores on the world's biggest digital signage, deploying mirrors in dressing rooms that magically display runway clips of the clothing items being tried on, and by arming store personnel with a customer's purchase history on an opt-in basis to ensure fashion consistency.

Solution Leadership

Solution leadership is a broad concept encompassing extensible, adaptable, smart digital products and services connected to cloud-based capabilities and an expansive partner ecosystem including social networks, which all together offer a unique, differentiated "product-service system" that can grow exponentially—in terms of features, customer adoption, and revenues—via network effects.

The original Apple iPod was a better *product*, thanks to its innovative click wheel, elegant design, and features such as random shuffle. It was also a better *solution*, thanks to iTunes and access to a near-infinite library of songs. The Apple iPhone was a better *product*, thanks to its innovative touchscreen, elegant design, and ease of use. It was a better *solution*, thanks to the App Store and the third-party app developer community. Thanks to network effects, more customers mean more apps, and more apps mean more customers. More of both mean more money: the Apple App Store crossed the $10 billion per year revenue threshold in 2013,[10] and grew another 50 percent in 2014.[11]

Services are becoming smart, digital, and connected, too: Pandora, TiVo, Netflix, and Shazam are connected services, driven by the cloud. Amazon.com is a connected retail service. But it isn't just virtual services: Domino's pizzerias are connected; the water and electric and cable utility services have points of presence such as smart meters and set-top boxes that are connected; Staples in-store copiers are connected; Uber transportation services are connected; FedEx and UPS delivery services are connected; and so on.

Products and services aren't limited to handheld devices or web applications running on PCs. BMW Group has driven past treating cars as standalone products and now views them as smart, digitalized[12] solutions that tie to a global cloud of data centers, offering solutions ranging from entertainment to real-time traffic information, access to social networks such as Facebook and Twitter and services such as Pandora and Yelp. Nike has sprinted past the idea of athletic shoes as just products, and now sees them as integrated with cloud-based activity trackers, digital coaching services, and social networks such as Facebook. GE sells aircraft engines and wind turbines, but is flying high by tying them back to engineers and customers who are fed enormous amounts of data to maximize performance and improve designs. Chapter 10 will delve into Nike's approach to solution leadership through the Nike+ flexible partner ecosystem, and Chapter 17 will examine GE in more depth.

Collective Intimacy

Firms know that social media should be a part of their strategy. Today's successful businesses are exploiting social media to engage with millions or hundreds of millions of customers, enhancing personal relationships with those customers 140 characters at a time. But collective intimacy is much more than that; at its heart it is about developing intimate, value-added relationships with every customer. Collective intimacy goes beyond mass personalization to develop a unique relationship with *each* engaged customer, based on insights derived from *all* customers using big data algorithms.

Only a few industry leaders are effectively integrating all the elements of a collective intimacy strategy—exploiting social media and communities together with customer relationship management, collection of data including not just stated preferences but also actual customer behavior, characteristics, and contexts, and using advanced algorithms to build virtually unassailable customer relationships that drive value for customers and the firm. Amazon.com is drowning its competitors, using a flood of information based on millions of customers and billions of purchases to recommend products using sophisticated algorithms. Better recommendations mean higher revenues through upsell/cross-sell, faster growth in customers, thanks to word of mouth and social selling, and higher profitability through reduced customer churn. The Mayo Clinic uses a voluminous repository of genomic, microbiomic, and epigenetic data across tens of thousands of patients to better prescribe personalized therapies for each patient. Chapter 13 will examine how Netflix uses advanced algorithms to pursue collective intimacy and thus provide better movie recommendations, increase customer satisfaction and loyalty, and maximize customer lifetime value.

Accelerated Innovation

Digital innovation is in many ways easier than physical: It can be easier to build and experiment with software than to build a full-size prototype. In either case, though, accelerated innovation uses the Internet, open innovation mechanisms such as contests, crowdsourcing, innovation networks, and idea markets, and cloud-based experimentation and platform as a service to dramatically accelerate the invention, commercialization, and adoption of improvements to processes, products, services, and solutions, and customer relationships. Netflix famously improved its *Cinematch* movie recommendation algorithm over 10 percent via an open contest, engaging scores of researchers around the world for the same cost as hiring a handful of them, and paying only upon attainment of a quantifiable improvement.[13]

Netflix then performed an encore with the Netflix OSS (Open Source Software) Cloud Prize, which used a somewhat different approach. There were multiple categories, rather than one objective. The goals were qualitative rather than quantitative. The results were dedicated to the improvement of cloud technology generally, with all entries treated as open source. Cloud computing technologies help Netflix but making them broadly available doesn't hurt Netflix's core differentiators, so an open-source approach garnered more entrants and better results.

Amazon Web Services has created challenges won by cities such as London, New York, and Asheville in implementing cloud technologies for better government; Goldcorp has run seismic analysis challenges on gold mine data to turn bankruptcy into, well, gold; Procter & Gamble complements its formidable internal R&D capability with crowdsourced and external open innovation to create new billion-dollar brands, as we'll see in Chapter 16; and GE has run them for improved airline and hospital operations, as we'll see in Chapter 17.

Exponential Value Creation

IT is an exponentially accelerating whirlwind that is feeding on itself. "Things" such as sensors, devices, equipment, vehicles, and buildings are creating an avalanche of big data, which is uploaded over networks to the immense computing resources of the cloud, which is running sophisticated algorithms to process and interpret it, linking to social networks, and driving real-time and predictive decisions implemented by people and things.

Estimates of the number of things that will be connected in the next few years range from tens of billions to trillions.[14] These estimates may seem far-fetched, but there are already billions of cell phones and smartphones in use. eReaders and tablets and PCs and smartphones and wearables and smart-watches and Wi-Fi cameras and light bulbs and toasters and refrigerators and video security cameras and digital photo frames and planes and trucks and traffic lights and who knows what else will connect to each other and the cloud over wireless (and occasionally, wired) networks. Even pills are becoming connected: the FDA-approved Proteus Pill already incorporates a wireless sensor the size of a grain of sand that signals—from inside the digestive system—when the pill has been taken.[15]

These devices, in turn, will generate massive and increasing amounts of data: purchase transactions, video streams, status updates, tracking data, oil pressure, turbine speed, and ambient temperature, on top of documents, slideshows, spreadsheets, songs, and photographs.

Data will increase in frequency and resolution. Netflix used to have a few data points for each movie: number of days out and possibly a rating. Now it knows the number of times you've watched it; on what device; at what time; where; and which scenes you've skipped or replayed. The stream used to be standard definition, then became high definition, now is becoming 4K, and eventually will be 8K, 3D, and holographic. Or consider this: reading utility meters every 15 minutes rather than monthly leads to 3,000 times more data. This means not just more data, but the ability to deduce when you are running the dishwasher or the air conditioning. The doctor used to know your gender, height, weight, temperature, and blood pressure. Then, your cholesterol and triglycerides. Now she can access your electrocardiogram or electroencephalogram on a continuous basis, not to mention your entire genome, which is about 700 megabytes.[16]

Multiply all these trends together: more devices, each generating more data, more often, and you are multiplying exponentials.

This is driving a global increase in data traffic. Wired data is growing by well into the double digits annually, but mobile data is growing at 60 percent per year.[17] Mobility is growing for many reasons, such as convenience and speed. The ability to do something *now* ties into our innate need for instant gratification, which surfaces in behavioral anomalies such as *hyperbolic discounting*, where immediate results are perceived as being of significantly higher value than those requiring a wait. And, time compression is important for businesses as well, whether to create differentiated customer value or to reduce supply chain costs such as inventory carrying costs. Consequently, the mere act of making a function available on a mobile device can be a market hit: CUNA Mutual developed a smartphone app allowing car buyers to get a loan while at the dealership—generating a billion dollars in loans in only two years.[18] Put differently, mobile *by itself* can support operational and information excellence, not to mention when used in conjunction with other technologies.

In turn, there is a need to store and process that data, helping accelerate the growth of cloud computing. Amazon Web Services, at the time of this writing the largest cloud provider, already stores trillions of "objects"—documents, photos, databases, movies, etc.—in its S3 Simple Storage Service.[19] Companies such as Amazon, Google, and Microsoft *each* are estimated to have hundreds of thousands, if not over a million servers.[20]

Underpinning it all is our innate, inescapable human need to be connected and to care about others and what they think. As UCLA professor Matt Lieberman, cofounder of a field of study called *social cognitive neuroscience*, puts it, "We are wired to be social."[21] Originating as a mammalian need for mothers and their infants to stay connected, he argues, this orientation drove language, growth in the neocortex, and ultimately *homo sapiens'* immense abilities in problem-solving, pattern detection, and collaboration. And social media is not broadcasting or marketing in a traditional sense. It is all about two-way interaction, connection, relationships, and engagement.

Social media increases the value of all four digital disciplines. It enhances collective intimacy, by strengthening bonds between company and customer. It accelerates innovation, by enabling collaboration, providing early customer and partner input into needs and wants, and supporting co-creation of solutions. Connection to social networks is often an essential part of today's leading solutions; even cars—and sharks—now connect to Facebook or Twitter. It impacts multiple touchpoints in driving information excellence, including product awareness, purchasing, delivery, use, billing, and return processes. In the old days, consumer purchasing decisions would be based on history with the vendor and word of mouth. Today, those decisions are based on vendor relationships and social selling, often created and maintained by social media, and referral marketing—that is, word of mouth, which has become word of Twitter, Foursquare, Instagram, Facebook, TripAdvisor, or Yelp.

The Leadership Agenda

The digital disciplines are not merely a matter for IT managers to squeeze in between discussions of approved mobile devices and upgrades to the email system, but a board-level agenda item. In fact, according to a recent McKinsey survey,[22] a majority of executives believe that the most important technology issue for the board to address is a strategic discussion regarding the impact of technology on the company's industry. Even the venerable *Wall Street Journal* just retitled its *Marketplace* section—after 27 years—to *Business & Tech*, explaining that " ... it's likely that your company's next CEO is currently a CIO ... "[23] If she isn't now, she will be soon: the most popular class at venerable liberal arts icon Harvard College is now "Introduction to Computer Science," handily surpassing "Principles of Economics."[24]

Unfortunately, only a quarter of CIOs self-report as true *chief* information *officers*. This minority focuses on driving innovation, aligning with the business units, and developing business strategy. A substantial fraction of the rest of CIOs are more like computing implementation organizers; managers, rather than leaders. Their focus is on IT operations improvement, systems deployment initiatives, and cost control.[25] The good news for all these CIOs and the companies that employ them is that the four digital disciplines can turn managers into leaders, cost-cutters into revenue-generators, and also-ran companies into market leaders.

Some have argued that "IT Doesn't Matter,"[26] because IT has become ubiquitous. Therefore, the thinking goes, it is accessible to all, and therefore can't be strategic, because everyone can employ it. But how could IT not matter when much of the greatest revenue growth and wealth creation globally has been through IT and IT-enabled companies: Alibaba, Amazon, Apple, Baidu, Facebook, Google, Instagram, Tencent, and Tesla? Sure, some IT doesn't matter: conference room reservation systems and expense reporting apps are probably not the key to competitive dominance.

But Mark Andreessen, one of the most successful venture capitalists,[27] serial entrepreneur and creator of Mosaic, the first usable browser, has declared that "software is eating the world."[28] He points out that newly hatched software companies are beating the incumbents: Amazon in books; Netflix in movie rentals; Apple (iTunes), Spotify and Pandora in music; Zynga (at that time) in entertainment; Shutterfly in photos; Google in direct marketing; Skype in telecom; LinkedIn in recruiting; Square and PayPal in payments.

Andreessen keenly observes, "Software is also eating much of the value chain of industries that are widely viewed as primarily existing in the real world." He points out, "In today's cars, software runs the engines, controls safety features, entertains passengers, guides drivers to destinations and connects each car to mobile, satellite, and GPS networks." And, he continues, software is critical in retail/distribution, logistics, oil and gas, agriculture, financial services, and so forth.

Mary Meeker, Internet guru and a partner at Silicon Valley's legendary venture capital firm Kleiner Perkins Caufield & Byers, calls this effect "re-imagination." In other words, longstanding industries are being rethought from the ground up. Of course, this also means that legacy players are in danger of being re-imagined into oblivion. The details of her annual Internet Trends report change each year, but the underlying message[29] doesn't: exponential growth of connectivity due to mobile and fixed broadband; exponential growth of data; previously unheard of adoption rates for new devices such as tablets and smartphones; new-age monetization through mechanisms such as mobile advertising.

Because of the effects of software and reimagination, digital strategies are now core to virtually any business and corporate initiative. This is one reason that Laura McClellan, an analyst with Gartner, the prestigious global technology research firm, predicted[30] that by 2017, the chief marketing officer will spend more on IT than the chief information officer. Although her conclusions have been fodder for debate,[31] they may not be much of a surprise to CIOs; after all, a substantial fraction of enterprise IT projects are already funded or approved by business units.[32]

A related force is the *consumerization* of IT, as employees desire the latest devices with the coolest features and the greatest flexibility at work that they already have at home. Long gone are the days when enterprises were the first to have expensive functionality such as mainframes and green-screen terminals or data communications gear, which eventually trickled down to consumers. Now enterprises eventually deploy what consumers already have.

And, the bars for usability and user experience have been raised by rich, elegant interfaces incorporated into today's leading consumer devices. It's not just usability, but engagement. The same tricks that make games so addictive are being applied to business applications as well.[33] Elements such as points, scorecards, badges, leaderboards, challenges, puzzles, reputation rankings, and progress feedback via levels and maps hit us in primal brain systems, as research in psychology, behavioral economics, and neuroscience has shown. By building these elements into products, processes, relationships, and applications—called *gamification*—companies can benefit through greater adoption and engagement, as we'll see in Chapter 18. We'll also take a look at Opower in Chapter 19, a company that is applying gamification to electricity consumption.

Information Technology in Context

All that notwithstanding, let us admit that IT isn't the only factor in competitive strategy. I purchase my groceries at Shop-Rite, not because its cash registers have patented, proprietary algorithms running on an advanced computing architecture but because it is the closest grocery store to me and its avocados seem to stay fresh a couple of days longer than those from the competition. So, let's clarify the context in which IT and thus digital disciplines matter.

At a high level, CEOs have a broad variety of tactics at their disposal. Going public, going private. Divestitures, mergers, and acquisitions. Global expansion, local focus. Cost-cutting, leasebacks, hedging, reverse takeovers, tax inversions, downsizing, and rightsizing. Stock sales, stock buybacks. Financial engineering, debt restructuring, organizational restructuring. Hiring, firing, training, compensation, and retention. Out-tasking, outsourcing, offshoring, onshoring, reshoring, insourcing.

Although these tactics may be helpful, they are not the essence of growth. Even a company that grows through acquisition has to acquire companies that are or can be successful. Companies need to look to innovations in business models, distribution, customer relationships, design, branding, endorsements, certifications, regulatory policies, positioning.

And, technology, of course.

But even if we restrict ourselves to technology, there are many technologies, not just IT. Nanotechnology is inventing new materials such as carbon nanotubes with unprecedented strength-to-weight ratios. Biotech is creating breakthroughs in everything from pest-resistant plants to new medical treatments. Chemistry breakthroughs are enabling new battery technologies and the manufacture of plastic literally from thin air.[34]

Even within IT, for every elegantly crafted application, there are many applications that are convoluted, unusable, late, overbudget, insecure, intrusive, or don't scale. Applications that ask you to press "3" for this and "#" for that or that offer cryptic Zen koans such as "Error: Unspecified Error." We'll address these issues and gotchas in Chapter 20.

Finally, let us admit that technology itself—information or otherwise—does not directly correlate with profitability at the industry level.

On the one hand, for example, one of the highest-technology industries is surely airlines. Computationally complex operational processes for global scheduling of crews and flights; modern jet airliners made of carbon composite frames and titanium alloy turbine blades; state-of-the-art dynamic pricing systems. These are complex amalgams of physics, aerodynamics, control systems, entertainment systems, navigational systems, information technology, and who knows what else. Yet, as strategy guru Michael Porter points out,[35] airlines are among the *least* profitable of all industries. Porter's Five Forces model—rivalry among competitors, threat of new entrants, threat of substitutes, bargaining power of customers, and bargaining power of suppliers—explains why.

On the other hand, the soft drink industry, which, after all, is just selling sweetened water—a century-old "technology," if one could call it that—is among the most profitable industries.

However, the point is not that higher information technology investments automatically lead to higher profitability. The point is that within a given industry and its profitability envelope, technology in general, and information technology in particular, *can* enhance performance and profitability relative to competitors. It can also enable new means of creating customer value, create barriers to entry, and reduce the appeal of substitutes.

We live in an era of immense technological change, thanks to the confluence of key technologies such as connected things, cloud computing, and social networks. While traditional elements of competition, such as brand and distribution channels, are still important, information technologies can be ignored only at the risk of ending up like Blockbuster and Borders, overtaken by new, digitally savvy entrants such as Netflix and Amazon.com. Ignore IT and risk irrelevance or death; exploit it and survive or thrive. This is true across verticals: healthcare, manufacturing, consumer packaged goods, aerospace, pharmaceuticals, and so forth.

Regardless of the vertical that your company is in, whether it's old or new, legacy or startup, SMB (small/medium business), Fortune 500, government, university, or garage shop, B2B (business to business), B2C (business to consumer), G2C (government to citizen), P2P (peer to peer), or X2X (anything to anything), understanding and applying one or more of these disciplines is likely to be vital for survival and growth. You don't need to be a hip Web 2.0 company to exploit these insights; many of the examples in this book come from century-old manufacturers who are transforming their processes, products, relationships, and innovation.

While there is no silver bullet, the same patterns—the digital disciplines—keep repeating across winners in these industries, and while they don't offer a simple recipe for success, they do provide a benchmark template to customize and adapt in the context of your own firm's strategy. In short, the digital disciplines are where digital technology meets value disciplines—the foundation of today's and tomorrow's strategies—and could be just what you need to help your company attain market leadership.

Notes

1. Michael Treacy and Fred Wiersema, "Customer Intimacy and Other Value Disciplines," *Harvard Business Review*, (January–February 1993): 84–93.
2. Michael Treacy and Fred Wiersema, *The Discipline of Market Leaders* (Reading, MA: Addison-Wesley, 1995).
3. Sunil Mithas, Ali Tafti, Indranil Bardhan, and Jie Mein Goh, "Information Technology and Firm Profitability: Mechanisms and Empirical Evidence," *MIS Quarterly* 36, no. 1 (2012): 214.
4. Lisa Arthur, "Five Years From Now, CMOs Will Spend More on IT Than CIOs Do," *Forbes.com*, February 8, 2012, www.forbes.com/sites/lisaarthur/2012/02/08/five-years-from-now-cmos-will-spend-more-on-it-than-cios-do/.
5. Robert Jensen, "The Digital Provide: Information (Technology), Market Performance, and Welfare in the South Indian Fisheries Sector," *The Quarterly Journal of Economics* 122, no. 3 (2007): 879–924.
6. Dan Pink, *Drive: The Surprising Truth About What Motivates Us* (New York: Riverhead Books, 2011).
7. David Zax, "Brown Down: UPS Drivers vs. the UPS Algorithm," *FastCompany.com*, January 3, 2013, www.fastcompany.com/3004319/brown-down-ups-drivers-vs-ups-algorithm.
8. Steven Rosenbush and Laura Stevens, "At UPS, the Algorithm Is the Driver," *Wall Street Journal*, February 16, 2015, www.wsj.com/articles/at-ups-the-algorithm-is-the-driver-1424136536.
9. Kim S. Nash, "State of the CIO 2014: The Great Schism," *CIO.com*, January 1, 2014, www.cio.com/article/744601/State_of_the_CIO_2014_The_Great_Schism.
10. "App Store Sales Top $10 Billion in 2013," Apple, Inc., January 7, 2014, https://www.apple.com/pr/library/2014/01/07App-Store-Sales-Top-10-Billion-in-2013.html.
11. AppleInsider Staff, "Apple's App Store Generated over $10 Billion in Revenue for Developers in Record 2014," *AppleInsider.com*, January 8, 2015, appleinsider.com/articles/15/01/08/apples-app-store-generated-over-10-billion-in-revenue-for-developers-in-record-2014.
12. As used in this book, to "digitize" is to convert an analog object to data, such as digits, as in scanning a photograph to create a JPEG. To "digitalize" is to convert an analog, biological, electrical, or mechanical function or mechanism within a product, service, or process to one that is digital (not "to administer digitalis").

13. Some complained that the algorithms acquired by the prize were not put into practice. Netflix transitioned to streaming services as the contest was run. However, insights gained have assisted in the new generation of recommendation algorithms.

14. Peter Lucas, Joe Ballay, and Mickey McManus, *Trillions: Thriving in the Emerging Information Ecology* (Hoboken, NJ: John Wiley & Sons, 2012).

15. Peter Murray, "No More Skipping Your Medicine—FDA Approves First Digital Pill," *Forbes.com*, August 9, 2012, www.forbes.com/sites/singularity/2012/08/09 /no-more-skipping-your-medicine-fda-approves-first-digital-pill/.

16. Reid J. Robison, "How Big Is the Human Genome? In Megabytes, Not Base Pairs," *Medium.com*, January 5, 2014, https://medium.com/precision-medicine /how-big-is-the-human-genome-e90caa3409b0.

17. "Cisco Visual Networking Index: Forecast and Methodology, 2013-2018," Cisco, June 10, 2014, www.cisco.com/c/en/us/solutions/collateral/service-provider/ip -ngn-ip-next-generation-network/white_paper_c11-481360.html.

18. Nash, "State of the CIO 2014."

19. Frederic Lardinois, "Amazon's S3 Now Stores 2 Trillion Objects, Up From 1 Trillion Last June, Regularly Peaks At Over 1.1M Requests Per Second," *TechCrunch.com*, April 18, 2013, techcrunch.com/2013/04/18/amazons-s3-now- stores-2-trillion-objects-up-from-1-trillion-last-june-regularly-peaks-at-over-1- 1m-requests-per-second/.

20. Rich Miller, "Estimate: Amazon Cloud Backed by 450,000 Servers," *DataCenterKnowledge.com*, March 14, 2013, www.datacenterknowledge.com/archives/2012 /03/14/estimate-amazon-cloud-backed-by-450000-servers/.

21. Matthew D. Lieberman, *Social: Why Our Brains Are Wired to Connect* (New York: Broadway Books, 2014).

22. Michael Bloch, Brad Brown, and Johnson Sikes, "Elevating Technology on the Boardroom Agenda," *McKinsey.com*, October, 2012, www.mckinsey.com/insights /business_technology/elevating_technology_on_the_boardroom_agenda.

23. "'Marketplace' Section Renamed 'Business & Tech,'" *Wall Street Journal*, February 16, 2015, www.wsj.com/articles/marketplace-section-renamed-business-tech- 1424138463.

24. Emmie Martin, "One-Eighth of Harvard Undergraduates Are Enrolled in the Same Computer Course, and It Says a Lot about the Future," *BusinessInsider.com*, September 11, 2014, www.businessinsider.com/most-popular-course-at-harvard -2014-9.

25. Nash, "State of the CIO 2014."

26. Nicholas Carr, "IT Doesn't Matter," *Harvard Business Review* (May 2003): 41–49.

27. Alex Konrad, "The World's Top 10 Venture Investors For 2014," *Forbes.com*, March 26, 2014, www.forbes.com/sites/alexkonrad/2014/03/26/midas-top-ten- list-for-2014/.

28. Marc Andreessen, "Why Software Is Eating The World," *Wall Street Journal*, August 20, 2011, online.wsj.com/news/articles/SB10001424053111903480904576512250915629460.

29. Liz Gannes, "The Best of Mary Meeker's 2013 Internet Trends Slides," *AllThingsD.com*, May 29, 2013, allthingsd.com/20130529/the-best-of-mary-meekers-2013-internet-trends-slides/.

30. Arthur, "Five Years From Now."

31. Michael Hickins, "Debunking the Ascendancy of the CMO IT Honcho," *Wall Street Journal* CIO Journal, July 3, 2013, blogs.wsj.com/cio/2013/07/03/debunking-the-ascendancy-of-the-cmo-it-honcho/.

32. Nash, "State of the CIO 2014."

33. Joe Weinman, "4 Ways to Win at Business by Playing Games All Day Long," *Forbes.com*, October 15, 2013, www.forbes.com/sites/joeweinman/2013/10/15/4-ways-to-win-at-business-by-playing-games-all-day-long/.

34. Jennifer Bogo and Emily Gertz, "Newlight Technologies AirCarbon: Plastic from Thin Air," *PopSci.com*, bestofwhatsnew.popsci.com/newlight-technologies-aircarbon.

35. Michael Porter, "The Five Competitive Forces That Shape Strategy," *Harvard Business Review* (January 2008), hbr.org/2008/01/the-five-competitive-forces-that-shape-strategy.

CHAPTER 2

Value Disciplines and Related Frameworks

The digital disciplines framework is a direct descendent of the value disciplines model conceived in the early 1990s by Michael Treacy and Fred Wiersema in their *Harvard Business Review* article titled "Customer Intimacy and Other Value Disciplines"[1] and their seminal, best-selling book *The Discipline of Market Leaders*.[2] Before delving into *digital* disciplines in the next chapter, it's essential to develop a baseline understanding of the original *value* disciplines and related strategy frameworks.

Perhaps business success is just serendipity, but over the past few decades, there have been hundreds—if not thousands—of attempts to determine why some firms succeed while others fail; why some companies or industries are highly profitable and others aren't; and to develop models, frameworks, repeatable processes, and insights that businesses can utilize.

Some strategists, such as visiting professor Gary Hamel of the London Business School and the late professor C. K. Prahalad of the University of Michigan, have argued for what might be called an inside-out view. They claimed that companies should build on their *core competencies* to offer new products and services or enter entirely new markets. One example that they highlighted is NEC, which identified three major evolutionary trends in the 1970s: from mainframe to distributed processing; from simple components to complex integrated circuits; and from mechanical/analog telecommunications to digital. By focusing on developing deep internal knowledge and skills including process technologies in these areas, and leveraging those competencies into interrelated products and businesses, NEC grew into a global leader.[3] Today, we see companies like Tesla taking a core competency such as lithium-ion batteries and using it to expand beyond cars into home energy storage.[4]

Other strategists, such as professor Michael Porter of the Harvard Business School, have been primarily concerned with a firm's competitive strategy, so their focus is outward, but primarily oriented to competition, not customers. In Porter's five forces framework, customers, often referred to as buyers, are just one of the five major considerations for strategy—others being suppliers, substitute products or services, the threat of *new* competitors entering the business, and the intensity of rivalry among *existing* competitors.

Yet another approach to strategy would be to work from the outside in, starting from the customer perspective backwards to the firm's positioning and strategic architecture. Treacy and Wiersema did just this, and after studying 40 companies for several years, concluded that companies could lead their industry through the delineation and delivery of differentiated customer value in one of three ways, which they called *value disciplines:* operational excellence, product leadership, and customer intimacy.

Value Disciplines

Treacy and Wiersema counseled that companies could advantageously differentiate themselves through better processes, better products, or better relationships. Their ideas about competitive strategy were structured according to three related components: the value discipline and its supporting value proposition and operating model.

According to Treacy and Wiersema, the *value proposition* is the implicit promise, that is, the *offer* that the company makes to its customers regarding the value—benefits less costs—that the customer can expect if he or she does business with the firm. Perhaps the simplest such proposition is Geico's famous "15 minutes could save you 15 percent." In other words, an investment (i.e., cost) of 15 minutes of your time could save you 15 percent on your car insurance premiums (i.e., benefit).

Value is not only measured in cost reduction, of course. It might include access convenience, purchase convenience, elegance, design, ego gratification, entertainment, emotion, user experience, or personal or business transformation, to name a few.

Treacy and Wiersema then defined the *value-driven operating model* as the integrated mechanism by which that value is delivered: processes, resources, data, plant, equipment, IT assets, location, organization, culture, leadership, management, governance, and employee skills and motivation. Different companies may have different approaches to delivering value: Toyota uses a very different model for manufacturing Camrys than Rolls-Royce does with its handmade Phantom Coupé. Each creates value for its target segments, but they are different kinds of value with different kinds of operating models.

Each *value discipline* is a combination of a generic value proposition with its corresponding operating model.[5] A company pursuing operational excellence through cost reduction, for example, will think about controlling costs everywhere, and is more likely to invest in automated self-service and interactive voice response (IVR) systems than in front-line account teams to build customer intimacy.

Treacy and Wiersema argued that value disciplines are very different from strategic goals. Whereas the same company can have different strategic goals one year versus the next, having a different value discipline requires rethinking all dimensions of corporate identity. So, to continue the example, an annual goal for an operationally excellent company might be to grow the proportion of customer service calls handled by the IVR system; whereas a customer intimate company might have a goal of increasing average customer satisfaction scores by 5 points, and incentivizing its dedicated account teams accordingly.

They also distinguished value disciplines from quick fixes. A company noticing a decline in market share might offer special promotions to win some deals that otherwise might be lost, but this is very different than reengineering core processes for lower cost. A CEO might desperately visit some top customers, but this is very different than customer intimacy that is deeply practiced throughout the organization. A company might paper over deep process issues by introducing expediters to speed some customer orders, but this is not a comprehensive process improvement approach leading to operational excellence.

Operational Excellence

Treacy and Wiersema defined *operational excellence* as "providing customers with reliable products or services at competitive prices and delivered with minimal difficulty or inconvenience."[6] They cited Dell, which at that time had disrupted the PC industry by offering a direct-to-consumer, make-to-order business model. The insight here is that the *product* itself—an Intel-based PC—was not really differentiated; it was the *processes* for configuring it, ordering it, paying for it, and taking delivery of it that were reimagined.

The concept of operational excellence can be broadly viewed as addressing process efficiency—doing things right—and process effectiveness—doing the right things. It can be viewed in terms of cost and convenience, but also in terms of *all* the ways in which processes can be differentiated: higher quality, higher reliability, shorter cycle times, lower risk and variance, greater flexibility. In some cases, internal process changes, such as maximized throughput, can contribute to customer value, such as lower cost.

Also of importance: accountability, transparency, and traceability; supplier employment practices; governance; sustainability, whether green data centers or sustainable forestry; environmental concerns, such as toxins and emissions; safety; social responsibility, such as offering living wages and eliminating child labor; locality, for example, locally grown food; ethics and fairness, such as fair trade coffee; and other values. Concepts like *convenience* have additional subtleties. In some contexts and for some segments, self-service is more convenient; in others, service delivery is. For some products and services, instant gratification is convenient. For others, such as using a car service to go to the airport, (delayed) synchronization between the firm and the customer process is more "convenient."

The value of different process metrics often depends on the specific type of process. For example, consider a sales process versus a manufacturing process. Important characteristics of a sales process might be close rate and sales funnel forecast accuracy. Important ones for a manufacturing process might be cycle time, yield, and compliance.

The notion of process excellence can then be further extended to include business effectiveness: greater customer advocacy and engagement in a customer relationship management process; higher revenues or forecast accuracy for a sales process; greater customer satisfaction for a service delivery process; and lower employee turnover for a talent acquisition process. We can extend revenue generation beyond sales, and also consider how existing processes can move from being cost centers to revenue generators by monetizing physical or information byproducts.

It should be noted that operational effectiveness and efficiency are not the same as operational excellence. To excel is to stand out and be the best—in other words, to be differentiated. Having efficient and effective operations is a good goal, but might not be enough to differentiate a firm.

Product Leadership

Treacy and Wiersema defined *product leadership* as "offering customers leading-edge products and services that consistently enhance the customer's use or application of the product, thereby making rivals' goods obsolete."[7] They offer the examples of Nike, which outran Adidas in footwear, and Johnson & Johnson's Vistakon unit, which clearly saw its way through to beating competitors to market with the first disposable contact lenses. Importantly, it is not just the invention or design of innovative products at which such companies excel, but also rapid product introduction processes, fast decision making, and an ability to experiment and adjust quickly during the product introduction process.

Product leaders, in Treacy and Wiersema's view, are those companies that continuously innovate. They referred to Intel. Today, we would also probably consider Apple as an iconic example of continuous market-disrupting innovation: iTunes, the iPod, the iPhone, the Retina Display, the MacBook Air, the iPad, and the Apple Watch come to mind, and perhaps someday the iCar. They propose that for product leaders, competition is not about price, but about performance. Picture a Lamborghini dealer trying to win a wealthy customer's business from a Ferrari dealer. She will not argue that the Lamborghini costs $20,000 less than the Ferrari nor that it's easier to select trim colors over the web. Instead, she will focus on more exclusive leather seats, a different center of gravity, greater sex appeal, or a faster 0 to 60 time.

Treacy and Wiersema illustrated the concept of product leadership primarily through the leading product manufacturers of the time such as Glaxo, Intel, Johnson & Johnson, Microsoft, Nike, and Sony. But they intended for the concept to apply equally to services, and highlighted companies such as Disney.

Customer Intimacy

Treacy and Wiersema defined *customer intimacy* as "segmenting and targeting markets precisely and then tailoring offerings to match exactly the demands of those niches."[8] Such companies have intimate knowledge of their customers' needs and use that knowledge to flexibly meet those needs. Importantly, such companies focus on relationships and lifetime customer value rather than individual transactions, and thus often segment their customers to provide the best service to their most profitable customers.

Treacy and Wiersema highlighted The Home Depot, Nordstrom, and Four Seasons as exemplifying customer intimacy. Home Depot will provide a personal consultant—a sales clerk wearing an orange apron—for hours, even for the purchase of a 15-cent screw, helping to recommend wood or metal, aluminum or steel, galvanized or not, and so on.

Or consider Nordstrom's legendary return policy: you can return anything. At any time. For any reason. With or without a receipt. Perhaps even if you bought the item somewhere else: one urban legend concerning Nordstrom is that a customer successfully returned tires there, even though Nordstrom doesn't sell tires.[9] Whether the story is true or not doesn't really matter; the legend underscores the brand's value proposition around customer service.

Customer-intimate companies, according to Treacy and Wiersema, are not focused on meeting the needs of the "market," but rather of individual customers. They provide the best customer value, based on best meeting the needs of each customer through greater in-depth knowledge of that customer's needs. Such an approach is clear for, say, a custom home builder or architect, who sits down with the family to better understand their lifestyle and preferences. Does the family want the family room open to the kitchen, encouraging togetherness? Or would Mom or Dad prefer to cook in peace while the kids play video games? A military contractor might use the same approach, better understanding the Army's objective for a new weapons system before designing it or bidding on it. But customer intimacy is not restricted to high-value goods, as the Home Depot example shows.

Importance of Focus

It is possible for a company to participate or excel in more than one discipline at a time, as we'll see with several of the highlighted companies, and in particular in Chapter 17 with GE. However, Treacy and Wiersema observed that straying from a disciplined focus is fraught with danger, partly because companies pursuing a value discipline need to align their culture, management, IT, organization, and processes.

It's a challenge to focus on one discipline. What company *wouldn't* rather have streamlined processes than cumbersome ones, great products rather than outdated, shoddy replicas, and delighted, loyal customers rather than high churn, lawsuits, and bad word of mouth? However, a key component of Treacy and Wiersema's argument is the need for focus. They argue that Sears tried operational excellence, offering everyday low prices and cutting costs. However, Sears didn't match Wal-Mart's single-minded focus on cost reduction through its innovations in supply chain management and logistics. In what Treacy and Wiersema considered a customer intimacy strategy, Sears then tried expanding beyond its Kenmore and Craftsman brands by carrying well-known ones, which merely matched competitors' product variety. Finally, Treacy and Wiersema pointed out that Sears attempted a product leadership strategy via celebrity endorsements, but didn't execute as well as a top competitor at that time, J.C. Penney.[10] Trying to be all things to all buyers—simultaneously pursuing operational excellence, product leadership, and customer intimacy—can be like trying to undercut Hyundai pricing with a custom-designed Lamborghini.

Their advice is still often valid. After the market close on January 28, 2015, McDonald's, the world's largest restaurant chain, ousted its CEO after a two-year tenure. McDonald's financial results had gone stale, but the CEO had gone from out of the frying pan and into the fire partly because of his attempt to simultaneously pursue multiple disciplines: operational excellence by offering low-cost Dollar Menu items and quick-service—i.e., fast food—convenience; product leadership through a broader selection of menu items including some "premium" items such as McWrap; and customer intimacy through a "make your own burger." As one investment advisory firm said, "Trying to please everybody is one of the issues that they're dealing with."[11]

There are multiple problems with such an approach. Product leadership conflicts with operational excellence as customers balk at items not on the Dollar Menu. Operational excellence conflicts with product leadership because food is partially prepared in factories and then flash frozen, pitting efficiency against freshness. Customer intimacy and product leadership conflict with operational excellence as customization and extensive menus slow down the drive-through lines.

Less than 40 hours after the McDonald's shake-up, Shake Shack sizzled as its IPO (initial public offering) opened at more than double its offering price. Shake Shack is focused on a 100 percent, all-natural product leadership strategy, offering fresher, higher-quality ingredients at premium prices: they advertise "100% all-natural Angus beef, vegetarian fed, humanely raised and source verified. No hormones or antibiotics—EVER. We pride ourselves on sourcing incredible ingredients from like-minded artisanal producers."[12] A double SmokeShack bacon cheeseburger goes for $9.49, compared to say, a McDonald's Bacon Clubhouse Burger: $4.99.

In short, Treacy and Wiersema's position was that companies should ideally pick one (although they also pointed out that some companies, such as USAA and Toyota, were excelling at more than one) value discipline, and do whatever is required to attain a leadership position in that discipline and at least maintain parity in the others. Today, the economics of information goods and technologies may enable more companies to pursue multiple disciplines. For example, Netflix can deliver individualized entertainment recommendations (customer intimacy) across a broad portfolio of titles including award-winning Netflix-produced content (product leadership) via convenient, streamlined delivery channels (operational excellence).

The Unbundled Corporation

John Hagel and Marc Singer, in a *Harvard Business Review* article titled "Unbundling the Corporation,"[13] took this notion of focus one step further. They argued in 1999, a few years after the value disciplines model emerged, that companies often have three separate virtual businesses, or core processes, related to operations, products, and customers, and should consider "unbundling" themselves—that is, splitting into those separate businesses. Or, if the company is not already integrated, continue to maintain focus on one area, and leverage other companies that have expertise in the others.

Hagel and Singer used slightly different terminology than Treacy and Wiersema, because they were focused on organizational entities rather than value disciplines—that is, strategies that deliver differentiated customer value. Thus, they argued for the separation of the *customer relationship management* business, which would appear to typically require a customer intimacy strategy; the *product innovation* business, which would presumably require a product leadership strategy; and the *infrastructure management* business, which would obviously benefit from operational excellence.

Hagel and Singer argued that the culture and competitive mandates for each business are often different. For example, they said that the customer relationship management business should have a culture of customer focus and service orientation. They argued that the product business should have a culture of innovation, rewarding creativity, and collaboration. The infrastructure business, in their view, should have a culture focused on cost, efficiency, and standardization.

Hagel and Singer argued that companies should not only choose which of these three to embrace as core strategy, but that they actually should split into three separate companies: one company per discipline, as it were. The customer relationship management business can achieve benefits through economies of scope—gaining a large fraction of wallet share by selling not only traditional products but those from partners. The product innovation business can achieve strategic advantage through speed. And the infrastructure management business should focus on economies of scale.

This is the exact opposite of the philosophy of a highly vertically integrated organization of a century ago—say, with Ford and automobile manufacturing, or Hollywood movie studios, which integrated production and distribution via company-owned theaters, or AT&T, which had a captive manufacturing unit, Western Electric, as well as owning its distribution business, the operating companies such as New York Telephone.

Representing the unbundled approach, consider Coca-Cola. Partly of necessity borne of the limited assets of its founder, it had a highly unbundled business from the very start. Most of Coca-Cola is water, which was acquired by soda fountain operators from municipal water infrastructure. When Coke became a bottled drink, it was independent bottlers who invested in bottling plants and machinery, and trucks and drivers for physical delivery to stores and restaurants, which were someone else's investment. And, in terms of materials such as sugar and corn syrup, these were not produced in Coca-Cola facilities, but were commodities bought from other firms, such as Monsanto and Cargill.[14]

As another example, consider Apple's iPhone. Apple itself is focused on product design and innovation. It does not own infrastructure such as manufacturing facilities; manufacturing is outsourced to Hon Hai Precision Industries, better known as Foxconn. And, although its retail stores are masterpieces of architecture and merchandising, in one recent quarter, only 15 percent of US iPhones were sold in the company stores. About 70 percent of the phones are sold through the four major carriers and another 10 percent at Best Buy.[15]

Or, consider a different Apple business, apps, which now generate $15 billion annually. Here, the product innovation business has almost completely been separated from the main corporation and given to app developers such as Rovio (Angry Birds), King Digital Entertainment (Candy Crush), and even a direct rival: Microsoft (Office). Although there are a number of Apple apps, such as Keynote for presentations and the Safari browser, product innovation for apps has mostly been outsourced to other businesses, while Apple retains customer relationship management through the hardware, the Apple App Store, Apple ID, and, of course, payments.

Information technology enables the unbundled corporation as never before. The App Store enables unbundled product innovation pure-plays to often thrive without any end-customer relationships, only a relationship with Apple. Uber, a "ridesharing" service, is arguably mostly a customer relationship app. Uber connects people who would need a ride somewhere with drivers that have vehicles, not unlike a taxi company. The infrastructure—drivers and their vehicles, but also roads, tunnels, and bridges, and cell phone towers and networks—is not owned or operated by Uber. Yet asset-less Uber recently had a valuation of $40 billion.[16]

The rationale for the unbundled corporation argument reverses a nearly century-old insight from economist Ronald Coase. He asked a deceptively simple question regarding why firms should exist. After all, it is not unheard of for individuals to band together to achieve a common goal, say, raising a barn, without formally incorporating.

Coase argued that firms exist as a way of minimizing certain kinds of costs. After all, in a loosely coupled network of individuals, there are costs not found in a standing corporate organization. These include costs such as those required to identify personnel with the right skills (search costs) and those to then contract for tasks (transaction costs). A company with a stable organization of employees could be more efficient over time than an *ad hoc* collection of individuals.

Hagel and Singer, though, said that information technologies reduce the need for such integration, enabling firms to be smaller yet still interact efficiently with those in complementary businesses. Consequently, firms could be smaller and more focused. Thus, they argued that an integrated firm could actually subdivide or unbundle into smaller firms focused on either operational excellence of their infrastructure, product leadership through innovation, or intimate customer relationships.

The bottom line: Whether or not a company does unbundle, it is important to understand the locus of strategic focus: operations, products, or relationships.

Business Model Generation

In *Business Model Generation*, Alexander Osterwalder and Yves Pigneur created what they call the *business model canvas*, which provides a high-level framework for specifying various choices to configure or restructure businesses. In their approach, they divide firm choices into nine major areas.[17]

The first three areas are *activities* (i.e., processes), *partners*, and *resources* (i.e., assets), which Hagel and Singer would presumably refer to as infrastructure; the relevance to operational excellence is clear.

Value propositions are another major category. As usual, the intent is to consider the benefit provided to the customer. It can be quantitative—say, a 10 percent reduction in heating bills—or qualitative—say, a not-to-be-missed entertainment experience. Since the value proposition is generated by the total product/service, including tangible and intangible elements, it's an area where product leadership or product innovation is essential.

Next, there are three areas of customer interaction: *customer segments, customer relationships*, and *channels*. The channels category includes *communication* such as marketing and advertising, *distribution*, and *sales*. Hagel and Singer would presumably consider these three areas in total to be customer relationship management, and Treacy and Wiersema would likely consider customer intimacy to be the relevant value discipline.

In addition, they delineate the underlying *cost structure* and *revenue streams* associated with these, which are areas for development of unique business and pricing models, such as, say, the "razor and razor blade" approach where the razors are low margin but the blades are highly profitable.

Each of the nine areas has a number of different options, and the total configuration of these options defines a business model. For example, customer segments might include the mass market, niche markets such as wealthy Brazilian expatriates with teenage children living in Ohio, or a diversified approach comprising multiple unrelated segments. Revenue streams might be based on physical product sales, delivery and ownership, or on a rental model, or based on third parties, such as advertisers. So, a particular business model might involve, say, online distribution (channel) of thermostats that can cut heating bills by 10 percent (the product and its value proposition) built by overseas manufacturers (partners) to wealthy Brazilian parents residing in Ohio (segment) that can display ads and therefore are free to homeowners because the advertisers pay (revenue stream).

While they identified a variety of business model patterns, such as the long-tail business (think Amazon.com and its broad portfolio of products), multisided platforms (think pay-walled or physical newspapers that sell subscriptions to readers and ads to advertisers), and freemium models (e.g., free-to-play mobile games that then sell virtual goods), the first pattern that they identify is based on this primary division into value disciplines or unbundled corporation components: basically operations/infrastructure/processes, products/services, and relationships.[18]

Michael Porter and Competitive Advantage

Another model worth reviewing originated with strategy guru Michael Porter. In his "five forces" model of competition, industry profitability depends on the bargaining power of suppliers, the bargaining power of buyers, the threat of substitutes, the threat of new entrants, and the intensity of industry rivalry.

Each of these forces has a variety of drivers. For example, buyers have greater bargaining power when they are concentrated or buy large amounts relative to the size of vendors, when their switching costs are low, when they can easily decide to backward integrate, when their profitability is low, forcing them to be cost conscious, when they have information about cost drivers, and when the firm selling to them has heavy fixed costs.

In light of these forces, Porter argued that "the best strategy for a given firm is ultimately a unique construction reflecting its particular circumstances."[19] In other words, there is no one-size-fits-all approach that all companies should take; they each must consider their industry, the five forces, and their unique positioning and capabilities.

However, Porter posited that there are three major generic strategies. Business units can compete either based on "overall cost leadership," "differentiation," or "focus." Retailing offers examples of companies utilizing these different generic strategies. Wal-Mart is a company that offers low cost; Neiman-Marcus is one that is differentiated through service; and Victoria's Secret is one that offers focus.

According to Porter, *overall cost leadership* means excelling at developing a product or service cost structure lower than competitors based on a variety of approaches. These may include economies of scale; experience curve effects (i.e., learning over time) and through high production volumes (i.e., experience, how to build products or offer services more cost effectively); rigorous management of costs, by, for example, renegotiating supplier contracts; and eliminating unprofitable customers or segments. Cost leadership is a competitive strategy, not a value discipline, in Porter's formulation. In other words, cost leadership *might* translate into lower prices to customers, but the company might leave prices at market parity and keep the outsize profits or use them to invest in, say, geographic expansion or new product offerings. As a competitive strategy, the point is that the cost leader can survive buffeting from the five forces. For example, strong buyer power that reduces pricing may impact the profitability of the cost leader, but will drive the cost laggard out of business.

Differentiation entails creating unique products or services in a variety of ways. Porter explained that such uniqueness can be based on functionality, design and aesthetics, brand, technology, distribution channels, or advanced technology. With cost leadership, even if pricing is identical, profitability is higher because cost structure is lower. With differentiation, profitability is higher even without cost advantages because customers are willing to pay for these unique capabilities. In some cases, higher prices may be based on perceived benefits such as ego value, such as a Prada bag or Bentley automobile. In other cases, higher prices may be justifiable because advanced product or service capabilities are more financially beneficial to the customer. Differentiation also insulates firms from the five forces. For example, brand loyalty can reduce buyer power by increasing perceived switching costs.

The third generic strategy is *focus*, either on a narrower product line, a particular customer segment, or a constrained geographic area. Such a strategy is not completely divorced from either overall cost leadership or differentiation. Porter says that a firm using a focus strategy can either better meet the needs of its target market (i.e., be differentiated) or can have lower costs than broad-based competitors *within* the constrained scope.

A superficial analysis might lead one to believe that Porter's approach is isomorphic to the Treacy and Wiersema framework. Low cost would seem to relate to operational excellence; differentiation to product leadership; focus to customer intimacy.

However, while there are similarities, the approaches are significantly different, because Porter is concerned with generic competitive strategies—ways in which companies in an industry can compete effectively based on the interplay of the five forces. Treacy and Wiersema's primary focus is on value disciplines, how companies can create unique customer value—and thereby ultimately be competitive and profitable.

Porter's model of differentiation fits nicely with the product leadership discipline. But, operational excellence can and should address a broad number of dimensions of differential process advantage. Cost is an obvious one, but time, quality, predictability, reliability, synchronization, convenience, and flexibility are means of differentiating processes and thus achieving operational excellence that have little to do with cost.

Focus is oriented to achieving cost or differentiation advantages by constraining scope, which is very different than customer intimacy. For example, a newsstand might only sell women's magazines such as *Vogue* and *Elle*—a focus strategy—but not know the names of any customers, nor whether they are buying primarily for the health articles, the fashion articles, or the beauty articles—and is therefore not pursuing an intimacy discipline.

In short, Michael Porter has created some of the most impactful models of competitive strategy, but they differ from both Treacy and Wiersema's value disciplines and from the digital disciplines described in the rest of this book.

Blue Ocean Strategy

Another popular perspective on competitive strategy comes from W. Chan Kim and Renée Mauborgne, professors of strategy at INSEAD, a business school in France, and the authors of *Blue Ocean Strategy*. They argued that most companies lock themselves into extreme competition within fixed market boundaries, leading to what they call red ocean strategy, so called because all competitors are bloodied in the battle.[20]

They argued that, instead, companies should look for Blue Ocean opportunities, i.e., uncontested market spaces. There are a number of good examples of innovators that have recently created entirely new markets. Uber created what has been called *ridesharing*, rather than, say, starting yet another taxi or limousine company with lower prices or plusher seats. Apple created a market for touchscreen, app-enabled smartphones, rather than battling things out with an incrementally better keyboard on a feature phone. Netflix created a new model for video rental pricing and delivery, rather than just opening another corner video store with a bigger selection or 10 percent off on Thursdays.

Beyond suggesting that it can be more profitable to create a whole new industry rather than battling it out in an existing one, Kim and Mauborgne provided some practical steps on how to do so. Contrary to Michael Porter, they argued for *value innovation*, by which they mean offering differentiated capability at a lower cost, a seeming oxymoron, like jumbo shrimp. The process by which they suggested achieving this is to break the rules and standard best practices of an industry, and to determine which elements of the standard offering can be eliminated or diminished, because they are of no or low value to customers. This can potentially enable both lower cost and the reallocation of capital investments or cost structure components into areas that *are* differentiating.

They illustrate this approach with Accor Hotels' development of the Formule 1 chain. Formule 1 did away with many amenities that just weren't critical to a majority of travelers, such as room decorations and a fancy lobby and restaurant. Instead, it focused on the things that were: comfortable beds and quiet, clean rooms. As a result, it excelled in the dimensions of differentiation that drove customer value, while achieving a dramatically lower price point.

Additional strategic moves are also necessitated by the value innovation approach. To maximize value requires a focus on lower cost. This requires scale. Pursuing scale often requires global expansion, which, in turn, helps reduce the threat of competition. Cost-effective scale also means avoiding customization, which increases cost structure. Kim and Mauborgne therefore argued that companies pursuing value innovation should avoid trying to grow by pursuing increasing segmentation and customization, and should instead focus on commonalities among customers. That said, such commonalities may attract new customers: Formule 1 did not just transform the value proposition for existing hotel customers, it also attracted truck drivers who had previously slept in their cabs and jet-lagged business travelers who could benefit from a few hours of sleep.

In a *rough* parallel to the value disciplines model, Kim and Mauborgne said that there are three platforms for value innovation: product, service and delivery. *Product platform* signifies the offered product or service; by *service platform* they mean customer service and support, warranties, and training; and by *delivery platform* they mean outbound logistics and channels. However, the value innovation model would be viewed through the lens of value disciplines as a combination of operational excellence and product leadership without customer intimacy. It is just one approach, and while value innovation may be useful for some companies in some markets during some time frames, one or more of operational excellence, product leadership, and customer intimacy would appear to more broadly capture the strategic options generally available to firms. To put it another way, there are more blue ocean opportunities than those restricted to value innovation as a combination of low-cost and differentiated products or operational excellence and product leadership. Netflix is a blue ocean case that includes customer intimacy and a high degree of micro-segmentation through personalized recommendations and specific genres, as we'll see in Chapter 13.

Moreover, as self-evident as *blue ocean strategy* seems, a recent study shows that 80 percent of self-made billionaires made their fortunes in hotly contested, mature red oceans. For example, Sir James Dyson went through over 5,000 iterations of his iconic bagless vacuum. The board of directors of a company in which he held a substantial stake withheld funding approval, saying, "If there really was a better type of vacuum cleaner, then surely one of the big manufacturers would be making it."[21]

Innovation: The "Fourth" Value Discipline

In the classic value disciplines model, *innovation* is firmly linked to product leadership. After all, leading products tend to have innovative features based on breakthrough technologies. Touch screens. Anti-lock brakes. High-resolution displays. Carbon nanotubes. Advanced search algorithms.

Hagel and Singer believed the same thing, arguing that the "product innovation" business can be unbundled from infrastructure and customer relationship management.

In blue-ocean strategy, a cornerstone of value innovation is the differentiated product.

However, there are several issues with limiting innovation to products. The first is that innovation applies to processes and customer relationships just as much as it does to products and services. While it's true that Mazda introduced the rotary engine, GM introduced OnStar, and Porsche introduced the first gas-electric hybrid (in 1901!), it was Toyota that drove to global dominance through *process* innovation(s): the Toyota Production System.

Other companies have innovated production and service delivery processes to achieve operational excellence: Consider new integrated circuit wafer fabrication technology from Intel, or Federal Express' introduction of an overnight delivery process. Companies also innovate customer relationships: Consider American Airlines' introduction of the first frequent-flyer program that offered mileage rewards, retailers' introduction of loyalty cards, migration of firms such as Gary Vaynerchuk's Wine Library to social networks, or Amazon's upsell/cross-sell recommendation engine.

Moreover, innovation can apply simultaneously to multiple value disciplines. For example, a product innovation can require process innovations, such as when the Boeing 787 Dreamliner required breakthroughs in carbon fiber and titanium graphite composite fabrication.[22]

Another issue with lumping innovation in with product leadership, or even operational excellence or customer relationships, is that innovation, *in and of itself*, can create customer value and thus brand loyalty. When customers select companies like Apple or Tesla, they are not just buying current products delivered by current processes across existing relationships; they are connecting with the overall brand and signing up for the potential embodied by the company. In other words, innovation can also be a value discipline. Effectively, the quantitative and qualitative value of the future stream of potential benefits is the value proposition; and the company's innovation culture, processes, creativity, and related elements of its strategic architecture are its value-driven operating model. Customer value is generated not only through a rational economic analysis of benefits, but also a behavioral economic association with innovation through cognitive biases such as illusory superiority and the assumption of uniqueness. In other words, there are rational customer benefits to innovation, such as the ability to do things faster, cheaper, or better, and irrational ones, such as the need to confirm superiority and uniqueness by having the latest, hottest products, processes, or engagement.

Innovation will be covered in depth in Chapters 14 through 16.

■   ■   ■

There are many strategy frameworks, but Treacy and Wiersema's value disciplines framework—especially if we expand it to innovation—is powerful and driven from the customer's perspective. The notion of differentiating based on unique customer value creation is hard to argue with, as is the notion that an operating model must be designed to deliver the value proposition.

Now that the foundational value disciplines framework and related approaches have been reviewed, the rest of the book will look at how digital technologies can create new opportunities to gain advantage.

Notes

1. Michael Treacy and Fred Wiersema, "Customer Intimacy and Other Value Disciplines," *Harvard Business Review* (January–February 1993): 84–93.
2. Michael Treacy and Fred Wiersema, *The Discipline of Market Leaders* (Reading, MA: Addison-Wesley, 1995).
3. C. K. Prahalad and Gary Hamel, "The Core Competence of the Corporation," *Harvard Business Review* (May–June 1990): 79–90.
4. Ucilia Wang, "Tesla's Elon Musk: On Creating a 'Cool' Battery System for Home Energy Storage," *Forbes.com*, May 7, 2014, www.forbes.com/sites/uciliawang/2014 /05/07/teslas-elon-musk-on-creating-a-cool-battery-system-with-a-beautiful- cover-for-home-energy-storage/.
5. Treacy and Wiersema, *The Discipline of Market Leaders*, xiv.
6. Ibid., 84.
7. Ibid., 85.
8. Ibid., 84.
9. "Return to Spender," *Snopes.com*, April 25, 2011, www.snopes.com/business /consumer/nordstrom.asp.
10. Treacy and Wiersema, *The Discipline of Market Leaders*, 92–93.
11. Katie Little, "McDonald's CEO Don Thompson Steps Aside, Stock Jumps," *CNBC.com*, January 28, 2015, www.cnbc.com/id/102376552.
12. www.shakeshack.com/ (accessed May 14, 2015).
13. John Hagel and Marc Singer, "Unbundling the Corporation," *Harvard Business Review* (March–April, 1999): 133–141.
14. Bartow Elmore, "How Coca-Cola Built a Sugary Empire, by Outsourcing as Much as Possible," *Fortune.com*, November 25, 2014, fortune.com/2014/11/25/coca -cola-capitalism/.
15. AppleInsider Staff, "Selling 50% of iPhones through Apple's Retail Stores Viewed as an Unrealistic, Lofty Goal," *AppleInsider.com*, July 17, 2013, appleinsider.com /articles/13/07/17/selling-50-of-iphones-through-apples-retail-stores-viewed-as -an-unrealistic-lofty-goal.

16. Dan Primack, "Uber Reportedly Valued at $40 Billion by Investors," *Fortune.com*, November 25, 2014, fortune.com/2014/11/25/uber-reportedly-valued-at-40 -billion-by-investors/.
17. Alexander Osterwalder and Yves Pigneur, *Business Model Generation: A Handbook for Visionaries, Game Changers, and Challengers* (Hoboken, NJ: John Wiley & Sons, 2010).
18. Ibid, 57.
19. Michael Porter, *Competitive Strategy: Techniques for Analyzing Industries and Competitors* (New York: Free Press, 1980), 34.
20. W. Chan Kim and Reneé Mauborgne, "Value Innovation: The Strategic Logic of High Growth," *Harvard Business Review* (July, 2004), hbr.org/2004/07/value -innovation-the-strategic-logic-of-high-growth.
21. Chunka Mui, "You Hardly Need to Discover a New Market to Make Billions," *Forbes.com*, February 9, 2015, www.forbes.com/sites/chunkamui/2015/02/09/all -oceans-are-purple/.
22. Martha Walz, "The Dream of Composites," *RDMag.com*, November 20, 2006, rdmag.com/articles/2006/11/dream-composites.

CHAPTER 3
Digital Disciplines

reacy and Wiersema's *value disciplines framework*—operational excellence, product leadership, and customer intimacy—is timeless. As long as there are companies, they will have processes, products or services, and customer relationships. These firms will need to differentiate themselves in the market to be successful enterprises, and to do so they'll need to create unique customer value.

Although the value disciplines approach is timeless, technology generally—and information technology specifically—is advancing so rapidly that there has been an evolution and revolution in each of the three *value disciplines* discussed in Chapter 2, leading to three corresponding *digital disciplines*. In addition, because of the exponential growth of both competition and technology, a fourth digital discipline—accelerated innovation—must be added.

The impact of these technologies is directly apparent to almost everyone, thanks to mobile devices and the Internet. We live in an always-on, always-connected mobile and multiscreen world, and the result of all this time spent on mobile and online has created immense wealth for high-tech companies that we all know: Facebook, Instagram, WhatsApp, Twitter, eBay, Yahoo!, Google, Apple, Amazon, and Microsoft, but also juggernauts in other countries: Alibaba and Tencent in China, for example.

But it isn't just the pure-play newly arrived Internet firms for whom digital technologies are relevant, but also the legacy firms that are redefining their strategies in light of technological disruption. The big story at *the New York Times* is how it has added a section to its business: nytimes.com; Wal-Mart is sold on adding Walmart.com to its assortment; 1-800-Flowers has blossomed into 1-800-Flowers.com.

If this book were written in 1999, that would be the end of the story. But what is truly fascinating is not the mere transmutation of physical entities such as newspapers and retail shelves and flower shops into their virtual World Wide Web equivalents, but the ability of virtually every firm to use digital technologies, including, but not limited to, the web, to rethink their processes, products and services, and relationships.

Thus, we see automotive firms, not just creating electronic catalogs showing different metallic color options on a web page instead of or in addition to a glossy brochure, but creating connected, intelligent vehicles, where digital technologies are used to manage hybrid or all-electric power trains, detect lane changes, deliver entertainment, monitor engines, and ultimately drive for us.

Thus, we see sporting goods firms not just manufacturing sneakers and apparel on automated lines, but becoming involved in the process of health management and athletic coaching through connected sensors, comparative databases, and personalized services.

Thus, we see medical equipment manufacturers not just using computer-aided design to engineer scalpels and computer-numerical controlled machines to manufacture x-ray machines or process shop floor orders, but enabling hospitals and physicians to offer patient-specific therapies to best enhance patient outcomes.

The digital disciplines provide a repeatable framework that captures the essence of the transformations underway in processes, products and services, relationships, and innovation. Excellence in physical operations is being complemented and enabled by information excellence; product leadership is evolving to leadership in solutions comprising cloud-connected smart, adaptive, digital products and services; mere transactions and minimal relationships are deepening not just to customer intimacy but collective intimacy, through optimized, individualized offers; and innovation is being innovated.

Information Excellence

Excellence used to be statically designed and built into operational processes. A good example is Henry Ford's famed assembly line, which was predated by centuries, if not millennia, in China in the manufacture of various items such as pottery and in Venice in the production of ships. The Ford River Rouge plant, a square mile of factory where iron ore and leather entered at one end and cars exited at the other, was anticipated about a millennium earlier in the twelfth century by the Arsenale di Venezia (Arsenal of Venice, or Venetian Arsenal), an enormous shipbuilding complex that ingested wood from nearby forests and fabricated ships, and its successor, Arsenale Nuovo (New Arsenal), basically Venetian Arsenal 2.0.

While ships date back to thousands of years BCE, the Venetian Arsenals (1.0 and 2.0) used improved processes and substantial resources to create competitive advantage. The Venetian Arsenal could produce a ship in a single day, compared to previous production practices that would take months. The Arsenal used interchangeable parts and a moving "assembly-line" based on a canal instead of a conveyer belt, where the ships that were in various stages of production moved to areas with specialists in that phase. The construction process differed from traditional practice: Using the old method, the surface of the hull was built first and then internal "ribs" added; at the Arsenal, the frame, including the hull ribs was built first and then the hull surface was attached. This dramatically cut cycle time for the manufacturing process. The Arsenal even owned its own forest and conducted maintenance on ships, so was as fully vertically integrated as one could imagine.

As impressive as the operational breakthroughs were for the Venetian Arsenal and its (relatively) modern day equivalent, Henry Ford's assembly line, they represent an offline, static process unrepresentative of information excellence. In traditional manufacturing process engineering, the idea was to design an assembly line or continuous process facility—such as an oil refinery, paper mill, or chemical plant—in conjunction with the product design. Thus, if chassis welding took 30 minutes and wheel assemblies took 20 minutes, the idea would be to speed up one or slow down the other, perhaps by adjusting conveyer speed or the number of workers so that they would come together at the same rate in what engineers call a *line of balance*. As a more mundane example, when ordering a burger and fries, you'd like for them to come out at the same time, rather than have the fries get cold while waiting for the burger to cook.

Operational excellence, at one extreme, involves static processes designed and implemented in advance of production. Unit after unit of products— paper clips, sirloin tips, or memory chips—or services—tax returns or insurance applications—flow through such a process in high volume, for years, or even decades. A closely related type of production has some customization through prebuilt or predesigned options: for example, tablets may be mostly the same, except for gigabytes of memory and network connectivity.

But at the other extreme, production or service operations are highly flexible and dynamic. Picture a busy port such as the Port of Hamburg, with tens of thousands of multimodal (sea-land-air) containers, thousands of trucks and scores of ships dropping off and picking up such containers each day. Now add in the complexity that containers are piled on one another, and that various issues arise at virtually every moment: congestion, drawbridges up or down, truck or ship breakdowns. Such an operation can be well-designed, but cannot be fully optimized in advance; it can only be optimized (or near-optimized) in real time, using up-to-the-minute information and sophisticated algorithms or heuristics to determine which trucks or ships should be loading or unloading, which cranes should be used to do so, and in what order.

Such complex, multiobjective optimization problems—which try and get ships into and out of port quickly, keep longshoremen busy, minimize crane effort, maximize safety, reduce fuel usage, and so on—cannot be statically designed ahead of time. They require complex calculations performed quickly enough to generate the best possible—even if not quite perfect—answers. In short, they require information excellence.

Information excellence has many dimensions. It includes the use of automation: conveyors or flexible material handling systems such as robots or drones to reduce labor costs. For example, Amazon.com has deployed (and acquired the manufacturer of) mobile robots in their distribution facilities. It includes substitution: replacing costly physical activities—such as traveling on jet planes—with efficient ones—such as video conferencing. It includes optimization of physical processes such as ports, but also package delivery, field support operations, flexible manufacturing, retail warehousing, and distribution. It includes rich virtual worlds offering new experiences, but also seamless fusion of the real and virtual worlds. It includes deriving new revenues from exhaust data derived as byproducts from various information-intensive processes.

To be fair, even back in the 1990s Treacy and Wiersema realized the importance of information and IT to operational excellence, using examples such as GE's Direct Connect system. However, the power of today's information technologies means that it is of value to draw a strong distinction between physical operations and virtual information.

Chapters 5 to 7 will address information excellence in depth.

Solution Leadership

A list of exemplars of product leadership might include the Rolex Daytona watch; the Bugatti Veyron supercar (the fastest production car in existence with a top speed closing in on 300 miles per hour); or the 1961 Grand Vin de Château Latour.

We'd also have to include service leadership. In the hospitality industry, a Four Seasons, Ritz-Carlton, or Mandarin Oriental would be obvious candidates, or perhaps the Gili Lankanfushi Maldives, on the Kaafu Atoll, rated the number-one travelers' choice in the world in 2015 by TripAdvisor.[1] In personal care, perhaps we would include the Ted Gibson salon, which charges about a thousand dollars for a haircut and boasts clients such as Angelina Jolie and Anne Hathaway.[2]

What makes such products and services leaders? Exclusivity. Luxury materials. Exquisite craftsmanship. Transformational user experiences. Unique production methods. Iconic brands. Historic traditions. Breakthrough innovation. Distinguished clientele.

But today, that might no longer be enough. Products and services are evolving from standalone entities to cloud-connected solutions. Tag-Heuer, facing competition from the Apple Watch, is partnering with Google and Intel; how long can Rolex hold out? Cars are becoming connected products, linked to navigation, entertainment, concierge, and security services as well as social networks. Hotels are beginning to compete not just on the luxurious-ness of their bedding, but instant check-in via mobile phones, personalization of the room, biometric door locks, and the like.

Solution leadership is dramatically different from product leadership. Rather than standalone products, solutions are product-service systems, with a physical product or service touchpoints and service delivery enablers connected over wireline and mobile networks to cloud services, partner ecosystems, and social networks. Revenue models have changed from a single sale to recurring revenues. Rather than pushing products, "vendors" and "service providers" are becoming focused on outcomes. This includes business outcomes for enterprises, such as enhanced profitability, and per-sonal outcomes for consumers, such as transformation into more educated university students or better athletes.

The control points of competition are changing as well. When you are selling a luxury watch, key elements include television advertisements with voice-overs in British or French accents. When you are selling a luxury car, fine Italian leather, or German engineering, television ads with sophisticated foreign accents and precision turns in woodland highways are critical.

But when you are offering a digital solution, control points such as user interfaces, APIs, software development kits, and partner and developer com-munity relations can make all the difference. Early momentum can lead to sustainable, defensible network effects.

Chapters 8 to 10 will address solution leadership in depth.

Collective Intimacy

Collective intimacy is my term for a new kind of intimacy, where a deep, value-adding individual relationship with each customer is based on insights derived from detailed knowledge of all customers.[3] This strategy is several steps removed from traditional customer intimacy.

Good examples of traditional customer intimacy in consumer markets are the butcher, the tailor, the hair stylist, the bartender. In each case, the provider knows your preferences: rib-eye or sirloin, cuff or no cuff, short or shoulder length, shaken or stirred. The provider knows your name, your kids' names, your personal issues regarding work and family. The same individual can sug-gest new experiences: Kobe beef, pleats, a new gel, the new craft beer.

The first phase of digital impact on traditional customer intimacy was through loyalty cards and programs. The web helped to move customer intimacy online. Brands could maintain "relationships" with customers through social media. Businesses could put strategic account plans, contacts, and opportunities into their customer relationship management systems.

But the true potential impact of digital technologies on customer relationships and engagement is more than merely migrating physical face-to-face relationships into virtual mouse-to-monitor or swipe-the-screen interfaces. It is the ability to use sophisticated algorithms to create new value for customers.

When Netflix recommends movies, Amazon.com cross-sells products, and Pandora or iTunes Radio streams songs, not only is there a base relationship, there are also creative recommendations. Sometimes these are fairly obvious: If you've bought *The Fellowship of the Ring* and *The Two Towers*, you are likely to want *The Return of The King*; if you've bought *The Godfather I* and *II*, you are likely to want *III*. But sometimes the recommendations are subtle, surprising, and delightful.

A concern with search engines is that they respond to exact queries essentially literally, and therefore are mere response engines. What one would like is a discovery engine that would open new horizons with delightful new experiences. The difference is simple: Upon asking for local Italian restaurants, rather than getting a rank-ordered list of Italian restaurants, such an engine—or user interface—might respond to the effect that, "You asked for Italian restaurants in New York City, but did you know that there is this new Thai fusion restaurant that just opened up in Brooklyn that you would really like?"

Currently, recommendations for books and movies are based on statistical analysis, which can use sophisticated algorithms, but is still essentially "brute force," based on mathematical calculations where *The Godfather I* is data point 372644 and *The Godfather II* is data point 837661 and The *Godfather III* is data point 271990 and those three numbers tend to show up together. This does not require knowledge of New York City criminal history or relationships in families of European descent—merely the ability to associate two numbers with a third. But increasingly, such insights will be based on rich models of human cognition and emotion. This will represent the best of human empathy, behavioral models, and *theory of mind*—that is, the realization that other people have thoughts and desires—together with analytics that only a computer (or cloud) can perform at scale.

Such collective intimacy in general requires deep subject matter knowledge, which is where statistical methods will meet deep *semantics* and *ontologies*—means of knowledge representation. Systems like IBM's Watson, which famously won at *Jeopardy!* against the best contestants humanity could offer, are being applied in areas such as medicine, but are still primarily statistical correlation engines. It is not that farfetched, however, to imagine a day when systems like Watson have a true understanding of human biology and physiology and derive diagnoses and therapies from a combination of deep knowledge, creativity, and comprehensive databases.

Chapters 11 to 13 will address collective intimacy in depth.

Accelerated Innovation

Innovation is often an imperative for business survival. The world of business is nothing if not an evolutionary ecology driving survival of the fittest and extinction of the weak—those without compelling value propositions.

While innovation means different things to different people and in different contexts, here we will generally consider it to be the conception and realization of new customer value through the *joint* activities of invention, commercialization by the firm, and adoption by customers. Invention may be incremental or transformational, but entails the creative act of ideation together with successful reduction to practice. Commercialization requires a viable business model and its successful execution. Adoption requires a compelling value proposition and the realization of the promise of that proposition through customer purchase, use, and the actual experience of benefits.

Innovation can apply to process innovation (i.e., improving operational and information excellence), product and service innovation (i.e., improving product, service, and solution leadership), customer relationship innovation (i.e., enhancing customer and collective intimacy), or *innovation* innovation—in other words, transforming innovation itself.

Innovation has experienced several major phases. The era of the individual, responsible for inventions and discoveries such as fire, the wheel, and the General Theory of Relativity, gave way to the first industrial laboratories, where tinkerers worked with company employees such as machinists. This was followed by a period where industrial labs moved beyond antagonism toward science, realized that theory had commercial value, and began partnering with and then hiring early scientists such as physicists and chemists.

The R&D lab matured to a pinnacle of "closed" internal innovation, conducted in giant labs such as Bell Laboratories, my prior employer and home to multiple Nobel Laureates, to "skunk works" such as Lockheed's famed secret facility, home of the SR-71 "Blackbird" reconnaissance and F-117 stealth aircraft. As the captive labs of industrial juggernauts of the time such as AT&T, IBM, Xerox, and Lockheed, the entire company had the resources to fund, invent, assess, and test nascent technologies and product or service concepts, and then bring them to market, including building manufacturing facilities, if needed.

A good example is AT&T. Scientists at its Bell Telephone Laboratories unit invented the transistor, built semiconductor fabrication facilities, designed and manufactured Electronic Switching Systems that each enabled tens of thousands of calls to be connected, deployed them in "central offices" around the country, and offered telephone service. Not that different a concept from the Venetian Arsenal, which grew its own wood, designed its own ships, built them, outfitted them with the weapons of the day, and offered maintenance and repair services.

That approach to innovation still exists today, to some extent, not only at traditional organizations such as AT&T, GE, and IBM, but also at newer companies such as Google and Apple. But according to Henry Chesbrough, an adjunct professor at the University of California–Berkeley Haas School of Business, companies need to complement this approach to innovation with a more open approach that includes leveraging external research and invention and also includes exploiting external paths to commercialization.

Utilizing external research could involve activities as significant as a multibillion-dollar acquisition, or as simple as a phone call with a noted expert. There again, the Venetian Arsenal was ahead of everyone else: It brought in Galileo as a consultant. Galileo acted as a product and process engineering consultant, helping to enhance the production processes of the arsenal, and as a scientist and product engineer, helping with navigation and weaponry. The benefits went both ways: Not only did Galileo help, but the practical problems of shipbuilders made their way into Galileo's creation of a new science concerning the strength of materials such as ropes, oars, and masts. This had practical implications, such as how large an oak boom or yardarm (the horizontal elements that keep the sail in place) could be made without cracking from its own weight.[4]

However, digital technologies open new possibilities for such open, external innovation and can make innovation better, cheaper, and faster.

Innovation can be made better, as open challenges and idea markets enable rapid access to global researchers with specific expertise to solve thorny technical problems.

Innovation can be made faster, as the process of hiring and onboarding subject matter experts who might or might not produce meaningful results is bypassed in favor of transactional engagements with individuals who may need to pass proof-of-concept or quantified performance tests to validate their contributions.

Innovation can be made cheaper, as fixed salaries are supplanted by contest economics, where payment may be made in cash or reputation, and such payment may be specified to only be paid in the event of a successful innovation.

Accelerated innovation is intended to encompass this approach of more cost-effective, results-oriented, timely, digitally mediated open external innovation. The contest approach is not new—it dates back to 1714 and even earlier, with contests such as for the *Longitude Prize*, intended to improve navigation at sea. What is new in the modern incarnation is the global, ubiquitous, instantaneous reach of the web to potential solvers, the ability to publish enormous data sets and have them instantaneously accessible, the maturation of intermediaries such as Kaggle and Innocentive that have made it easy to run a contest or intermediaries such as Kickstarter and Quirky that have made it easier to crowdfund or prioritize funding for commercial introduction.

Chapters 14 to 16 will address accelerated innovation in depth.

All of the Above?

It is traditional in strategy books to explain that unless a company focuses on a single strategy, it will be doomed to mediocrity and "stuck in the middle," as we discussed in Chapter 2 with Sears and McDonald's as examples. However, the economics of information and of IT may enable companies to pursue multiple disciplines simultaneously, and there can be synergies between them.

Moreover, although we present the disciplines as if they are separate, they are interrelated, not disjointed. When Intel introduces a new generation of chip, there are often improvements to the product itself—product leadership, say, the memory capacity of an integrated circuit. But, there are often also improvements to the processes used to manufacture and test the chip (i.e., operational excellence). For example, the components may be spaced closer together, or manufactured in three dimensions as opposed to the traditional two. And, some design decisions may be made based on input from customers (i.e., customer intimacy).

Brad Power, a consultant in innovation and business transformation, in a piece for the *Harvard Business Review*, writes that customer intimacy and operational excellence are increasingly intertwined. A company such as L.L. Bean, which has "survived through heroics," according to Terry Sutton, its vice president of business transformation, has been making investments in IT to foster operational excellence.[5]

One level of customer intimacy uses existing products and processes to meet customer needs, say, the way The Home Depot helps customers select from standard inventory to meet their home needs. A next level uses standard processes to create never-before-seen products—for example, in the way that Nike allows customers to select various colors and monograms for footwear through NikeID. A next level creates custom processes to create custom products based on customer intimacy: Architecture, engineering, and construction firms often do this for special projects. And at the ultimate level, firms redefine their innovation process and create other custom processes to create custom products to meet unique needs. Examples include the Manhattan Project to build the first atomic bomb in utmost secrecy, or the overall NASA *Apollo* mission, which led to the first moon landing.

High technology is not restricted to high tech: For example, food companies devise new processes to introduce new products as well. The Pringles stackable chip was intended to be a better product, solving issues with the traditional potato chip such as broken chips at the bottom of the bag and consumer's receipt of more air than chips as the bag contents settled. However, the product required new preparation and cooking processes and a specially designed machine to make them.

It is also clear that innovation relates to processes, products, and relationships: Whether the chips are branded Intel or Pringles, innovation of the product often requires innovation of the process. And, of course, intimate customer relationships can be used to drive innovation: Consider customer focus groups, test labs or agile co-creation.

Companies can apply the disciplines together or in separate business units to achieve separate objectives.

Netflix, for example, used accelerated innovation to engage the world's top statisticians to identify improvements to its Cinematch movie recommendation engine in the days before streaming. This engine was focused on collective intimacy—using movie ratings and rental habits to improve movie recommendations. Netflix also has pursued information excellence—developing and implementing a streaming architecture that delivers movies over a backbone network and then over the Internet into millions of homes simultaneously.

In Chapter 17 we examine GE, which is successfully pursuing multiple disciplines simultaneously.

Even if a company is pursuing only a single value or digital discipline, there are common levers and traps. All digital disciplines require not just insightful strategy formulation but successful execution, including successful adoption by customers, employees, and partners. *Gamification*—the use of principles of human behavior such as those that make games so enjoyable—accounts for not just rational human cognitive processes but irrational, emotional, ones. People are not just often irrational, they are, as author and Duke professor Dan Ariely says, *predictably* irrational.[6] Chapter 18 examines the secrets to human motivation, exploring numerous cognitive biases and anomalies, and tactics to employ those quirks to maximize execution success. Chapter 19 looks at Opower, a company that is dramatically reducing energy consumption using those behavioral insights.

The traps include everything from poor IT project management to inability to scale to security and privacy issues. As bad as those are now, the Internet of Things will make them worse if steps aren't taken to make them better. For example, everything from Wi-Fi light bulbs to smart TVs to nannycams has *already* been exploited. It isn't just an irritating inconvenience; motion picture studios and steel mills have been harmed or destroyed by such actions. Chapter 20 overviews pitfalls to beware.

■   ■   ■

Michael Treacy and Fred Wiersema created a timeless framework for companies to identify, crystallize, and deliver strategic differentiated value to customers through operational excellence (i.e., better processes), product leadership (i.e., better products), and customer intimacy (i.e., better customer relationships). However, their approach can benefit by being updated for the modern digital era, where digital technologies combine with value disciplines to create digital disciplines.

Excellence in physical operations can be complemented, enabled or replaced by excellence in information. Leadership in products or services is often no longer enough, because standalone offers are giving way to cloud-connected product-service systems, in turn driving shifts to ecosystems, subscription models, and a focus on outcomes. Customer intimacy is evolving from face-to-face personal and organizational relationships to data-driven relationships at scale, where advanced algorithms can drive better relationships with each customer, thanks to relationships maintained with all customers. And the nature of innovation is shifting, with virtual experiments replacing real ones and collaboration moving beyond the four walls of the enterprise into external, open collaboration.

Notes

1. "Top 25 Hotels—World," *TripAdvisor.com* (accessed March 2015), www.tripadvisor.com/TravelersChoice-Hotels-cLuxury-g1.
2. "Bazaar's Little Black Book of Stylists," *HarpersBazaar.com* (accessed March 2015), www.harpersbazaar.com/beauty/g1629/little-black-book-of-stylists/?slide=2.
3. Joe Weinman, "How Customer Intimacy Is Evolving to Collective Intimacy, Thanks to Big Data," *Forbes.com*, June 4, 2013, www.forbes.com/sites/joeweinman/2013/06/04/how-customer-intimacy-is-evolving-to-collective-intimacy-thanks-to-big-data/.
4. Matteo Valleriani, *Galileo Engineer* (New York: Springer, 2010), 117.
5. Brad Power, "Customer Intimacy, Meet Operational Excellence," *HBR.org*, September 6, 2013, https://hbr.org/2013/09/customer-intimacy-meet-operati.
6. Dan Ariely, *Predictably Irrational: The Hidden Forces That Shape Our Experiences* (New York: HarperCollins, 2008).

CHAPTER 4
Digital Technologies

A Cambrian explosion of digital technologies underpins the digital disciplines, driven by developments in science and technology, an increasing economic shift from physical to virtual, accelerating global competition, and increased venture capital and government investment.

Advances in these technologies are too numerous to list, and would be immediately out of date as technologies showing early promise fail to pan out or gain user adoption, and new entrants arrive. Some, such as 3D printing, 4K displays, and drones have captured the popular imagination as volume and learning curve effects begin to drive down prices to consumer levels; others—such as quantum cryptography, machine learning, artificial intelligence, and neuromorphic computing, memristors, electroholographic displays, and optical satellites—are emerging.

It can be argued, though, that there are five key categories of information-related technologies: people and things, data and processing, and the networks to tie them all together; hence the list in the subtitle of this book: cloud, big data, social, mobile, and the Internet of Things. All of the digital disciplines—information excellence, solution leadership, collective intimacy, and accelerated innovation—rely on these building blocks. Complex solutions, such as artificial intelligence or machine cognition (computers that think like we do, or better) use a mix of advanced algorithms running on massive data sets.

The core technologies defining today's world fundamentally echo a basic architecture for information processing. Logically, information processing begins with data. Data from a broad variety of sources generally must be collected to be processed, requiring networks, whether wireless or wireline, storage of the data, and processing of the stored data or live datastreams to detect trends or anomalies and develop actionable insight. Decisions must then be executed, requiring transmission back out to the edges of the network, to the people who execute the decisions or actuators that invoke them.

For example, consider a smart electric grid. Power usage from a variety of devices, household temperature, ambient temperature, and electric load on the grid, and policies, such as "never let the temperature in my house be less than 64 degrees or more than 76 degrees," can be fed into a central decision support capability. This, in turn, can be used to adjust thermostats across households and business facilities within the grid area, potentially remaining within the constraints of each policy while minimizing the likelihood of brown- or black-outs. An untethered thermostat could keep the temperature in range, but wouldn't be able to coordinate with other electrical devices in light of real-time grid conditions.

For information excellence, real-time data is acquired from sensors in things, fed over networks to dynamic optimization systems in the cloud, and then used to feed actuators (things) such as cranes or to inform people. For solution leadership, things such as pacemakers link across networks to the cloud in a variety of different services configurations, such as monitoring, archiving, and so forth, and from there on to social media and the rest of the ecosystem. For collective intimacy, data on customer behavior, characteristics, and preferences is collected by things such as medical scanners or DNA sequencers or television set-top boxes, fed across networks to big data/analytics engines, and used to generate recommendations or offer better services. And, for accelerated innovation, challenges are advertised and data sets are published in the cloud, accessed via solvers across networks, and then uploaded to contest evaluation mechanisms in the cloud.

Because these digital technologies are essential to the digital disciplines, it's worth overviewing each of them briefly.

The Cloud

There are many definitions of *cloud computing*, but we can think of it simply as applications, computing, storage, and networking resources acquired on a rental, subscription, or service basis, rather than through ownership. What taxis and rental cars are to automobile ownership, what hotel rooms are to home ownership, and what tax preparation services are to filing your own returns, cloud computing is to computer system ownership and application licensing and use. Whether we are talking about computers, automobiles, or rooms, resources are shared across multiple customers, and each customer pays in proportion to the quantity of resources and amount of time used.

The cloud is typically viewed as either encompassing low-level elements, such as computer hardware, platform as a service, web services, and microservices, where components that are the software equivalent of Lego® blocks can be rapidly assembled, and software as a service, where programs such as Google search, H&R Block accounting, Salesforce.com customer relationship management, or Twitter, Instagram, and Facebook remote software services may be used.

In previous writings, I've defined the cloud very exactly.[1,2] For our purposes here, however, we'll use the term *cloud* very expansively, to mean any type of computing—and related functions such as storage, data and database management, and applications—performed in a data center; typically far away from the manufacturing process, service operations, physical product, data collection device, or customer touchpoint.

Increasingly, complex functions will be performed locally, at the device, whether it be a toaster or a car. As microprocessors increase in computing power, formerly intractable functions such as language and image recognition, logical deduction, and collision detection and autonomic vehicles (self-driving cars) will be feasible, and eventually commonplace. However, there are many reasons to perform such functions remotely. Cloud providers can exhibit economies of scale and specialized expertise and gain utilization benefits by sharing resources across customers. Also, data from multiple sources can be aggregated and interrelated. After all, having your own *private* Facebook or your own telephone system that no one else could access would not be very useful; social networking, communications, collaboration, gaming, and processing large volumes of data and drawing correlations with other data inherently require a cloud approach.

Although there are still plenty of untethered, smart, digital products, such as greeting cards that play songs or the CHI digital ceramic blow dryer with a touchscreen display, connecting such products to the cloud offers new functions. For example, a wearable or implantable device may be able to tell you that your heart rate was at 150 for 37 minutes during your workout today, but only through networks and the combined processing that the cloud offers can it tell you that the workout was in the top 7 percent of people of your age and gender today. A standalone GPS device and database may be able to tell you to turn *right* up ahead to get to your destination, but only a cloud-connected one can tell you to turn *left* instead, because otherwise you'll end up in the middle of a traffic jam.

Thus, rather than merely thinking of the cloud as computing resources for hire, it is important to realize that it is a nexus for the flow of information among many different entities: people, devices, and applications. A smart digital device unconnected to a network is like someone reading a book or playing solitaire in their secluded mountain cabin. The cloud is like a cocktail party, with information flowing dynamically among all involved parties. Facebook, Instagram, and Twitter are examples of cloud applications, where hundreds of millions of people exchange information. In a way, so is the air traffic control system, where tens of thousands of planes exchange information with controllers, or a package delivery system, where thousands of delivery trucks are optimally routed.

In the case of information excellence, the cloud acquires information from people or devices, and executes sophisticated algorithms to perform dynamic optimization or fuse digital and physical worlds.

For solution leadership, the cloud is part of the complete system—physical endpoint(s), network, cloud, and social—that together comprise the complete solution and make it more than a standalone product or service.

In the case of collective intimacy, the cloud is the central collection point for the data, such as movie-watching behavior, ratings, and context, and then executes the algorithms that generate personalized services, such as movie recommendations.

For accelerated innovation, the cloud is the intermediary that, for example, can match solvers with challenges, distribute data for solvers to analyze, and serve as a computing resource to evaluate innovative algorithms.

Big Data

Just as there are many definitions of the cloud, there are a number of definitions of **big data**. One popular one, from Doug Laney of research firm Gartner, is that big data is data that has volume, velocity, and variety.[3]

Volume means that there is a lot of data, which may arise through a number of factors, such as acquiring *all* data rather than merely sampling; monitoring large numbers of customers or large numbers of things; processing large quantities of transactions per customer; or massive detail per transaction. For example, merchandisers don't just want to know that you bought the gray sweater in size medium, but the exact series of bends, reaches, and steps taken and counters and aisles visited in the physical store, or web page navigation and mouse moves on your desktop browser. This enables them to maximize revenue.

Velocity means that this data is changing rapidly—say, a live datastream from weather sensors; sales data from Amazon.com during Cyber Monday; in-flight data from the plane and jet engines; or what's trending on Twitter. While there is a high volume of social security numbers, their velocity is low. Conversely, the price of a share of Apple is a single entity, but has a high degree of velocity.

Variety means that, rather than, just, say, a traditional "structured" relational database of employee names, home addresses, and social security numbers, it might include "unstructured" data such as YouTube or surveillance videos, device telemetry, images, tweets, Facebook status updates, 3D models, documents, and metadata—data about data—such as timestamps and geographic location.

Others have added different Vs over time, such as *veracity*—that is, the notion that the data should be correct and factual, which is often a challenge due to either multiple data sources or sources such as social media, which may not be verifiable. *Variability* is the idea that the data changes over an extremely wide range of values, and *value* is the concept that it must have value to the business.

While the Vs are helpful, we don't need to make such fine distinctions for the purposes of this book. An application that enables information excellence is not going to be ruled out because it doesn't include video data or doesn't have enough velocity. The point is that as the costs of processing and storage have plummeted, and as a projected tens of billions of devices ranging from pacemakers to toasters to cans of soup start generating massive quantities of data, such data can be collected, processed, analyzed, and communicated in real time to provide insight that can aid decision making. Examples range from which customers should receive coupons to which plane should land at Runway 06 to whether a jet engine is about to fail or a patient is about to have a heart attack. That insight can be provided to people to drive action, or used to direct machines, or both. And the action can be as trivial as turning right in 100 feet or manufacturing another paper clip, or as impactful as creating a new billion-dollar brand.

Big data sometimes appears to be solely the realm of marketing, but it applies to a broad array of processes, including basic science, research and development, and production and service delivery. It is also key to the latest generation of products and services, and customer relationships.

A few major themes are worth noting about big data.

First, new software technologies are being devised to efficiently process such data sets. A good example is the technology originally developed by Google to be able to respond rapidly to any random search query, no matter how unique, misspelled, or poorly formatted, such as "chinees restorant time sq.," which serves up Ruby Foo's in a half second. The speed of such technologies means that applications can respond in real-time and interactively, whether for such search queries, driving directions, or business purposes such as fraud detection or construction site safety.

Second, with enough data, as AT&T's former chief scientist Dave Belanger says, even weak signals can support strong inferences.[4] An example he uses is a web search on "flu." If one person searches for it, it might mean that he suspects that he has the flu, mistyped "fly," or might be the rare case of an author looking for an interesting factoid to end a paragraph like this one, such as that neuraminidase inhibitors can be an effective flu treatment.

But, if *thousands* of people in a given area suddenly start searching on "flu," there is a high likelihood that there is an epidemic. This is the premise behind Google Flu Trends.[5] It turns out that searches on Google closely track actual flu incidence as monitored by the Centers for Disease Control.

People don't even need to be involved. If one cell phone shakes, it might have been dropped or be a muscle tremor. But if many do within a given region, synchronously and with an ever-widening radius, it's probably an earthquake. CalTech's Community Seismic Network uses a phone-based app to report centrally on vibrations detected by the phone's accelerometer.[6] Obviously, the same approach using other types of sensors could measure smog, temperature, or humidity. In another approach, the videos that each spectator takes at sporting, concerts, or similar events could be merged to create a movable perspective.

A third theme is the ability to process live data flows rather than data sets. This is something like the difference between watching the stock ticker rather than perusing the financial section of a printed newspaper. The ability to actively query live streams (how has the average sale price of AAPL been trending since lunch time?) can lead to faster response times (Buy! Sell!) than by looking at static historical data sets.

A fourth theme, enabled by the plummeting price of data storage, is the opportunity to engage in what might be called fishing expeditions or treasure hunts. If a company knew in advance *exactly* the questions it would ask over the next decade, it would be easy to design an architecture that threw away unneeded data and left only data key to answering those questions. However, like a forensics expert at a crime scene, maintaining the integrity of all possible data is key to enabling future open-ended questions—the treasure hunts. The price-performance of today's storage enables both cost-effective storage and cost-effective processing of the data stored therein. This has two dimensions: the degree of granularity of the data and the length of time the data can be successfully processed. For example, if we are trying to make decisions on an investment portfolio, we need to not just know the value of the Dow Jones Industrial Average; we'd like to know the prices of individual stocks. And, we don't just want to know their value now; we'd like to be able to see every transaction since the stock began trading.

A fifth major theme is that leaders in using data tend to use a mix of proprietary data and externally sourced data. For example, a beverage company might have data on sales by region by week, day, or even hour. However, to gain insights, say, for running marketing promotions, often requires looking not just at that data, but also data such as the weather, the economy, or demographics. It's not just marketing. If a jet engine company wants to understand engine performance or devise algorithms for predictive maintenance, it benefits from knowing the speed and altitude that the engines were flown at. But it also benefits from weather and atmospheric data, including, for example, airborne particulates.

Analysis of big data leads to insights that often contradict "obvious" conclusions. It turns out, for example, that swimming pools are deadlier than guns and car seats are no better than seat belts in protecting kids, as statistically valid studies have shown.[7] However, sometimes, intuition can be a helpful complement to machine intelligence. Sometimes it's superior to machine intelligence, at least for now. Often, though, deep analysis of data at a scale that dwarfs any human or organization is required; hence, the value of big data. A popular example of this is the IBM Watson victory at *Jeopardy!*. Perhaps less well known is the victory of "Pocket Fritz 4," a chess game running on a smartphone, in a chess match in Argentina, demonstrating play at the level of a chess grandmaster.

Data is the fuel for the engine of information excellence. It helps to optimize processes in terms of better performance, better asset utilization, and greater availability through predictive and proactive maintenance. For example, voltage issues detected by smart electric meters can signal the need to replace a transformer; variations in a jet engine's speed can signal that it needs maintenance.

It supports solution leadership, as devices that generate data can provide their customers better value—for example, lowering their electric bill or helping with their athletic training.

It supports collective intimacy, as deeper insights are derived based on examining granular customer behavior such as which scene in a movie is replayed and which one is skipped, or which section of a DNA sequence predisposes the patient to react in a certain way to a certain treatment.

In addition, publishing big data can help with innovators who use it to test new process algorithms, such as airline scheduling, or new relationship algorithms such as retail upsell, or new products such as smart thermostats. In addition to aiding human innovation, machines are already beginning to innovate. For example, IBM's Chef Watson creates new recipes by analyzing existing ones.

Mobile

Moving data from things to the cloud and back requires networks. Often these are wired, like traditional telephones or cable or fiber connections, but increasingly they are mobile. "Feature phones," like the old flip phones, smartphones, tablets, and laptops often come to mind when people think about mobility, and it is true that these are critically important parts of the digital economy.

But wireless technologies are important in many other contexts as well, including smart tags such as RFID (Radio Frequency Identification Tags) on products or pallets, connected devices such as "smart" light bulbs and toasters, connected cars, and so forth. There are many different technologies at play. Some are very familiar, like Wi-Fi and Bluetooth; others less so, like Near-Field Communications and contactless chips for secure mobile payments; ultra-wideband (UWB), which enables wireless short-range transmission of TV signals; optical wireless such as "Li-Fi," where, for example, a light bulb can transmit data; and wireless power such as through "Qi," which enables cable-free charging.

Sometimes the means of connection is subtle. Bazooka Joe bubble gum includes an 8 character alphanumeric code in each "comic" to unlock rewards and link each piece of gum to the cloud. Webkinz stuffed animals have a secret code linked to a virtual toy on the web accessible through a browser. Bottles of Heinz ketchup have QR (quick response) codes linking them to the cloud via smart phones.

Although most people use "mobile" and "wireless" interchangeably, there are subtle differences. A water meter that is attached to a house may be wireless, but isn't very mobile.

As with big data and the cloud, we are less concerned with exacting definitions such as for specific network technologies, and more concerned with the impact that such cost-effective, always-on, ubiquitous connectivity has in enabling better processes, products, relationships, and innovation.

Mobile technologies enable a range of improved processes. One of my favorite examples is the fishermen of Kerala, India, who, using nothing more sophisticated than voice-only feature phones, can determine which shore markets are offering the best prices for their catch and deliver them there rather than to markets that are already overstocked. Or consider Amazon's use of mobile Kiva robots to improve warehouse logistics, or Uber's use of GPS and smartphones to efficiently match drivers with prospective passengers.

Many products can benefit from mobile technologies, such as cameras with connections to upload pictures to services such as Shutterfly or cars linked to insurance or vehicle emergency detection and response services.

And, no firm can truly be intimate with customers unless it has a "presence" everywhere the customer is. Perhaps the most intimate mobile devices are implanted medical devices, such as connected pacemakers.

Mobility is also unleashing multiple waves of innovation. More global innovators can participate in the new economy, since their Internet connection is often through their mobile phone. And, of course, the unique capabilities of mobile devices and their omnipresence are driving a Cambrian explosion of innovation in apps and their functionality.

The Internet of Things

Everyone is familiar with the Internet, which connects people to other people (e.g., via email, messaging, or chat or through social networks) and also people to machines (e.g., people to search engines, mapping tools, or movie streaming services). The Internet of Things is the popular term used to add "things" into this mix, and is often intended to encompass not just the things, but the networks, data, and cloud processing that enhance and invigorate them. These can be very small, such as "smart dust" or nanoparticles, or much larger: light bulbs, thermostats, garage door openers, video cameras, digital signage such as electronic billboards, store shelves, refrigerators, toasters, autonomous robots, driverless cars, farm tractors, buses, planes, jet engines, clothing, cans, bottles, boxes, pallets, air conditioners, washing machines, smart buildings, smart cities, or a smart planet.

The Internet of Things is also referred to by many similar or related terms: smart, connected products, the Industrial Internet, cyber-physical systems, embedded systems, the Internet of Everything, pervasive computing, intelligent machines, brilliant machines, machine to machine, and sensor networks, for example. Regardless of what it's called, the general notion is a combination of sensors and/or actuators, power, software and hardware, which connects over networks to other systems or people.

The sensors may be videocameras, image capture devices, those for pressure, touch, motion, humidity, moisture, vibration, infrared, or what have you, and the actuators may be electromagnets, motors, valves, switches. These work with other mechanical, electrical, and electronic or optical components such as gears, lenses, networking elements, and power supplies. At one extreme, a jumbo jet or a ship or a building can be a thing; at the other, an ingestible pill with a small sensor and wireless connection can be.

Smart, connected things enable information excellence by providing the data needed to make smart decisions, as well as the mechanisms to implement those decisions. Logistics optimization, for example, may require information on trucks and intermodal containers, and the ability to use cranes to move those containers around.

Smart, connected products are the core enabler of solution leadership. A good example is wind farms, where the turbines perform optimally by communicating with each other, a master controller, and the electric grid.

Connected things enable the capture of data on customer behavior that enables intimacy. Smart TVs, set-top boxes, or other streaming devices can capture data on movie watching, gene sequencers or pathology equipment on DNA or tissue samples.

Finally, connected things can support innovation, by acquiring data by which to gain insight into customer and user needs, behaviors, and contexts that, in turn, can be a first step in creating a commercially viable solution to those needs.

Social

Social technologies cover a broad range of capabilities. One obvious example is social networks, such as Facebook. But there are other ways of engaging groups of people through technology. For example, crowdfunding sites such as Kickstarter enable the collective financial resources of many people with small donations to support a creative idea; emerging crowdfunding sites such as EquityNet enable investors essentially to bypass investment banks and act as venture capitalists. Crowdsourcing sites such as Quirky let anyone suggest an idea, or vote for someone else's idea, with the idea being that the collective wisdom of the participants is both more inventive than any individual and is an effective proxy for market reaction to new product ideas. Airbnb is a means for people to match up available real estate, whether a home or a spare bedroom in an apartment, with people who need to stay somewhere. Any time that resources—financial, intellectual, information, entertainment, or otherwise—are being contributed or shared by people, social technologies are at work.

Social is important for information excellence, since people plus algorithms often are better than just algorithms. Moreover, customers often benefit from social elements. Knowing the restaurants or books or music that your friends like or that strangers have positively reviewed has more weight in purchasing decisions than generic lists.

Solution leadership gains from social network integration. For example, Nike+ ecosystem products often upload activities to social networks, so that personal bests or running a race can generate accolades from friends. Smart TVs will increasingly add a social dimension to what was previously a solitary or family activity.

Collective intimacy benefits from the social element as well: upsell/cross-sell can be enhanced when the customer's friends made similar purchases, and recommendation engines increasingly include the social element under the theory that if all of your friends liked a movie, book, or song, you are more likely to as well.

And accelerated innovation can often require a mix of collaboration, competition, and co-creation, which at their heart, are social technologies.

Such interactions were traditionally geographically constrained, but can now be global.

While social technologies—perhaps restated as those technologies that support interaction, engagement, and relationship-building among people—represent a key driver for individuals, there are many additional rational and irrational drivers of human behavior. Some, such as a need for status, are inherently a result of the fact that people are social primates. But there are other behaviors that are not as closely tied, such as *loss aversion*, the idea that an economic loss is perceived as worse than an equivalent gain is perceived as beneficial. There are dozens of cognitive biases that fall under the broad areas of behavioral economics, neuroeconomics, human psychology, motivation, gamification, and so on, which we'll discuss in Chapter 18.

■ ■ ■

There are hundreds of important information technologies that have the potential to drive strategic advantage through better processes, products, and services, relationships, and innovation. The big five discussed here—cloud, big data, mobile, social, and things—are just a start.

At some level, though, the five cornerstone elements of this book, which may be generically thought of as things, people, connectivity, information processing, and data, are unlikely to be displaced. Emerging technologies will merely enable still-greater process improvements, new types of connected solutions, more intimate relationships, and more, well, innovative, innovation.

Notes

1. Joe Weinman, *Cloudonomics: The Business Value of Cloud Computing* (Hoboken, NJ: John Wiley & Sons, 2012).
2. Joe Weinman, "Axiomatic Cloud Theory," Working Paper, July 29, 2011, www.JoeWeinman.com/Resources/Joe_Weinman_Axiomatic_Cloud_Theory.pdf.
3. Doug Laney, "3D Data Management: Controlling Data Volume, Velocity, and Variety," META Group, February 6, 2001, blogs.gartner.com/doug-laney/files/2012/01/ad949-3D-Data-Management-Controlling-Data-Volume-Velocity-and-Variety.pdf.
4. David Belanger, "Making Big Data Work for Your Organization," *KnowHOWE* 16, no. 2 (Fall 2013), https://www.stevens.edu/howe/sites/howe/files/Belanger.pdf.
5. "Google.org Flu Trends: Explore Flu Trends around the World," www.google.org/flutrends.

6. Matthew Faulkner, Robert Clayton, Thomas Heaton, K. Mani Chandy, Monica Kohler, Julian Bunn, Richard Guy, Annie Liu, Michael Olson, Minghei Cheng, and Andreas Krause, "Community Sense and Response Systems: Your Phone as a Quake Detector," *Communications of the ACM* (July 2014): 66–75.
7. Freakonomics, "Are You Ready for Swimming Pool Season?" http://freakonomics .com/2006/04/16/are-you-ready-for-swimming-pool-season/, April 16, 2006; Stephen J. Dubner and Steven D. Levitt, "The Seat-Belt Solution," *New York Times*, July 10, 2005, www.nytimes.com/2005/07/10/magazine/10FREAK.html.

PART TWO

Information Excellence

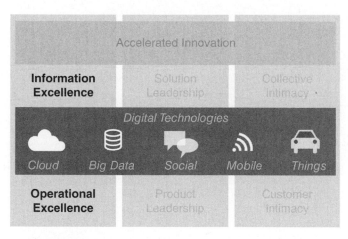

CHAPTER 5

Operations and Information

Operational excellence is one of Treacy and Wiersema's three value disciplines, which we've extended to information excellence as one of the digital disciplines. But what exactly do we mean by *operations* and *information*, and how do they relate to each other?

We can think of operations as broadly encompassing a network of interlinked processes together with the assets or resources they use to generate outputs. These processes can either enable the creation, sales, support, and production of products or delivery of services. To illustrate the breadth of these elements, processes can include manufacturing, sales, marketing, returns, service and support, patient admission, aircraft maintenance, lawn mowing, and so forth. Assets can encompass things like cash, stores, factories, equipment such as mills, drills, and computers, trucks, ships, and inventory, human resources in some sort of governance and organizational structure, and also intangible resources such as information, including internal data, externally acquired data, customer data, intellectual property, and trade secrets.

Process improvement often seems to be viewed as synonymous with cost reduction; resource management with asset utilization; organization improvement with downsizing; and information management with budget cutting. While cost control and optimization can be useful and help drive competitive advantage, other approaches to processes, resources, how they are organized, and information can be strategic as well, impacting revenue, profitability, and market position.

To understand the potential *top-line* value of evolutionary and revolutionary improvements to operational processes, one needs to look no further than Federal Express, now FedEx. It created an entirely new industry—express distribution—generating tens of billions of dollars in revenue globally each year, through "mere" process change. That process change was *not* focused on cost reduction; in fact, FedEx services were priced at a premium; their advantage was based primarily on *speed* but also on reliability and visibility through real-time tracking. FedEx didn't invent the airplane, trucks, conveyor belts, or packaging; it was how it employed them in an accelerated, reliable, visible *process* that caused it to not only succeed, but to become one of the fastest companies to reach one billion dollars in revenue. In addition to innovative logistics—an integrated system for air cargo rather than "interlining" between air carriers with its resultant delays and the use of a "superhub" in Memphis—FedEx also made use of innovative information technology. It was the first shipping company to use IT to manage and optimize its resources and processes such as trucks, planes, crews, and drivers, incorporating information such as shifting weather conditions.

There are many other examples of process changes that have created industries or helped firms create competitive advantage. Michael Dell innovated, accelerated, and lower-cost processes for ordering, configuring, and delivering PCs; eBay, the process for selling used goods; Wal-Mart, cross-docking; Netflix, the processes for selecting, recommending, distributing, and paying for DVD rentals; Uber the process for acquiring and paying for transportation.

Uber is a particularly interesting example because it combines two separate major strategies for information excellence: process optimization and asset optimization. Rather than standing in the street to hail a cab, or calling and hoping for one to show up, Uber dramatically improves the "ordering" process by using a mobile client together with GPS tracking to make the process faster and more convenient. In addition, it optimizes assets, largely by dispensing with them. Rather than incurring huge fixed leasing costs or capital expenditures to acquire a large fleet of vehicles and hiring an army of drivers for them, it relies on on-demand, pay-per-use acquisition of both.

Processes

The constellation of interlocking activities that firms conduct goes by many different names: business processes, operations, workflows, value chains, value networks. These processes vary by industry, but at a high level have substantial similarities. For example, most companies have inbound and outbound logistics, including supply chain management, procurement, distribution and delivery, and channel management; inbound and outbound marketing such as competitive analysis, customer satisfaction management, and advertising and promotions.

There is a process for hiring employees, consisting of getting headcount and budget approval, writing a job specification and/or requisition and getting it approved, and so forth. There is a process for expense reporting, including attaching a copy of the receipts, having the expense report approved, and getting reimbursed. There is a process to launch a product, acquire a company, restructure financing, issue a press release, manage a customer complaint, and on and on.

Although often a process is defined as a sequence of activities, it is better described as a network of activities that may occur sequentially, in parallel, conditionally, iteratively, or a combination of these. Consider baking a cake, which is, after all, a process. Sequential activities include mixing the ingredients, *then* pouring them into the cake pan, *then* baking. Parallel ones include preheating the oven *while* mixing the ingredients. A conditional activity might involve adding more sugar *if* you want it sweeter. And an iterative activity would be to *repeatedly* take bites from the finished product. The act of baking and eating a cake is a structured network combining individual activities such as breaking an egg into an end-to-end process that creates value.

Often, there is substantial interplay between resources and processes that impacts value creation and performance. The total throughput (i.e., cakes produced per hour), whether of a family or commercial bakery, will be a function of the number of chefs, baking pans, mixers, and ovens. Suboptimal process design—say, waiting until the oven is preheated before beginning to assemble ingredients—can reduce productivity, as can insufficient resources.

Competitive differentiation and business model innovation can often be achieved solely through process innovation, together with the supporting resources, organization, and information. For example, prepaid services have now gained 20 percent of the US mobile phone market,[1] based on a simple process change from "make calls, then pay" to "pay, then make calls." Of course, such simple process changes often require additional changes, for example, in payment processes and systems, and can create important shifts in the value proposition ranging from anonymity to a reduction in the risk of bill shock.

In addition to the structure of the activities, a broad view of processes includes how they are controlled, including decisions that are made that alter decision paths taken, how those activities are resourced, how the resources—information, energy, physical, and especially human—are organized, acquired, directed, and motivated, and how information is generated or used by those processes, and taken together, these can be a rich source of competitive advantage.

Process Advantage

What makes a process *better*, and how can companies gain strategic competitive advantage through better processes?

At a high level, organizations often categorize process improvements in terms of efficiency and effectiveness. Process efficiency can be addressed through the elimination of waste and better asset utilization. Process effectiveness varies by industry—for example, how good the process is at meeting objectives such as on-time, accurate delivery for transportation and logistics companies or medical outcomes such as long-term survival rates for healthcare providers.

As we have already noted, efficiency relates to doing things "right;" effectiveness to doing the right things. For example, one can drive from New York to Los Angeles "right," by not getting any speeding tickets, minimizing fuel costs, and with perfect posture. However, if Houston was the intended destination, not LA, those metrics wouldn't really matter.

But efficiency and effectiveness are too high level to be of real use in crafting strategy. Instead, it is important to realize that there are many dimensions by which one process may be "better" than another, and such an advantage depends on the segment, the client, and often the context, as well. There are a number of ways to differentiate processes.

Cost. Wal-Mart rose to prominence by having *lower cost* for retail supply chain and logistics processes than its competitors did. Cost can be reduced by eliminating unnecessary activities, such as checking for a boarding pass multiple times rather than once, or using less expensive or more productive resources, such as using nurse practitioners rather than board-certified physicians for some procedures, offshoring insurance claims processing, or outsourcing activities to an organization with greater economies of scale or skill.

Convenience/Experience. In addition to hard dollar costs, there are soft costs such as physical, cognitive, and emotional costs. A process might be physically difficult for a customer, user, or stakeholder; too complex to understand, use, or control; or emotionally harrowing: consider customer complaint processes or the process of testifying against a felony murder suspect. Various areas are relevant: decision convenience (ease of purchase or use decisions), access convenience, benefit convenience (ease of realizing results), and so forth.[2]

Quality. Although we all have a view about what *quality* is, it is a surprisingly rich term. Quality can mean closer conformance to manufacturing tolerances; a greater fit or perceived fit with customer requirements; lower cost due to lower *cost of quality* (i.e., lower cost of defects associated with poor quality). Often, these different dimensions are related: Toyota differentiated itself through higher-quality manufacturing processes to rise to become a leading global automobile manufacturer.

Relevance. One particularly important definition of quality is "fitness for use as perceived by the customer." Although this may include several aspects, one important one is surely relevance. Relevance can mean the quality of search query results, the appropriateness and efficacy of a course of medical treatment for a given patient, the correct size for clothing, or in real estate sales processes, a basket of dimensions such as proximity to shopping, quality of schools, low crime rate but also price, rooms, architectural style, and yard size.

Time. Amazon.com is an example of a company that has been focused on intervals from intent to ordering, accelerated through its famous "one-click" ordering process, and from order to delivery, through overnight delivery, most recently, its introduction of one-hour delivery in select markets, and eventually, possibly, drones or distributed 3D printing on roving trucks. Time can sometimes imply higher cost, for example, getting a package across the country using a dedicated private jet. However, time compression can also be aligned with lower cost: reduced work-in-process inventories go hand in hand with reduced manufacturing cycle times; they also reduce carrying costs associated with inventory. Time can be compressed by speeding up existing activities, either with faster resources, like Lucille Ball on the candy conveyor line, more resources, such as additional cashiers at the bank or grocery store, or different resources, such as substituting planes for ships. As with cost, time can be compressed by eliminating unnecessary or overly repeated activities or ones that don't add value.

Reliability and Performance. Offering more reliable processes can be a differentiator. Airlines—and passengers—obsess over their on-time arrival rate. Medical treatments should be reliable. Internet, cable, and phone service delivery should be reliable. A process with substandard performance may be indistinguishable from an unreliable process.

Availability. Some service processes are available only during limited times: banks are open from 9 a.m. to 3 p.m.; standard postal delivery is not available on Sundays; and so on. Creating 24/7 availability of processes can be a means for staking out a market position; limiting availability can enhance urgency.

Visibility. Customer visibility into process status can be a differentia-tor. A good example is package delivery tracking, which represented an improvement over mere delivery confirmation. It is only a matter of time before customers have visibility into the exact location and velocity of their package (say, "at the intersection of 3rd and Main, headed south at 27 mph"). Visibility is important in other domains as well: the state of a manufactured product, health metrics, exact batch or production characteristics (82 degrees Fahrenheit, 37 percent relative humidity), and so forth.

Control. Beyond visibility comes control. Some delivery firms allow cus-tomers to have a package held or even change destination after the package is *en route*; home construction companies allow varying degrees of customization after ground is broken. For some time, leading manufacturing companies have allowed employees to "stop the line" if there are quality or safety problems. Visibility and control are important to customers, because people fear uncer-tainty and exhibit a "need for control."

Synchronization. Firm processes that are better synchronized with customer processes can achieve advantage. Being able to select a delivery window for the arrival of, say, a new dishwasher, can be more advantageous than mere speed. If a customer will only be home Thursday afternoon, the ability to schedule delivery for then is to be preferred to it being rapidly left on the front steps on Monday.

Self-Service. One dimension of the need for control, together with individuals' "need for achievement," is for processes to enable at least the option for customer self-service. This is why people use ATMs (automated teller machines) even when there are bank tellers free.

Consistency. Generally, consistency is desirable in a process. If each Toyota Camry came off the line looking different, some looking like Mercedes SLK55s, and some looking like Smart Cars, Toyota and its customers would have a problem. And, if the horsepower or seat firmness or gas mileage varied randomly, that would be an issue as well. Consequently, process managers go to great pains to monitor processes and use techniques such as statistical process control to minimize unintended variation.

Predictability. If consistency can't be achieved, the next best thing can be predictability. The weather is a good example. It obviously is inconsistent. However, with predictive models now extending out reliably a few days for many weather phenomena, steps can be taken such as alternate routing of flights or pre-planned school closings.

Individuality. That said, there is often the desire to produce and consume semi-custom, custom, or truly individual and artisanal works. People have a "need for uniqueness," which might be better expressed as a belief—true or not—that they are unique. Simply put, they want products and services tailored to their needs that make them feel special.

Context-Sensitivity. Individuality is one dimension of context sensitivity. Processes also need to incorporate information about other contextual elements, such as ambient temperature, weather, local regulations, federal laws, cultural preferences, community sensitivities, and so forth. For example, McDonald's restaurants in India do not sell bacon cheeseburgers, because they do not sell beef or pork.[3] Airline flight preparation processes include de-icing if weather conditions suggest it is necessary.

Flexibility. While *unintended* variation is generally undesirable, process and resource flexibility can be very desirable. Production processes that can assemble different models of vehicles, for example, can adapt to shifting order volumes for sedans versus convertibles or cars versus SUVs (sport utility vehicles). Flexible resources, such as computer numerically controlled (CNC) machines or cross-trained workers can aid in such flexibility. Allowing auto buyers the flexibility of different colors, performance packages, sunroof options, and entertainment and navigation systems is an example of value-added flexibility.

Adaptability. Often, such flexibility is built into the design of the process and its equipment and facilities. Ideally though, firms would like processes with the capability to adapt to shifting conditions and learn. While traditionally such adaptability has been the domain of knowledge workers and their processes, such as strategy formulation, today even machines and devices adapt. A search engine, for example, can learn as you search. If your query is "models," it should know whether to return Golf rather than Gisele or Cabriolet rather than Claudia.

Safety and Security. Safety is important in virtually all physical processes: manufacturing, mining, farming, fishing, transportation, and so forth. Security and related process requirements such as privacy are important for those processes, as well as partly or wholly virtual ones. It also arises in perhaps-unexpected situations. For example, the interrelated operations of construction cranes in Dubai are coordinated by real-time anti-collision software.

Sustainability. Sustainability has rapidly increased in importance. This includes sustainable farming and forestry, reducing carbon footprint, using sustainable energy sources such as solar and wind, and using recyclable and recycled materials in manufacturing.

Ethics and Fairness. Processes may be more just, as with fair trade coffee. They may support social goals, such as avoiding use of child labor or ensuring safe working conditions and fair wages. A process may employ, enroll, pay, or promote based on or without regard to gender, minority status, or other demographics.

Empathy and Humanity. Although much of making processes better can be based on quantitative methods, often a process is better because of the culture and individuals involved. Processes ranging from healthcare to selling shoes over the web can be enhanced by caring individuals.

Compliance. Processes may achieve advantages associated either with marketability, process performance, or eliminated fines through compliance with government regulations, legal and regulatory bodies, or industry or social mores or norms. The list here is extensive and often industry dependent—for example, HIPAA (Health Insurance Portability and Accountability Act), OSHA (Occupational Safety and Health Administration), FAA (Federal Aviation Administration), or FINRA (Financial Industry Regulatory Authority).

Transparency. More transparent processes can be more efficient, whether because more stakeholders are able to suggest improvements or because they are less prone to corruption. For example, water utilities can report on levels of contaminants; cities can report on where the snow plows have been using GPS and data aggregation.[4]

Other. There are at least as many ways of differentiating processes as there are companies, customers, and their individual needs. One might add in employee satisfaction, individual comfort, self-actualization, love, economic opportunity, diversity, and more.

Of course, companies can differentiate based not only on a single dimension, but multiple ones. For example, FedEx created a whole new industry by deploying *faster*, more *reliable* package delivery processes with greater *visibility*. W. Chan Kim and Reneé Mauborgne argue in *Blue Ocean Strategy* that "value innovation" can enable differentiated products at lower cost. On the other hand, some would argue that it is better to excel in and be known for one differentiator than to muddle the messaging about what your brand stands for.

Strategic alignment is important, not just for a single process, but among all of them. Michael Porter, a professor at the Harvard Business School and one of the best-known strategy thought-leaders, argues that the activities (i.e., processes) in a business need to "fit" together for a strategy to be successful. Southwest Airlines was able to carve out a meaningful position in the airline industry by aligning multiple process and resource trade-offs into an aligned activity system: limited service to passengers, efficient ground, gate, and flight crews, frequent departures, high utilization of aircraft, a standardized fleet of aircraft, short-haul underserved routes that those planes could efficiently serve, and very low ticket prices complementing aligned "low-fare" branding.[5]

Defining segments, customers, and contexts can be important: delivering a kidney for a transplant requires a different model of aligned processes than transporting coal does. Depending on the strategy and process, standardization and repeatability may be important, as with toaster manufacturing, or flexibility and creativity may be, as with legal defense. To reduce variability, techniques ranging from Statistical Quality Control to "Six-Sigma" have arisen and been broadly deployed to ensure the repeatability of processes. Models such as the Capability Maturity Model, originally designed for software but broadly applicable to any type of process, rate processes according to five levels of increasing maturity: initial, or *ad hoc*, that is, random, chaotic, and uncontrolled; repeatable; defined with some level of standardization; managed, with metrics and controls in place; and optimized, that is, improved or reengineered for cost, time, quality, or reliability.

Process Optimization

Some of the dimensions just described that are useful for strategic differentiation can be implemented through specific actions such as leadership appointments, governance, organizational designs, and single-purpose programs. One example is enhancing transparency through the use of multiple outside director appointments to a board, or through a compensation committee that does not report to the CEO.

However, many process differentiators, such as cost and time, require quantitative optimization. Sometimes both qualitative and quantitative approaches can make sense. For example, cost optimization can be based on complex algorithms to maximize asset utilization, as well as, say, moving from sole source to dual source supplier arrangements to, among other things, provide greater negotiating leverage.

Optimization is a rich and complex field in mathematics, economics, operations research, and computer science. Roughly speaking, however, strategies may be considered to fall into two categories. At one extreme, you are trying to solve a problem once and for all, or at least for a relatively long period of time. What is the best place to build a bridge across the river? How thick do the girders and cables on the bridge need to be? What should the factory layout be? How many milling machines should it have? How should the pressure on the paint sprayers be set? How many conveyor belts should there be? Where should the airport be built? How many gates should it have? How many runways does it need?

At the other extreme there are dynamic, constantly shifting problems. Which flights, if any, should be allowed to take off on runway 08 given that the wind is now gusting to 20 knots from the southwest? In what order should they take off given that there is congestion over Chicago? Should flight UA15 level off at 33,000 feet?

Information technology is useful in both cases, but has completely different incarnations. In the first case, data can be collected manually, and calculations can proceed relatively slowly. Such calculations can even conceptually be performed by hand, or with a slide rule or abacus.

The second case is much more challenging, because results must be available in real time based on data that are collected in real time. This generally requires some sort of automated data collection through sensors, high-speed networks to bring the data to a central point, and enough computational capacity to analyze the data and provide an answer in seconds, or even milliseconds.

One of the challenges is that many of these types of optimization problems are "computationally complex." Problems that are very simple to describe and conceptually understand have answers that can't be calculated exactly in the time that such answers are needed. A classic example is the "Traveling Salesman Problem," which asks what the shortest route is to visit a number of cities. In simple cases, such as when the cities are New York, Kansas City, Los Angeles, Chicago, and Denver, the answer is straightforward: Start at one coast and move towards the other. When more cities are added, the problem becomes increasingly difficult, and eventually intractable—too hard to solve exactly in a practical amount of time.

Fortunately, there are often *heuristics*, such as the ones used by UPS's ORION system, which don't necessarily provide exact answers but often can provide good enough answers, and provide them within useful time frames.

Information is a requirement for both one-time and dynamic problems. Knowing where the river is the narrowest or the deepest or has the most stable ground may be helpful in determining where to build a bridge. However, timely information is particularly important in solving real-time, dynamic problems to achieve operational excellence.

Asset Optimization

In addition to process optimization, improved asset utilization can directly drive improved profitability, as measured by metrics such as return on assets or return on invested capital. A recent Boston Consulting Group study of nearly 3,000 firms spanning 24 verticals showed that "asset-light" models almost always generate better financial results, as one might expect.[6] But even companies with assets can find more productive ways to employ them and do more with less.

There are a number of ways to better use assets:

Process Improvement. Because processes utilize assets, streamlining processes—say by eliminating rework or waste by building quality in, or by eliminating unnecessary, non-value-adding process steps—has the effect of reducing wasted assets that support them.

Asset Optimization. Even if the process remains the same, there can be opportunities to more efficiently utilize resources. Earlier, we discussed UPS's ORION system, which can optimize the route taken. The high-level process remains the same, but by determining the best order for pick-ups and drop-offs and using the best navigation between locations and using tricks like minimizing left turns, such a system can reduce the number of trucks and drivers and amount of fuel needed. Other mechanisms include reducing unplanned downtime through predictive maintenance, and scheduling planned downtime for off-peak periods.

Asset Substitution. One asset or asset class can be substituted for another, such as automating operations and thus substituting capital for labor and machines for people. This can go the other way, too. When quality, empathy, and intimacy are the objectives of a customer service process, it makes sense to replace interactive voice response systems or Frequently Asked Questions lists with actual people. Assets can be replaced by lower-cost ones, such as when nurse practitioners take over some of the work formerly performed by doctors, or by higher cost oncs, as when a single superstar can replace multiple less capable teammates. A higher-cost machine or better-trained worker may cost more, but can enhance process flexibility, either creating value directly or enabling a lower total cost than separate operations using less flexible resources.

Asset-light Strategies. Assets don't need to incur fixed operating costs or require capital expenditures. Instead, they can use flexible, pay-per-use, on-demand mechanisms. Because on-demand resources can sometimes cost more than dedicated ones, a hybrid strategy of fixed and variable cost resources can sometimes be best. Uber was mentioned as an example of a company that uses such an approach. It leverages independent drivers who are financially responsible for their vehicles, whether by ownership or lease. Most companies use a mix of dedicated and on-demand employees, such as contractors, temps, consultants, seasonal hires, or day laborers.

Uber can be thought of as an asset-light transportation service, but it can also be considered to be a services market, matching drivers and passengers. It is not that different from a product market, such as eBay. The same way that Uber could, theoretically, acquire assets by purchasing vehicles and employing drivers, eBay could, theoretically, purchase goods from its millions of sellers and inventory them for future sale. However, the asset-light approach that they both use obviously confers benefits. Inventory risk is lower, and the return on assets is clearly greater by acting as a marketplace, intermediary, agent, or whichever term you'd like to use. The key element in many of these strategies is decoupling the physical asset from the information elements, such as product, quality, price, seller, and so forth.

Payor Changes. Even if the payment doesn't change, the payor can, or a third-party can offset payments. These include R&D and other tax credits, special economic zones, research grants, and so on. Search engines aren't paid for by searchers but by advertisers. The Vestergaard LifeStraw water purifier isn't paid for by customers but by a global carbon credit trading infrastructure.

Cost Offsets. Another means is to offset costs, ideally generating more revenue from an asset than it costs. An asset that is already paid for but repurposed is essentially available at zero marginal cost for the new purpose. One popular example is personal data, which needn't be surreptitiously gathered but can be a clear part of the terms of service such as the DNA data that 23andMe collects. Many 23andMe customers want the firm to sell their data, in the hope that treatments for genetically-based diseases may be found.

Free Assets. The ultimate asset optimization is when assets are acquired for free. An example is Google and other web search providers, who leverage a free asset, namely the entire World Wide Web and information contained therein. Although they do incur a cost to crawl and index it, they do not pay any websites to view their content—unlike, say, Apple iTunes or Amazon Kindle ebooks, which do pay a portion of revenues to content providers such as Lady Gaga or John Wiley & Sons.

Another free asset strategy is to crowdsource the assets at minimal cost, the way Yelp.com and TripAdvisor.com acquire reviews and YouTube acquires videos. Such reviews have no cost to Yelp, beyond the minimal cost to maintain computer resources, but they cost the reviewer time and effort, although provide psychological benefits.

Even better than *acquiring* assets at no cost is to do so in such a way that is at either minimal cost, no cost, or zero marginal cost to the asset provider. An example of this last approach is Waze, which effortlessly and frictionlessly convolves information from many users to develop insights into traffic patterns, congestion, and map accuracy.

It isn't just data assets that can be acquired for free: Open-source software such as Linux and OpenStack is produced thanks to free contributions, either because the work is done on a volunteer basis or because a third party is paying a salary yet giving permission for such contributions.

Business Value of Information

All business processes benefit from information: Sales processes benefit from information about customer needs and budgets; order fulfillment benefits from information about customer creditworthiness and inventory status; hiring from information about candidate skills and potential; and so on for end-to-end processes such as those that Cisco utilizes: market to sell, lead to order, quote to cash, issue to resolution, forecast to build, idea to product, and hire to retire.[7]

Information also has costs: the costs to create, acquire, maintain, process, distribute, and consume it. Although the economics of information have unique qualities, in a way, these costs parallel those for physical goods such as corn: There are costs to grow (create), harvest (acquire), store (maintain), mill (process), and distribute and consume it.

In the case of information, there are also indirect costs, such as the cost to create models of how the information fits together (which IT professionals refer to under terms such as database schema and information architectures), and to plan, architect, procure, manage, and dispose of physical assets such as data centers and servers, storage, and network equipment.

In a world of increasing complexity, competition, customer demands, and uncertainty, the value of information is increasing. Meanwhile, the costs of managing information are plummeting exponentially. The net result is that the (net) value of IT is increasing exponentially.

There is a rich body of literature on what information is, and how to model its value. Here, we will just touch on some of the main insights.

Some have created structured hierarchies, beginning with raw data, which is processed to create information, which leads to knowledge, and thence to wisdom.[8] For example, raw data regarding temperature, humidity, and wind speed and velocity can be used to generate information regarding cold fronts or high-pressure areas, which can be used to generate knowledge regarding weather predictions, and ultimately wisdom regarding theories of storm formation.

There is a model is called the Expected Value of Perfect Information (EVPI), which essentially values information based on how much better an outcome is expected to be with the information than without it. Whether the process involves hiring the best candidate, setting a price for an airline seat, rerouting a truck, or actuating a speed control on a train about to traverse a curve, there are a few key elements for information to have value: action-ability, predictive and prescriptive value, choice, goals, timeliness, accuracy, uncertainty, and a net benefit.

Actionability. Information needs to be actionable to be of value. Clairvoyance regarding stock market fluctuations over the next few days doesn't matter much if you are trapped in a cave with no way to communicate with the outside world to place orders. Unless the information is actionable, there may be psychological benefits, but no business benefit.

Predictive value. Big data analysts categorize insights gleaned from data into three categories. "Descriptive" says what *did* happen; "predictive" says what (probably) *will* happen; and "prescriptive" is a type of predictive data that offers guidance as to what *action* to take.[9] Predictive models can be based on things like trend analysis (e.g., sales of snow blowers have grown 4 percent every year over the past five years so probably will again this year) or correlations (e.g., sales grow by 4 percent whenever there is a blizzard before Thanksgiving, so probably will again given the recent snowstorm).

Because information has value in the context of future decisions and actions, it has to have some predictive value, based on insights gleaned through, say, statistical analysis. Having detailed information regarding the outcomes at a fair roulette table, unfortunately, has no predictive value in determining where to bet on the next spin, although it does have prescriptive value in deciding whether to play the game.

Prescriptive Value. To understand prescriptive value, one can look at online media site Buzzfeed.com. It has convincingly surpassed *The New York Times* online in terms of unique visitors per month, doubling that metric within one year, and now rivals CNN. Buzzfeed's publisher, Dao Nguyen, connected the dots: Views come from sharing stories, women share more than men, Pinterest is a social network frequented by women, and the nature of Pinterest is to "pin" (collect) items onto "boards" (visual folders), leading to a "slow burn" for stories, suggesting early publishing of seasonally themed stories.[10]

Choice. An action that will be taken regardless of any information means that the information was unnecessary. If you are planning on taking your umbrella anyway, you really don't need to check the weather forecast.

Goals. Choices need to be compared in the context of one or more goals. Typically, this involves reducing cost or maximizing revenue or profitability, but often includes social goals such as safety or employee welfare. When there are multiple goals, balancing priorities is also important.

Timeliness. In an environment with multiple competitors, it is not only important to have information, but to acquire it and act on it sooner than others. Some contests are winner-take-all, or provide outsized profits to early movers, so the company that can determine the optimal choice and successfully execute on it more quickly than the competition can wins. A good example of this is high-frequency algorithmic trading.

Even in the absence of competition, timeliness has value. Consider a pipe that is leaking a valuable liquid, say, jet fuel, into the ground. Even ignoring environmental impact and fines, the speed with which that information is acquired and acted on directly relates to the savings in lost fuel.

Accuracy. Generally, the more accurate the information, the more useful it is, although imperfect information can also be of use.

Uncertainty. The world is full of risk and uncertainty. Information can have value even if all it does is lower the uncertainty in nondeterministic situations. Not every male aged 18 to 24 plays *Call of Duty*, but knowing that that demographic is more likely to play than, say, healthcare industry CEOs, helps target advertising more effectively.

Net benefit. The costs to acquire, maintain, and act on the information must be lower than the value of the information, which itself must be netted out from the expected value of the outcome in the absence of the information. In other words, the value of information is not the same as the value of the outcome of the decision based on that information, but how much better that outcome is versus the outcome that would be achieved without the information. This might be a default option, including doing nothing or what the boss said to do, or the expected value of a random selection. To make all this even trickier to analyze, information may not only be used for "internal" purposes, but sold or resold to third parties, further increasing the net benefit.

The Role of Information Technology

In virtually all of the possible ways to differentiate operations and processes and utilize information, information technology plays a role. There are relatively straightforward tasks, such as cost reduction by sourcing from suppliers with the lowest price, which can be aided by online markets or commerce networks. Then, there are mathematically complex tasks such as dynamic optimization problems.

Whether it's for doing the right things, process efficiency, or process flexibility and creativity, information and information technology can help. It can help identify customer requirements and how those requirements are evolving. It can help brands engage with those customers. It can reduce time through automation, eliminate process bottlenecks through elastic resource scaling, and enhance process control through workflow management. It can also enable greater creativity, by enabling experimentation and A/B testing, where two alternatives are both implemented and results compared, and through data science, where hypotheses are constructed and evaluated based on a mix of data and intuition. And, it can enable greater process flexibility, through the creation of software platforms which conceptually are not that much different from flexible manufacturing systems, which are platforms enabling small-batch or highly custom production. It can accelerate the process of process improvement itself, as measurements and analyses that formerly occurred in a *post mortem* after quarterly book close can be conducted in real time. Such flexibility can also extend to business partners, through systems such as the SAP Ariba Commerce Network, which is a sort of eBay for supply-chain partners to find each other and set up commercial relationships.

Caveats

All that said, it is worth putting information in context. There is more to the world than just information. Insight and intuition, as well as dumb luck, can potentially lead to "best" outcomes: The fact that information exists to show that splitting tens is a bad idea in Blackjack doesn't mean that occasionally someone won't get double Blackjacks a result of doing so. One can introduce the iPhone without asking for any customer opinions. On the other hand, one can also introduce the Lisa or Newton that way.

Information *per se* does not provide a value system with which to evaluate alternatives.

Insight can lead to models, frameworks and theories into which information can be interpreted and understood, and information can be used to validate or disprove theories, but such theory-generation has traditionally lain outside of the framework of information processing. This has been true generally in science. For example, Aristarchus of Samos had the insight around 300 B.C. that the Earth revolved around the sun and the stars were very far away, contradicting the conventional wisdom not only then but for the next two thousand years. He presumably arrived at this without detailed astronomical data. Rather than being a curiosity, it also points out one of the conundrums in data science—basically, that the creative process of theory formulation (say, customers will prefer this to that) has traditionally existed largely in the realm of human intuition as opposed to brute-force machine processing.

However, some have argued that science is shifting to a fourth paradigm where *theories* are unnecessary, merely the determination of *correlations*. In this paradigm, there is no need to determine, say, that aspirin relieves pain through a reduction in inflammation due to its inhibitory effect on the enzyme cyclo-oxygenase, which in turn reduces the formation of prostaglandins, which cause inflammation. Instead, there is only a need to identify a correlation between aspirin consumption and freedom from headaches.

There is also a new realm of information processing where machines are beginning to formulate theories and hypotheses. For example, computers have scanned tens of thousands of research papers to formulate insights regarding which molecules might suppress cancer.[11]

■   ■   ■

All areas of the business can benefit from better processes and better use of assets. One such asset is the information needed to develop insights that can support decision-making action: to select among suppliers, to site new locations, to optimize inventory levels; to determine prices that maximize profitability; to identify new markets; and so forth. Information technology is increasing in value as information becomes more usable and the unit and total costs of IT plummet. And, besides process and resource optimization, operations and information can be seamlessly integrated, offering tighter bonds with customers and partners and reflecting today's world, which is a mix of virtual and physical.

Notes

1. Justinas Laskinsas, "Growing Popularity of Prepaid Mobile Services Reshapes US Telecommunications Market," *Euromonitor.com*, August 3, 2014, blog.euro monitor.com/2014/08/growing-popularity-of-prepaid-mobile-services-reshapes-us-telecommunications-market.html.
2. Kathleen Seiders, Glenn B. Voss, Andrea L. Godfrey, Dhruv Grewal, "SERV-CON: Development and Validation of a Multidimensional Service Convenience Scale," *Journal of the Academy of Marketing Science* 35, no. 4 (2007): 144–156.
3. Candice Choi, "McDonald's to Beef up in India with Meatless Menu," *Yahoo! Finance*, March 4, 2015, finance.yahoo.com/news/mcdonalds-beef-india-meatless -menu-220612075--finance.html.

4. Marc Santora and Michael M. Grynbaum, "Facing Outcry on East Side, Mayor Admits Snow Removal Efforts Fell Short," *New York Times*, January 22, 2014, www .nytimes.com/2014/01/23/nyregion/east-coast-storm-brings-snow-and-disruptions -to-the-new-york-region.html.

5. Michael Porter, "What Is Strategy?," *Harvard Business Review* (November–December 1996): 61–78.

6. Nicolas Kachaner and Adam Whybrew, "When 'Asset Light' Is Right," *BCG Perspectives*, September 30, 2014, https://www.bcgperspectives.com/content/articles /business_unit_strategy_value_creation_growth_when_asset_light_is_right /#chapter1.

7. Andrew McAfee and Erik Brynjolfsson, "Investing in the IT That Makes a Competitive Difference," *Harvard Business Review* (July 2008), hbr.org/2008/07 /investing-in-the-it-that-makes-a-competitive-difference/ar/1.

8. Russell L. Ackoff, "From Data to Wisdom," *Journal of Applied Systems Analysis* 16 (2010): 3–9.

9. Jeff Bertolucci, "Big Data Analytics: Descriptive vs. Predictive vs. Prescriptive," *InformationWeek.com*, December 31, 2013, www.informationweek.com/big-data /big-data-analytics/big-data-analytics-descriptive-vs-predictive-vs-prescriptive/d /d-id/1113279.

10. Mat Honan, "Inside the Buzz-Fueled Media Startups Battling for Your Attention," *Wired.com*, December 17, 2014, www.wired.com/2014/12/new-media-2/.

11. Spangler, Scott, Angela D. Wilkins, Benjamin J. Bachman, Meena Nagarajan, Tajhal Dayaram, Peter Haas, Sam Regenbogen et al., "Automated Hypothesis Generation Based on Mining Scientific Literature." In *Proceedings of the 20th ACM SIGKDD International Conference on Knowledge Discovery and Data Mining*, pp. 1877–1886. ACM, 2014. dl.acm.org/citation.cfm?id=2623667.

CHAPTER 6

The Discipline of Information Excellence

The discipline of information excellence entails strategically leveraging information to drive unparalleled customer value and customer experience and thus achieve competitive advantage, through better processes and resourcing. Processes and their enabling resources can be made cheaper, faster, higher quality, more reliable, more flexible, more sustainable, or improved in any of dozens of other dimensions.

Because information intensity varies by industry and company, the concept of information excellence spans a broad variety of practical implementations. The use of information by a pure virtual company, say, a developer of online games, will of necessity be different from that of a capital-intensive company such as an aircraft manufacturer, which will be different from another aircraft manufacturer or a package delivery company. *Information excellence* sometimes supplants *operational excellence*, as when videoconferencing replaces air travel, and sometimes complements it, as when better flight scheduling algorithms improve airline operations through fuel efficiency or more on-time arrivals.

Processes and resources are subject to improvement in purely virtual, purely physical, and hybrid virtual-physical domains. For example, even purely virtual Internet movie delivery can be differentiated on video quality, response times to start and stop movies, and cost, through better use of the cloud, data centers, and networks for websites and content transcoding and delivery. More subtly, the recommendations of such movies, and the decisions of which movies to make, benefit from better algorithms.

As just one example of the complexities of information excellence, consider modern international container terminal (i.e., shipping port) operations, where tens of thousands of containers, stacked on one another, must be moved onto and off of hundreds of ships, trucks, and rail cars, in the presence of various delays due to weather, traffic congestion, drawbridges, or accidents.

Information is critical to the safe and efficient operation of cranes that load and unload the transport vehicles, and do so to minimize waiting times for vehicles and to ensure accurate routing of containers as various trucks, trains, and ships arrive and depart with containers destined for each other. There can be little optimization without timely information: information on the containers, the vehicles, the roadways, arriving and departing ships, bills of lading, ports of call, customs documents, weather, tides, currents, and so forth. To acquire this information requires things such as video surveillance cameras, container tracking devices, mobile networks, GPS, optical character recognition, sufficient processing and storage, and so forth. Information and optimized logistics are increasingly the basis for competitive advantage, since ports compete with each other and with substitutes such as truck and rail for business. Hong Kong doesn't compete with Los Angeles, but it does with Singapore and Yantian, in nearby Shenzhen. Similarly, Hamburg competes with Rotterdam and Antwerp.

In addition, the growth of the global economy means growth in international shipping leading to additional logistics and computational challenges. The Hamburg Port Authority has developed a Smart Port Logistics system, in conjunction with partners, to handle an expected threefold growth in containers from the current 9 million containers annually, on constrained acreage.[1]

Information excellence is not limited to operations within a port. True optimization requires global coordination among ports, because if a ship is delayed at one port, it has to determine whether to speed up to the next port, requiring extra fuel; arrive late at the next port, causing a cascade of further problems; or skip the port, causing issues with the cargo that was to be picked up or dropped off there. Alternate routes for the cargo can cause additional fuel costs, trucking, or transshipment fees. These kinds of problems are also opportunities: Xvela is a start-up that is deploying cloud-based software to address this problem, intending to aid information sharing, collaboration, and analytics to support information excellence.[2]

Competitive advantage is often thought to be strategic only if it is sustainable, but it can be strategic yet perishable. Apple bested Research in Motion (now named BlackBerry) and Nokia in smartphones with the iPhone, then Samsung overtook Apple with Android devices, then Xiaomi and LG took share from Samsung, then Apple regained its prominence in the last quarter of 2014, only to have Samsung regain the lead the next quarter.

Such turbulence is not restricted to the smartphone industry, of course. MIT professor Erik Brynjolfsson and principal research scientist Andrew McAfee have studied how IT relates to competitiveness for years. Their analysis shows that industries are becoming more concentrated—fewer firms are responsible for a greater proportion of revenues—yet there is greater turbulence—a company that is the market leader in a given quarter or year might not be in the next one. Finally, the "performance spread," which they define as the difference between profitability among firms, has been growing, rather than settling down to some long-run average.

Brynjolfsson and McAfee trace these effects to a single source: increased spending on and adoption of IT. Their analysis shows that increased merger and acquisition activity, research and development expenditures, and globalization had relatively minor effects. Moreover, they argue that it is "Not because more *products* are becoming *digital* but because more *processes* are ... a company's unique business processes can now be propagated with much higher fidelity across the organization by embedding [them] in enterprise information technology. [emphasis added]"[3]

McAfee and Brynjolfsson make the case that IT-based processes enable standardized process improvements to be deployed quickly. Software changes should be easier to make, say, than re-laying out pipe in an oil refinery. A logically centralized IT environment such as one enabled by the cloud means that software updates containing business process logic changes can instantly propagate across a far-flung global enterprise. McAfee and Brynjolfsson contrast this with one based on rolling out a training program, where results may vary as individuals vary in their learning, adoption, and successful execution of the new process. They relate the example of CVS, where merely switching the order of two screens in the prescription fulfillment process reversed a decline in customer satisfaction and drove an improvement in scores from 86 percent to 91 percent. Anyone who has ever measured or had a bonus impacted by customer satisfaction results knows just how enormous an increase this is.

The trends McAfee and Brynjolfsson identified now come into focus. The rapidity of information systems deployments can cause temporary advantage, leading to greater turbulence. Or, if competitors don't respond quickly enough, they may exit the industry through liquidation or acquisition, leading to greater consolidation. And, gaps between IT leaders and laggards help explain the performance spread.

Information excellence can replace (physical) operational excellence, when processes go completely virtual. However, for physical businesses, typically information excellence can be used to complement and achieve operational excellence.

From People to Machines

The most straightforward evolution from pure operations to those enhanced by information technologies is from muscles to motors and from minds to machines.

Automation, including the replacement of physical labor by machines, can reduce cost, speed processes, and improve quality. Robots and algorithms don't get tired, can work to extremely fine tolerances, and are now capable of mimicking capabilities that traditionally were only found in biological systems, such as touch sensitive enough to pick up an egg and the ability to balance themselves well enough to walk or run on two legs. Robots have expanded beyond the factory, and the technology is increasingly found in home vacuum-cleaning robots and operating-room surgical robots and will be used for driverless cars and drones.

Machine cognition, the replacement of mental labor by machines, such as through machine learning and artificial intelligence, had not lived up to its promise until recently. After half a century of trying, we are finding cognitive capabilities approximating, and in some cases exceeding the capabilities of humans. In May, 1997, a computer—IBM's Deep Blue—beat the reigning grandmaster of the time, Garry Kasparov. Then, in January 2011, IBM's Watson beat the reigning "grandmasters" of *Jeopardy!*, Ken Jennings and Brad Rutter. The technology behind Watson is being extended to other domains, such as healthcare and cooking.

While these are spectacular accomplishments, they represent only the tip of the iceberg. The replacement of mental and physical labor is so ubiquitous that we no longer recognize it. Software calculates our taxes, email replaces a trip to the mailbox or the post office, ecommerce replaces trips to the mall. Advanced algorithms schedule and manage airline crews, planes, trains, trucks, traffic lights, home thermostats, automobile cruise controls, carburetor air-fuel mixes, equity trades, newsfeeds, search results, ad placement, and every other dimension of society.

Of course, other elements that seem distinctly human are getting machine assists or being replaced. Driverless cars have vision systems that can detect lanes, other vehicles, pedestrians, and obstacles. Shazam can recognize songs. Various systems are getting better at speech to text, translation, and semantic analysis (i.e., understanding spoken queries), most notably as with Apple's Siri; conducting sentiment analysis (i.e., understanding the emotion behind spoken or written phrases); and not only doing facial recognition (i.e., determining who someone is from a captured image), but also understanding the emotion behind facial expressions. In addition, self-service portals can displace costs to customers (or partners) while increasing their satisfaction.

It is possible to take this too far. Often, the best performance comes when people work with machines. Retailer Belk, rather than implementing a fully automated labor scheduling system using algorithms based on demand predictions, weather predictions, and, say, optimizing paths taken down the aisles at the stores, enabled store managers substantial autonomy to account for things such as an employee's doctor appointment. The result was that in contrast to competitors using fully automated scheduling, the system achieved a return on investment, with a notable 2 percent increase in gross profit.[4] On the other hand, people can sometimes be a barrier to successful implementation of systems.

From Physical to Virtual

Besides augmenting or substituting for human labor, information technology can augment or substitute for other physical assets and processes.

Substitution of physical for virtual—replacing atoms with bits—is increasingly usable and relevant. The *New York Times* took its back issues, which existed only in microfilm form, and managed to use the cloud and optical character recognition software to create a searchable database: the *TimesMachine*. A "face-to-face" meeting, which used to require an ocean voyage of weeks and later required plane travel of hours, now can be held with a couple of mouse clicks or screen taps. Substitution can decrease time, cost, and increase sustainability. For example, airfare, parking, meals, hotel, and taxis running into the thousands of dollars for a single person to attend a meeting can be replaced by free software as a service. Moreover, this greatly reduces the carbon footprint: powering a computer monitor, network, and server is nothing compared to jet fuel.

Similarly, physical meetings, and the cost to own or lease space, acquire office furniture and equipment, and the transportation required to get to and from the office, can often be replaced by virtual equivalents. It is true that face-to-face meetings have advantages, but surely not all such meetings are required, and moreover, virtual meeting technology is becoming increasingly immersive.

The mere act of making a physical process and/or its supporting assets virtual creates significant value, and wealth. It does so by reducing costs, by replacing atoms with bits, and also by making the process faster, easier, of higher quality, and so on. It's no surprise, but digital games are replacing board and card games, digital songs, movies, and books are replacing their physical counterparts, digital mail (email) is replacing physical, and physical transportation of goods will be in part replaced by digital transport with local manufacture through 3D printers.

When moving from physical to virtual, it's important to not merely create a virtual replica of the physical world but to rethink assumptions and processes. For example, when Burberry moved its fashion shows online, it didn't merely put the show that one might have seen in person onto YouTube. It recognized that the show was no longer open to just the fashion press, but also VIPs who could participate globally in stores, and the public, who could participate online. It opened up behind-the-scenes videos. It made it possible to order merchandise while viewing the shows. In short, it recognized that information goods have different economics, and that online technologies can, paradoxically, make exclusivity ubiquitous.

In the physical world, machines such as lathes and drills became more flexible by becoming computer controlled. In the virtual world, software is becoming more flexible, too. Technologies such as platform as a service, composable apps, and microservices are intended to move software development away from line-at-a-time coding to the assembly of components that have already been tested, like replacing hand woodcarving with Lego block assembly. This increases the flexibility of virtual, digital elements, since they can be assembled or customized as needed.

From Virtual to Digical

Although it might appear that virtual operations would be the end-state, the truth is that reality is not going away any time soon. Fused digital and physical operations—which Darrell Rigby, a partner at consulting firm Bain & Company calls *digical*—are important in both business and consumer markets.[5] An obvious area is multichannel and omni-channel marketing and retailing: being able to, say, find something on the web, try it on in the store, order it via your mobile phone, pick it up in the store, and then return it via the Postal Service. Unfortunately, in many businesses, things aren't that simple. As Rigby laments, many companies "tend to run their digital operations as independent business units—the way companies prefer to manage them, as opposed to the way customers expect to use them."[6] For many companies, even digital operations aren't consistent; features vary significantly and capriciously across mobile devices.

Digical processes are relevant to a wide variety of verticals across consumer and enterprise markets, and to many processes, not just marketing and sales.

Domino's uses an integrated order management system to tie together customers, pizzas, restaurants, and delivery personnel. A customer can order pizza online, either accessing her favorite or designing one from scratch: small, medium, large, thin or thick, gluten-free or Brooklyn-style crust; a variety of sauces such as marinara or BBQ; and a couple of dozen different toppings, including peppers, sausage, onions, bacon, and feta. There's no point in merging virtual and physical if you can't visualize your pizza in real time, so Dominos.com graphically depicts the pizza as you are constructing it. Then, Domino's Tracker illustrates progress to the customer—order placement, preparation, baking, a quality check, and delivery—while workers are provided order details and do their part.[7]

In the old days, handling goods was easier than handling information. "Information lags," from retailers to distributors and then on back to manufacturers and their suppliers, meant that it was easier to stockpile inventory to handle unknown demand.

Now, increasingly, leading companies are eliminating inventory, taking orders from customers and delivering the order information upstream to the manufacturer to deliver, rather than delivering the product downstream to a warehouse for the retailer to deliver. Such "stockless distribution" is what happens when Amazon.com says "This order will be fulfilled directly by Acme International."

This eliminates the bullwhip effect, where information lags regarding minor demand fluctuation create huge and unnecessary stockpiles or stockouts, as well as eliminating all of the extra materials handling.

From Processes to Experiences

Disney is merging the physical experience of theme parks with various virtual elements.[8] FastPass has been a way to avoid the long lines for some attractions, but required a physical presence the day of the reservation to acquire a FastPass at a kiosk. FastPass+ is now available remotely, over the web, in advance. MagicBands are wristbands that allow access to rides, parks, and hotel rooms, as well as mobile payments. Moreover, they can enable personalized experiences, such as a Disney character greeting the guest by name. My Disney Experience enables scheduling for yourself and family across a range of theme park activities: rides, dining, hotels.[9]

MagicBands are just a portion of a billion dollar investment that Disney has made in streamlining and personalizing the park experience. They use an embedded radio that can transmit 40 feet and link to a broad cloud-based service called MyMagicPlus to enable unique experiences. For example, a family can order food in advance, sit down at a table, be subtly triangulated, and have the food arrive nearly instantaneously. Similar to UPS's ORION system, Disney algorithms use your ride preferences to optimize routing through the park and enable entry to the park and rides, and help "turn the park into a giant computer." By minimizing time spent waiting in lines, among other things, MyMagicPlus and MagicBands create customer value by enabling guests to maximize their experience and enjoyment, but this in turn also means that they will partake in more activities and thereby see more opportunities to spend (e.g., on memorabilia), and be more likely to return.[10]

Burberry, which we'll review in detail in the next chapter, takes both in-store and online shopping beyond mundane processes and into the realm of memorable experiences. In-store processes use digital signage that comes alive through RFID (Radio-Frequency Identification) tags embedded in select merchandise; online processes include streaming live runway shows, while providing the opportunity to order select goods such as apparel, nail polish, and fragrances.

Both Burberry and Disney were already offering experiences: theme parks and luxury retail environments. In both cases, they use information technology in subtle ways to enhance these experiences.

From Operations to Improvement

Information began to be used to support formal process management and improvement perhaps as early as the construction of the ancient Egyptian pyramids, but certainly as of nearly a century ago, when manual methods of statistical process/quality control—such as control charts—were implemented. Such charts then drove root cause analysis to determine the causes of variations and defects. Today, such management and improvement activities benefit from more data, available sooner. Cars collect speed, location, interior temperature, and more. Wearables and related devices collect location, accelerometer, pulse, body fat, and glucose. Even television remote controls are a source of data on keypresses, which can help cable or satellite providers optimize onscreen menus and even the layout of the remote. In the purely virtual world, every click, button push, touch, keystroke, hover, swipe, or mouse move is potentially fodder for data collection.

Domino's is an example, examining data such as orders per minute, detailed transactions, and coupon usage.[11] Domino's provides real-time statistics to its restaurants, including on-time deliveries and number of new customers. The data are gamified to show how restaurants are doing relative to each other, to help maximize individual facility performance.[12]

Disney data can be used to not just merge the physical and virtual worlds, but as a basis for customer experience and process improvement. The MagicBands described earlier are not just useful for helping guests get into theme parks or their hotel rooms, but also can track how they move through the park. Mapping this to customer demographics can lead to lots of helpful changes: determining where additional personnel are required in real time, determining the kinds of rides that appeal to which customers, or determining where to place an ice cream stand to maximize revenue. This is clearly a very different scenario than the kind of coarse information available previously, which showed that the park had, say, 20,000 visitors that day, the wait at Space Mountain was an hour at lunchtime, and ice cream sales grew 2 percent over the same period last year.

Metrics for process improvement can range from high-level business results—revenue, profit, market share—to the root causes and drivers of these, pageviews, sentiment analysis, net promoter score, or highly granular customer behavior.

Information, in short, can be used to improve processes, and thereby enhance the customer experience, reduce costs, increase productivity, and generate additional revenue.

From Static Design to Dynamic Optimization

Process improvement has typically had a connotation of an activity conducted over the long term, but with real-time data comes an opportunity for real-time control and optimization.

Optimization of existing physical processes is becoming more pervasive thanks to the synergies of sensors, mobility, and the cloud. Physical processes as local as a single retail outlet or as wide-reaching as a global supply chain can leverage sophisticated algorithms to squeeze out additional costs or reduce cycle times. Sometimes the improvements are enormous and disruptive, sometimes they are minor—say, only a percent or two. However, a mere 1 percent improvement to a multibillion-dollar process is, of course, worth millions.

Goldcorp was able to use detailed geological data to improve the efficiency of its mining process, reducing production costs from $360 an ounce to under $60, while increasing production from 53,000 ounces to over half a million.[13] Harrah's famously used data on gamers to run targeted promotions and boost profits. New talent management software can maximize the effectiveness of hiring, training, and retention processes. Ports can optimize operations; railways can run both individual trains as well as their transportation networks better. Manufacturers and distributors can run their supply chains more efficiently and flexibly. Real-time demand management can be used to ensure that enough inventory is on hand to meet customer requirements, but no more.

Navis offers software that optimizes operations at container terminals—that is, shipping docks that load and unload intermodal containers onto and off of trains and trucks. It uses sophisticated algorithms to route "straddle carriers," which move containers around the yard, and to place and stack ("stow") containers around the yard and on the ship. For example, the software considers the port where the cargo will be discharged, container size and weight, and the cost of usage of various cranes, to optimize cost and productivity.[14]

Or consider Wal-Mart. For many retailers, a large portion of investment is not so much in the store itself as in the inventory. Too little inventory and sales will be lost. Too much, and inventory carrying costs will eat up profit. Wal-Mart improves its gross margins through the use of "Retail Link" and SPARC[15] (Supplier Portal Allowing Retail Coverage), which provide real-time inventory visibility to suppliers and shift the onus of inventory management onto them.[16]

From Mass Production to Mass Personalization

In addition to processes that are optimized dynamically through access to real-time data, processes are moving away from one size fits all to customization and even personalization at scale. Henry Ford's famous quip about the Model T was that a customer could have it painted any color he wanted as long as it was black.

Although Burberry is known for its signature camel, red, black, and ivory check, through Burberry Bespoke customers can design their own trench coat, selecting among fabrics such as gabardine and sateen, different sleeves, epaulette, and cuff patterns, various lining colors, fabrics, and detachability, collars, buttons, belts, and monograms.

Nike enables choices in athletic shoe design. Besides different colors for various elements such as tongue, heel, swoosh, and so forth, customers can also customize performance aspects of the shoe, such as lateral stiffness, which are then implemented through fibers with different tensile characteristics.

When done properly, such capabilities create a trifecta of gains: greater customer satisfaction together with the seeming paradox of reduced (unintended) process variability with greater (intended) process agility.

From Cost Reduction to Revenue Generation

Information acquisition and retention has been traditionally viewed as a cost and information technology as a cost center. Cost reduction of processes is certainly relevant, and always will be, through optimization or cost displacement.

In addition to reducing cost, however, information and information technology can be used to increase revenue in many ways: increasing process yield, not just for manufacturing but also areas one might not expect, such as mining, book publishing, or movie production; enhancing customer experiences and optimizing merchandising, leading to greater ability to conclude transactions or propensity to repurchase; or driving upsell and cross-sell. Disney and FedEx, discussed previously, and Burberry, which will be covered in the next chapter, are just a few examples.

In addition to those strategies, where information is used to enhance a process, information itself is a good that can be sold.

Information goods are a pure-play way to create value. Selling information predates the Information Age. After all, newspapers and book publishers have been around for hundreds of years, and other forms of entertainment, such as selling LP records or making movies are information goods as well. Today, sales of information have merely expanded beyond physical media to virtual: eBooks, market data, online search and advertising.

With the shift to virtual media, sales of a different type of information good—software such as applications, apps, games, and microservices (software components that are used by other software)—have also become possible. This includes selling the apps themselves, as well as virtual goods including in-app purchases.

Production of goods entails a mix of fixed and variable costs. With physical goods, the cost of those goods is typically nontrivial, varying due to scale economies and learning curve effects. With information goods, the economics shift entirely. The cost to acquire or generate the information is typically fixed, so after that investment is recouped, the sold product has close to zero marginal cost, due to relatively minor costs for replication and distribution.

There are more ways to monetize information goods than putting a sales tag on them. The information can be free, but the player profitable, as with some of the free apps or content available on various brands of "smart" TVs; the information can be free in virtual form but for a fee in physical; there can be various freemium models, such as 10 free articles per month with an upsell to a paid subscription model for more; there can be two-sided monetization, equivalent to when newspapers sell ads but also sell subscriptions; or complementary goods can be sold, such as free content being used to drive both services and products.

From Direct to Indirect Monetization

Like someone finding a masterpiece in their attic, companies can sometimes be sitting on a gold mine that can monetized directly or by a third party. There are three ways to exploit process data.

Exhaust data monetization. Companies can monetize data that is an intentional or unintentional byproduct of their processes. This is like a company that sells cedar lumber to the construction or furniture business who realizes that it can sell the stripped off cedar bark to landscapers or homeowners, rather than paying to have it hauled off as waste. A package delivery company could sell real-time data on traffic congestion derived from its fleet, for example. Foursquare can leverage check-ins to provide information to urban traffic planners or to restaurateurs trying to site a new trendy bar.

Perhaps the best example of this is 23andMe, which supposedly was founded to help individuals understand their risks for various genetic diseases[17] by offering a "personal genome test" based on a saliva sample. While this business may be a profitable one, a byproduct of their core business was the creation of a massive database of genetic data. In 2015, it announced the sale of the data to pharmaceutical and biotech firms. One such deal, with Genentech, was valued at as much as $60 million, roughly on par with the revenue from what ostensibly was 23andMe's core business.[18]

Capabilities. A lawn service company with truck "capabilities" can extend its business to snow removal. Similarly, companies can also monetize their software capabilities, rather than data *per se.* A complete reservations system business, SABRE, now perhaps better known through its online version Travelocity, was spun out as a separate company from American Airlines. Amazon.com's software capabilities to handle a variety of tasks for their retail business became the Amazon Web Services cloud service provider business, now generating billions of dollars in revenue. And Google was able to take APIs it had developed as part of its Google Maps application and offer them to others; for free for low use or for fee for high volume. One example: a geocoding API that converts addresses to geographic latitude and longitude coordinates, and a geolocation API that determines where a user is by using data such as cell tower and Wi-Fi hotspots.[19]

Touchpoints. In addition, companies can monetize their customer relationships based on the increased volume, interactivity, and quality of touchpoints that they now have with customers. Traditionally, a customer might come into the store once every few months. They also might read your newspaper ad or insert, but you might not know that they had. As a consumer packaged goods manufacturer, you never saw your customers; that was the retailer's role. Now, between the web, mobile devices, email, social media campaigns, and the like, you can touch the customer every day, every hour, or even more frequently. Moreover, digitalized products can provide info on the customer and how they are using the product; the same for connected services. There are many ways to monetize these interactions: selling ads, in-app purchases, messaging that the product needs maintenance, or upselling complementary services.

From Touchpoints to Integration

Traditionally it was simple to determine the touchpoints a customer had with the firm: a customer might view an ad, talk to a salesperson, purchase a product in store, or return it. The firm and its resources, such as employees and corporate proprietary information, had clearly demarcated boundaries separating it from the customer, her resources, and her information.

Now, however, those boundaries are becoming less clear. When a customer makes suggestions for new products or product changes, hasn't she become part of the product management team? When a client co-creates a new offer or capability through close partnering, isn't she part of the research and development organization? When customers are brand ambassadors, aren't they acting like marketing employees? When product users provide helpful instructions via an externally facing product support wiki, aren't they part of the technical support organization? When they research and then conclude an online purchase, aren't they doing part of the work of the salesperson?

Processes, in short, are becoming jointly resourced by customers and employees.

Moreover, it's getting harder to determine who owns the data. If a parent uploads a family photo to Facebook or Instagram, who does it belong to? If someone checks in on social media, does his geolocation data belong to him or the social media firm? If a woman's DNA is sequenced, whose DNA sequencing is it? The fine print in the terms of use often presents surprises.

And, if firms are focused on successful customer outcomes, as GE Aviation is in terms of trying to maximize airlines' flying time and minimizing unplanned outages, or as Nike is in offering coaching services to maximize athletic performance, these shared goals seem very different from traditional economic views of consumer surplus versus producer surplus, that is, the idea that a firm's gain is the customer's loss and vice versa.

From Firms to Networks

The traditional view of a process is something that happens within the firm boundaries, for example, quote to cash. Company processes interact with customer, supplier, and stakeholder processes. For example, a customer's learning process touches the firm's outbound marketing process; a customer's purchase process touches the firm's sales and order fulfillment process, and so on.

However, we are entering a world where opportunities lie beyond the four walls of the enterprise, into what Don Tapscott calls the Open, Networked Enterprise and has also been termed the Virtual Corporation.

We are also increasingly seeing these partnerships outside of the enterprise become highly dynamic. Some call this the Hollywood organizational model, because of the way that film production moved beyond the vertically integrated, standing organizations of the studios of the 1930s with actors, screenwriters, and directors on payroll, to a dynamic model where every film has a different executive producer, cast, screenwriter, director, and cinematographer.

The networked organization—a virtual corporation that focuses on its core mission, say game design, and outsources many other functions to partners—is evolving to the *dynamic* networked organization, where those relationships shift frequently based on the needs of the business. Uber is one example. Other examples include CrowdPlat and (Appirio's) TopCoder.com, which do contract software development work using dynamically engaged programmers and project managers, thus competing with traditional systems integrators. Freelancer.com lets anyone hire someone to, say, translate an article or clean up a term paper. Among firms selling physical goods, Li & Fung has close to $20 billion in revenue, yet owns no factories. Instead, it dynamically sources its goods and production from an ever-changing matrix of thousands of international suppliers.

Such dynamic networked organizations can also be realized through the software development kit, application programming interface, and app store model. A company like Apple or Google could insource development of all of its own applications, but the new model is to let the market pick winners and losers from millions of apps generated by a Hollywood model of participants—a variety of software developers and content producers—while taking a cut of the proceeds.

This, in turn, is giving rise to intermediaries such as agents and markets that are creating ecosystems that enable this high level of dynamism.

In one type of market, say the commodity market for frozen concentrated orange juice, there are many buyers and many sellers, but only one undifferentiated good. One major function of such a market from an information—and information technology—perspective, is to determine the price at any given point based on supply (availability) and demand. Another is to manage payments. In a different type of market, such as for dating or matching kidney donors and recipients, a more important function is optimally matching "buyers" with "sellers," even if no monetary transaction occurs.

A good example of an intermediary that has grown to enable this kind of matching is the SAP Ariba Commerce Network, where procurement agents can identify potential suppliers, receive bids, and make a purchase, all electronically.

Companies may outsource design or advertising to IDEO or R/GA and manufacturing to FoxConn; others like Li & Fung adjust their partner mix every few days; and increasingly, individuals can compete with corporations, thanks to firms like Etsy and Quirky, not to mention development platforms for coding and app stores for distribution.

There are also opportunities to leverage suppliers, partners, and competitors by addressing a larger span of activities in the customer's process. For example, companies in the airline and train business such as Virgin and SNCF have begun to incorporate ground transportation on the origin and destination side.[20] This is more than just stapling together disconnected processes; a fixed fee covers the taxi or limousine ride, including potential delays.[21] Firms that just offered package delivery are now embedding themselves with their customers and integrating themselves into information flows, offering overnight delivery of spare parts inventoried not at the manufacturer, but at the logistics hub, and even moving into maintenance.

It is typical to view distributors, end-customers, and end-users as "customers." But if you are a distributor, suppliers can also be customers, in the sense that they have choices as to who to distribute through, and can easily choose a competitor. Consequently, demonstrating value is essential. BuildDirect is an online building products supplier. It can offer dramatically lower prices to its customers, by minimizing inventory costs. It has lower costs because suppliers provide inventory on consignment, based on predictive analytics and insight provided by BuildDirect, which enables the suppliers to optimize production planning and inventory management based on better predictions of which products are likely to sell. Rather than merely being a channel, it provides value to suppliers through monthly meetings with BuildDirect category managers, which enable the suppliers to tune their production mix.[22]

At the other extreme, there are opportunities to digitally disintermediate or reintermediate existing industry structures. Dell is the poster child for disintermediating the computer retailing channels that existed at the time, going direct to consumer. Amazon has enabled authors to reach their audiences more directly, thus re-imagining existing publishing industry practices and processes.

From Data to Actionable Insight

Sometimes, the purpose of data is just to ensure the proper operation of a low-level system. For example, cruise control takes data on current speed relative to target speed and adjusts the automotive powertrain accordingly. But at its most powerful, data can be analyzed, possibly in combination with other data, and used to derive insight, with that insight being used to drive action.

Decision making—which markets to enter, in which products to invest, who to promote—is usually improved when based on data. Not always: there is still a role for intuition, and the world is stochastic and chaotic; in other words, defined by randomness and by the ability of small catalysts to create large impacts, such as when World War I began due to the assassination of Archduke Ferdinand when he turned down the wrong street. Information-enabled decision making can range from use of data to select website colors, to determine a course of medical treatment, or even whether to irrigate grapevines.

Fruition Sciences exemplifies information excellence in vineyards in Napa Valley and around the world. Using water-flow sensors attached to vines, it is managing to overturn millennia of "best" practices in the noble art of viticulture. In other words, its data-based insight beats thousands of years of allegedly expert human insight, such as that when leaves wilt, the vines are thirsty. The overall solution connects the flow sensors wirelessly to the cloud, uploading data and correlating it with information such as weather, soil moisture, and vineyard layout. To conduct A/B testing, Ovid Vineyards divided its acreage in half, one side using traditional visual means—if the leaves appear wilted then the grapevines need to be irrigated—with the new Fruition Sciences data-based approach. The new approach led to fewer, later, deeper irrigations and earlier harvests. Bottom line: better-tasting wine, made with less water and at less risk. The first vintage from Ovid incorporating these techniques received one of its highest scores ever from noted wine luminary Robert Parker, and if these techniques were more broadly used, the savings could be almost 10 billion gallons of water each season in California alone. According to Fruition Sciences' wine expert Thibaut Scholasch, the problem with vintners eyeballing the vines is that "plants aren't designed to tell the human eye what they need. They have over 400 million years of evolution on us and very subtle ways of coping with heat and water regulation."[23]

In entertainment, companies such as Epagogix use "advanced artificial intelligence in combination with [a] proprietary expert process … to provide studios, independent producers and investors with early analysis and forecasts of the box office potential of a script."[24] In other words, they can predict whether a final motion picture will end up steaming ahead like the movie *Titanic* or sinking like the RMS *Titanic*, often with surprisingly accurate predictions of box office receipts. This is information excellence to the tune of a billion dollars a year or more per major studio.[25] Not only that, but Epagogix can help fix scripts to make them more profitable; both costing less and generating higher revenue.

If analytics can be used to effectively forecast and predict, great. But if not, fast reaction time can be just as effective. For example, Zara has implemented *fast fashion*. Rather than attempting to predict what consumer fashion preferences will be a year from now—the traditional fashion house interval—it responds to what is selling through rapid replenishment, based on local preferences. Analytics can also support corrective action for problem spots, shifting mixes of products and styles, and altering pricing. For example, Amazon.com makes more than 2.5 million price changes every *day*.[26]

From Answers to Exploration

Finally, it should be noted that having the processing power of the cloud and big data from pizza delivery trucks and MagicBands and grapevines and what have you does not just mean feeding existing algorithms to optimize existing processes.

It offers the possibility of unfettered exploration, visualizing and identifying new patterns, asking new questions and finding unexpected answers.

Donald Marchand, a professor at the Institute for Management Development in Lausanne and Joe Peppard, a professor at Cranfield University in the United Kingdom, argue that big data and traditional IT systems deployments are very different from each other.[27] Based on a study of 50 international firms, they argue that big data implementations should focus on opportunities for the "exploration of information." They also say that done right, the two approaches can be complementary: Data that are a byproduct of standard production systems can be used to explore hypotheses and create new value.

Tesco, a UK grocer, adjusted its processes for direct marketing, leading to a 20 percent redemption rate for coupons compared to an industry benchmark of only 2 percent.[28] Jonathan Goldman, a data scientist at LinkedIn, began "forming theories, testing hunches, and finding patterns"[29] as he analyzed members' networks and behaviors. This led to the popular "People You May Know" feature, and spectacularly reversed what had become a slowdown in LinkedIn's growth rate. Harrah's found that its target customers had a higher promotion redemption rate to an offer of $60 in casino chips than to a free room, two steak dinners, and $30 in chips, rationally worth three to five times as much.[30]

Trying two alternatives—so called A/B testing—is the foundation of any scientific, data-driven experiment, such as a trial of a new drug's efficacy. 1-800-Dentist used such testing to determine which web page photo would garner more clicks.[31] Two alternatives is the minimum, but Google at one point tested over 40 different shades of blue for its toolbar to find the one with the highest click-through rate.[32]

■   ■   ■

While these are the major areas where IT can impact processes, the power of IT is such that its ability to transform operations continues to grow and will no doubt become applied in currently unforeseen ways.

Leading companies are applying these new capabilities individually and in combination. And startups are creating new business models by selecting one or two areas or industries on which to focus these approaches.

Notes

1. Tatjana Geierhaas, "Always on the Go," T-Systems, March, 2012, www.t-systems.com/news-media/special-feature-cloud-steers-containers-in-the-port-of-hamburg/1010888.

2. Manuel Pérez Núñez, "The Shipping Industry: A Risky Business," *From the Crow's Nest* blog, November 18, 2014, community.navis.com/t5/From-the-Crow-s-Nest-Blog/The-Shipping-Industry-A-Risky-Business/ba-p/24538.

3. Andrew McAfee and Erik Brynjolfsson, "Investing in the IT That Makes a Competitive Difference," *Harvard Business Review* (July 2008), hbr.org/2008/07/investing-in-the-it-that-makes-a-competitive-difference/ar/1.

4. Ethan Bernstein, "The Transparency Trap," *Harvard Business Review* (October 2014): 65.

5. Darrell Rigby, "Digital-Physical Mashups," *Harvard Business Review* (September 2014), hbr.org/2014/09/digital-physical-mashups/ar/1.

6. Ibid.

7. Domino's website, https://order.dominos.com/en/pages/tracker/#/track/order/.

8. Rigby.

9. "Unlock a New Dimension of Disney Magic with MyMagic+" https://disneyworld.disney.go.com/plan/my-disney-experience/my-magic-plus/.

10. Cliff Kuang, "Disney's $1 Billion Bet on a Magical Wristband," *Wired.com*, March 10, 2015, www.wired.com/2015/03/disney-magicband/.

11. "Slicing Data for Domino's Pizza," [Video], www.splunk.com/view/SP-CAAAH8H.

12. Elise Hu, "Domino's Becomes a Tech Company That Happens to Make Pizza," *NPR.org*, November 4, 2014, www.npr.org/blogs/alltechconsidered/2014/11/04/359829824/dominos-becomes-a-tech-company-that-happens-to-make-pizza.

13. Linda Tischler, "He Struck Gold on the Net (Really)," *Fast Company*, June 2002, www.fastcompany.com/44917/he-struck-gold-net-really.

14. "Navis Terminal Operating Systems: The Global Technology Standard," NAVIS, www.navis.com/solutions.

15. "Walmart's SPARC Initiative in Spotlight Again," *RetailingToday*, October 10, 2013, www.retailingtoday.com/article/walmart%E2%80%99s-sparc-initiative-spotlight-again.

16. Chris Petersen, "Walmart's Secret Sauce: How the Largest Survives and Thrives," *Retail Customer Experience* blog, March 27, 2013, www.retailcustomerexperience.com/blog/10111/Walmart-s-secret-sauce-How-the-largest-survives-and-thrives.

17. Anna Edney, "FDA Tells Google-Backed 23andMe to Halt DNA Test Service," *BloombergBusiness*, November 25, 2013, www.bloomberg.com/news/articles/2013-11-25/fda-tells-google-backed-23andme-to-halt-dna-test-service.

18. Matthew Herper, "Surprise! With $60 Million Genentech Deal, 23andMe Has a Business Plan," *Forbes.com*, January 6, 2015, www.forbes.com/sites/matthewherper/2015/01/06/surprise-with-60-million-genentech-deal-23andme-has-a-business-plan/.

19. "The Google Geocoding API," https://developers.google.com/maps/documentation/geocoding/; "The Google Maps Geolocation API," https://developers.google.com/maps/documentation/business/geolocation/.

20. Virgin Atlantic, "Je ne sais quoi. Defined," www.virgin-atlantic.com/us/en/the-virgin-experience/upperclass/arrive-in-style.html.
21. Av Simon Matthis, "SNCF Extends Its Door-to-Door Service," *RailwayBulletin .com*, September 16, 2013, www.railwaybulletin.com/2013/09/sncf-extends-its-door-to-door-service.
22. GigaOm, "Structure Data 2013: Future Impacts of Big Data Insights on Your Organization," [video] *YouTube.com*, April 10, 2013, https://www.youtube.com/watch?v=Z_qFbvfSX0o.
23. Jeffrey M. O'Brien, "The Vine Nerds," *Wired.com*, October 21, 2012, www.wired.com/2012/10/mf-fruition-sciences-winemakers/.
24. Epagogix website, www.epagogix.com/.
25. Ian Ayres, *Supercrunchers: Why Thinking-by-Numbers Is the New Way to Be Smart* (New York: Random House, 2007), 146.
26. Vivian Gomez, "Amazon's Quest to Be Most Price-Competitive Retailer on Web," *RetailingToday.com*, December 11, 2013, www.retailingtoday.com/article/amazon%E2%80%99s-quest-be-most-price-competitive-retailer-web.
27. Donal A. Marchand and Joe Peppard, "Why IT Fumbles Analytics," *Harvard Business Review* (January 2013), hbr.org/2013/01/why-it-fumbles-analytics/.
28. McAfee and Brynjolfsson.
29. Thomas H. Davenport and D.J. Patil, "Data Scientist: The Sexiest Job of the 21st Century," *Harvard Business Review* (October 2012), hbr.org/2012/10/data-scientist-the-sexiest-job-of-the-21st-century/ar/1.
30. Gary Loveman, "Diamonds in the Data Mine," *Harvard Business Review* (May 2003): 111.
31. Antonio Regalado, "Seeking Edge, Websites Turn to Experiments," *MIT Technology Review* (January 22, 2014), www.technologyreview.com/news/523671/seeking-edge-websites-turn-to-experiments/.
32. Laura M. Holson, "Putting a Bolder Face on Google," *New York Times*, February 28, 2009, www.nytimes.com/2009/03/01/business/01marissa.html?pagewanted=3.

CHAPTER 7

Burberry—Weaving IT into the Fabric of the Company

R egent Street in London is one of the most famous streets in one of the greatest cities in the world. Known now to tourists for its shopping, it dates back almost two centuries and is so architecturally important that *every* building along its route is protected as a "listed building," meaning it has special architectural or historic interest and requires government permission for any kind of alteration. 121 Regent Street is home to the Burberry flagship store. Upon entering, you might be impressed with the classic British ambience: the bronze lanterns, elegant furniture, Corinthian marble, wood flooring, stone staircases, dramatic balustrade, or the plaster details.

Chances are, however, that your eye will be drawn to the enormous digital display, stretching from the ground on the first floor to the ceiling on the second, one of one hundred in the shop, and perhaps the tallest indoor retail display screen in the world.[1] This is only the most visible element of a store that juxtaposes old with new and is so brimming with digital technology that it practically needs its own data center. The store is incredible on its own merit, but is especially fascinating given the building's listed status. As Burberry's Chief Creative and Chief Executive Officer Christopher Bailey put it, "In renovating this iconic London building we have worked with some of the UK's finest craftsmen to restore a wealth of historic features, at the same time as pushing the boundaries of digital technology."[2] This is just one element of a comprehensive strategy. According to Bailey, "a determined and unique focus on making digital integral to everything we do will be a key growth driver and source of competitive advantage."[3]

Burberry predates the dawn of commercial computing by a century. It was founded in 1856, before the telephone, Edison's light bulb, and the U.S. Civil War. Although today we tend to think of Burberry as a fashion and beauty house, with its trademarked camel, ivory, red, and black check, it actually rose to prominence as a technology innovator. Thomas Burberry invented and patented gabardine, a fabric woven from cotton that is weatherproofed *before* weaving, leading to a unique combination of water resistance and breath-ability. This material, first used in raincoats, was used to outfit and supply expeditions to the South Pole such as those of Ernest Shackleton, Robert Falcon Scott, and Roald Amundsen; to Mount Everest, by early record-setting aviators; and also in World War I, when the raincoats became known as "trench coats."[4]

The use of information excellence to optimize port logistics, flexible manufacturing production lines, railway and airline network operations, and even vineyard output has been discussed in the previous chapters. Nothing could seem farther from those use cases than a luxury brand that is focused on intimacy, inspiration, experiences, luxurious materials, and exclusivity. But Burberry has achieved what might seem impossible: seamlessly fusing high touch, high tech, and high fashion.

It accomplished a major transformation under the leadership of then Chief Executive Officer Angela Ahrendts, who has since become senior vice president for retail and online stores at Apple, and Chief Creative Officer Christopher Bailey, who added the CEO title and continues to build on digital. John Douglas, former CIO and then CTO, was the linchpin in much of the conception and execution of these initiatives.[5] CEO Bailey sums up Burberry's approach: "Technology is an intrinsic part of most people's lives. All we've done is make sure to weave technology into the fabric of the company."[6]

Before Ahrendts took the helm in 2006, Burberry was growing at below 3 percent annually even though the luxury fashion market was growing at 13 percent.[7] Burberry had not only lost its association with luxury customers, but worse yet, even its own employees weren't wearing its product. During the time of Ahrendts's and Bailey's collaboration—2006 to 2013—sales and operating income just about tripled and market capitalization almost quadrupled.[8,9] The digital course that they charted had momentum: revenue growth continues to far outpace the segment norms.

Interbrand indicates that Burberry was the luxury fashion brand with the greatest increase in brand value each year during these years.[10] Part of this change represented a reversal in segment focus, away from mass market and returned to luxury, as well as an increased focus on millennials. But, it also was based on a strategic imperative to become a digital leader. These two strategies are in reality one: Burberry has a digital presence anywhere and everywhere that its target affluent millennials and digital immigrants are.

Burberry seamlessly fuses tradition and technology, inspiration and aspi-ration, retail and theater, elegance and execution, and virtual and physical.

Operational Excellence and Product Leadership

Burberry has focused on operational excellence in a number of ways that have little to do with information management *per se*, such as consolidating distribution centers and headquarters offices into expanded space and insourcing ecommerce operations. Besides organizational elements, a focus on brand authenticity also required shifting production: A factory in New Jersey making product for the US market was closed, to consolidate production of all "heritage" trench coats in the United Kingdom.[11] In addition, Burberry has been transitioning out of licensee arrangements and opening dozens of new stores so that it can have a direct presence in key luxury goods markets.[12]

Operational excellence also extends to sustainability, gender-equality, and ethical trading. Burberry has programs to reduce the environmental impact of cotton and leather, reduce chemical use in manufacturing, sustainably source packaging, and reduce energy use and carbon emissions within Burberry and water and energy use across its suppliers.[13]

Its strategy also is based on product leadership; as Burberry puts it, "As a global luxury brand, product excellence—craftsmanship, innovation, design—remains central to the business." To help ensure this, Bailey was made the chief creative officer for Burberry, responsible for brand consistency, centralizing all design decisions, including some that until that point had been made by licensees or local in-country organizations.

From Operational Excellence to Information Excellence

There are a number of areas where investments have been made in information excellence to support current operations and process improvements. This includes basic blocking and tackling such as accurate, timely order fulfillment, but in addition, Burberry worked with SAP and Salesforce to design several custom systems that link together sales, service, and partners through a single digital social platform called "Burberry World." The platform enables employees and key business partners to connect and to access brand information and news as well as group conversations focused around specific initiatives or business areas. There are bimonthly Chat Live webcast interviews with some of the organization's key leaders, and frequent video broadcasts to employees, previewing ad campaigns, for example.

Burberry doesn't just digitally market by giving customers a web-based storefront with a shopping cart and credit card entry form. It became the first major fashion brand to livestream its shows on its Burberry.com website and to millions of social media followers across platforms such as Facebook, Twitter, and WeChat. It also broadcasts coverage to digital screens at iconic "out of home" locations in flagship cities around the world, such as New York's Times Square and London's Piccadilly Circus. It converts excitement to sales by making select items worn on the catwalk immediately available via its "Runway Made to Order" service, with the interval from show to consumer delivery reduced to a fraction of the industry standard time.

Burberry is also a heavy user of analytics to understand shifts in consumer preferences and behavior, such as changing product or color preferences, items bought together, or growth in online purchasing.

From Physical to Virtual

Burberry moved many dimensions of the physical embodiment of the brand into the virtual world. It was an early entrant into the world of ecommerce, launching its first transactional website in the United States in 2004. Ahrendts and Bailey crafted the vision to make Burberry "the first company who is fully digital"[14] back in 2006—the same year Facebook was opened to the general public.

This strategy, to be first and foremost, has been successfully executed, according to L2, a research firm that evaluates how well brands ranging from Absolut and Acura to Zara and Zenith are doing in the digital world. L2 has rated Burberry among the top fashion brands for several years in a row and number one from 2011–2013 based on a metric composed of its website, digital marketing acumen, mobile strategy, and social media presence.[15,16]

Burberry.com clearly communicates—in images, sounds, and videos—the elegance and exclusivity of the brand in a way that mere words can't describe. Since Burberry is global, the site currently exists in 11 languages, and offers live customer service chat in over a dozen languages and dialects as well. It isn't just a single ecommerce site, though, but a variety of microsites offering not just fashion and beauty, but also social interaction and music.

In addition to a presence on popular social media, in 2009 Burberry launched its own platform: the Art of the Trench. It enables Burberry customers around the world using six languages to upload photos of themselves wearing the iconic coat. Thousands of photos have been uploaded from faraway places ranging from Armenia to Azerbaijan and Seoul to Shanghai, and since its launch, there have been 25 million page views from users in over 221 countries.

Another microsite—Burberry Acoustic—taps into Burberry's British identity and the universal enjoyment of music by showcasing various emerging British musical artists playing a variety of acoustic instruments—guitars, pianos, and violins—in uniquely British contexts, such as on the lawn in front of a centuries-old manor.

Burberry Kisses enabled customers to literally kiss their mobile device to generate an image of their lips, color it with a shade of Burberry lipstick, and send the image to a paramour. An animation showed the kiss traveling across the globe to its destination.

In addition to its own properties, Burberry has been extremely effective in leveraging popular social platforms, not just maintaining a presence there but being on the cutting edge of innovation in partnership with them. It was among the first to join Facebook, Twitter, Instagram, Google+, and VSCO, a mobile camera app and curated photography site.

Given the importance of Asia as a global luxury market, Burberry also maintains a presence on platforms such as Sina Weibo (a microblogging site not unlike Twitter), Youku (comparable to YouTube), mobile messaging medium WeChat (a bit like WhatsApp), and LINE. LINE is less well-known in the West, but is something like a roll-up of WhatsApp, Skype, and Facebook, together with gaming, and in a short period of time has grown to well over a half a billion users.

The brand has maintained a reputation for pioneering new ways to leverage social media, becoming the first luxury fashion brand to livestream on Facebook, Twitter, and LINE, and helping platforms launch new functionality such as Instagram's video roll-out. Burberry was the only fashion brand to participate in the launch of Twitter's in-tweet purchasing,[17] and it's announced strategic partnerships with both WeChat and LINE to help develop and launch new platform functionality.

Burberry has more than 30M fans across these various sites and platforms. Its accounts present unique views of Burberry stories and media customized for each platform, so, while a new campaign might launch on Facebook, Instagram might be the platform with the unique behind-the-scenes content.

From Virtual to Digical

According to CEO Bailey, Burberry is "focused on continued innovation at the intersection of our physical and our digital worlds."[18] This is not just a fuzzy vision, but a commitment based on hard data on customer behavior. According to Burberry's Chief Operating Officer John Smith, research shows that half of all purchases had at least one digital "step," say, perusing a new item on an iPad before heading over to buy it at the store. Burberry.com receives twice as many visitors as do their hundreds of stores, with additional reach through social media.[19]

One simple component of *digital-physical fusion*, also called *digical*, that customers want is the ability to order online and pick up in store, or, conversely, order in store and have the product delivered. As recently as 2013, only 6 percent of retail brands offered such channel-agnostic functionality,[20] yet Burberry has managed to achieve a high degree of integration. Offline and online channels are integrated in several ways. "Collect-in-store"—available at 140 stores in 23 countries—enables customers to order online and pick up the merchandise the next day in a store. The reverse is also enabled: Retail sales associates are armed with iPads to access the full Burberry assortment at Burberry.com for customers even if a particular product is not carried or is out of stock at that store. One could think of this as order in-store and pick-up online. Finally, inventory pools are shared between virtual and physical channels, to streamline total inventory resource requirements. As a measure of the importance of an omni-channel perspective and the value of instant gratification, almost a quarter of Burberry's online sales are picked up in store.

But digital-physical fusion at Burberry is much more than in-store pickup or ordering. In-store events are synchronized across the multimedia platform, so, for example, at the global flagship store on Regent Street, all 100 digital signs and 500 speakers will come to life simultaneously to create a multimedia show, such as an acoustic guitar concert or fashion show.

Flagship stores are physically laid out to reflect navigation at the website. Unlike men's, women's and kids' clothing, as at many stores, the layout reflects unique characteristics that Burberry has fostered, such as Burberry Heritage, for which the dedicated section online is mirrored in-store, celebrating the relaunched collection of iconic trench coats and customizable cashmere scarves, and even the unique Burberry Acoustic, where recording artists play acoustic instruments while wearing Burberry apparel.

The #tweetwalk hashtag was created by Burberry to take behind-the-scenes photos and videos and post them to Twitter before the fashions appear on the runway, giving the online audience a slight head start over the in-person one. But Burberry did even more to leverage Twitter. During the launch of Twitter's in-tweet purchasing, Twitter customers in the United States were able to buy a limited number of nail polishes, as they appeared on the runway during the Spring/Summer 2015 fashion show. It also offered *My Burberry*, its new women's fragrance, lipsticks, and additional nail polishes through in-tweet purchasing.

Burberry Beauty Box is a stand-alone concept store initially opened in London and Seoul. Among other features, there is a Digital Nail Bar, where customers can examine different shades of nail polish. Putting a polish down on the bar triggers an RFID (Radio Frequency Identification) tag to activate a digital display showing a model's hand with those colors. Setting five polishes and a lipstick on the bar shows each nail in a different shade and the model's lips colored accordingly.

Burberry's Runway to Reality is a creative rethinking of ecommerce. Normally, a client might view an article from the fashion press about a recent runway show, closed to the general public, and months later, possibly remember to go online or visit the store to see if the item was available and order it. Instead, Runway to Reality streams the catwalk directly into flagship stores, live, and enables customers to order items immediately for delivery within weeks. Even better, the general public can watch—and does watch, to the tune of millions of simultaneous viewers—the live stream on the Burberry.com website and can then click to order those items. The videos are also available for delayed playback and purchasing on the Burberry.com site.[21]

In September 2009, Burberry was the first major fashion brand to livestream, enabling online viewers to not only watch the Spring/Summer 2010 show from virtual front row seats at Burberry.com, but also to interact with the brand by sharing personal comments on the collection. It was also the first luxury fashion brand to livestream a fashion show on Twitter. It continues to broaden its platforms, streaming in HD on Facebook and WeChat, and posting on YouTube.

In addition to fusing live experiences with online ones, various products such as clothing, accessories, and beauty and fragrance products are enabled with RFID tags. Mirrors that are used in the usual way for trying on clothes might suddenly display "weather moments" with virtual rainstorms, evoking the company's iconic trench coats,[22] musicians singing and playing, or live fashion shows. Then, based on the tag, they might display fashion designer sketches of the item, multimedia clips of the item from a runway show, or product information, and then become mirrors again.[23]

From Processes to Experiences

Being a luxury fashion and beauty retailer involves more than just selling items on a website or in store and folding them neatly to be taken home or delivered. It is all about creating an elegant ambience and an aura of exclusivity, together with excellent customer service and unique experiences.

Fashion shows are perhaps the experience most unique to luxury apparel. They have become as involved as any live theater production. It used to be an exclusive experience only available to very few insiders, reported on by the fashion press, eventually diffusing to customers and prospects and perhaps leading to a customer order many months later. Burberry has been a leader in managing to continue to maintain close relationships with VIP customers while also connecting with large numbers of customers and prospects through mechanisms that manage to combine broad reach, maintain exclusivity, and yet provide an immediate, engaging experience.

As discussed above, shows are livestreamed over the web and through social media with interactive engagement. Special experiences occur live at the shows and in stores via digital signage, but also through select outdoor venues.

In February of 2010, Burberry broadcast its runway show live in 3D to simultaneous events held in New York, Paris, Dubai, Tokyo, and Los Angeles, the first brand ever to do so. The Autumn/Winter 2011 Womenswear show was livestreamed onto the enormous 100+ foot (32 meter)-long digital screen in Piccadilly Circus. Other events have been streamed to digital screens in London, Hong Kong, and New York.

The shows have also become events transcending fashion and including music. For example, the Autumn/Winter 2013 show included a live performance by Tom Odell, a musician featured at Burberry Acoustic. Subsequent major menswear and womenswear shows have included other uniquely British artists, reinforcing the brand heritage and promise.

These artists sometimes perform live at the flagship store, on a hydraulic stage that rises in front of the enormous digital display, creating a unique and compelling in-store experience.

From Mass Production to Mass Personalization

Although Burberry is virtually synonymous with the "Haymarket Check"—its camel, black, ivory, and red pattern—Burberry Bespoke lets customers select their own colors and designs. For example, one can select a coat design, such as Ardleigh, Winbourne, or Yarmouth; a material, such as cotton gabardine, washed cotton gabardine, cotton sateen, bonded cotton, or Nappa Leather; various designs for sleeves, epaulettes, and cuffs; assorted linings, such as the traditional design, a khaki block check, or a blue "dégradé" check; assorted undercollars, overcollars, and "throat latches" (i.e., neckline closures); and different buttons, belts, and monograms. Software logic ensures that fashion faux pas are impossible. Burberry has even considered offering "made-to-measure," that is, garments that are tailored to the customer during manufacture, rather than altered in store.[24]

Burberry "Smart Personalization" and Runway Made to Order provide an engraved nameplate sewn into various products. More than just a name tag, it incorporates a digital RFID tag personalized to the customer and can activate in-store digital signage.

In September 2014, Burberry released a new women's fragrance, *My Burberry*, and relaunched its Heritage line of trench coats and related accessories such as cashmere scarves. With this, Burberry introduced a monogramming offer, where customers could have their initials engraved onto the *My Burberry* bottles or embroidered on scarves. Customers and prospects were able to have the monogramming done in store or through online channels, but also were able to virtually monogram their initials and share the virtual bottle across social networks including Twitter, Facebook, and Google+.

Not only that, but customers could use their mobile devices to have their personalized virtual bottle displayed on giant digital billboards in New York and London, such as the one at Piccadilly Circus, and via interactive digital window displays during a special campaign held at the famed Printemps department store in Paris. Customers could control elements of the display through their mobile phone, and then share digital screen grabs from the display socially.

As if that weren't enough, Burberry television advertising was personalized on an on-demand channel, where the ad ended with not just a generic video clip of a *My Burberry* fragrance bottle but one where the image had a digitally inserted monogram personalized to the viewer.

In addition to messaging and product personalization, a tool called Customer Value Management is used by Burberry Private Client services to provide highly personalized service to VIP clients. It and an opt-in tool and service called Customer 1-2-1 help provide personalized sales, including product preferences and purchase transaction history.

From Cost Reduction to Revenue Generation

Burberry is certainly focused on operational excellence; it's one of Burberry's five core strategic priorities. To reduce costs, it has taken a number of steps, such as reducing the range of variability in the product assortment, leading to greater volumes and purchasing power. Burberry deployed SAP enterprise resource planning, helping to reduce costs by tens of millions of dollars and to improve inventory visibility.[25]

However, the most strategic arena for digital technologies, as should be clear at this point, is revenue generation. There is less financial benefit from, say, driving down the cost of cotton for gabardine by a few percent than in selling higher-value products more frequently to more customers in more places.

It's not news that ecommerce is growing, but specific data in Burberry's case are instructive. According to COO John Smith, in interim results posted 6 months into Burberry's 2014 fiscal year, Burberry grew adjusted profits by 6 percent and grew revenues by 14 percent. This occurred in the context of a luxury sector growing only a third as fast, at 5 percent. But the ecommerce segment of that sector has been estimated to be growing at 25 percent. Revenue from Burberry.com alone grew at almost 60 percent annually over a three-year period.[26] If there was any doubt as to the importance of mobile, it's worth noting that a quarter of the Burberry.com sales come from iPads.

Riding the wave of digital growth is not about, say, just sending more emails, but using digital to help meet two of Burberry's key strategies, which are to "Inspire with the Brand" and "Realise Product Potential," as well as connecting with target customers such as millennials where those customers reside, which is online and on social media. Brand and product are inseparable, because products are differentiated through the heritage of the brand, and desirable products strengthen the brand. Burberry Prorsum, which is the "fashion-forward" runway show collection, generates only 5 percent of retail apparel revenue, but is the "design inspiration" for the other labels that generate revenue, and is also the key generator of excitement across social media, the press, and in-store VIP shows.

Although inspiring customers with the brand might seem separable from or even antithetical to operational excellence, it need not be. In Burberry's case, having a clear brand message is aligned with a focused product assortment and the supply chain efficiencies that are part of the operational excellence thrust.

As should be clear, realizing this comprehensive approach to information excellence requires investments. Various applications ranging from Burberry.com to those running on in-store iPads and supporting Burberry Private Client Services don't just display electronic catalogues of images or videos of models at fashion shows, nor just support standard shopping carts. Flexibility in selection of fabrics, designs, and devices such as epaulettes are one level of complexity; rules engines ensuring that faulty stylistic combinations are impossible to order are another layer, and integration with back-end systems for custom production requires nontrivial application development and integration.

From Touchpoints to Integration

As we've seen in the preceding pages, Burberry touches customers, prospects, and influencers in numerous physical and virtual ways. Stores are an obvious physical touchpoint, but so are fashion shows, magazine and print ads, including specially placed magazine back-cover ads at retailers such as Printemps, print media with fashion show or news coverage, and physical retailers with Burberry merchandising including interactive digital displays. It touches them digitally at Burberry.com, and through all the key social media channels, including microblogs like Twitter, messaging services like LINE, social networks such as Facebook, and video distribution platforms such as YouTube. It offers personalized and exceptional experiences, touching its audience through personalized TV ads, and by livestreaming to giant billboard displays, in-store displays, and mobile devices.

Regardless of device or channel, virtual or physical, handheld or building-sized, Burberry has integrated all these touchpoints to the extent possible, across the customer purchase journey from brand awareness through customization and delivery, and across nonpurchase activities that involve customers generally engaging, identifying, and bonding with the brand.

In addition to now-typical customer service options such as phone, email, in-store, and website and social media chat, Burberry maintains a strong brand and customer service presence on Twitter. Moreover, as mentioned, customers could click on a buy button in Twitter to do in-tweet purchasing of new nail polishes in new colors, as they appeared on the runway, and subsequently, the *My Burberry* fragrance and other cosmetics. Customers can order select items as they are first launched during streamed fashion shows.

Through Customer 1-2-1, retail and private client sales associates can see all purchases that the customer has made, their clothing sizes and product preferences, and view the purchases not just as a list of SKUs, but as a visual wardrobe. This capability is omni-channel, integrating the customer data across online and offline purchases and other touchpoints.

From Firms to Networks

Finally, Burberry has broken down the firm's boundaries, building a network of suppliers, retailers, social networks, customers, prospects, and other stakeholders into a *social enterprise*.[27] It has been tying together legacy and emerging systems, websites, social media, sentiment analysis, events, licensees, franchisees and their scores of stores in dozens of countries, investors, its hundreds of directly operated stores and hundreds of concessions (mini-stores in department stores) in dozens of countries, "travel retail" (airport stores), customers, private clients, prospects, over 10,000 employees, suppliers, almost 1,500 wholesale department and specialty stores, distributors, channels, tablets, smartphones, laptops, desktops, digital tags, and video streams.[28]

This network has physical and virtual dimensions. Operationally, Burberry works with suppliers in a variety of areas, for example, to streamline supply chain and logistics processes and increase supplier sustainability. Digitally, Burberry World, an application based on SAP and Salesforce.com's Chatter, is an internal global resource for employees to connect and collaborate with each other and also with key global supply chain partners more easily. Between it and related systems, Burberry has become the nexus of a network of participants.

For example, in-store and online sales and customer service personnel can view their customers' posts on social media, and then comment on them. Customers can make suggestions, whether for new products or changes to existing ones. Burberry also works closely with select retailers to integrate marketing outreach efforts.

As Ahrendts said when she was Burberry's CEO, "You have to be totally connected with everyone that touches your brand."[29]

■   ■   ■

Burberry has successfully been implementing a growth strategy in which all the elements are aligned. It has refocused on a clear brand identity and moved beyond operational excellence to become a role model of information excellence. It targeted affluent, aspiring millennials, who are digitally savvy, social, brand ambassadors, and influencers. It seamlessly fused digital and physical domains to create a compelling, inspirational brand. It also hitched a ride on the coattails of exponential growth in luxury ecommerce, flawlessly delivering unique customer experiences and many technology firsts in the luxury retail industry—or any industry. Finally, it has a 10-year track record of dramatic growth in revenues, profitability, and market capitalization, even after accounting for the costs of resurrecting a brand that had been having trouble weathering the storm at the turn of the millennium.

Notes

1. Emma Hutchings, "Burberry Launches Interactive, Multimedia Store in London [Pics]," *PSFK.com*, September 13, 2012, www.psfk.com/2012/09/burberry-interactive-multimedia-store-london.html.
2. "Burberry Flagship Store, London," *RetailDesignBlog.net*, September 17, 2012, retaildesignblog.net/2012/09/17/burberry-flagship-store-london/.
3. "World Television: Burberry: Interim Results Presentation 12th of November," *BurberryPLC.com*, November 12, 2014, www.burberryplc.com/documents/results/2014/burberry-interim-report-2014-transcript.pdf.
4. "Company History," *BurberryPLC.com*, www.burberryplc.com/about_burberry/company_history.
5. Leo King, "Burberry Struts Ahead with Tech Transformation Begun by Apple's Angela Ahrendts," *Forbes.com*, May 21, 2014, www.forbes.com/sites/leoking/2014/05/21/burberry-struts-ahead-with-tech-transformation-begun-by-apples-angela-ahrendts/.
6. Sophie Doran, "How Burberry Does Digital," *LuxurySociety.com*, January 9, 2014, luxurysociety.com/articles/2014/01/how-burberry-does-digital.
7. Colleen Leahey, "Angela Ahrendts: The Secrets behind Burberry's Growth," *Fortune.com*, June 19, 2012, fortune.com/2012/06/19/angela-ahrendts-the-secrets-behind-burberrys-growth/.
8. Andrew Roberts, "Burberry Designer Bailey to Be CEO as Ahrendts Goes to Apple," *BloombergBusiness*, October 15, 2013, www.bloomberg.com/news/2013-10-15/burberry-says-bailey-to-become-ceo-as-ahrendts-leaves-for-apple.html.

9. Angela Ahrendts, "Burberry's CEO on Turning an Aging British Icon into a Global Luxury Brand," *Harvard Business Review* (January 2013), https://hbr.org/2013/01/burberrys-ceo-on-turning-an-aging-british-icon-into-a-global-luxury-brand/.

10. Putri Arinda, "Brief Analysis on Digital Marketing Strategy of Burberry, Anthropologie and Beacon's Closet," *SlideShare.net*, October 5, 2013, www.slideshare.net/putriarinda/brief-analysis-on-digital-marketing-strategy-of-burberry-anthropologie-and-beacons-closet.

11. Ahrendts, "Burberry's CEO."

12. Burberry Annual Report 2013/14, www.burberryplc.com/documents/ar-13-14/burberry-annual-report-2013-14.pdf

13. Ibid.

14. "Why Is Burberry's Digital Strategy So Good?" *Parallax Blog*, April 28, 2014, https://parall.ax/blog/view/3047/why-is-burberry-s-digital-strategy-so-good-.

15. Homa Zaryouni, "Behind Digital Genius Burberry," *L2Inc.com*, December 5, 2013, www.l2inc.com/behind-digital-genius-burberry/2013/blog.

16. Laura Black, "The Top 10 Fashion Brands in Digital," *L2Inc.com*, January 21, 2015, www.l2inc.com/top-10-fashion-brands-in-digital/2015/blog.

17. Tarun Jain, "Testing a Way for You to Make Purchases on Twitter," *Twitter Blog*, September 8, 2014, https://blog.twitter.com/2014/testing-a-way-for-you-to-make-purchases-on-twitter.

18. "World Television: Burberry."

19. Ibid.

20. Joe McCarthy, "Burberry Leads Digital Fashion Pack for Third Straight Year: L2," *LuxuryDaily.com*, December 6, 2013, www.luxurydaily.com/burberry-leads-digital-fashion-pack-for-third-straight-year-l2/.

21. Doran, "How Burberry Does Digital."

22. Retail Design Blog.

23. Doran, "How Burberry Does Digital."

24. Paul Sonne, "Mink or Fox? The Trench Gets Complicated," *Wall Street Journal*, November 3, 2011, online.wsj.com/articles/SB10001424052970203804204577013842801187070.

25. King, "Burberry Struts Ahead."

26. Calculation based on "fourfold growth in three years" from Burberry Interim Report, www.burberryplc.com/documents/results/2014/burberry-interim-report-2014-transcript.pdf.

27. Salesforce video, "Angela Ahrendts on Burberry's Social Enterprise," [Video], *YouTube.com*, September 14, 2011, www.youtube.com/watch?v=BlMBxhP1abc.

28. Ibid.

29. Ahrendts, "Burberry's CEO."

PART THREE
Solution Leadership

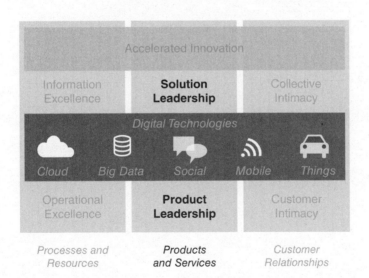

CHAPTER 8

Products, Services, and Solutions

There are a number of useful frameworks with which to better understand competition in products—such as paper clips, blenders, jumbo jets, and flat-screen televisions—and services—such as hairstyling, entertainment, pest control, and transportation. These frameworks are helpful in understanding the basis for competition, benefits offered to customers, and why some products and services succeed while others fail. In particular, they help clarify *value creation*—how products create value for customers—and *value capture*—how they make money for firms.

Services, in contradistinction to products or goods, it has been argued, are *intangible*—they can't be touched; *perishable*—they must be consumed as they are produced; *inseparable*—the consumer must be present for the service to be delivered, as in a haircut; and *variable*—each case of service delivery is unique.

Unfortunately, these classic criteria, while plausible, are not as clear as they might appear. An information product such as online news is intangible, yet a personal massage service is very tangible. Many products, ranging from apples to Apples, are perishable; in the first case due to biochemistry, in the second, due to technology advances. A remote data archiving service is separable from the customer whereas a pacemaker product is not. And products can vary, too, such as a customized car with a choice of doors, seats, exterior color, and trim package, or due to manufacturing or natural variation, say in wood grain or marbling.

Rather than get wrapped up around definitions and criteria, we'll think of products as tangible or virtual goods and services as activities that create value for customers.

Products and services often combine to form product-service systems. Examples include a telephone and telephone service; a tablet and app store retail service; a radio and broadcast or satellite service; a wearable device and activity tracking services.

When such a product-service system *solves* a specific customer need, say, the wearable and cloud-based activity tracker helps an individual attain a fitness objective, it is a product-service system solution. One of the major premises of this book is that standalone products are evolving to product-service system solutions, or just solutions, which we'll address in the next few chapters.

First let's review some of the major insights that have been developed around products and services.

Competitive Strategy

Harvard Business School professor Michael Porter is perhaps the most well-known business strategy guru.[1] As we introduced in Chapter 2, Porter observes that corporations don't compete, business units do. In other words, General Electric Company doesn't really compete with Rolls-Royce Holdings Plc or Citigroup, Inc., but rather, GE Aviation competes with Rolls-Royce Aerospace, and GE Capital competes with Citi's Global Consumer Banking unit.

Porter says that in such competition there are five forces that affect profitability: the bargaining power of suppliers, the bargaining power of buyers (customers), the intensity of industry rivalry, the threat of substitutes, and the threat of entry by new competitors.

For example, Amazon.com has had protracted negotiations with publishers. In this case, the bargaining power of one particular customer—Amazon—is quite high, because publishers derive a substantial portion of their revenues from this customer, and are being offered a tough choice: accept lower margins or lower revenues.

The threat of substitutes is also a type of customer buying power. If oil customers can switch to natural gas, oil companies are limited in their ability to raise prices, as are natural gas suppliers. The threat of new entrants can dampen industry profitability as well, whereas barriers to entry can raise it. At one extreme, consider cellular phone service: Limited radio spectrum, which is auctioned off to competitors, means that a new entrant cannot just begin offering service. The same is true with airport landing slots. At the other extreme, consider pizzerias in New York City. There are plenty of sites suitable for restaurants, and virtually anyone can learn to make pizza and buy an oven. This is why pizza generally is inexpensive.

Porter argues that, in light of these forces, companies or units can either compete through lower price, differentiation, or by focusing on particular market niches. As discussed in Chapter 2, Porter's primary focus is on competition between business units, not products, but the two are clearly related: business units offer product lines. In the retail clothing business, for example, Wal-Mart probably offers the lowest cost and Neiman-Marcus the most differentiated (and expensive) product. But if you are interested in, say, luxury leather handbags, Prada (due to its focus on the luxury segment) may be the best choice.

Information technology can help products become less expensive. The cost structure of a product is based on its design, on its components, and on the production processes that build it. Design can often be optimized through information technology. As one example, simulation techniques such as finite element analysis can help remove material without impacting strength, resilience, or stability. Digital components can replace mechanical ones, offering a reduced cost structure. And, various approaches can be used to improve the design or operation of physical manufacturing lines: process simulation, software-driven flexible manufacturing equipment, and so on.

Information technology can also help differentiate products. Examples include talking dolls, smart door locks, and learning thermostats. Differentiation sounds like a single strategy, but in reality there can be dozens if not hundreds of ways to differentiate a product in a given industry: classic design or innovative; freshness or timelessness; flexibility or standardization; disposability or durability; low cost and ubiquity or high cost and exclusivity; or high value (benefits less costs). Also: cool and hip or conservative; global consistency or local adaptation; emotion; ego, status, power and prestige; anonymity and fitting in or identity and individuality; customer experience; customer service; bundling or unbundling; transparency; convenience; breadth of assortment; simplicity or feature-richness; environmental friendliness; social meaning; spiritual meaning. The list can go on and on, depending on the specific domain. For hotels, the list might include cleanliness and location. For televisions, remote control layouts, image resolution, brightness and contrast. For cars, miles per gallon, colors, heated seats, and in-vehicle entertainment and navigation systems.

The list shows the challenges of the marketplace but also the opportunities for differentiation. Everyone values product attributes differently; these preferences shift over time; many attributes are mutually exclusive; different factors weigh differently during evaluation, purchase decision, and product or service use. The good news is that with so many attributes on which to differentiate, and such a wide variety of customer preferences, most industries have room for many competitors and many product offerings.

Product Elements

Somewhat more granular than the Porter model is the *marketing mix* model—an attempt to characterize the rich dimensions of how products can compete and be marketed, devised by E. Jerome McCarthy, a professor at

Michigan State. In this framework, the notion is that a firm's proposition to a customer isn't just the product itself, but the "4 Ps" of marketing: product, price, promotion, and place. The last "P" is sometimes considered to be physical distribution.

The point is that the total offer is not just the product itself, say, the blender, but the price at which it is offered, where it can be purchased, and outbound marketing (the "promotion"). Each of these can be broken down further: promotion includes advertising, brand identity, sales collateral, executive briefings, public relations efforts, etc. Moreover, while "price" used to just mean a particular fixed price, today there are many options for how to charge for products, which we'll cover later in this chapter.

There have been a number of variations on this core model. For example, one takes the corresponding customer viewpoint: matching the producer's Ps with the customer's Cs: product relates to consumer, price to cost, promotion to communication, and place to convenience. Others have added various other Ps such as people, processes, programs, and performance, and other Cs such as corporation, competitor, compliance, commodity, and channel.

Even if we ignore price, promotion, and place, the concept of product is a very rich one, and not just for iconic products such as Apple iPhones, Aston-Martin DB9s, or Rolex Daytonas, but even commodities. Products, after all, do not exist in a vacuum, but in an envelope of positioning, support services, and contract terms, even without considering how they integrate with the services that make them product-service systems.

This insight led marketing icon and Harvard Business School professor Theodore (Ted) Levitt to claim decades ago, "There is no such thing as a commodity." Companies selling pork bellies, paper clips, or scrap steel, say, may differentiate themselves on price, terms, responsiveness to inquiries and so forth, so that what they are offering is not undifferentiated, but something completely unique. He points out that merely looking at the minimal common denominator of even a product category such as scrap steel misses the fact that the *total product* has four levels: the generic product, which delivers the core benefit, the expected product, the augmented product, and the potential product.[2]

Consider a toaster. The core benefit of a toaster is to provide tastier bread, Pop Tarts, or other items. The generic product is the basic version of the toaster: a box with slots, a lever, heating elements, and a power cord. This doesn't mean that one can actually buy such a toaster, but that conceptually, any toaster has such a skeleton inside. Levitt calls the generic product table stakes: merely offering a chance to play, but in no way guaranteeing any kind of win. "Generic" does not mean "identical." As Levitt says, one vendor's "commodity" steel might meet specifications just as well as another's, but differ, say, in how well it accepts coatings. Nevertheless, by meeting the requirements needed to deliver the core benefit, it can be considered to be generic.

The expected product includes features or characteristics that buyers expect, but may not necessarily vocalize. For the toaster, this might include Underwriters' Laboratories (UL) certification or dual slots. The expected product represents the customer's minimal purchase conditions (e.g., delivery, pricing and discount terms, support and solution consulting). But, as Levitt says, "differentiation is not limited to giving customers what they expect," offering opportunities to differentiate an expected product through augmentation.

The augmented product extends the expected product through, for example, additional features such as defrost settings or wide slots for bagels. The augmented product goes beyond what was "required or expected by the buyer," and might be called the "unexpected" product. These are the differentiators that delight and surprise the customer, since they were unanticipated. These differentiators might be product features, such as a touchscreen instead of physical buttons, or ultralight weight or longer battery life. Or, it might include special financing, different delivery logistics, or additional services and features that can help differentiate the offer.

Finally, the potential product represents what the product may become in the future. The potential product comprises product or complementary service features or attributes that don't yet exist, but could someday, as a result of innovation, new applications, extension, or discussions between the vendor and the customer (e.g., a change to product design or how to engineer it into a customer's assembly or process). As Levitt says, for the potential product, "Only the budget and the imagination limit the possibilities."[3]

However, Levitt recognizes that "Not all customers for all products and under all circumstances, however, can be attracted by an ever-expanding bundle of differentiating value satisfactions."[4] In other words, some people just want to save money, not pay for additional "augmentations."

In addition to the core benefit from the generic product, the other layers of the total product deliver benefits as well, although Levitt doesn't detail these. One can presume, however, that the expected product delivers typical benefits from industry-standard features, the augmented product delivers unique benefits from differentiated features and services, and the potential product delivers future benefits associated with the firm itself and its broader ecosystem. For example, the potential product embedded in an iPad includes all of the applications that Apple or that the development ecosystem building apps for the platform might create. In addition, the various layers of the product deliver a variety of cognitive, behavioral, and emotional benefits such as a need for status or novelty and societal or value benefits such as sustainability or charitable contribution.

Levitt's insights align with those of Professor Noriako Kano of the Tokyo University of Science, who observed that product characteristics can be expected or unexpected by customers, and they also may be spoken or unspoken. Unspoken expected elements don't generate positive differentiation by their presence, only negative through their absence. For example, if a customer is asked what she wants in a car, she is likely to say something like "gas mileage" or "sporty styling," not "it shouldn't have airbags that may explode in shrapnel" or "it shouldn't have an ignition switch that occasionally cuts all power off while traveling at highway speeds." At the other extreme, unspoken, unexpected elements are those that delight customers, and loosely correspond to the potential product.

Levitt's Total Product concept was promulgated initially in 1960; well before mobility, the World Wide Web, or the Internet of Things. However, it is even more relevant today, thanks to digital technologies.

The potential product now can be realized through upgrades to fix bugs or improve performance, machine learning and adaptability, user personalization, and so on. The Nest Learning Thermostat is a good example. The generic thermostat lets you set a temperature. But Nest learns about your preferences, and has already been upgraded with new software that reduces heating and air conditioning bills compared to the original release.

In Levitt's model, conceptualized well before the digital era, the potential product was the universe of possible future (real world) applications that human creativity could add after the fact; now, the potential product comprises physical and software applications that human creativity complemented by computing and networks can realize.

Many of these benefits and product elements relate to place and promotion and can be considered part of the total customer experience, which can include merchandising, including layout, aesthetics, colors, and furnishings of a retail outlet, such as a Renovation Hardware or Apple Store, or a McDonald's PlayPlace; the packaging a product comes in, whether Tiffany blue or Apple white; the music on hold on the customer service line, and so forth.

Leonard Berry, a distinguished professor of marketing at Texas A&M and expert in customer service, says that the "clues" that make up a customer experience are of two types. One is the function performed, such as a car moving and braking or whether a dishwasher repairperson fixes the problem, and its success or failure can be interpreted logically and rationally. The other type of clue is sensory and emotional, and can include the smell of the leather seats, the marble in the dealership, and ego gratification—whether the car stands for "safety" or for "ultimate driving experience."[5] Today, products must consider both types of clues.

The Experience Economy

In their seminal book, *The Experience Economy*, Joe Pine and Jim Gilmore partition what Levitt would call total products into a hierarchy of increasing value: commodities, products, services, experiences, and personal and social transformations. As value increases to customers, they argue, profit opportunities expand for firms.[6]

In the *experience economy* model, commodities generally are extracted, farmed, or fished; products are manufactured; services are delivered; experiences are staged; and transformations are the highest form of experiences. McDonald's is just a restaurant; Medieval Times is an experience. Ringling Brothers is just a circus; Cirque de Soleil is an experience. Coursera offers free college courses over the web, enabling personal transformation. Kiva boosts the economy of developing countries through cloud-mediated micro-loans, enabling societal transformation.

Experiences can be impactful, yet delivered regularly, as with the twice-nightly performance of the Cirque de Soleil show *KÀ* at the MGM Grand. They can also be limited duration or once in a lifetime events such as ringing in the new millennium at Times Square. STORY, as an example somewhere between the extremes, is a retailer described as "monthly magazine, meets art gallery, meets retailer." It completely renews all merchandising on a monthly basis, including product selection, theme, and décor.[7]

Pine and Gilmore use coffee to illustrate increasing value and profit potential. Whereas raw coffee beans might sell for 10 or 20 cents per pound, when roasted and packaged as products, they can be sold for several dollars a pound. When offered as a service in a corner coffee shop, several dollars of coffee-as-a-commodity can generate perhaps a hundred dollars' worth of coffee-as-a-service—*ventis*, *grandes*, and talls. Instead of selling a cup of coffee for a few dollars at the corner coffee shop, a cup might cost 10 dollars or more at an elegant restaurant offering not just the coffee as a *product*, not just coffee *service*, but a dining *experience*.

There are many different types of experiences: one example that Pine and Gilmore explore is Cirque de Soleil. If you've been to a Cirque de Soleil show, you'll immediately understand. Otherwise, it defies description. It is a concert, a costume extravaganza, a play, an acrobatics and athletic exhibition. There is a plot, but it may or may not really matter. There are surprises, delights, and a continuing sequence of impossible acrobatics. The sets are out-of-this-world constructs, comprising contraptions and devices that have never been seen before, including stages that are pools and stages that can rotate to be vertical. The performers interact with these bizarre constructions in a sequence of gravity-defying feats of split-second timing. There is no way to confuse Cirque de Soleil with anything else. It is not merely an entertainment service; it is an experience that will cause you to question the bounds of reality.

However, in the Pine & Gilmore model, the pinnacle of value is not an experience, but a *transformation*. It is the ultimate experience; one that doesn't end when the show is over, but continues on forever. Education is a service; attending college may be an experience; but graduating from medical school and becoming a physician is a transformation. Visiting a doctor as a patient may be a service or an experience, but having her perform life-saving surgery on you is a transformation. The corner gym may sell supplements as products, offer spin class as a service, or even yoga as an experience, but a meditation retreat may be life-transforming.

Although they are focused on consumer transformations, the model is clearly extensible to business or societal transformations. A consulting group that can redirect a business's strategy and organization leads a business transformation not unlike the way that a medical school can lead a personal transformation. A movement that can cause societal change is yet another type of transformation.

Digital products and services can help create experiences as well as transformations. A product that ties to back-end educational, weight loss, or fitness services can create a transformation: MyFitnessPal has reportedly helped lose over 200 million pounds for its customers in aggregate—in just one year.[8] IT can also help with business transformation. This can include mundane products that help manage supply chains or customer relationships better. It can include algorithms that enable high-frequency trading. And it can include connected industrial products that transform performance in generating electricity, running transportation networks, or in manufacturing other products.

Pricing and Business Models

Price is one of the elements of the marketing mix, but *pricing* models, and more broadly, business models, are of even greater importance today. Product pricing traditionally was cost-plus, competitive, or value-based. Whereas a corner store of a century ago only had to determine at what price a jar of pickles should be sold, today there are dozens of pricing models, including many forms of "free."

One model is to offer leasing or rental instead of outright sale. Wikipedia is free, but remains in operation through charitable donations, also known as "pay what you like" pricing, and a low cost structure, thanks to volunteer contributors and editors. Use of Google or Microsoft Bing search is free, but not to advertisers, for whom advertising slots are auctioned off. Newspapers, country clubs, and software as a service mostly use subscription models. Amazon Web Services offers "pay-per-use" pricing, often called a linear tariff. But it also offers reserved instances, which are a discount for committed future use. The Google Cloud offers "sustained use" pricing, which offers a discount for consistent use over time. The Vestergaard LifeStraw, which filters drinking water, is free to users, but paid for—behind the scenes—through the exchange of carbon credits. The razor and blade model was applied to Gillette razors a century ago, and to printers and ink cartridges today.

Free and "freemium" are powerful pricing models. Research conducted by Dan Ariely, a professor at Duke and one the world's leading behavioral economists, suggests that free goods and services offer an irrational perception of outsized benefit to customers.[9] Customers would rather accept a free ten-dollar gift certificate than pay $7 for a twenty-dollar one, even though the latter offers a greater rational economic value.

Most of these models would be difficult with physical products: Imagine a car dealership selling cars via "pay what you like" pricing. However, with perishable capacity such as hotel rooms and airlines seats, "pay what you like" within acceptable bounds can be viable, as with Priceline. And, when the marginal cost of a product is essentially zero, as with pure digital goods, free is often the first step toward monetization, either through two-sided or multisided models such as advertising-supported, or in-app purchases, upgrades, or virtual goods. The economics of digital services can leverage open source software, pay-per-use pricing for cloud services, and therefore, after upfront software development costs, can largely align costs and revenues.

Professor Stefan Michel, of the International Institute for Management Development in Lausanne, Switzerland, has organized 15 generic pricing strategies into five major groups.[10] They include changing the price-setting mechanism, such as from fixed price to auctions; changing who pays, such as from user pays to two-sided monetization; changing the price carrier, such as from a la carte to all-inclusive; changing the timing of payments, for example, via a razor-and-razor-blades approach; or changing who the target customers are.

There are a few major insights one can derive from his analysis. First, there are a broad number of innovative pricing approaches one can use. Second, pricing can make all the difference between survival and bankruptcy. One could argue that Netflix's victory over Blockbuster was primarily one of pricing models, repositioning onerous late fees into a flat-rate subscription.

But the most important insight for the purposes of this book that one can glean from Michel's analysis is the importance of information technology in enabling many innovative pricing models, such as the following.

Dynamic pricing, with which we are all familiar—thanks to the seeming randomness of airline ticket prices—requires yield management and dynamic pricing software to forecast future demand, understand current reality, and either incent demand or extract maximal value accordingly.

Auctioning—such as when Google auctions off search results ranking for various keywords to the highest bidder, rather than merely setting a single rate—requires sophisticated, high-performance real-time systems. These systems match a product ad, such as for baby carriages, to target prospects, such as pregnant women with American Express cards, in milliseconds, using sophisticated algorithms and detailed customer data.

Changing the price carrier is another category Michel suggests. For example, he points out that McDonald's offers Wi-Fi and PlayPlaces for free; it makes its money on fast food. And, he argues, prior to Netflix, video rental stores made their money on rentals, and any recommendations from the clerk came for free. Netflix included recommendations as part of the total value proposition of the subscription, thus altering the monetization of the overall offer. In this case, digital technologies are key to several elements of the offer—recommendations, movie delivery, ordering, queue management, payment—and so successful implementation of such a pricing strategy requires IT.

Bundling or *unbundling* is another way of changing the price carrier—for example, charging for parking, meals, drinks, room, and entertainment, vs. an all-inclusive resort. In an unbundled offer, of course, metering, audit trails, and other data-intensive tasks are required.

The value of a valid business model is perhaps best understood through Pets.com. It advertised during the Super Bowl. It had $300 million of venture capital from prominent investors with sterling track records. It had an easy-to-pronounce name that was also easy to type into a browser. It had cost structure advantages from being online rather than needing to operate bricks and mortar stores. It had a memorable mascot, the Pets.com sock puppet. It won awards for advertising and site usability, including a Super Bowl ad with the highest recall of that year. It was one of the first movers in the then-burgeoning business of online sales, and acquired its only real competitor, Petstore.com. It had a killer customer value proposition, offering unbeatable prices.

It had everything, in short, except a viable business model. Pets.com sold merchandise for one-third of what it cost, even before considering sales, general, and administrative costs and other operations costs such as shipping.[11] It went from IPO to liquidation in less than nine months.

■   ■   ■

The concept of a "product," apparently so simple, is actually quite rich. A variety of models, including the total product model—generic, expected, augmented, and potential products—and the experience economy model—commodities, products, services, experiences, and transformations—can help inform and ultimately enable product, service, and business unit differential advantage and competition.

Today's "products" can be enriched and differentiated via IT. Integrated services can be provided by the cloud to create product-service systems. The product can be augmented by such services. And, when one buys any kind of applications platform, one is not just buying the physical device, or even the back-end service, but all potential upgrades and future apps that may come along in the future, free or paid. Such rich capabilities can evolve from commodities to transformations, with business unit profitability accompanying such evolution.

Notes

1. Michael Porter, *Competitive Strategy: Techniques for Analyzing Industries and Competitors* (New York: Free Press, 1980).
2. Theodore Levitt, "Marketing Success Through Differentiation—Of Anything," *Harvard Business Review* (January–February 1980): 2–9.
3. Ibid.
4. Ibid.
5. Leonard L. Berry, Lewis P. Carbone, and Stephan H. Haeckel, "Managing the Total Customer Experience," *MIT Sloan Management Review* (Spring 2002).
6. B. Joseph Pine II and James H. Gilmore, *The Experience Economy: Work Is Theater & Every Business a Stage* (Boston: Harvard Business School Press, 1999).
7. Babs Ryan, "Trends That Will Revolutionize The Retail Industry," *TechCrunch .com*, November 6, 2014, http://techcrunch.com/2014/11/06/trends-that-will-revolutionize-the-retail-industry/.
8. Kleiner Perkins Caufield & Byers, "Behind the Scenes: The MyFitnessPal Story," *YouTube.com*, February 4, 2015, https://www.youtube.com/watch?v=g1vjIpPmMlo.
9. Kristina Shampanier, Nina Mazar, and Dan Ariely, "Zero as a Special Price: The True Value of Free Products," *Marketing Science* (November–December 2007): 742–757, people.duke.edu/~dandan/Papers/PI/zerofree.pdf.
10. Stefan Michel, "Capture More Value," *Harvard Business Review* (October 2014).
11. Kirk Cheyfitz, *Thinking Inside the Box: The 12 Timeless Rules for Managing a Successful Business* (New York: Simon & Schuster, 2003), 29–32.

CHAPTER 9

The Discipline of Solution Leadership

The discipline of solution leadership entails competing not just with better standalone products but with better solutions: product-service systems encompassing "things" connected to cloud-based services; which are customized or customizable to solve customer problems; have virtually unlimited potential via platforms and ecosystems; and that maintain a long-term relationship with the customer rather than being sold in a single transaction, further enabling a joint focus on customer outcomes.

Formerly standalone services are becoming connected to the cloud as well. Consider the difference between the traditional corner pizzeria and today's, where ordering the pizza and selecting toppings can be done online, the restaurants are connected to the ordering system and display gamified performance metrics, and the trucks increasingly have GPS tracking.[1]

Moreover, the boundary between products and services is blurring. In one room of my house, I get cable *service*, which is delivered through physical objects such as a set-top box. In another, I have a purchased *product*—a TiVo personal video recorder—which, through a CableCard, is connected to a back-end cable and TiVo scheduling and recommendation services. The same core benefit is delivered either way.

Product-service-ecosystem combinations per se are not new. They include televisions, broadcast networks, and television programming; electrical devices and appliances, electrical transmission and distribution networks, and power generation utilities; or cars, repair shop services, service stations (gasoline distribution networks), and petroleum exploration and refining. What *is* new is digital intelligence, two-way network connectivity, and the frictionless growth of cloud-based or cloud-distributed applications. This also is driving new options for the location of value creation, for example, from the firm to ecosystem partners or from the device to the cloud, and control points, for example, from distribution channels to app licensing criteria.

The difference between products and solutions can be seen in the evolution of the wristwatch. The first watches were mechanical; using various springs and gears to keep time, more or less. They still exist. Today's Rolex Cosmograph Daytona is a canonical example of product leadership, made of 18-karat gold, a water-resistant case, and a 44-jewel chronometer movement. Then along came electronic watches, such as from Seiko, which used a battery-driven quartz piezoelectric oscillator. Then, in 1970, the first digital (electronic) watches came on the market from companies such as Pulsar and Texas Instruments. In 2004, the first Microsoft "SPOT" (Smart Personal Objects Technologies) watches arrived, with information such as weather and stocks beamed into the device over an FM radio channel. But it is only recently that the watch has become a solution, not only digital and electronic, but connected to limitless cloud services and a world of apps. The Apple Watch is perhaps the most notable entrant in this field.

Watches also exemplify how solution leadership can drive ecosystems, revenue growth, and sticky customer relationships. You can always put that Rolex back in the drawer and strap on the Tag-Heuer, or switch to a Swatch. But changing out an Apple Watch for a Samsung Gear S (or vice versa) is more difficult. The challenge is not the device itself, which is like the proverbial visible portion of an iceberg. It's the personal data that reside in the cloud, such as photos, contacts, calendars, and videos, the unique experience, characteristics, and personalization of the interface, and the integration with other devices such as your phone.

A "solution" is also something that solves a customer problem and thus generates customer value. GE Aviation is no longer just in the jet engine business, but in the flight performance optimization business. Netflix is not in the movie rental business, but the entertainment (i.e., consumer emotion evocation and mental diversion) business.

Product or service "leadership" is often viewed as that having the highest quality. Rolex in watches, Bentley in automobiles, Four Seasons in hotels, Neiman-Marcus in department stores. But, as marketing and strategy professionals are likely to realize, there often are many market segments in which a company, or its products, can lead. Bentley, Tesla, Prius, Lamborghini, Mini, Tata, and Volvo have all carved out leadership positions in specific market niches: say, British luxury, all-electric high-performance, hybrid family, Italian exotic, trendy, lowest cost, and greatest safety.

It is possible to lead a segment by focusing on attributes such as cost, value, reliability, safety, performance, user experience, convenience, green/sustainability, transparency, values, and dozens if not thousands of others, like HIPAA compliance, LEED certification, gluten-free, fair trade, UL-listed. The good news is that most companies can stake out a leadership position in *something*, often, the only constraint is imagination.

Intelligent products or services connecting to the cloud is an approach that is applicable in just about any industry. Plummeting costs of digital technologies increasingly enable innovative capabilities. Jet engines with oil pressure, temperature, and vibration sensors connect to back-end services for monitoring and optimizing engine performance and uptime. Packages, instead of being tracked, will report their own position, temperature and shocks in real time. Disposable greeting cards, which can now record and playback sound, will play video and connect to remote well-wishers.

CT (computed tomography) scanners, or someday, nanobots floating in your blood, will report anomalies to an intelligent cloud such as an IBM Watson system for diagnosis, to help your doctor treat disease. Wireless pacemakers are already reporting patient status, potentially alerting a caregiver in the middle of the night that an emergency is unfolding.[2] Sharks are being tagged so as to alert swimmers via Twitter that they are shorebound.[3]

Much more than a mere change in nomenclature, there are several interlocking components of a solution leadership strategy: product, service, connection, platform, ecosystem, and social presence. Each of these breaks down further: a "product" or "service" may include packaging, design, place/distribution, pricing/promotion, ego gratification benefits, convenience benefits, and even offer value through the "potential product" that it might become in the future. Ideally, these components help engender network effects, and beyond mere commodity products, become part of a total customer experience that is not just an economically rational decision, but creates emotional bonds. Emerging solution leadership strategies leverage the comfort and familiarity customers have with digital technologies and in being digitally connected.

There are a number of variations on this core theme. One, for many products, is that the product is a set of functions that may be encapsulated as a physical product or virtual one. The Kindle is a device that can be held in your hand, but it is also an application that runs on Android, iPhones, laptops, and iPads. Eventually, it may run on billboards, televisions, and connected digital contact lenses. The service can come before the product, as with Amazon.com's book distribution preceding the Kindle, or vice versa, as when the iPod was launched two years before the iTunes store.

And, besides individual solutions, companies can compete on a family or portfolio of solutions. Then, breadth, interoperability, accessibility, elegance, simplicity, or integration can be a basis for leadership. Products from companies such as Apple, Google, and Microsoft are a clear digital example, with calendar entries, music libraries, or photos available across the solutions. But so are Nike+ athletic solutions or Amazon Kindle and Netflix apps or emerging families of home appliances and devices or medical equipment.

Everything from sneakers to sports cars is becoming digital and connected to the cloud. In Nike's case, pressure sensors in the Nike Hyperdunk+ athletic shoe were linked to cloud services ranging from activity tracking to digital coaching services.

In Tesla's case, the product exploited a technology—lithium-ion batteries—to dramatically rethink a trunkful of product parameters: performance, acceleration, fuel economy, and environmental considerations. Other elements of the total product experience, sometimes also referred to as the "whole" product, were aligned with this, such as style, ego, and exclusivity. Others, surprisingly, also might be, such as cost and convenience.

But behind much of this is software. If all it took to design an electric car was plugging a motor into some batteries, someone could have done it long ago. However, as Tesla puts it: "One of the greatest benefits of starting a revolutionary car company in the heart of Silicon Valley is the direct access to the best and the brightest software engineers in the industry."[4] First of all, on-board software runs on multiple processors for everything from simple tasks, such as monitoring and displaying tire pressure, to more complicated tasks requiring sophisticated algorithms. This includes controlling the temperature of the batteries by heating or cooling them, disconnecting them in the event of a car accident, optimally charging them based on charging preferences for that specific location, and continuously "topping off" the charge when the batteries remain plugged in.

Also, advanced algorithms are at the heart of a Tesla's unmatched 0–60 acceleration on the one hand, and environmental friendliness on the other. The "Power Electronics Module" controls torque, based on whether the driver is accelerating or braking, whether the battery charge is full or low, and the temperature of the motor.

So far, those are all elements of a digitalized and informationalized product. What makes it a connected solution? For one thing, these systems are tied in to remote diagnostics. Tesla engineers and mechanics can access car data, determine the problem, and provide a fix. Better yet, the owner can be predictively alerted to imminent problems. And even better, data gathered from all the Teslas on the road are used to improve the software specifically and the product generally. Software changes can be quickly developed and applied over the Internet and your home Wi-Fi network. Tesla says that changes that might take a traditional manufacturer months to implement can be applied by the Tesla team in hours. These changes include new functionality, such as collision detection, extended battery life, routing to the nearest charging station, and even driverless car functionality.

The essence of competition has shifted from product leadership to solution leadership. Multiple interrelated transitions define this profound transformation.

From Products and Services to Solutions

The first step in the journey to solution leadership is to evolve a simple, standalone product (or service) into a smart, digital product or digitally enabled service connected to a cloud-based back-end. Sometimes the product itself is smart, sometimes it's just a window to a smart cloud-enabled service.

Smart products don't *necessarily* need to connect to the cloud. The Haiku ceiling fan from Big Ass Fans comes with "SenseME" technology. Sensors determine whether you are in the room, saving energy if you aren't there. It adjusts fan speed based on temperature and humidity, and adapts to the homeowner's preferred room conditions.

However, there are many advantages to being connected, including visibility into product usage for predictive maintenance purposes or future solution upgrades or streamlining; remote control of the product, as with Wi-Fi door locks; tuning or comparison of products such as individual wind turbines in a wind farm or users such as competitive runners; and the ability to leverage massive cloud-based databases and their updates.

For example, the MyFitnessPal app helps dieters measure caloric intake, by leveraging a database of 3 million foods; Google Street View has tens of millions of images, and it and automobile navigation systems exploit massive databases of roads, street addresses, and places of business.

Navigation services built on top of the road database are a great illustration of the value of connectivity. When navigation systems ran off of in-vehicle DVDs, they could do a decent job of plotting a route. However, if they are cloud-connected, they can immediately route around congestion due to an accident that just happened. Data can flow the other way, as well. For example, car velocities can be uploaded to the cloud. If one car slows down, it could be that the driver wants to check for a flat. If hundreds do, it's a sign of an accident or other issue to be fed into the routing subsystem. And such connections can enable new pricing models, such as insurance premiums based on real-time driving habits, or new services, such as Waze. Waze tracks driver's routes and times to determine where there is congestion and then suggests alternate routes, as well as providing additional features such as where to find the least expensive gas.

Creating a connected product-service system can require attention to the capabilities and pricing of the connection. For example, Amazon introduced Whispernet, a free cellular connection, to enable ebook downloads at no cost to customers, rather than requiring customers to purchase, say, a hundred-dollar-per-month cellular plan for each Kindle, whether they downloaded any books or not.

Often, rather than a standalone product, there is a product family—such as Nike+ ecosystem elements including wearables and apps, or Netflix apps running on a variety of devices such as TVs, tablets, and smartphones—and the connection can enable synchronization among family members. A Netflix movie that is partially watched on a Smart TV can be continued without fast forwarding on a tablet; an e-book that is partially read on a Kindle device can be continued on a smartphone Kindle app.

Similarly, for business markets, John Deere has created a family of products that work together. Multiple combines and tractors interoperate intelligently with each other through a capability called Machine Sync. For example, equipment that is planting a field can ensure that 100% of the field is covered without any overlap, increasing efficiency. Or, combines, which are used to harvest wheat and other grains, can coordinate with grain carts, which transport the harvested grain off the field.

As industry leaders have shown, product design and customer experience are still primary concerns. The iPhone, the Nest thermostat, and the Tesla Model S roadster are not just smart, cloud-connected products, but aesthetically pleasing in every dimension and designed for simple, intuitive use.

From Generic and Expected to Augmented and Potential

The total product model we discussed in Chapter 8 teaches that there are four layers to a product: generic, expected, augmented, and potential. The generic product delivers the core function and benefit. For example, a drill makes holes, an aspirin relieves a headache, a thermostat keeps the temperature comfortable. The expected product comprises the features that are now standard in the market: drills are all reversible, aspirin all comes in tamperproof packaging, thermostats all have day-of-week settings. IT increasingly enables the expected product: say, through drill speed or thermostat temperature control, which represents a transition from electronic, mechanical, or electromechanical control systems.

But IT can have a still more powerful role. It can enable differentiation through intelligence in the augmented product, service, or solution, and can enable the flexibility and evolvability that enables its "potential" to manifest itself.

The Nest Learning Thermostat is a great example of differentiation—as both an augmented and potential product—through IT. Unlike typical (expected) thermostats, Nest is augmented through remote control. It also achieves its "potential" as it learns your preferences for heating and cooling, and accepts upgrades from the cloud that improve its performance.

Augmented products can embody a variety of IT-enabled features. Harvard Business School's Michael Porter and James Heppelmann, CEO of PTC, argue that smart connected products can conduct monitoring, enable control, including personalization, optimize, and become autonomous.[5] These low-level functions can enable higher-level functions and thus benefits. For example, monitoring can enable visibility into use, which can lead to product improvements. It can also enable predictive maintenance, and thus less downtime. All of these might be generally considered under the heading of intelligence, or as GE calls such smart devices, "brilliant machines." Digital technologies greatly increase the intelligence available before the digital era, such as irons with built-in electromechanical shut-off timers or mechanical centrifugal speed governors. Porter and Heppelmann restricted their analysis to products, but the physical instantiation of service solutions, such as in retail, healthcare, or food service, offers similar benefits.

When we consider the *potential* product as a component of a solution leadership discipline—where the product you are using is not the product you unwrapped—there are four major possibilities: extensibility, adaptability, modifiability, and upgradability.

Extensibility is enabled through connectivity and, often, platformization. App stores are a great example, where the product side of the solution can be extended, in this case by downloading new apps. Or consider Tesla adding new features such as collision detection and ultimately self-driving capabilities. But there is also the cloud side of the solution, where extensibility can be achieved without any client-side changes. Google, for example, keeps improving its search algorithm and extending the range of services available online: from search, to documents, to computing services. Or, both can happen. For example, the *New York Times* added online recipes to its formidable repository of information, *and* created a new tablet app to sort through them. Extensions can be solely created by the firm, or enabled through a partner ecosystem and APIs (application programming interfaces).

Adaptability and *flexibility* through machine learning and artificial intelligence can occur within the device, the cloud, or both. The Nest thermostat has capabilities that enable the device to learn more about your behavior and adjust accordingly. Google personalized and social search technologies use capabilities in the cloud to better understand the semantics and context of your searches based on previous behavior such as website visits: a search on "cloud" will return different results if you are a meteorologist than if you are a CIO (chief information officer). Advanced cognitive systems such as IBM's Chef Watson offer adaptability and flexibility by using extensive databases upon which it applies creativity to devise never-before-seen elements: unique recipes now, but unique patient treatments, theories of quantum physics, and previously undiscovered mathematical proofs tomorrow.

Modifiability is not new, but software offers the ultimate in plasticity. Hot rodders have been "modding" cars for years: painting flames on the body and adding headers to the exhaust system. Now, though, modding cars can mean tweaking the processors and software in the car to force a different carburetor mix of fuel and air for higher performance than the manufacturer originally could achieve. Lego Mindstorms EV3 is another example. It's a Lego robotics kit that works with a smartphone remote control app, a PC, and is able to download programming and instruction software to a PC. Microsoft Kinect is another example. It's a motion-sensing accessory that uses video, audio, and depth sensors and connects to an Xbox to serve as a game controller. However, various groups have been able to create entirely new applications by modifying the back-end software, for example, to teach skills to autistic children.

Upgradability is enabled through connectivity and the cloud. While extensibility is focused on adding new features, functions, or services, upgradability is oriented to fixing issues with or enhancing the performance of existing ones. One example is "service packs" or "patches," which are euphemisms for fixes for software bugs and vulnerabilities. But beyond righting wrongs, upgrades can also enhance existing capabilities. For example, the Nest Learning Thermostat 4.3 software update included enhanced algorithms that react more quickly to shifting patterns of heating and air conditioning use, leading to a 6 percent reduction in energy consumption.[6] Such algorithm improvements can be based on human invention or based on learning. Tesla cars can be tuned remotely; aircraft engines can be tuned based on studies performed through thousands of flights and millions of flight hours, as well. For example, data might show that aircraft engines are inefficient or more prone to failure when flying at a given altitude at a given speed and a given level of humidity.

From Transactions to Relationships

Consider what happens when a consumer products manufacturer sells a standalone product such as a vacuum cleaner or pair of sneakers through a retailer such as Wal-Mart. The product gets shipped on a pallet to a distribution center and ends up on store shelves in some far-flung region of the Earth. The retailer sells the product either to an anonymous consumer who pays cash, or to an identifiable—to the retailer—customer who has a loyalty card or uses some means of payment such as a credit card that can be used to identify the consumer going forward. Either way, unless the customer calls the manufacturer for customer service or support or fills out a warranty card, the manufacturer generally won't have any relationship with the customer. The manufacturer won't know which demographic loves its products, nor which hates them, and won't know whether to advertise in *Seventeen* or in *AARP* to grow its business. The revenue from the sale is one-time. And, since the manufacturer doesn't have a relationship with the end-customer, the retailer may well cut out the manufacturer or reduce shelf space in favor of a competitor or store brand. And, even if the retailer remains loyal, or at least fair, to the manufacturer, fickle consumers can make a product selection based on the latest in-store promotion or celebrity endorsement.

However, when the product is connected to back-end services, the service can become a source of relatively stable, recurring revenue instead of a momentary blip, or at least a means to maintain a relationship with the customer. From a revenue perspective, moving from products to solutions can have the beneficial result of transforming a transaction into a relationship, and therefore a one-time product sale (perhaps with ongoing maintenance or support contracts) into a recurring revenue stream, enhancing the predictability of cash flow, depending on the exact nature of the product and the contract.

Even if the service is free, because there is a relationship in place, information such as updates can flow from the provider to the consumer, and information such as usage can flow from the consumer back to the provider. Such information can be used to upsell and cross-sell, to get better results from targeted advertising, to connect the consumer to a community of other customers with shared goals such as to get in shape, and thus help the manufacturer bond with the customer. A relationship also facilitates the sale of additional premium services that provide more value, such as maintenance and support.

Customers can defect from one product vendor or service provider to another relatively easily, but less so from one solution provider to another. In the latter case, a customer might need to not just change out the endpoint product, but often the back-end services as well, any data collected by those services, and vendor-based as well as social network communities. These are difficult, if not insurmountable, switching costs.

There are opportunities to move beyond mere relationships into a high degree of intimacy, which we'll cover in Chapters 11 to 13, but for now the point is that a continuous *physical* connection to the customer's product or service delivery elements enables an ongoing *business* connection with the customer.

From Sales Results to Customer Outcomes

A solution is something that solves a problem. Solution leadership involves smart products or service delivery components connected to cloud services, but also, ideally, solves customer problems. A digital map is a product, a navigation service that takes the customer to her desired destination is a solution. A scale that displays weight is a product, a scale connected to activity tracking and trend analysis software that helps a customer achieve fitness and weight objectives is a solution. Products are pushed from inside the firm out to the customer; solutions begin with the customer and her needs and wants.

Solutions don't just address "rational" customer problems such as optimal routing to a destination, but potentially irrational needs as well: ego, status, instant gratification, fear of uncertainty, social connection, emotion, novelty, alignment with values. Needs like transparency and values can be incorporated into digital solutions. For example, automotive dashboards such as the Ford SmartGauge display and EcoGuide program help drivers achieve higher miles per gallon and thus align with values around sustainability; GPS tracking on snowplows can help city governments with transparency around snow removal services and thus voter approval, a type of customer satisfaction.

The mindset of a traditional product manufacturer is to push as much product as possible through distribution channels. The solution leadership mindset is to help customers to solve problems, help customers to exploit opportunities, and partner with customers to create win-wins that maximize successful outcomes, even if this means recommending a *competitor's* product or service. To accomplish this often requires a more intimate knowledge of customer requirements, a collaborative approach to helping the customer solve those problems or grasp those opportunities, and putting the customer first. These in turn often require an ongoing relationship.

Every company measures its sales results on a quarterly, monthly, or even more frequent basis. However, product-focused companies often stop there, or perhaps measure additional related metrics such as churn and profitability by segment. But companies embracing solution leadership don't stop with outbound metrics, they also focus on customer outcomes.

Perhaps this is nowhere more clear than in pharmaceuticals, where maximizing sales could result in overdoses, while maximizing outcomes results in the healthiest possible patients. In 2011, GlaxoSmithKline eliminated bonus pay for its sales professionals for meeting sales targets in parts of its business. According to Deirdre Connelly, president of North America Pharmaceuticals for GSK, they changed their compensation systems to begin to reward sales reps for "patient focus, understanding of their customer, problem solving, and level of scientific knowledge."[7] Another healthcare example is CVS Health, which stopped carrying tobacco products, thus eliminating $2 billion in annual sales of tobacco products, as well as sales of additional products a customer might pick up while at the store. However, such an assortment decision is more aligned with patient health outcomes.[8] Such a decision to carelessly throw away billions in sales has, well, led CVS Health's revenue to grow by about 10 percent or over $12 billion, and market cap to steadily increase over 50 percent in the year since, partly thanks to new partnerships with hospitals and other healthcare systems.[9]

Solution leadership can leverage analytics to adjust the marketing mix and fulfill needs, such as convenience, arising in different segments. For example, Tesco realized that they could offer smaller stores closer to customers offering a limited range of products—something like A&P deciding to open 7-Elevens. To provide such a solution required segmentation of customers based on demographics as well as on purchasing behavior.

Solutions can be co-created with customers, perhaps with the assistance of agile development, rapid prototyping or simulation, virtual experiments, 3D visualization, augmented reality, or 3D printing. This can enable upfront participation or at least feedback from customers early and often to help them be partners in the conception and evolution of the solution.

Such win-wins must begin with a focus on the customer's success: doing well (profitability) by doing good (helping customers). GE Aviation, as we will explore in Chapter 17, is not just trying to sell more jet engines. Sure, they'd like to sell as many as they possibly can, but they realize that the way to do this is to help their customers—airlines—achieve business outcomes, such as "time on wing," in other words, minimizing or eliminating unscheduled downtime to achieve maximum utilization of their aircraft, on-time arrivals, and lowest possible fuel consumption. This greatly expands the boundaries of relevant technologies and skill sets: GE needs not just metallurgists for better or cheaper alloys for jet engine turbine blades, but software engineers and data scientists to devise better algorithms for routing planes and predictive maintenance.

Being focused on outcomes makes a vendor not just another bidder to be awarded a contract if it provides the lowest bid, but a strategic, irreplaceable business partner that helps the customer meet its objectives and its downstream customers and end-users meet their objectives, thus enhancing customer satisfaction and creating a virtuous cycle.

The shift in focus from products to outcomes also necessitates different metrics. The basis of product competition is better products; the basis of outcome competition is better outcomes. Product competition requires more and better features and attributes or lower prices. But outcome competition requires better outcomes at competitive prices, which relates to what W. Chan Kim and Reneé Mauborgne call "value innovation." A customer value proposition is the net benefit that the customer will receive by using a product or service. According to Jerry Alderman, an entrepreneur and author, a "differential value proposition" is how much better that net benefit will be by using that product or service versus a competitors'.[10]

To understand the difference, consider two jet engines. If they have more or less the same performance but one costs $100,000 less, that represents a hundred-thousand-dollar differential that does generate customer value of a sort. But if the more expensive one results in $5 million less fuel consumption and unplanned downtime savings than the less expensive one, there is a much more significant differential in the value propositions between the two engines. This is not just an ROI (return on investment) or TCO (total cost of ownership) calculation, but a financial assessment of outcomes relative to the competition.

Of course, this approach is not limited to jet engines. A more expensive surgical procedure which has a higher likelihood of extending life or increasing quality of life creates a differential value proposition. A more expensive hybrid that offers much better fuel economy can offer a compelling differential value proposition.

In other words, a value proposition is "spend this, get that." A differential value proposition is when your "spend this, get that" is a much better deal than the competition's.

This should be more than a boldfaced claim. As authors D. Keith Pigues and Jerry Alderman say, the differential value proposition is "a measure of a company's competitive advantage in measurable financial terms."[11]

From Standard Products to Custom Solutions

Rather than just pushing a standard product through the usual distribution channels, digital solutions can creatively combine and customize preexisting components and capabilities.

The intelligence, adaptability, modifiability, upgradability, and extensibility addressed earlier offer a powerful means of customizing solutions. Nest thermostats and Big Ass Fans ceiling fans adapt to user preferences and behaviors. Many websites can be customized to user preferences. Broadcast radio and television meant one size fit all, whereas streamed, personalized channels on YouTube and iTunes Radio automatically adapt to your preferences and behaviors to offer a high degree of customization.

New production mechanisms, such as Nike Flyknit knitting machines and 3D carbon fiber printers mean that not only can the software components of the product-service system be customized, but so can the physical product itself. Of course, implementing such customization begins and ends with software: software for the customer to help visualize the final product in a 3D image as it is customized, software to price the total, software to place the order, software to ensure the materials are on hand, and software to drive the computer-controlled machines that produce the product.

Custom solutions are not limited to consumer goods and services. While all airlines or railway operators may have similar equipment, each will have a different mix of objectives around business outcomes such as cost, on-time performance, asset utilization, and operating expenses such as salaries and fuel.

While one might be trying to have the best on-time arrival rate, another might be trying to carve out a niche as the lowest cost provider. As a result, a business partner must be able to develop and customize unique solutions with customized outcomes tailored to each customer's needs based on continuous data acquisition and analysis.

From Products and Services to Experiences and Transformations

As discussed in the last chapter, Joe Pine and Jim Gilmore have proposed a hierarchy of value, with commodities and products at the bottom, services in the middle, and experiences and transformations on top. Digital solutions can help drive experiences and transformations.

In the Pine and Gilmore model, while an experience is one time and enjoyable, a transformation is the pinnacle: an experience, such as a college education, that lasts a lifetime. A good example of the difference between a product and a solution-based transformation is the difference between a video game and the Nike+ Kinect Training. Xbox's Kinect offers an enjoyable entertainment experience. With the Nike+ Training component, which offers coaching, long-term performance tracking, and support for competition, it helps to bring about a fitness transformation.

Often, the best kinds of offers are ones involving co-creation, where the customer is engaged in the construction of the product or the delivery of the service, or participates in the experience or transformation. Recording a song on a greeting card represents co-creation of a product; working with an architect or rating a restaurant co-creates a service; going on stage during a magic act co-creates an experience; doing exercises with a physical therapist co-creates a transformation.

There are numerous examples of physical, mental, emotional, health, and other personal transformations across that spectrum: calorie counting and weight-loss apps such as FitNow's Lose It! app; HAPIfork Bluetooth®-enabled smart forks which signal if you are eating too quickly and record data through a smartphone or tablet; Fitbit Wi-Fi activity, sleep quality, and wake-up alarm wristbands; Withings Smart Body Analyzers which connect over Wi-Fi and measure not just weight but body fat levels, heart rate, and air quality. At the business level, imagine a customer firm working with consultants to transform its strategy during a turnaround; or co-creating new software to optimize operations.

There are those that enable cognitive or emotional transformation: Massive Online Open Courses (MOOCs) and other online training, such as the Khan Academy, the University of Phoenix, Coursera, and Stanford

University classes available on YouTube; any of hundreds of thousands of puzzles and games including social games available in any of the app stores; or "Brainwaves—The Unexplainable Store®," which is an app for "spiritual, meditation, sleep, relaxation, positive life, and brain training." The sky's the limit on health solutions for prevention, detection, and treatment of various disorders: ingestible pills with micro-cameras, connected pacemakers, robotic and tele-surgery, and DNA sequencing on a USB stick or as a service, such as 23andMe offers. A 30-second phone call or free iPhone app could be all it takes to diagnose or monitor the progress of Parkinson's disease.[12,13]

From Standalone to Social

As today's standalone products and service delivery capabilities evolve to solutions, social elements are essential, whether through dedicated communities or through connections to existing social networks. Such connections are important to both customers and firms.

In terms of customer value, the social dimension plays to customers' innate needs for social relationships, community membership, novelty, curiosity, and intermittent rewards. Social and community elements existed, but were limited in the era of standalone products, when the community was detached from the product. You might own a Harley and also be a member of HOG, the Harley Owners Group, or a BMW and the BMW Car Club. Now, because the product ties over a network connection to cloud-based services, membership in a community can be a continuous, inseparable facet of the solution experience.

In terms of firm value, such connections strengthen customer engagement, in terms of both the time spent with the brand and the stickiness of the bond. Such engagement affects traditional financial metrics by increasing customer lifetime value and reducing churn and thus customer acquisition costs. The connections can lead to increased impressions through network effects and virality, especially when the solution requires social elements to achieve full value, such as group coupons, social games, or collaboration. Social games need not be restricted to the virtual world: Nike+ products enable friends and friendly competition in the real world, mediated by the virtual one.

Network effects benefit both customers and firms. Facebook and Instagram were initially popular due to innovative capabilities, but increasingly, they are popular because they are popular. It is simple for an individual to change to a different social network, but much harder to convince all of that individual's friends to move, as well as the friends of friends, and so on.

Once the networks are in place, virality can occur, as when a tweet is retweeted and then re-retweeted and so forth in a chain reaction. Thus can an insight, witty observation, news item, or brand or product recommendation from a single person reach millions of followers or friends: Ellen DeGeneres' 2014 Oscar selfie was retweeted over 3 million times, ultimately reaching perhaps millions more.[14]

From Product to Platform

A common way to enable standard products to become customizable solutions and to expand their market reach and enable ecosystems is to convert closed products into open, extensible platforms.

Platforms can enable ecosystems, but either can occur without the other. A platform can be used even within a closed community at a single firm to encourage reuse, reduce costs and development time, and enhance quality; an ecosystem can be constructed as a static entity without platforms and their innate extensibility.

A classic example of a platform is the Microsoft Windows operating system, but platforms don't need to be software: the Chrysler K-car was a platform underpinning the Chrysler Lebaron, Dodge Aries, and Plymouth Reliant. Intel processors are a platform for many computer vendors. The Internet is a platform as well. Google's YouTube.com is a platform for video upload, discovery, and streaming; Amazon's Kindle is a platform for authors to write and readers to discover, purchase, and read books; Apple's Xcode is a platform (an Integrated Development Environment) for software developers to design graphical user interfaces and write code for Apple products.

Platforms can be a double-edged sword. Competition in the digital space seems to constantly accelerate, and thus platforms are updated and extended on an accelerated basis as well. They can enable developers to rapidly build products, but too-frequent changes can also cause problems for those developers when working code "breaks," leading to the reassignment of creative lead developers from new features and services to maintenance tasks.[15]

Platform pricing is also a matter of interest to partners: the price to develop a solution on the platform, to make it ready for sale, and the proportion of revenue kept by the third party versus the platform/solution provider, whether through commissions on real goods, virtual goods, content or applications. Apple, for example, takes a 30 percent cut as well as a $99 listing fee for apps sold through its app store.

Conversely, according to one analysis, eBay takes roughly 10 percent of the revenues its sellers generate. One might think that most pure online services might be at about that level, but estimates of fees charged range from 1.9 percent for OpenTable to 70 percent for Shutterstock. As Bill Gurley, a venture capitalist with Benchmark and a member of the board of directors of numerous Silicon Valley firms observes, lower fees can lead to dramatic ecosystem growth and platform adoption. On the other hand, he argues, "The most dangerous strategy for any platform company is to price too high—to charge a greedy and overzealous rake that could serve to undermine the whole point of having a platform in the first place." In other words, it's better to have a portion of a lot than all of nothing.

He argues that high margins not only disincent partners but also offer competitors an opportunity to disrupt the industry and gain share. Gurley quotes Jeff Bezos, the CEO of Amazon, who has stated that "your margin is my opportunity." He provides examples of companies that became dominant by entering a market where 30 percent fees were standard and charging only 10 percent: Booking.com, which is now the number one online travel provider in Europe, having grown rapidly to displace Expedia and Travelocity, and oDesk, which became dominant in the "temp" software developer business.[16]

To incent partners to join your platform-based ecosystem, even a relatively attractive 10 percent fee can be trumped by "free." This is one reason that the Linux operating system has achieved meaningful share in a variety of segments, including 97% share in supercomputers. It's also one reason that Google's Android (based on Linux) achieved a vast majority of the share of global smartphones in 2014: roughly four-fifths of all shipments.[17,18]

Platforms and ecosystems enable emergence—that is, behaviors, components, and capabilities that were never originally envisioned. A good example is the World Wide Web. It is unlikely that Tim Berners-Lee, who invented the browser and the web, envisioned YouTube.com, Yo, Facebook, Twitter, or Etsy, anymore than Johannes Gutenberg, the inventor of movable type (often confused with the invention of the printing press) envisioned the narrative of this book.

But, this is what happens when you create a platform that can be extended, and engage a community or ecosystem that has its own motivations—financial or self-actualization—to build on the platform, say, editing a Wikipedia entry, or improve it, say, editing the MediaWiki software upon which Wikipedia runs. Sometimes, the boundary between the platform and its extensions blurs: the emergence of the hashtag on Twitter was originally a convention for marking a tweet, and then became part of the platform.

From Engineered to Ecosystem

There are two types of constellations of products and services: within a single company, and beyond it. One is best described as a product family or suite, the other an ecosystem. In some cases they may both be present: the Nike+ family at various times has included shoes, sensors, wearables, apps, and services that are part of an engineered family, but also an ecosystem stretching beyond Nike to companies such as Microsoft, Garmin, Withings, Twitter, and Facebook, and an integrating principle—a focus on fitness based on activity tracking via NikeFuel. Apple also has both: engineered products such as smartphones and tablets that are extensible via an ecosystem of apps.

A perennial dilemma in solution design can perhaps best be described as the trade-off between engineered families and ecosystems open to partners. For example, Apple engineered hardware (such as the iPhone, iPad, and Mac) to work together with an operating system (iOS and Mac OS, later OS X). On the other hand, Windows (and DOS before it) was intended to be cross-platform, running on PCs from IBM, HP, Compaq, and Dell, for example, and Android runs on phones from LG, Motorola, and Samsung, to name a few. The Apple hardware plus operating system software may be viewed as an engineered platform that enables an application ecosystem.

The benefit to an engineered solution is tight control over design, function, performance, user experience and revenues. The benefit to an ecosystem is the ability to gain market share by magnifying one's own efforts through partners and network effects. Apple and Google's results in smartphones illustrate the trade-offs. Apple maintains high profitability, whereas Android has the highest market share.

Research has shown that an engineered solution drives higher levels of satisfaction and loyalty. In a way, this is not surprising: there is no single brand to be loyal to in an ecosystem. Satisfaction may be due to greater simplicity in procurement, fewer interoperability problems, and greater vendor-customer intimacy through a broader set of touchpoints, but also due to inferences regarding greater value, which may be perceived, rather than actual.[19]

Ecosystems, though, can be difficult to avoid joining, and once joined, hard to leave, as Nintendo and Samsung show. Nintendo, after years of trying to keep its games on its own hardware, decided to begin offering games on mobile devices. Samsung, which had had a leadership position in smartphones, had to "indefinitely" postpone the release of a phone—the Samsung Z—which was a highly regarded *product*. The reason: the Z was Samsung's first attempt on a smartphone to replace Google's Android operating system with its own operating system—Tizen—although Tizen apparently works just fine. Samsung blamed "ecosystem" problems (i.e., presumably, difficulty in attracting app developers).[20] Samsung's challenges were not for lack of trying: Samsung hosted developer conferences and otherwise attempted to foster a community. The main challenge is network effects: developers flock to the platforms where they think they can make the most money.

The other issue with ecosystems is that they enhance partner success, and encourage virality and network effects, but leave money on the table. Some partners plan their exit around acquisition by the platform or ecosystem provider. On the other hand, other companies in the ecosystem can have the rug pulled out from under them due to a change of strategy or acquisition of a competitor by the platform provider. As Al Hilwa, an analyst with IDC put it, "It is typical for players in the new age tech economy to start with permissive and free access to gain share and users and then progressively curtail it to monetize the audience they have gained."[21]

LinkedIn, after fostering a fairly robust ecosystem, reversed course a bit, limiting use of the more advanced elements of its API to enrolled partner companies such as Samsung and Evernote. Twitter, after encouraging a robust ecosystem, acquired popular app Tweetdeck in 2011, making it more challenging for some participants in the ecosystem who were now simultaneously relying on and competing with Twitter.

Platforms and their enabled ecosystems enable third parties to innovate. Some will fail, but for the ones that don't, innovations can drive further innovations, which may be incorporated into the platform or become new platforms themselves, to the benefit of the platform provider and the next wave of ecosystem innovators.[22]

Ecosystems theoretically can be formed not just with friendly partners, but also competitors. In practice, however, that can be challenging to manage. Toys "R" Us formed a trailblazing partnership with Amazon.com in 2000 to market its toys on the retailing giant's online platform. This ended in an equally trailblazing lawsuit a few years later, dissolving the partnership.[23]

■ ■ ■

Solutions are the connected, cloud-enabled evolution of standalone products and services, but are much more than simply gluing on processing and networks. Instead, they can transform low-value anonymous transactions to strong relationships and drive additional value for firms and customers. Instead of merely measuring sales, solutions focus on differentially maximizing customer outcomes. They can be ever further strengthened when they become platforms and ecosystems and engender network effects, virality, and winner-take all dynamics.

Notes

1. Angus Kidman, "Domino's Planning GPS Tracking For Every Pizza," *Lifehacker .com*, February 11, 2015, www.lifehacker.com.au/2015/02/dominos-planning-gps-tracking-for-every-pizza/.
2. Reuters, "New York Woman Receives Wireless Pacemaker," *PCMag.com*, August 10, 2009, www.pcmag.com/article2/0,2817,2351371,00.asp.

3. "Sharks Tweet to Swimmers in Australia," *TechEye.net*, January 3, 2014, news
   .techeye.net/mobile/sharks-tweet-to-swimmers-in-australia.
4. "A Silicon Valley Approach to Vehicle Software," *TeslaMotors.com*, www.tesla
   motors.com/roadster/technology/firmware.
5. Michael Porter and James Heppelmann, "How Smart Connected Products Are
   Transforming Competition," *Harvard Business Review* (November 2014): 64–88.
6. Barclay Ballard, "Nest Thermostat Gets Software Update to Help Lower Energy
   Bills Even More," *ITProPortal.com*, April 11, 2014, www.itproportal.com/2014/11/
   04/nest-thermostat-gets-software-update-help-lower-energy-bills-even-more/.
7. Deirdre Connelly, "Bonuses Should Be Tied to Customer Value, Not Sales Targets," *Harvard Business Review* (April 16, 2014), https://hbr.org/2014/04/bonuses-
   should-be-tied-to-customer-value-not-sales-targets.
8. Jayne O'Donnell and Laura Ungar, "CVS Stops Selling Tobacco, Offers Quit-
   Smoking Programs," *USA Today*, September 3, 2014, www.usatoday.com/story/
   news/nation/2014/09/03/cvs-steps-selling-tobacco-changes-name/14967821/.
9. Bruce Japsen, "CVS Anti-Tobacco Stance Boosts Hospital, Health System Deals,"
   Forbes.com, February 13, 2015, www.forbes.com/sites/brucejapsen/2015/02/13/
   cvs-anti-tobacco-stance-boosts-hospital-health-system-deals/.
10. Jerry Alderman, "Overview: Winning with Customers: Do Your Customers
    Make More Money Doing Business with You?," *Valkre.com*, 2012, valkre.com/
    papers/Winning_with_Customers.pdf.
11. D. Keith Pigues and Jerry D. Alderman, *Winning with Customers: A Playbook for
    B2B* (Hoboken, NJ: John Wiley & Sons, 2010).
12. Parkinson's Voice Initiative, "Two New Studies in Which You Can Participate!"
    ParkinsonsVoice.org.
13. "Apple Introduces ResearchKit, Giving Medical Researchers the Tools to Rev-
    olutionize Medical Studies," *Apple.com*, https://www.apple.com/pr/library/2015/
    03/09Apple-Introduces-ResearchKit-Giving-Medical-Researchers-the-Tools-to-
    Revolutionize-Medical-Studies.html.
14. Shea Bennett, "Ellen, 1D and the President—The 3 Most Retweeted Tweets
    in History," *AdWeek SocialTimes*, www.adweek.com/socialtimes/most-retweets-
    twitter/612320.
15. Andrew Chen, "Why Developers Are Leaving the Facebook Platform,"
    AndrewChen.co, April 22, 2013, andrewchen.co/2013/04/22/why-developers-
    are-leaving-the-facebook-platform/.
16. Bill Gurley, "A Rake Too Far: Optimal Platform Pricing Strategy," *AboveTheCrowd
    .com*, April 18, 2013, abovethecrowd.com/2013/04/18/a-rake-too-far-optimal-
    platformpricing-strategy/.
17. Troy Wolverton, "Despite Apple Gains, Android Rules Smartphones," *The Mer-
    cury News siliconbeat*, January 29, 2015, www.siliconbeat.com/2015/01/29/despite-
    apple-gains-android-rules-smartphones/.

18. Some handset manufacturers may pay a small fee to Microsoft due to the resolution of an intellectual property dispute.

19. Jason Kuruzovich, Shu Han, Nevena T. Koukova and T. Ravichandran, "Testing the Steve Jobs Hypothesis in a B2B Context: Will a Portfolio of Hierarchically Related Technology Products Improve Customer Outcomes?," *Journal of Service Research* 16, no. 3 (2013): 372–385, www.researchgate.net/profile/Nevena_Koukova/publication/258158779_Testing_the_Steve_Jobs_Hypothesis_in_a_B2B_Context_Will_a_Portfolio_of_Hierarchically_Related_Technology_Products_Improve_Customer_Outcomes/links/0a85e53383bf120125000000.pdf.

20. Jonathan Cheng, "Samsung Postpones Launch of Tizen Smartphone in Russia," *Wall Street Journal*, July 28, 2014, online.wsj.com/articles/samsung-postpones-launch-of-tizen-smartphone-in-russia-1406531740.

21. Joab Jackson, "LinkedIn Restricts API Usage," *PCWorld.com*, February 12, 2015, www.pcworld.com/article/2883992/linkedin-restricts-api-usage.html.

22. Simon Wardley, "Lifecycle," *Bits or pieces?* blog, November 30, 2009. blog.gardeviance.org/2009/11/lifecycle.html.

23. Martin Wolk, "Toys 'R' Us Wins Suit against Amazon.com," *NBC News*, March 2, 2006, www.nbcnews.com/id/11641703/ns/business-us_business/t/toys-r-us-wins-suit-against-amazoncom/#.UvvIwWuYbb0.

CHAPTER 10

Nike—A Track Record of Success

Nike, named for the Greek goddess of victory, has consistently been the top-ranked global brand in apparel and sporting goods, and one of the top global brands, period.[1,2] Its more than 50,000 employees generate close to $30 billion in annual revenue. Its stock price has resembled its own iconic swoosh in terms of consistent, exponential growth, with its market capitalization increasing threefold to approximately $80 billion in the past decade.

Nike's growth is due in no small part to innovation. The textured rubber sole that now exists in one form or another on a variety of athletic shoes was originally prototyped in the early 1970s by Nike co-founder Bill Bowerman, by pouring rubber into a waffle iron.[3] Numerous product introductions and thousands of patents later, *Fast Company* named Nike *the* Most Innovative Company of 2013—ahead of Amazon, Google, and Apple—for its Flyknit athletic shoe and FuelBand wearable.[4]

The Flyknit radically reimagines shoe design and manufacturing, replacing labor-intensive cutting and stitching with computer-controlled knitting, thus dramatically reducing waste in the manufacturing process while enhancing product customizability. The Nike+ FuelBand was one of the first "wearable" wristband activity trackers. If that were all it was, we might consider the FuelBand to be an example of product leadership. But from the time of its launch, it was engineered to link to back-end services, and it and other members of the Nike+ family, such as the original Nike + iPod, the Nike+ Running App, and the 2012 Nike Hyperdunk+ basketball shoe, have represented a comprehensive, evolving ecosystem of wirelessly linked, cloud-connected, big-data-analyzed, socially connected Nike and partner products, services, and communities.

Over the past few years, the Nike+ solution has evolved from a product connected to back-end services, to a family of products connected in an integrated and interoperable approach, to a solution framework heavily focused on partners.

The Nike Hyperdunk+ was not just a basketball shoe, but a solution—a cloud-connected product-service system to help athletes achieve desired outcomes such as athletic skills development and improvement. Pressure sensors in the sole linked wirelessly through Bluetooth to activity tracking and performance-monitoring services—logging how active you were and how high you jumped—and from there to popular social networks, the Nike community, and coaching services. The activity and performance metrics were time-stamped, so they could be synchronized with and automatically superimposed on a smartphone video in what Nike called "Showcase Mode" and then uploaded to social networks. Typical engineered performance footwear is intended to help athletes perform at their best, under challenging conditions such as uneven surfaces, slippery conditions, and temperature extremes. But former products such as the Nike Hyperdunk+ shoe and current ones such as the Nike+ Training Club app enable athletes to not just perform at their *current* best, but to become even *better* through coaching and feedback.

Nike has strategies that address all the digital disciplines. It has invested in multiple labs, university partnerships, and a startup accelerator to speed innovation. The Flyknit illustrates information excellence since it uses new computer-controlled knitting machines to make Nike's manufacturing process simultaneously more precise, more efficient, and more flexible. NIKEiD enables a high degree of personalization and customer intimacy; it enables customers to design their own shoe for style and performance, order it, and share the design on social media. Products ranging from the Nike+ FuelBand to the Nike+ Running App, and related Nike+ offers illustrate solution leadership. Although various individual elements have been discontinued while new ones have been introduced by Nike or its partners, the Nike+ framework and ecosystem provide continuity to the overall solution. Taken together, Nike has significantly evolved from the waffle iron to big iron.

The man at center court in Nike's entry into the digital era is Stefan Olander, Nike's VP and General Manager of Nike+, as well as a published author. Olander, a Swede who relocated to Oregon, assembled a small team at Nike's headquarters to quietly develop these digital products, and then grew the Digital Sport business unit from an idea to a full-blown P&L center. As Olander says, the mission of Nike hasn't really changed; it's always been about inspiring athletes—whether celebrity or weekend—to get better, with its well-known message of "Just Do It." But, he says, customers don't just want inspiration, but also help, so "the role of the [Nike] brand changes from one of inspiration purely to inspiration and enablement."[5]

From Products to Solutions

Nike, Inc. is a leader in product design, engineering, and manufacturing, including style, aesthetics, performance, user experience, efficiency, and sustainability. Nike+, however, is not a single *product*, but a family of products from Nike and its partners woven into a cohesive *solution* ecosystem and unified customer value proposition centered on athletic performance and the quantifiable self: metrics and analysis of athletic activities and progress against goals. It all began in 2006 with the Nike + iPod, a sensor inserted into athletic shoes that communicated with an Apple iPod, and then from there sent data to a website—Nikeplus.com—via iTunes.

The Nike+ solution ecosystem has comprised a dynamically evolving set of Nike and partner devices, cloud services, and apps. The ecosystem has evolved as Nike has introduced leading-edge products, learned from market experience, developed partner relationships as core technologies have matured, and as partner and competitor product lines have evolved. The ecosystem has at various times included wearable devices such as the Nike+ FuelBand SE and Nike+ SportWatch GPS; connected footwear such as Nike+ Basketball, Nike+ Hyperdunk+, and Nike+ Training shoes; apps that can turn devices such as iPhones and Nanos into Nike+ trackers; and console "games" and web apps that complement these sensors and wearables but provide athletic training and personal coaching, such as Nike+ Training Club, Nike+ Running App, Nike+ Running Coach, and Nike+ Kinect Training. For the Microsoft Xbox, the Kinect video capture capability tracks movements, making it a virtual wearable. And, those devices that link to mobile devices or iPods generally offer some sort of integration with music and social networks, providing an additional energy boost.

Real and virtual Nike+ products and services have different capabilities and purposes, but all have mechanisms oriented to tracking activities and results in some fashion: for example, global positioning system (GPS) for location and route; accelerometers for vertical jumps and lateral acceleration. Nike computer models help determine whether the athlete is running, doing jumping jacks, knee raises, or what have you.

The unifying principle that spans the ecosystem is a common activity metric called "NikeFuel," which is intended to normalize activity levels across Nike+ products and across athletes and sports with different characteristics. This enables a football player, for example, to compare himself to a marathoner in terms of workout intensity and energy expenditure. It also lets an athlete make comparisons, say, between the energy spent in yesterday's run relative to today's run or tennis match.

It took Nike two years to develop NikeFuel, which is based on "oxygen kinetics," a means of measuring aerobic activity. The basic idea is that the greater the level of activity, the harder you breathe, and the more you weigh, the greater the energy used, but it took detailed studies at an Arizona State University exercise physiology lab to develop algorithms that converted various sensor readings into an activity, and the intensity of that activity into NikeFuel.

Simplistically viewed, NikeFuel is a rough proxy for exercise duration and intensity, but strategically, it offers an advantage in thought leadership and as a *de facto* industry standard. Practically, it converts what would otherwise be disjoint products measuring random activities such as hand-motions per minute into a uniform, meaningful metric aligned with personal goals. Fundamentally, it is the overarching principle that unifies the Nike+ ecosystem solution. Lastly, it ties into deep psychological needs and cognitive biases in the areas of status, recognition, competition, social relationships, and self-actualization, which will be addressed further in Chapter 18.

Ultimately, cloud services provide all of the rich functionality that enlivens the individual products and mobile apps, acquiring data from one or more of an athlete's Nike+ devices, and slicing and dicing it, showing timelines, routes, activity levels, trends, progress toward goals and offering the means to share that data through social networks. Much of the social network integration happens in real-time, so friends—and celebrities—can virtually cheer you on while you are exercising.

From Generic and Expected to Augmented and Potential

The total product concept described in Chapter 8 delineates the generic, expected, augmented, and potential product. Nike+ solution components such as footwear certainly incorporate the generic product and its core benefit of protecting the foot, as well as expected product features such as traction on wet surfaces and fashion elements. They are also augmented, through digital functionality such as activity and route tracking.

Most importantly, as a solution incorporating both smart, digital products and cloud services, the potential product is infinitely extensible. The product side can incorporate upgrades, such as better Nano software or new Nike+ Training Club modules, and the cloud side can be enhanced with further capabilities and gateways to other services.

Moreover, if we think of the entire ecosystem as the solution, the family of physical and virtual products has the potential to expand to an unlimited number of activity tracking sources in the future; not just wearables, but, say, home video streaming cameras, acting like Kinect, or a connected carpet that measures footfalls. Similarly, the cloud services have unlimited potential for new tracking or coaching software, as well as helping connect to Nike and partner innovations.

From Transactions to Relationships

The shift from selling products to delivering solutions also drives a shift from an anonymous sales transaction to a long-term customer relationship. As Olander says, "It used to be that when you bought a product, that was the end of the relationship … and I [as a marketer am] going to say 'great, you bought the product; see you in a year, when our next campaign comes along.'"

Now, however, due to the evolution of standalone products into a product and service solution, a single transaction can become a long-term relationship. Olander observes that "the purchase of any Nike product needs to be the beginning of the relationship we have with the consumer." In Nike's case, this relationship is a particularly strong one, because the Nike+ ecosystem, Olander says, is the means to create an emotional connection to one's self, one's achievements, and one's friends.

An athlete buying running shoes or a sweatshirt at a multibrand retailer might switch to a competitor at the next purchase. But one who has spent years getting data into Nikeplus.com will not be so hasty. The basis of competition shifts then, away from pricing and features, to the management of relationships and the creation of both immediate and long-term value.

Besides the stickiness of historical data and familiarity with interfaces and functions, the community aspect of Nike+, both in terms of the Nike community and integration with social networks, also increases mental and emotional switching costs.

From Sales Results to Customer Outcomes

The evolution from product to solution has an additional dimension. Nike, like any other firm, can measure success traditionally, in terms of revenues and profitability, perhaps broken down by region, channel, and product line. To understand customer needs, Nike could always conduct focus groups and surveys, and attempt to analyze data self-reported by customers, which is notoriously inaccurate.

But now, Nike is intimately involved, in real time, in helping its customers achieve their exercise and activity goals, their personal well-being, and their identity as a member of a global community. By playing a more central role in helping customers achieve their desired outcomes, Nike becomes a more central part of its customers' lives. As long as Nike maintains an ecosystem and a full set of capabilities around monitoring and coaching, it can maintain a preferred position with the customer.

Pitting one athletic shoe against the other is based on features and attributes such as style, price, fit, performance, and celebrity endorsements. But the shifts from product to solution, sales results to customer outcomes, and differentiated features to differential value proposition mean that the basis of competition encompasses not just better individual footwear or wearables, but a better ecosystem and the delivery of better outcomes, such as through personal coaching services.

From Standard Products to Custom Solutions

An important part of the complete Nike offer is the ability to customize products, experiences, and transformations. For example, NIKEiD enables customers to design their own footwear, selecting colors for the upper or swoosh, placing logos or text on the shoe itself or even its laces, and so on.

In addition to aesthetics, customers can alter performance attributes as well. Someone that exercises outdoors, for example, might select an outsole that performs better on wet surfaces; other requirements such as lateral acceleration might drive different selections of, say, firmness.

This customization is all driven by a unified experience tailored to fit retail store digital signage, the web, and mobile devices. This experience ties to social networks, and can be embedded in other sites. Customers can tap to select options, share their designs, search for designs, or scroll through others' designs. And, these designs can be seen not just from one viewpoint, but in high resolution from any angle; a digital selling capability that required the development of innovative graphics technologies in conjunction with Adobe.

But customization doesn't end with the physical product. Various Nike+ training programs can also be customized in different ways: changing the intensity of the workout, focusing on toning versus flexibility, lower body versus upper body, and so forth.

From Products to Experiences and Transformations

Recall that in Joe Pine & Jim Gilmore's *Experience Economy* framework there is a five-level hierarchy of offers—starting with commodities, continuing through products and services, and culminating in experiences and transformations—with increasing customer value and profit potential and increasing customer engagement and impact. Nike has climbed this hierarchy very effectively, beginning with athletic shoes, which are products, and activity tracking, which is a service. Some might argue that athletic activity is an experience at its core, and Nike has always been part of that. However, there are even more engaging ways to tap into human values and desires, such as the need for novelty, relatedness and community.

As *experiences* go, there aren't many that can rival the 2008 Nike+ Human Race, in which nearly 780,000 runners from all over the world participated in a simultaneous virtual and physical experience. Runners ran routes in person in various cities, and also participated virtually through Nike+. To further enhance the impact, race-goers all wore the same red T-shirt, enhancing the sense of community. The campaign incorporated channels such as Facebook and Twitter, and video captured on mobile cameras during the race was uploaded, edited, and played back on large digital screens, leading to a rich, memorable, participatory and thus co-created global experience.

Another important dimension of a compelling experience is novelty. With Nike+, an athlete can pick a workout intensity level, and the app will generate a plan for each day of the week. Each day's workout might consist of two to four 15-minute activities, with leading athletes taking the user through each 15-minute long session.

In addition to visual feedback, some Nike+ products provide audio feedback for specific achievements, including congratulatory messages from personalities such as LeBron James and Serena Williams. Achievements can also be shared on social networks, which, in turn, can generate additional feedback, enhancing the overall experience.

In the Pine & Gilmore framework, experiences are unique and memorable, but ephemeral; the highest value comes from *transformations*, which are personal and permanent. One could argue that Nike has always played a role in physical and emotional transformations: helping customers to be active, lose weight, get in shape, see beautiful views of mountains and coastlines up close, and achieve inner peace. However, Nike's role in this transformation has ramped up.

The coaching services within Nike+ can have advantages over human coaches or personal trainers. Nike has exact data to provide clear feedback in real time and long-term trend analysis. The incorporation of video or motion capture through capabilities such as offered by Nike+ Kinect, augmented by exact metrics, pressure sensor data to improve biomechanics, and the ability to examine trends all provide substantial valuable feedback. Biohacking by linking to calorie counting software and weight and body composition devices provides further advantages.

Nike+ software first offers an assessment of your current capabilities, such as range of motion. Then it lets you set constraints, such as a trainer, a goal, and specific days to work out. During workouts, the software corrects your form, just like a real trainer would: slow down, hold it, don't sway, and so on. As the weeks pass and your body gets fitter, Nike+ keeps pushing you. As Olander says, you now have a personal trainer in your pocket.[6]

From Standalone to Social

A person who happened to have Nike running shoes could always go running with other people that also owned them, but the Nike+ solution ecosystem digitally mediates social engagement in entirely new ways, not just during special events such as the Nike+ Human Race. It offers the ability to connect with others as friends or competitively.

Nike+ supports challenges against other people anywhere in the world. One might be a sprint that covers a particular distance. Another might be high knee stepping. The point is that beyond doing exercise yourself; beyond even comparing the "you" of today with the "you" of last week, extra motivation and entertainment can be gained through a competition.

Nike+ also supports the need for maintaining social connections, and not just by "uploading" your status. You can have a workout with a friend anywhere in the world, and even if they aren't exercising, Nike+ enables friends to cheer you on remotely as you are doing your workout, with simulated cheers being heard through your device's headphones.

Athletes are not just customers, nor just limited to their existing connections, but can also become part of the Nike+ community of other exercise enthusiasts. As I write these words, the community has reportedly[7] run a total of over a billion miles.

In addition to the online community, numerous real-world activities complement all of the above, ranging from store merchandising to launch events. In addition to the Nike+ Human Race 2008, Nike has held a series of events called "We Run" in multiple cities.

Finally, Nike+ has enabled integration with third-party social networks such as Twitter, Facebook and YouTube.

From Engineered to Ecosystem

If corporate capabilities are insufficient to deliver desired customer outcomes, either internal skills need to be enhanced or partners and ecosystems need to be activated. For example, both weekend and professional athletes desire optimal weight and muscle/fat composition, but athletic activity alone, while Nike's central competency, needs to be complemented by diet and results monitoring.

NikeFuel is the unifying high-level principle in the Nike+ ecosystem. But at the level of actual product design and engineering, Nike has created a site—developer.nike.com—to enable partners to build products that can access Nike customer data through a predefined application programming interface (API), using tools contained in a software development kit (SDK).

APIs are how programmers build on other programmers' work in a standardized way, similar to how a general contractor might rely on a plumber when building a house. Nike offers third-party developers access to data such as whether the user is currently running, walking, or cycling, the Nike+ product in use, NikeFuel earned, the distance traveled, and so forth. Users then opt in to allow secure access to the data. Nike could have hidden this data, but by loosening its grip on NikeFuel and device data, Nike has made the solution much more powerful.

The API and SDK are then used by partners such as Withings, which makes both the Smart Body Analyzer scale—which can measure weight and fat—and Health Mate—the app to track that data. This made Withings a natural fit for a relationship with Nike: Withings measures outcomes, Nike measures activities. NikeFuel points earned the day before show up on the bathroom scale's display and in the Health Mate app.

On March 6, 2015, Nike announced additional partners and interoperable components to further expand the Nike+ ecosystem.[8] Garmin and TomTom offer GPS sportwatches, which can be used as a source of activity via both accelerometers and GPS tracking of routes and distances, as with existing choices such as Apple, Google, and Samsung. Netpulse enables better linkages to health-club equipment. Another announced partner is Wahoo Fitness, which offers heartrate monitors, indoor cycling trainers, and the ability to evaluate not just running pace but *motion analytics*—that is, running form.[9]

The API and SDK are the enablers, and a business development organization can help structure deals such as the ones with Withings and Wahoo. In addition, Nike called on Silicon Valley legend TechStars to create the Nike+ Accelerator to nurture, fund, and mentor startups.[10]

From thousands of entrants, the inaugural Nike+ accelerator selected 10 startups, with business ideas such as tying virtual reality games to real-world physical activity, focusing on physical activity for families and kids, and using a playing card metaphor to mix up workout routines by dealing out ever-changing digital fitness "hands."

Nike and the Other Digital Disciplines

The Nike+ ecosystem is so intriguing that it's been highlighted in this chapter as a sterling example of solution leadership. However, it would be an unforced error to assume that Nike isn't an all-around athlete; it also excels in information excellence, collective intimacy, and accelerated innovation.

Information Excellence. Nike uses information technology creatively. For example, it was awarded a patent in 2015 for an invention that uses augmented reality to design footwear, and used 3D printing technology to rapidly prototype and manufacture the carbon-fiber-soled Nike Laser Vapor Talon.[11] But one of the most interesting examples of information excellence at Nike is the Flyknit shoe, made possible only because of a radical new computer-controlled manufacturing process.[12]

Producing footwear has traditionally been labor-intensive, involving cutting, molding, stitching, and gluing dozens of pieces of cotton, leather, rubber, and plastic. Because of this high labor content, footwear production is generally offshored to exploit labor-cost advantages, with a predictable lengthening of supply chain intervals, in turn potentially leading to either stockouts and lost revenue or excess inventory and write-downs.

Nike reverse-engineered knitting machines that make socks and sweaters, and built one that could make the Flyknit, which replaces dozens of pieces with a woven upper attached to a sole. This has multiple implications. A labor-intensive process becomes a computer-controlled one, potentially increasing flexibility in locating production.

The new computer-controlled process is also more flexible. Each shoe can be not just aesthetically customized but also "micro-level precision-engineered," as Nike calls it. As the shoe is being constructed, varying quantities of threads with different thickness or stretchiness can be used, leading to extremely fine differences in performance, transforming a mass-produced make-to-stock product to a customized make-to-order one.

As if all that weren't enough, the new process also reduces waste dramatically, because only a bit of thread is lost in the production of each upper. This is a good example of information excellence, because ultimately all of the customer experience, sustainability, time, cost, and flexibility improvements in the softwear rely on the software.

Collective Intimacy. NIKEiD is a personalization service than enables customers to design their own footwear via a web interface. For example, for the Jordan Flight 45 High iD basketball shoe, virtually every element of the shoe can be customized: upper, accents, underlay, strap, tongue top logo, lining, lace, midsole, midsole topline, outsole, heel logo, personal ID, and size.[13] This plays to a customer's innate need for control, and is also, well, just plain fun. The web interface interactively updates 3D visuals of the shoe as the elements are changed. Moreover, *even without making a purchase,* prospects can post their designs to social networks.

These capabilities increase the intimacy of the relationship between Nike and the customer. Nike can learn each customer's preferences, and the customer can engage more deeply with the company. It fosters social selling, as customers brag about their designs and orders. Nike can use data on preferences to make product design and market segmentation decisions, as well as optimize marketing, in a way dramatically different from when an anonymous customer buys a pre-manufactured shoe off a retailer's shelf.

Olander says that customers are brutally honest and clear about their needs. He says that Nike has always been obsessed with helping people to achieve their goals, and has always had intimate knowledge of athletes, dating back to when the founders were selling running shoes from the back of a van at track meets.[14] Moreover, Olander claims that the data Nike collects have a different purpose than typical analytics, helping Nike serve consumers better rather than trying to upsell them.[15]

In most other companies' approaches to collective intimacy, *all* customers' preferences become the fodder to determine *each* customer's preference. In the Nike model, working intimately with top athletes in each sport can also be the basis for defining solutions. These solutions then have a core based on best practices, with additional customization opportunities based on customer preferences (e.g., Flyknit performance tuning).

Accelerated Innovation. Olander says that usually, in a company of Nike's scale and mass-market orientation, production is driven by best-selling items and satisfying the needs of the retail channel. But, as an innovation company, he argues that it's important to organize to incubate new product ideas. A key part of innovation is having the right individuals with the right motivation collaborating within the context of the right culture.[16]

In 2014, Nike was awarded 546 US patents, Adidas 36, and Under Armour 19. Such a continued investment in innovation has led Nike to amass the largest patent portfolio in the shoe and apparel industry. Such innovation begins at the top. Nike co-founder Phil Knight reportedly has observed that "it's really risky not to take risk,"[17] and current CEO Mark Parker says Nike is "an innovation company ... innovation and design [are] at the epicenter of all we do."[18]

Parker is no stranger to innovation. He is a co-inventor of US Patent #4,439,936, "Shock Attenuating Outer Sole," and US Patent #4,817,304, "Footwear with Adjustable Viscoelastic Unit," better known as the Nike Air. Perhaps as a result, while most CEOs might focus on the minutiae of the business case when being presented with a new idea, Olander said that Parker's first question upon seeing the FuelBand prototype was, "How fast can you build that?" (i.e., bring it to market).[19]

Nike has numerous teams focused on innovation, such as the Nike Explore Team, Materials Science Innovation, and Sustainable Business & Innovation. Nike often co-creates products by working with top athletes at the Nike Sport Research Lab, a multidisciplinary laboratory where "the focus is on biomechanics, physiology, perception and athletic performance."[20] While athletes exercise in special temperature and humidity controlled chambers, a massive amount of data is collected and analyzed, using techniques such as pressure sensors, oxygen uptake tracking, and 3D motion capture technology using video cameras that operate at up to

30,000 frames per second, as compared to a normal video capture rate of 30 frames per second.

Internal efforts in these labs often go to market. The Flyknit began that way, and the sensors inside the Nike+ Basketball athletic shoe began as internal lab equipment used for measuring top athletes.

But increasingly, as "apparel" becomes more multidisciplinary, Nike is complementing its internal innovation with external and sometimes open innovation, which will be discussed further in Chapter 15. It launched the Nike+ Fuel Lab and the Nike Accelerator. It also contracts with companies such as Astro Studios, which "creates...brand experiences that...incite lust....," Synapse Product Development, to support design engineering activities for firmware, embedded systems, wireless communications, and more, and Whipsaw Product Design, for industrial design and engineering including concept development.

R/GA, a "digital advertising agency" that does much more than advertising, is one of Nike's important partners.[21] It ensures that users can intuitively and easily interact with the product or service, writes the copy, copywriting, and visual design, for products, websites, commerce, and apps, digital signage and interactive elements, and so forth. These are not as unrelated as they might seem, because the same emotional elements that make a product and supporting applications engaging to use need to be uniform across advertising, branding, and tutorials.

Some elements of Nike's digital game plan are likely to continue to be adapted over time as conditions change due to customers, competitors, and partners. For example, Apple and other companies have introduced smartwatches, which will limit the long-term potential for a special-purpose activity wristband. Under Armour bought MyFitnessKeeper for almost half a billion dollars. There are plenty of other fitness and health apps, and new ones launching every day.

However, smartwatch manufacturers and app developers are unlikely to enter the apparel and sporting goods industry. Nike's strategy builds on its strong position in that industry—including brand, customer relationships, and endorsements—and extends into adjacent digital market spaces through a strong solution ecosystem.

■　■　■

Nike's evolution offers real-world lessons in implementing a solution leadership strategy. It began with standalone products, then connected those products to back-end services, and evolved the end-to-end solution into an ecosystem with both its own and partner elements. Like a pick-up game of basketball, where individual players may enter or leave but the game continues, the individual endpoint "things" such as wearables and fitness equipment from Nike and its partners may come and go, as may back-end services, but the Nike+ solution ecosystem remains.

Nike is stretching beyond its core apparel business into the digital and virtual world. Nike offers pure apps, such as Nike Golf 360°, which tracks scores and skill progress, but the Nike+ ecosystem, which has included components such as the Nike+ FuelBand, Nike+ Running, and Nike+ Training Club, unified by NikeFuel and nikeplus.com, offers a winning example of solution leadership. In addition, Nike has exemplified information excellence, collective intimacy, and accelerated innovation in many areas of its operations, product line, customer interfaces, and internal and external research collaborations.

The lessons from Nike's approach are relevant to many firms: imagine the massive increase in customer value by going beyond selling athletic shoes to managing a customer's transformation to health and fitness. It is the difference between a product and a solution; between one-time anonymous sales intermediated by a retailer and an ongoing relationship; between a finite product and an infinitely extensible universe; between an easily interchangeable item and a sticky ecosystem; between anonymity and an engaged, disintermediated community.

Notes

1. "Rankings," Interbrand. bestglobalbrands.com/2014/ranking/.
2. "BRANDZ Top 100 Most Valuable Global Brands 2014," Millward Brown, www.millwardbrown.com/docs/default-source/global-brandz-downloads/global/2014_BrandZ_Top100_Chart.pdf.
3. John Kim, "Nike Showcases Bill Bowerman's Original Waffle Iron," *Sneaker News.com*, March 1, 2011, sneakernews.com/2011/03/01/nike-showcases-bill-bowermans-original-waffle-iron/.
4. Austin Carr, "Nike: The No. 1 Most Innovative Company of 2013," *FastCompany.com*, February 11, 2013, www.fastcompany.com/most-innovative-companies/2013/nike.
5. "Building a New Ecosystem … ," [video] Part 2, *RGA.com*, www.rga.com/nike-and-rga-building-a-new-ecosystem-for-consumer-experience/.
6. "Building a New Ecosystem … ," [video] Part 3, *RGA.com*, www.rga.com/nike-and-rga-building-a-new-ecosystem-for-consumer-experience/.
7. The data at nikeplus.com is animated, but does not appear to change over longer periods.
8. Nike, "Nike+ Running Expands Global Partnerships to Motivate More Runners Around the World," *Nike.com*, March 6, 2015, news.nike.com/news/nike-running-expands-global-partnerships-to-motivate-more-runners-around-the-world.
9. "Why Tickr?" Wahoo Fitness, www.wahoofitness.com/devices/hr.html.

10. Nike, "Nike+ Accelerator Companies Pitch Investors at San Francisco Demo Day," *Nike.com*, June 20, 2013, news.nike.com/news/nike-accelerator-companies-pitch-investors-and-leaders-at-nike-whq-demo-day.

11. Nike, "Nike Debuts First-Ever Football Cleat Built Using 3D Printing Technology," *Nike.com*, February 24, 2013, news.nike.com/news/nike-debuts-first-ever-football-cleat-built-using-3d-printing-technology.

12. Matt Townsend, "Is Nike's Flyknit the Swoosh of the Future?," *Bloomberg Business.com*, March 15, 2012, www.bloomberg.com/bw/articles/2012-03-15/is-nikes-flyknit-the-swoosh-of-the-future.

13. "Jordan Flight 45 High ID," *Nike.com*, store.nike.com/us/en_us/product/jordan-flight-45-high-id/?piid=39411&pbid=374405716#?pbid=374405716

14. "Building a New Ecosystem ... ," [video] Part 5, *RGA.com*, www.rga.com/nike-and-rga-building-a-new-ecosystem-for-consumer-experience/.

15. "Building a New Ecosystem ... ," [video] Part 4, *RGA.com*, www.rga.com/nike-and-rga-building-a-new-ecosystem-for-consumer-experience/.

16. "Building a New Ecosystem ... ," [video] Part 5.

17. Allan Brettman, "Nike Designer Describes Life Inside the Innovation Kitchen," *OregonLive.com*, May 11, 2011, blog.oregonlive.com/playbooksandprofits/2011/05/nike_designer_describes_life_i.html.

18. Stephanie Ruhle, "Nike's Just Getting Going: CEO Parker," *Bloomberg Business*, October 9, 2014, www.bloomberg.com/video/nike-s-just-getting-going-ceo-parker-OdYc8j3aRr2fiNMbiNvpfg.html.

19. "Building a New Ecosystem ... ," [video] Part 3.

20. Nike, "Nike Sport Research Lab Incubates Innovation," *Nike.com*, July 16, 2013, news.nike.com/news/nike-sport-research-lab-incubates-innovation.

21. "Building a New Ecosystem ... ," [video] Part 1, *RGA.com*, www.rga.com/nike-and-rga-building-a-new-ecosystem-for-consumer-experience/.

PART FOUR
Collective Intimacy

Accelerated Innovation

Information Excellence | Solution Leadership | **Collective Intimacy**

Digital Technologies

Cloud | Big Data | Social | Mobile | Things

Operational Excellence | Product Leadership | **Customer Intimacy**

Processes and Resources | Products and Services | Customer Relationships

CHAPTER 11

Customer Experience and Relationships

W e've discussed processes and resources, products, services, and solutions, but what about customers? Customers are obviously important to business success, but beyond the fact that they are the ultimate source of revenue, why do the customer experience and customer relationships matter?

It helps to understand what customer experience is. Forrester Research vice president and principal analyst Kerry Bodine and research director Harley Manning use a three-layer approach to what they call the *customer experience pyramid*.[1] For an excellent customer experience, they argue that a product or service must first meet needs—that is, deliver what we earlier called the core benefit. After all, tasty snacks and courteous flight attendants won't matter much if the airline flies you to the wrong destination.

In addition, though, they argue, it must be easy and convenient, and then, ideally, must be enjoyable. While there are other ways to evaluate customer experience, Forrester's customer experience index then averages the net difference between customers that report good experiences versus those that report bad experiences in each area. In a six-year period that included the recent recession, while the S&P returned 14.5 percent, customer experience leaders' stocks returned three times that—43.0 percent—whereas laggards' lost 33.8 percent.[2] Correlation doesn't imply causality, but there are numerous examples of companies that have radically improved in this arena and reaped financial rewards as a result, through higher revenues or lower customer service costs. Differences of such enormous magnitudes lead Forrester to argue that we are now in the *age of the customer*.

There are numerous concepts that relate to how customers interact with firms: customer intimacy, customer relationships, customer engagement, customer loyalty, customer satisfaction, customer acquisition and retention, customer advocacy, customer experience, and customer service, to name a few. These all fit together, sometimes in complex ways.

Customer relationships are often better than independent transactions for a number of reasons. First of all, repeat customers purchase more. They not only purchase more because they make repeat purchases, but because as customers stay with the firm their order size or, more generally, value to the firm tends to increase. This is true across multiple verticals: Zappos sells more shoes and accessories; retail-banking customers increase the size of their account balances. This happens as customers experience the firm's products and services and the value that they create first hand, and as customers are upsold and cross-sold.

Profitability is affected as well as revenue. Although it varies by industry, the cost to acquire a customer can be quite sizable; at an extreme limit, consider the cost to bid on a large government project such as Healthcare.gov or a new fighter jet. But even customers for more mundane products and services such as retail banking, groceries, apparel, and fast food are costly to acquire. There are television, radio, billboard, and magazine advertising campaigns, online marketing campaigns, guerilla marketing events, event sponsorships, discount coupons, sales inquiries, and so forth.

Customer acquisition is not only expensive, it's much more expensive than the cost to retain a customer—up to five times more expensive, according to one study.[3] Because of all of these factors, a small increase in customer retention has been typically found to correlate with outsized gains in profitability.[4] There are additional benefits in surprising areas. For example, the better the relationship, the less likely customers are to cause legal problems. Research has shown that one of the best ways for doctors to avoid malpractice claims involves nothing more than spending more time with their patients.[5]

Additionally, loyalty is associated with advocacy. Long-term customers act as brand ambassadors and referral marketers, telling their friends, family, social contacts, and strangers—through dinner chats, grocery-line conversations, online reviews and ratings—how great the firm is.

IBM suggests that there are three types of customers—antagonists, apathetics, and advocates—and suggests measuring advocacy using three main dimensions: willingness to recommend to a friend or family member; willingness to buy from the firm if it offered a product currently bought elsewhere; and willingness to stay with the firm if another company introduced a competitive offer.[6]

In a similar classification, consultancy Bain & Company focuses on a concept they call the *net promoter score*, which refers to advocates as "promoters." At the other extreme are "detractors," who wouldn't recommend the firm or its products, and may go out of their way to bad-mouth the firm and relate their horrible experience(s). In the middle are "passives," who don't have a strong opinion.[7,8] Unlike IBM's three dimensions, Bain relies on what it calls the Ultimate Question: "Would you recommend us to a friend?"[9]

Promoters can act something like what author Malcolm Gladwell calls *mavens*—information brokers that accelerate the spread of ideas, including sentiment toward specific brands.[10] In 2000, when Gladwell wrote *The Tipping Point*, a maven might have spread the word to dozens of people, or perhaps hundreds. Now, armed with YouTube.com, Facebook, Instagram, Snapchat, or Twitter, a maven can reach millions, so the importance of maximizing promoters and minimizing detractors is magnified.

For example, according to Dave Carroll, a musician, United Airlines broke his expensive guitar on a flight from Halifax to Omaha, and then apparently was unresponsive to his complaint. So he put a music video on YouTube with a song he wrote called "United Breaks Guitars." It has been viewed almost 15 million times.[11] Because detractors tend to share their views with more people than promoters, and also perhaps because people love a good story more than plaudits, detractors arguably have an outsize effect relative to promoters.

Advocacy by promoters can include not just posting a tweet or status update but also writing reviews, which are particularly important because they are often read when a prospect is considering a purchase. Advocates also populate wikis and upload how-to videos, reducing customer support costs.[12]

Clearly, it's better to have more promoters than detractors, and Bain research provides additional color as to why. Promoters have a higher retention rate than detractors, leading to higher profitability due to the economics of customer acquisition outlined earlier. Promoters are less price-sensitive, because they have internalized the underlying value of the relationship with the firm. Promoters spend more, because they buy more frequently, buy more expensive items, and are more likely to acquire new products. The relationship costs less to maintain, because they complain less and are less likely to cause credit/accounts receivable problems. Their advocacy makes them act as extensions to the marketing team, reducing the effective cost of customer acquisition. All of this is reversed for detractors. According to Bain, this means that firms with the highest net promoter score (i.e., normalized number of promoters vs. detractors) are likely to grow, profitably, much faster than their competition, although, as with everything else in business, nothing is guaranteed.

But all of this begs the question of what makes customers loyal to begin with. Perhaps more importantly, since a mere lack of competitive options may be misconstrued for loyalty, what makes them promoters rather than detractors? It basically is, as the song says, a matter of accentuating the positive and eliminating the negative. According to Rob Markey, global practice leader of the Customer Strategy and Marketing practice at Bain, it requires "fixing defects, the issues and problems that create dissatisfaction," and on the other hand, "creating differentiating 'Wows' that really impress your customers and earn their deep advocacy."[13] The first includes not only customer service, but also relates to product and service quality. Shoddy merchandise that falls apart out of the box is unlikely to drive satisfaction, much less promotion. The second clearly relates to the total customer experience. Often, the two go hand in hand: A deft recovery from a bad experience can actually lead to a more satisfied customer than a mere good experience can.

Markey further points out that merely having more promoters than detractors does not assure competitive success. The key is to translate those sentiments and attitudes into results, such as greater sales through greater purchase frequency and engagement and greater advocacy by promoters. Specific tactics to turn sentiments into outcomes include better target marketing to promoters, gaining deeper insights into customer needs, tailoring offers to meet those needs, understanding the dimensions of the total customer experience that were extraordinary, and offering platforms for them to share their "Wow" experiences such as user groups or social networks.[14]

As might be expected, there are both promoters and detractors of the Bain approach.[15] However, even if there is no perfect mathematical formula that correlates net promoter score and growth rate, this kind of thinking helps clarify how all the pieces of the customer puzzle fit together. Great customer service and customer experiences lead to loyalty and advocacy. Customer intimacy and engagement help resolve issues, develop better insights into customer needs, and create and replicate excellent experiences. When coupled with the economics of customer retention and acquisition, it means that satisfied, loyal customers who are willing to be advocates can translate into profitable growth for the firm. In today's world of instant everything, customer service and experience are even more directly revenue impacting: One ridesharing service allows customers to dispute fares based on the quality of service.[16]

Legendary retailer Zappos, since acquired by Amazon.com, provides some hard numbers around the value of loyal customers. According to founder and CEO Tony Hsieh, each day, three quarters of purchases are from returning customers. These customers expand their initial purchases, ordering more than two and a half times as much over the next year. And, just as many new customers come from word of mouth as from online advertising. To help instill such customer focus, Zappos has put together a *culture book*. Everyone goes through five weeks of training on culture, values, and customer service; and both hiring and employee performance reviews are weighted heavily toward culture and values.[17]

Moreover, Hsieh points out that building customer relationships is an investment, not an expense. This shift in outlook is critically important for customer-oriented companies. A company that is not customer-focused will want to minimize customer service costs by taking every possible step to avoid those annoying customers. It will make their contact information difficult, if not impossible, to find. Then, its customer support telephone lines will have the most convoluted menus possible, requiring NSA codebreakers to determine the sequence of entries leading out of the maze and to a human operator. Should an occasional lucky customer actually manage to connect with a human being, that customer service representative will be measured on how quickly he can get the irritant off the line. Asking for the same information over and over again, and an inability to communicate in the customer's language, can also help incent the customer to drop.

Conversely, according to Hsieh, at Zappos, there are no call hold time metrics on service reps. The 800 number is prominently displayed right next to the logo. This might not seem atypical, but Amazon.com, which now owns Zappos, has no such number displayed. I couldn't find it by navigating from the home page, so finally had to consult a search engine. This is not to say that one is necessarily better, just that the two brands embody different value disciplines. Zappos is focused on customer intimacy, so invests in it. Amazon.com is more focused on operational and information excellence, so customers benefit through lower prices, rather than strong interpersonal relationships.

Customer Intimacy

Today, when we think of leaders in computing we might think of companies such as Apple, Google, Amazon, or Microsoft. But in the 1970s, the undisputed market leader was IBM. Why was it so successful? Treacy and Wiersema say that it was not because IBM was the price leader nor the most innovative company in the space: Many innovations in computing came from competitors such as Burroughs and Univac or universities such as Dartmouth, MIT, and the University of Illinois, and were later adopted by IBM.

No, Treacy and Wiersema argue that IBM was dominant in that era due to its focus on *customer intimacy*: customer-focused account teams and sales and support professionals that could offer a broad range of services to help customers with challenging problems with newfangled, tricky technology to achieve meaningful business outcomes.

Treacy and Wiersema would argue that long-term relationships and customer intimacy should not necessarily be the objectives of every firm, but that if and when they are, there are certain clear principles to follow. Perhaps the most central is that in a relationship, not every transaction or touchpoint needs to be profitable. Firms don't have to charge for consulting or design services when they do consultative selling or work with customers to design complex solutions, say, nor have complicated policies for accepting returns, because they are focused on the overall, long-term relationship with each customer. It is for this reason that The Home Depot can consult for hours on a small hardware purchase, and that Nordstrom accepts returns even for used items, no questions asked.

A self-contained transactional approach can win the battle but lose the war. Wine retailing and social media icon Gary Vaynerchuk relates the situation of a store manager who wouldn't retroactively honor a recently issued dollar-off coupon for a bottle of previously purchased Chardonnay. The manager was legally and procedurally correct, the dollar was retained by the firm, the original transaction remained profitable, but that customer and what was left of his lifetime value was lost—forever.[18]

In customer-intimate relationships, since a company does not require that every transaction and touchpoint be profitable, it can invest in resources that support the relationship, such as onsite account teams embedded with the customer, executive briefings, custom prototypes, and collaborative dialogue and engineering sessions to understand each customer's objectives and create or co-create solutions. This leads to a virtuous cycle: Better understanding the customer's requirements enhances the personal and emotional bonds of the relationship, which leads to more trust and a more open kimono, which leads to further insight into requirements. It also leads to the opportunity to craft customized and personalized solutions, which inject greater value into the relationship. In truly customer-intimate relationships, the firm will refer the customer to another company, even a direct competitor, if that is in the customer's best interests.

Customization and personalization are necessary but not sufficient for intimacy. After all, junk email may be personalized to you, but that doesn't make it intimate. At a fast-food counter, saying "no onions, extra mayo" is custom, but it isn't intimate, either.

In customer-intimate relationships, the customer integrates the product or service into her own lifestyle or business processes. Today, that integration may be digital, as when an electronic retailer incorporates a link to the shipping firm's tracking capability in the order confirmation email. The integration may be physical as well, as when consumer packaged goods manufacturers are responsible for restocking inventory at retailer locations. With such close operational integration, the firm can even better understand the needs, long-term objectives, purchasing habits and usage patterns of the customer.

It's worth noting that both the firm and the customer invest in a long-term relationship. A firm invests in personnel, facilities, and attention to understanding customer wants and needs, long-term objectives, usage patterns, and issues, and delivering exceptional, tailored products, services, experiences, and issue resolution or service recovery. Various relationship touchpoints can be areas of firm investment: diagnosis, consulting, service quality management, on-site customer support, dedicated account teams, a special escalation hotline, or partner, community, and ecosystem development.

Customers make investments as well: time to evaluate and comprehend vendor offerings, detailed customer or partner training, traveling to executive briefings, dedicated market development or business development personnel, learning a new user interface, or paying above-market prices based on the overall benefits the relationship brings.

These investments, though, bring a payoff to both parties. Customers get solutions that better meet their needs over time and reduce their search and switching costs; firms reduce costs such as churn and customer acquisition, build long-term bonds, and can increase margins and share.

A Broad Spectrum of Relationships

While this all sounds good in principle, one challenge about customer relationships is that they are all different. Not only are customers and their needs and priorities different, but the relationships that they desire to have with different brands and at different times differ as well.

Two decades of research led Jill Avery, a senior lecturer at Harvard Business School, Susan Fournier, a professor at Boston University, and John Wittenbraker, a global director at GfK, to argue that many firms lack *relational intelligence*.[19] These firms don't realize that different customers want different relationships, and they don't know how to develop mutually beneficial ones.

While the nature of these differences might appear to be simply described on a one-dimensional scale from short-term, anonymous transaction to committed, intimate, long-term relationship, these researchers identified 29 different types of desired relationships, to which they assigned names such as "dealer-addict," "star-groupie," "annoying acquaintance," "old friends," and "marriage on the rocks," all with salient differences, with different willingness to pay a premium price, with different opportunities to evolve to deeper relationships, with different correlations to market share, and with different impacts and definitions of what relationship "success" means.

A "one-night stand" is not looking for a long-term relationship, but is willing to pay a high premium, not unlike a once-in-a-lifetime trip to Paris to celebrate an important birthday. On the other hand, "marriage partners" are looking out for each other's best interests, and behaving as a team for the long term. At the other extreme are "complete strangers," who are just looking to complete a basic transaction.

Some customers are looking for a "master-slave" relationship, where they are the master and the firm is the slave. For these customers, a critically important aspect of the relationship is the need to be listened to and treated with respect. Whether in a face-to-face interaction or an online one, they expect immediate acknowledgment and a complete response to issues raised. Avery, Fournier, and Wittenbraker describe the case of one such high-value, long-term customer, who instead of being treated with the dignity she felt she deserved as a loyal customer invested in the relationship and offering helpful suggestions, was read a standard script by a customer service representative, then offered a gift card for her troubles by a senior executive. Dismayed by their lack of responsiveness, she then canceled a $7,000 order.

Avery and her colleagues argue that companies need to be sensitive to the fact that customers can fall into any of these 29 categories, and treating them monolithically can lead to disaster. In normal relationship terms, a casual sidewalk passerby is unlikely to want to immediately depart for a four-week vacation in Europe, and conversely, a spouse is unlikely to be satisfied with just a short text message once a week.

Avery and her colleagues argue that companies need to recognize these different relationship styles and leverage customer understanding to move them along to deeper relationships. In the same way that a first date can turn into a lifelong marriage, smart companies can turn "fleeting acquaintances" into "teammates."

Dimensions of Interaction

The types of desired relationships reviewed in this chapter are one way to partition relationship styles, but four additional dimensions have become increasingly relevant:

Activities vs. outcomes. Real intimacy does not merely entail learning all about the customer, but a genuine dedication to customer outcomes, whether business or consumer. It is not about vacuuming as much personal data from a customer or prospect as possible and then monetizing it, but having the customer's best interests at heart. Systems to implement this can include everything from quantifying a differential value proposition—how much more the customer gains from using your solution—to hiring, training, and motivating employees and fostering a culture based on these concerns, to measuring and rewarding actual customer outcomes. One challenge is that extrinsic financial motivation can often interfere with intrinsic motivation and values, hence the importance of the right customer-focused culture and core values, as Zappos shows.

Physical, virtual, or digical. A relationship can be physical (e.g., visiting your physician or hair stylist, going to lunch with your account rep, or talking to the store clerk about your hardware project). It can also be virtual (e.g., buying something at an ecommerce site, or "liking" a brand on social media). For many businesses, a *digical* relationship that seamlessly fuses digital and physical interactions is ideal. In Burberry's case, this can include being able to order online and pick up in store, or being able to watch live fashion events delivered over digital networks into physical stores and then try on clothes in the store, while the clerk reviews prior purchases on an iPad to check for fashion integrity. In such a digical, omni-channel world, the relationship transcends the medium.

Human vs. algorithmic. Traditional examples of customer intimacy might include Home Depot clerks, who patiently discuss your project with you in the plumbing or lumber aisle, your hair stylist, who knows how you like it done but can suggest new trendy styles you might like, or the corner butcher, who you've patronized for decades, and knows which cuts you like, and whether they should be marbled or lean.

But if relationships move from physical to virtual or digical, the knowledge of customer preferences can also move from human to algorithmic. Human relationships can still be virtual; that's what Facebook is all about. But some virtual relationships can be algorithmic. Sophisticated algorithms at Amazon.com help you find items based on presumed relevance, and they help you understand other items that you might like. A blend of human customer reviews, editorial reviews, performance data, filtering algorithms, and revenue and profit maximization techniques that optimize based on financials and propensity to purchase become the new embodiment of intimacy. Even companies such as Zappos that are heavily biased toward human customer service use the web for ecommerce, use IT to manage warehouse inventory, and have back-end order fulfillment systems.

Individual vs. collective. Algorithmic mediation of relationships means that an entirely new type of intimacy is possible. A customer-intimate individual such as a tailor, butcher, or doctor has two main limits. The first is that she can only interact with and humanly remember a limited number of individuals, and there is an inverse relationship between quantity and quality: more patients means less time with each patient. In addition, the small number of interactions limits the ability to derive statistically significant insights. Is the high fever related to the abdominal pain, a recent trip, a chronic condition, a specific gene, or an emerging pandemic?

However, algorithms can do just that—moving beyond simple analyses of small numbers of individuals, to strong inferences and an understanding of interaction complexities at a scale of millions or hundreds of millions of customers. With algorithmic collective intimacy, scale is not only manageable but advantageous, because these subtle inferences are more statistically significant and thus more conclusive when based on more data points.

Netflix's recommender accentuates the positive by recommending movies that you are likely to enjoy. CVS Health's Drug Interaction Checker attempts to eliminate the negative by warning of potential drug interactions that can change the way the body reacts in combination to drugs that might be fine if taken independently, say, by increasing strength or unwanted side effects. Google's Waze recommends individual routes based on insights derived from collective analysis of all users.

Collaborative and Content Filtering

Customers originally had intimate relationships with their providers, based on small town or neighborhood ethics. You walked to the corner butcher or saloon, and you really couldn't switch providers, because there was only one in town, and because both your kids were on the same baseball team.

When Web 1.0 came along, it ushered in a new era of choice. If you didn't like Lycos, there was Altavista, or you could switch to Yahoo!, and eventually Google.

But now, stickiness is making a return, in part due to the way technology is enabling network and community effects. As websites became not just one-way advertising and information media, but enabled a variety of interactions, people invested energy into relationships with providers (e.g., setting up music channels on Pandora, or entering movie ratings into Netflix). Companies like LinkedIn and Facebook drove network effects.

The perhaps-unexpected surprise of such virtual relationships was the opportunity to analyze weak signals from massive quantities of relationships, possibly combined with external datasets such as demographics or weather, to generate strong inferences that could enhance the quality of each relationship. Netflix uses many different data points, ranging from partly external data such as movie metadata—the actors, director, length, date of release—as well as customer behavioral profiles—what movies they ordered, which ones they watched or rewatched, skipped, stopped or rewinded, on what device, at what time. It can then balance out general recommendations, based on aggregate statistics such as the most popular or most highly rated, and based on surprising its customers with insightful suggestions based on big data analytics across all of its data.

Such recommendation algorithms generally fall under the categories of collaborative filtering and content filtering.[20] *Collaborative filtering* is a technique where recommendations or other selections are made based on patterns of shared preferences. Recommendations follow the general rule that if Alice and Bob both like the same things, then they are also both more likely to both like—or dislike—a different thing. This general rule can be extended to more things, and to common friends.

One issue with filtering is access to valid data. People don't necessarily do what they *say* they do. For example, most Netflix customers say that they love highbrow foreign movies, but according to Netflix data, hardly anyone ever actually watches them. Similarly, dating and interpersonal harmony sites based on attempting to match what you consciously specify in your profile that you'd like in a mate against the characteristics that others specify in their profiles evidently don't work well, according to a recent study. However, collaborative filtering based on users' dating site *activities* evidently can offer better recommendations, increasing the chance of a response by a notable 40 percent.[21]

The good news for today's IT-based collaborative filtering is that it can get much more granular and accurate data. Take Netflix. When DVDs arrived in the mail, Netflix had to take your word that you even watched *La Vie en Rose* or *Jean de Florette*, much less that you were serious about your rating. With actual behavioral data, such as that you've streamed them each over a dozen times—or not at all—firmer conclusions can be drawn.

Content filtering is a technique where recommendations are made based on the actual content of the object or its metadata. For example, if you like science fiction, chances are good that you will like a movie with the term *star* in it. That will work fine for any of the *Star Trek* or *Star Wars* or even perhaps *Buzz Lightyear of Star Command: The Adventure Begins*, but not so well for *The Star Chamber*, *Dancing with the Stars*, or *Dickie Roberts: Former Child Star*.

Given the complex nuances of movies—actors, scripting, cinematography, timing, directors, producers, lighting, sets, costumes—one can appreciate that predictions based on collaborative or content filtering are not guaranteed to always be successful. However, even a slight improvement in the quality of recommendations means that customers are likely to perceive more value from Netflix; more likely to purchase based on an upsell or cross-sell on Amazon.com; more likely to be cured based on personalized medicine; more likely to follow a revenue-generating ad inserted into a web page or app; or more likely to enjoy a wine recommendation.

In a world of infinite, highly accessible content of which a vast majority is unknown and unknowable, the winner is not the provider who offers yet more undiscoverable content. It's the one that can filter through infinity to find those nuggets that create the most value for customers, which is a mix of the comfortable with the unexpected pleasant surprise.

In retrospect, this is the way business should always have been conducted. Like a spouse or significant other bringing home a bottle of wine from an unknown vineyard or a surprise chocolate treat, meeting unique personal requirements and occasionally creating a "Wow!" is at the heart of a quality relationship. Unexpected surprises tickle the brain's dopamine system, and create the strongest type of addiction and reinforcement, through what psychologists call variable ratio intermittent rewards. Even pigeons would rather get rewarded on such a basis than predictably.[22]

What's good for the individual can be good for the employer and for society. News articles and opinion pieces that occasionally surprise with differing viewpoints help reduce the risk of succumbing to *confirmation bias*, where information is filtered to remain consonant with prior beliefs. This can help firms avoid stagnation due to drinking their own Kool-Aid, and help individuals and societies become more tolerant.

■　■　■

Understanding, respecting, and managing customer relationships is a critical part of any business. Even for companies that don't excel in processes or products, it is possible to maintain or improve market position by focusing on customers.

To do so requires evaluation and exploitation of the opportunities in five dimensions: desired relationship; virtual, physical, or digical embodiments of that relationship; evolving toward a focus on customer outcomes and value; balancing human insight with algorithmic speed, scalability, and precision; and moving from individual transactions to collective intimacy, to offer customers solutions that are of the highest value.

Notes

1. Harley Manning and Kerry Bodine, *Outside In: The Power of Putting Customers at the Center of Your Business* (New Harvest, 2012).
2. Kyle McNabb and Josh Bernoff, "The CIO's And CMO's Blueprint for Strategy in the Age of the Customer: Four Imperatives to Establish New Competitive Advantage," *Forrester.com* (no date), https://solutions.forrester.com/age-of-the-customer/cio-cmo-strategy-3115Q-3763IK.html.
3. Alex Lawrence, "Five Customer Retention Tips for Entrepreneurs," *Forbes.com*, November 1, 2012, www.forbes.com/sites/alexlawrence/2012/11/01/five-customer-retention-tips-for-entrepreneurs/.
4. Typical claims span a broad range from 25 percent to 100 percent.
5. David C. Dugdale, Ronald Epstein, and Steven Z. Pantilat, "Time and the Patient-Physician Relationship," *Journal of General Internal Medicine* 14 (Suppl 1) (1999): S34–S40, www.ncbi.nlm.nih.gov/pmc/articles/PMC1496869/.

6. Maureen Stancik Boyce and Laura VanTine, "Why Advocacy Matters to Online Retailers," *IBM Institute for Business Value* (Somers, NY: IBM Corporation, 2008), www-935.ibm.com/services/us/gbs/bus/pdf/gbe03050-usen-00_advocacy_online.pdf.

7. Frederick F. Reichheld, "The One Number You Need to Grow," *Harvard Business Review* (December 2009), https://hbr.org/2003/12/the-one-number-you-need-to-grow.

8. Rob Markey and Fred Reichheld, "The Economics of Loyalty," *Insights Loyalty* (March 23, 2012), www.bain.com/publications/articles/the-economics-of-loyalty.aspx.

9. Fred Reichheld with Rob Markey, *The Ultimate Question 2.0 (Revised and Expanded Edition): How Net Promoter Companies Thrive in a Customer-Driven World* (Boston: Harvard Business Review Press, 2011).

10. Malcolm Gladwell, *The Tipping Point: How Little Things Can Make a Big Difference* (New York: Little, Brown, and Company, 2000).

11. Sons of Maxwell, "United Breaks Guitars," *YouTube.com*, July 6, 2009, https://www.youtube.com/watch?v=5YGc4zOqozo.

12. Gary Vaynerchuk, *The Thank You Economy* (New York: HarperBusiness, 2011), 56.

13. Rob Markey, "The Economics of Loyalty," [Video], *Insights Loyalty* (December 22, 2014), www.bain.com/publications/articles/rob-markey-the-economics-of-loyalty-video.aspx.

14. Rob Markey, "Converting Loyalty Into Economic Advantage," [Video] *Insights Loyalty* (October 1, 2014), www.bain.com/publications/articles/rob-markey-converting-loyalty-into-economic-advantage-video.aspx.

15. The approach is credited to Bain, Fred Reichheld, and Satmetrix.

16. Sam Biddle, "Uber and Lyft Both Sued for Allegedly Ripping Off Drivers," *Gawker Valleywag*, September 6, 2013, valleywag.gawker.com/uber-and-lyft-both-sued-for-allegedly-ripping-off-drive-1264430943.

17. Tony Hsieh, "Building a Customer-Focused Culture," *SlideShare.net*, February 7, 2008, www.slideshare.net/Thor/zappos-lessons-building-a-customerfocused-culture.

18. Vaynerchuk, *The Thank You Economy*, xiii.

19. Jill Avery, Susan Fournier, and John Wittenbraker, "Unlock the Mysteries of Your Customer Relationships," *Harvard Business Review* (July–August 2014): 72–81.

20. William W. Cohen, "Collaborative Filtering: A Tutorial," www.cs.cmu.edu/~wcohen/collab-filtering-tutorial.ppt.

21. "New twists for love in age of big data," *AsiaOne.com*, February 12, 2014, digital.asiaone.com/digital/news/new-twists-love-age-big-data.

22. Stephen B. Kendall, "Preference for Intermittent Reinforcement," *Journal of the Experimental Analysis of Behavior* 21, no. 3 (1974): 463–473, www.ncbi.nlm.nih.gov/pmc/articles/PMC1333219/.

CHAPTER 12

The Discipline of Collective Intimacy

The discipline of *collective* intimacy is ultimately based on the perhaps surprising synergy between digital technologies and *customer* intimacy. Treacy and Wiersema said that companies pursuing customer intimacy offer "unmatched value … not in product or price, but in the extraordinary level of service, guidance, expertise, and hand-holding" that they provide to each client.[1] A customer intimacy strategy entails an intimate relationship with each customer; but collective intimacy entails an intimate relationship with each customer *enhanced by value-adding insights derived across all customers.* To derive these insights requires applying sophisticated, processing-intensive algorithms against massive datasets acquired from customers on characteristics, preferences, behaviors, and contexts, such as genetic sequences, movie and music preferences, electric power consumption, and, well, just about anything.

The evolution to collective intimacy is happening among companies with intimacy strategies in virtually every vertical.

The private-practice physician may not exactly say, "Take two aspirin, and call me in the morning," but, "Take this broad-spectrum antibiotic and call me in 10 days," is not that much more advanced. It is being replaced at hospitals such as the Mayo Clinic by personalized medicine, based on data collected from all patients—ranging from lab tests to biopsies to DNA sequences—and evidence based on analysis of pharmaceutical and treatment efficacy, to better treat each patient in a unique way.

The video store with the top-rental list is mostly gone, replaced by the Netflix recommendation engine, one of the most sophisticated "computers" ever built. This engine literally processes billions of data points across tens of millions of customers to maximize your entertainment experience.

The corner bookstore's front table of best sellers and maze of aisles with shelves that may or may not have what you were looking for has been supplanted by the infinite virtual book store of Amazon.com, where the books—and other merchandise—you are most likely to purchase are clearly on display at your personal virtual front table—the home page.

A standard route from point A to point B is being replaced by an individualized one from Waze that incorporates real-time congestion, calculated from data collectively crowdsourced from other users.

The wine store clerk's recommendations—which just might possibly have been based on which wine had been overstocked or had just received promotional market development funds from the vineyard—are being replaced by computerized suggestions. Tasting Room by Lot18 uses a personalization technology it calls "WinePrint," which generates a custom "Wine Profile" based on how you've rated wines that Tasting Room has sent you.[2]

Twitter's suggestions for "Who to Follow," LinkedIn's for "People You May Know," Match.com's "Daily Matches," and Facebook's "Do You Know…?," to varying degrees offer a mix of algorithms looking at the *social graph*—the giant web of connections recording who knows whom, collaborative and content filtering, and other secret sauce. "People You May Know," for example, is partly based on the realization that the friend of a friend may well be a friend, too.[3]

The value discipline of customer intimacy remains as vital and valid as ever, but digital technologies can take it to a whole new level. As the preceding examples illustrate, the discipline of collective intimacy entails maintaining and deepening a broad range of customer relationships, using algorithms to identify, create, and deliver meaningful customer solutions across all channels and touchpoints to each customer as an individual, based on intimate relationships with and inferences drawn from all customers collectively.

Ultimately, the intent of an intimacy strategy is to generate customer value, attain market leadership, retain customers, and grow profitably. For Netflix, it's better movie recommendations; for Waze, it's better navigation; for the Mayo Clinic, it's better patient outcomes; for WinePrint, it's a better drinking experience.

There are several evolutionary steps to move to collective intimacy.

From Transactions to Relationships

The process of deepening customer engagement can be described as moving from anonymous transactions to ongoing relationships, but it's important to recall that different customers want different relationships with different firms at different times, so a single approach won't work. Business relationships are like personal relationships, in all their variety. Businesses need to be cognizant of those differences and match customers' preferences rather than attempt to force all customers to maintain the same level of intimacy.

As described in the previous chapter, some customers prefer anonymous transactions like "one-night stands," others are looking for deeper, longer term, more engaging relationships reminiscent of "marriage partners."

Assuming that both partners want a long-term relationship, investments made up front can pay off for both the firm and the customer. Consequently, as Treacy and Wiersema argue, companies pursuing intimacy strategies are willing to spend time and money to understand customer needs and to develop unique solutions for customers. This is very different from independent transactions, which each need to be profitable. It's also different from freemium approaches, where a small set of paying customers subsidizes the nonpaying ones.

Increasingly, these investments are becoming digital.

Today, relationships and engagement often seem to be defined and measured within the context of social media: friends, followers, likes, tweets, and retweets. A stronger way of viewing the intensity of engagement is the extent to which such relationships are two-way—for example, what percentage of tweets mentioning a particular company receive direct responses, or, better yet, how many simple comment/responses turn into longer-term relationships with measurable financial results. More sophisticated techniques can understand the sentiment of the interactions, and the reach of such sentiments due to network effects.

Of course, one means of determining the intensity of engagement is incremental revenue, and therefore the ROI (return on investment) of social media. One such case is when a single tweet turned into $250,000. A customer tweeted to his follower community that he was interested in Avaya but also in a competitor. Thanks to a rapid response by an alert Avaya employee, this quarter-million-dollar sale was closed within two weeks.[4]

But there is more to digital engagement than social networks; digital technology offers new ways of deepening relationships beyond just apps and likes.

Digitalized *products* and *services* offer the opportunity to maintain a deep relationship with the customer, such as when Nike+ products help derive insights into personal fitness status and trajectories. The Zeo Personal Sleep Manager is even more engaged. It's partly an alarm clock, but one linked to online sleep quality analysis and coaching services. It uses a soft headband worn during sleep, wirelessly connected to a bedside alarm clock, to gently wake you when your brainwaves indicate that you are no longer in deep sleep.

Digitalized *processes* offer another massive opportunity to drive engagement by measuring and tuning company processes and by integrating—that is, linking, coordinating, synchronizing, and optimizing—customer processes with firm processes. Wal-Mart links its stock replenishment processes with its suppliers' distribution processes. FedEx offers critical inventory management and logistics and fulfillment services, which enable tight integration and outsourcing of customer order fulfillment, supply chain, and maintenance spares processes, through information systems which manage inventory and provide supply chain visibility globally. When airlines provide an estimated time of flight arrival updated in real time, it helps spouses and limo drivers.

For mail-order retailer Harry & David, customer engagement can be quantitatively measured through ecommerce analytics, objectives, and metrics: (1) customer counts—get more people to order; (2) order frequency—get them to order more often; (3) order size—have them put more items in their online shopping cart; and (4) shopping cart value—try to get those items to be higher-priced.

Based on metrics trends, tuning the approach, reallocating spend, or training or replacing personnel may be called for. As Paul Lazorisak, head of customer marketing at Harry & David, says—applying Newton's laws to the marketing of figs—"An object at rest stays at rest unless acted upon by an equal and opposite force ... Apply that universal law to customer metrics, such as re-buy (retention) rate, frequency of purchase or shopping basket value. These metrics will not change unless you put programs and investments in place to move them. What customer relationship management strategies are you going to put in place to move the metrics?" By tracking customer cohorts over time, Harry & David is able to validate that its marketing strategies are effective in moving transactional customers into loyal repeat customers, and that these loyal repeat customers are increasing their spend.[5]

From Relationships to Intimacy

Face-to-face customer relationships can evolve to customer intimacy, and digital relationships can evolve to digital intimacy. Take a classic example of a customer-intimate relationship: doctor-patient. This was always intimate. Doctors would endeavor to determine a patient's needs, such as eliminating chronic abdominal pain. They would then try to solve the problem using the best possible solution. They would then follow a course of treatment to devise and deliver a solution to meet the customer's (i.e., patient's) needs.

The degree of intimacy was traditionally based very much on personal relationships, such as knowing the family and remembering that the patient fell off a horse many years ago. As methods improved, additional diagnostic tools arose, such as EKGs (electrocardiograms), EEGs (electroencephalograms), X-rays, and so on. Increasingly, patient-doctor intimacy is digitally derived, such as from CT (computed tomography) scanners and DNA sequencers. Much more data are becoming available to further increase intimacy: pills that report whether they have been taken; video surveillance to monitor changes in gait; connected pacemakers; watches and other wearables that monitor skin conductance, body fat, and pulse; and deep brainwave data such as from the Zeo.

Personal and organizational intimacy leverage digital technologies across other industries, not just medicine. As one example, GE Aviation and Taleris, a joint venture with Accenture, are concerned with the "health" of airlines and their aircraft, monitoring numerous vital signs through aircraft sensors and engine sensors.

Target uses data mining to better understand its customers, even to the point of knowing whether they are pregnant and even when they're due. Pregnant women stop buying scented lotions and soaps and start buying cotton balls and taking vitamin supplements. Other clues include browsing for baby items online, the age and sex of the customer, and whether they have other children.[6,7] Or consider electric utilities. Customers used to need to call in power outages; the Internet of Things can report such issues in real time.[8]

Information from any intimate relationship needs to be kept private. All of the efforts to build trust, loyalty, and engagement can be lost if that trust is betrayed. This can happen unintentionally, through data breaches such as Anthem's, which reportedly affected 80 million customers, and Target's, which reportedly affected 100 million.

Intentional intimacy strategies can also unintentionally turn from helpfulness to creepiness. Samsung Smart TVs, for example, were alleged to "listen in" on living room conversations, and the Samsung privacy policy did not explicitly preclude such activities.[9] Target's insights into pregnancy caused problems when the father of a teenage girl complained that his daughter was being sent inappropriate promotions, only to then find out that Target was correct—his daughter was in fact pregnant.[10]

Even if not creepy, insights need to be reasonably accurate, or at least come with a disclaimer. Pinterest sent emails to unattached or at least unaffianced women saying "You're getting married!," then inviting the women to examine the Pinterest "boards"—the virtual pinboards that Pinterest runs online—for stationery designers and wedding photographers. The response from Pinterest's Barry Schnitt, their Head of Communications and Public Policy: "We're sorry we came off like an overbearing mother who is always asking when you'll find a nice boy or girl."[11]

From Physical to Virtual

It's not news that as technology has matured, physical customer relationships—and interpersonal relationships—have gone online. Social networking is the number-one online activity in the United States, with each person spending over half an hour each day on average. It's not just to catch up on photos of friends' vacations or restaurant activities; almost half of Internet users look to those friends before making a purchase decision. A majority of small and medium businesses leverage social media to gain customers, increase brand exposure, increase web traffic, and/or gain insights into markets and customers. And social media is not just good for companies. Customers benefit in multiple ways: gaining access to promotions and discounts, product information, and customer service, including offering feedback to companies.[12]

Smart companies listen to that feedback very carefully, respond immediately, attempt to resolve the underlying issue as quickly as possible, and identify trends and recurring issues and take action to systemically address the opportunities or issues. But that general approach disguises some of the unique ways in which companies creatively leverage social media to create "Wows," as Bain's Rob Markley calls them, and thus enhance engagement and advocacy and build long-term relationships.

Autodesk, a computer-aided design software company, tweeted during the Oscars about its technical support for various winners. Kimpton Hotels listens and responds to social media during the customer service experience (i.e., hotel stay): A guest who mentioned that she was sick received soup, tea, and a get-well card; one celebrating a 50th birthday received a birthday cake specially prepared by a pastry chef. Whole Foods Markets, the organic grocery store, maintains "local social" Twitter accounts for each of its stores. This helps build relationships between customers and not just an abstract national brand, but actual physical stores and the people that work there. Moreover, it analyzed social media inquiries about genetically modified food to help design a customer education program.[13]

In addition to moving or complementing offline customer relationships themselves with online ones, online social media has the additional critical benefit of enabling monitoring and management of those relationships. For example, besides easy things like monitoring the sheer number of Facebook likes or Twitter followers, advanced tools can monitor customer sentiment and track how it is changing, helping to clarify the relative balance of promoters and detractors, i.e., advocates and antagonists.

Another critical difference between face-to-face and virtual relationships is that the former can generally only be expressed in person. However, virtual relationships can exist around the clock; on the firm side, social media channels can be monitored 24/7; on the consumer side, continuous engagement can be enabled by pervasive access through mobile and embedded channels.

Digital technologies can support virtual customer intimacy in other ways, too, such as loyalty programs that track purchases or enable consumers to connect with various communities. Embedded devices can enable continuous engagement as well. A patient-doctor discussion might last three minutes; a connected pacemaker enables customer engagement 24 hours a day.

From Virtual to Digical

Customers expect a seamless hybrid of digital and physical, or *digical* services, as Bain & Company's Darrell Rigby calls it. If they buy a shirt online, they expect to be able to return it in a store, or if it's out of stock in the store, they expect to be able to easily order it online. Relationships exist between firms and customers, not specific channels, which shouldn't impact the relationship *per se*, merely alter some of the characteristics of the experience. Representatives can be physically present, as with store clerks, or virtual, as with online support representatives or even engaged customers who respond to other customers' questions in online forums.

A customer continues to exist whether or not she is on the phone to your customer service line or offering kudos or complaints on Twitter. Engagement should be continuous across all moments of truth. Staying in touch with customers across all moments of product and service use in an integrated fashion is important, and can now be amplified via digital technologies. A good example is the Amazon Kindle Mayday button, where a product—the Kindle—incorporates an easy-to-use feature—the Mayday button—to instantly connect with the brand.[14]

Target collects data from customers (whom it calls "guests") across multiple channels. As Andrew Pole, a Target statistician, says, "If you use a credit card or a coupon, or fill out a survey, or mail in a refund, or call the customer help line, or open an e-mail we've sent you or visit our Web site, we'll record it and link it to your Guest ID. We want to know everything we can."[15] Beyond those touchpoints, Target also maintains data about your age, marital status, parental status, location, driving distance from the store and recent household moves, financial information such as income and current credit cards, recent purchases, coupon redemption, competitors within the trade area, email click-throughs, store and online purchases, and which websites you've visited.[16]

In addition, as author Charles Duhigg observes, Target or any other retailer can "buy data about your ethnicity, job history, the magazines you read, if you've ever declared bankruptcy or got divorced, the year you bought (or lost) your house, where you went to college, what kinds of topics you talk about online, whether you prefer certain brands of coffee, paper towels, cereal or applesauce, your political leanings, reading habits, charitable giving, and the number of cars you own."[17]

To understand customer behavior across channels requires a consistent view of both customers and products. This means some way to tie customer data acquired online with that acquired offline, and consistent product iden-tification and product hierarchies regardless of channel.

From Company to Community

A relationship between a firm and a customer is, perhaps paradoxically, strengthened, rather than weakened, through expansion to a community. Bonds between the customer and the community strengthen the bonds between the customer and the firm, because it is easier to defect to a competitor than to also have to change out the entire community. The balancing act for firms offering virtual communities is to foster such relationships to the extent possible without being intrusive.

Some of the most powerful corporate brands today have a business that arguably is primarily focused on facilitating relationships *among* customers ("arguably" because their primary focus really is monetization of those relationships and engagement). Facebook builds communities among friends. Twitter builds communities among those with shared interests. Match.com is a community of singles seeking love. eBay is a community of buyers and sellers. LinkedIn is a community of professionals and firms, who may be job seekers, recruiters, or looking to collaborate or share interests.

But perhaps the most powerful model is when a company combines business-to-customer or business-to-business relationships with community facilitation. Netflix and Amazon.com have direct-to-consumer models, but also foster and enable a community of reviewers, which further enriches their offers to those consumers. The EMC Community Network has hundreds of thousands of employees, customers, and partners. Information on existing products flows outward, new product ideas flow inward—a sterling example of greater customer intimacy mediated by a digitally enabled community.[18]

A large portion of customers make their purchase decisions based on recommendations from friends and family and the rest of their social network(s), as well as reviews. Consequently, engaging customers to write reviews is second in importance in social media marketing only to actual purchases. Target was able to generate tens of thousands of new reviews through a campaign targeting customers who had previously written reviews and had recently made purchases.[19]

From People to Algorithms

As intimacy evolves from individuals and organizations to algorithms and data, there are opportunities and requirements for greater scale, greater accuracy and granularity of collected data, and more data from more sources, providing a richer understanding of the customer, and, ultimately, the delivery of greater customer value.

In addition, the algorithms that can be applied can be much more complex than people can possibly apply. Our human pattern detection and causal logic is known to have "bugs" in it—cognitive biases and anomalies. *Illusory correlation* is based on our innate orientation to find patterns, such as creating constellations out of random starfields, and leads us to find relationships where none exist. A related bias, the *hot-hand fallacy*, leads us to treat random, independent events, such as free throws in basketball, as if there were dependencies between the events; *herding* causes us to follow along with the group. Computer algorithms can avoid all of these, although, of course, they don't offer insight into emotion, human drives, or intuition, which is, after all, just a rapid approximation algorithm that humans use. So algorithms, whose creation is guided by data scientists and intuition, operating on massive amounts of data, in real or near-real time, can offer advantages over the traditional mechanisms used by the corner butcher, tailor, or country doctor.

Another key difference is more subtle: Doctors and lawyers are expected to have a high degree of confidentiality with their patients and clients: medical data privacy and attorney-client privileged communications. A hair stylist or bartender is presumed to exercise common-sense discretion. Businesses selling to businesses often have related privacy practices, for example, enterprise account teams working to strategically partner with clients generally must have nondisclosure agreements in place to ensure not only that they don't divulge customer proprietary information to competitors or the public but also that they don't divulge such information to others in the same firm that are servicing competing accounts. In the era of algorithms, personally identifiable and customer proprietary information must still be appropriately protected, but the algorithms must be able to (privately and securely) process data from all customers collectively.

In the old days, Nielsen, the TV audience measurement company, would ask audiences to fill out paper booklets to log their television watching. This took effort and was fraught with errors. Focus groups would watch children at play. Directors and producers would screen films to small groups to see which ending they preferred.

Now, such data collection can be performed with 100 percent of the customer group, rather than a sample, and frictionlessly, with no additional effort on the customer's behalf. Rather than trying to recollect and note what one watched after the fact, smart TVs, set-top boxes, and mobile devices can determine viewing behavior with perfect accuracy in real time. Rather than bringing together a focus group at the studio, Netflix or TiVo can see *exactly* what you watched, when you watched it, where you paused it, where you rewound or fast-forwarded, where you abandoned it. The important point is that companies can increasingly collect important data that benefit users at essentially zero marginal cost to them or to users.

Understanding consumer behavior will soon become even more intimate. Nielsen has moved from paper record-keeping to online and mobile. Not only can it use "on-device meter panels to record every interaction users have with measurable mobile devices,"[20] it even considers mobile network performance, phone bills, and network service provider records. Next, Nielsen plans to use "consumer neuroscience methods to measure brainwave activity in real time, capturing purchase considerations at the moment they are formed in the brain."[21]

With a deeper understanding of *each* customer, firms can now create a deeper understanding of common requirements, issues, and behaviors, enabling better targeting, segmentation, and customization of solutions, and overcoming preconceived notions. Harrah's famously data mined its customer database and determined that 26 percent of its gamblers generated over 80 percent of its revenues. It turns out that these profitable customers didn't fit a high-roller stereotype like James Bond but were former teachers and blue-collar workers, as well as doctors and bankers. Focusing on these customers turned out to be the key to brand differentiation and many successive quarters of profitable growth.[22]

The use of such algorithms, however, is a bit of a double-edged sword. Currently, the algorithms are, one might say, using statistical tricks to substitute for true insight. These statistical tools can tease out the needle in the haystack (i.e., the relationship or recommendation or upsell opportunity embedded in a mass of 1s and 0s). However, some argue that what distinguishes leading organizations from below-average ones is not customer data per se, but the ability to understand that data in terms of basic human needs and motivations, such as need for achievement and need for social connection.[23] In other words, it is a combination of human insight and machine processing.

Sometimes, that human insight is encoded in the algorithms. For example, movie-recommendation algorithms might understand the differences between romance and comedy and that there are rom-coms, or the difference between George Lopez and George Clooney, but that might be due to their human programmers more than any capabilities unique to computer algorithms. Kevin Slavin, of the MIT Media Lab, argues that while algorithms can do more and more sophisticated things, they function best when combined with such insight. As we have already noted, a machine—IBM's Deep Blue—beat then World Champion Garry Kasparov for the first time in match play in 1997. But in 2005, a couple of amateur chess players with PCs beat the best human players—grandmasters—and beat the best computer players—supercomputers.[24] It's been argued that the best chess "player" in the world is not a man or a machine, but a man-machine hybrid.[25]

One of the most advanced combinations of human and machine is Palantir Technologies, which has its origins partly in fraud detection techniques used at PayPal and partly in the US intelligence community. Palantir's core theme is that because human adversaries rapidly adapt to countermeasures, really thorny problems require a mix of human intuition and exploratory analytics, together with the power of computers to process large data sets, which they call "intelligence augmentation" and "human-computer symbiosis."[26]

Even though Netflix uses advanced recommendation systems to suggest what you might like to watch next, it still uses human intuition in conjunction with data to help decide which content to create. As Ted Sarandos, chief content officer at Netflix, admits, it's "probably a seventy-thirty mix.... Seventy is the data, and thirty is judgment.... But the thirty needs to be on top, if that makes sense."[27]

From Individual to Collective

Insights can now flow both ways: data about individuals can be aggregated to understand commonalities and devise insights regarding segments or the overall group; and insights about each individual can be derived by analysis of all customers, collectively. And, paradoxically, rather than relationships with other customers diluting the quality of any particular relationship, they strengthen it. Amazon.com can make better and more relevant product recommendations to you *because* of insights derived from the relationships it has with everyone else. The recommendations are also better for Amazon.com, because they maximize revenue and profits. iTunes Radio or Pandora can make better music recommendations for the same reasons. And so it is with Netflix and movie recommendations, as we'll see in the next chapter; the GE Medical MultiOmyx system and tissue pathology, as we'll touch on in Chapter 17; and even messaging to reduce power consumption, as we'll see with Opower in Chapter 19. The Mayo Clinic can better understand the treatment implications of your unique genetic makeup *because* of the genetic profiling that it has conducted on everyone else.

The Mayo Clinic is at the forefront of a critically important area for collective intimacy: personalized medicine, where patient-specific therapies are engaged to cure, relieve, or delay symptoms of chronic diseases and acute illnesses. The Mayo Clinic, rather than looking at data on movie-watching habits or power usage, gets as intimate as one can imagine by examining individual physiology in depth.

Mayo's Biomarker Discovery Program analyzes genetic data to enable better diagnosis and treatments that are specific to that individual. For example, a particular genetic biomarker may be associated with a specific type of lung cancer, which responds well only to a specific chemotherapy, whereas another biomarker might suggest radiation, and another might include both. To better understand these correlations, Mayo has a biomarker repository with data from hundreds of thousands of patients.

Mayo, in other words, has evolved to complement a century and a half of customer intimacy between doctors and patients with collective data-based intimacy. Big data analytics against the repository can be used to tailor treatments to each patient based on the most precise possible diagnoses. According to Mayo, there are additional benefits: one can use such biomarkers to predict and take preventive measures; for example, a greater genetic risk of lung cancer might be a strong incentive to quit smoking. And, such data can also be used to eliminate treatments that would be ineffective for that patient at that time with that diagnosis, reducing the cost of medical treatment or allowing available funds to be apportioned where they can do the most good.[28]

Although we tend to think of bacteria as nasty pests that cause an infection, only one-tenth of the human body is made up of "our" cells. The vast majority of our "selves" is actually comprised of the "microbiome," 100 trillion microbes, mostly bacteria, residing in or on areas such as our intestines, mouth, and skin. These exist in a delicate balance, and therefore the correct approach to issues with harmful bacteria might not be antibiotics, but probiotics for the friendly and essential bacteria. As a result, Mayo is also using genetic analysis to understand individuals' microbiomes, and collectively determine correlations between markers, diseases, and treatments.[29]

This kind of data-based intimacy doesn't stop there. Mayo's Pharmacogenomics Program looks to correlate genetic makeup with drug efficacy and optimal dosages. Some people break down drugs more quickly than others, others respond differently or not at all to them, still others have deadly side effects. A rapid genetic test devised by Mayo can determine how to optimally dose—or not use at all—30 oft-prescribed drugs, such as statins.[30]

Collective intimacy is useful not just for Mayo, but also for mayo. McCormick FlavorPrint develops a profile of an individual's flavor preferences in terms of 33 basic building blocks like bitter, cheesy, tomato-ey, salty, and so forth. It also maps thousands of recipes in terms of those building blocks, creating a match between preferences and recipes. In about a minute, one can respond "like," "dislike," or "skip" to sample food items such as red wine, blueberry pancakes, and guacamole. In less than a second, FlavorPrint will suggest "Peppercorn Mélange Chicken and Udon Noodles in Lemon Grass Sake Broth," noting a 93 percent match thanks to its umami and citrusy elements.

This is a terrific example of collective intimacy. McCormick could have pursued an operational and information excellence strategy and developed more efficient processes for drying and transporting spices (which they very well may have). It could have pursued product leadership and offered some exotic breed of Madagascarian vanilla beans (which it also very well may have). But FlavorPrint is a way of engaging intimately with customers in a way that benefits them—who wouldn't like suggestions for tasty food?—and also sells more McCormick spices. It also spices up the McCormick brand.

A different type of heat is the focus of Opower, reviewed in Chapter 19. Opower is a fascinating example of the use of gamification techniques by business, but it is also an excellent example of how collective intimacy can help influence individuals to spend *less* and have a positive environmental impact. Opower acts as an intermediary between and enabler of power utilities and their customers. It collects data from utilities and customer smart meters every few minutes, and feeds it into a "data integration system," which also acquires demographics, weather, and even tax assessor data. The data are maintained for tens of millions of homes. This then feeds an analytics engine that can compare usage among neighbors, provide personalized bills and consumption forecasts, conduct what-if analyses such as the usage impact of rate increases, and adjust all these for weather variation.[31]

All of this information is then used to make decisions and drive or at least influence action. Because different customers have different devices such as smart meters and Wi-Fi thermostats, behavioral styles, personal objectives, values, and times of day where they can effectively take action, messages are highly personalized. Messages are based on "social proof" (i.e., what everyone else is doing), indicating, for example, that 72 percent of your neighbors with comparable homes use less electricity than you. This kind of message has been proven to be most effective at influencing behavior.

All these steps together lead to collective intimacy, in which Opower in partnership with the utility can process massive amounts of data to generate an individual relationship with and recommendation for each customer that benefits that customer, delivered via a messaging medium most effective for that customer.

The data used by Netflix, the Mayo Clinic, McCormick's, and Opower are not only structured but typically numerical: a 5 rating, 37.2 kilowatts, a DNA sequence. But other applications can use a similar approach against video, or image, or text data. IBM, for example, is looking into scanning psychiatrists' notes. There is little *collective* learning across patients or psychiatrists because patient interview notes are filed away in a cabinet. Soon, speech to text and voice analysis will be used to predict episodes based on variations in speech patterns.[32] Images are another source of data. GE's MultiOmyx scans images of tissue biopsies; and IBM can scan photographs for evidence of melanoma. The computer is able to identify melanoma 95 percent of the time, compared to 75 to 84 percent of the time for manual methods.[33] It is obviously not long before there is an app on your phone enabling early diagnosis and therefore early treatment of melanoma. From there, it's not much of a stretch to imagine an app in your showerhead or other medical diagnostic capabilities in common household products.

■   ■   ■

At a high level, the customer intimacy value discipline is as valid as ever. In today's world of outsourced processes, the Hollywood organization model, dynamic supply chains, and global innovation, some might argue that strong customer relationships are the only hope for success.

However, digital technologies provide new opportunities to implement customer intimacy. Collecting stated preferences and actual behaviors from customers at scale can enable better recommendation and higher customer satisfaction, thus enabling collective intimacy, where, paradoxically, having more customers can mean more intimate relationships with each customer.

Notes

1. Michael Treacy and Fred Wiersema, *The Discipline of Market Leaders: Choose Your Customers, Narrow Your Focus, Dominate Your Market* (Reading, MA: Addison-Wesley, 1995), 122.
2. "About Us," *Tasting Room by Lot 18*, https://www.tastingroom.com/about.
3. Thomas H. Davenport and D.J. Patil, "Data Scientist: The Sexiest Job of the 21st Century," *Harvard Business Review* (October 2012), hbr.org/2012/10/data-scientist-the-sexiest-job-of-the-21st-century/ar/1.
4. Casey Hibbard, "It Pays to Listen: Avaya's $250K Twitter Sale," *SocialMedia Examiner.com*, November 12, 2009, www.socialmediaexaminer.com/it-pays-to-listen-avayas-250k-twitter-sale/.
5. SAS, "From Growing Pears to Growing Connections: Three Keys to Cultivating Customer Relationships at Harry & David," 2013, www.sas.com/en_us/white papers/from-growing-pears-to-growing-connections-106557.html.
6. Charles Duhigg, "How Companies Learn Your Secrets," *New York Times Magazine*, February 16, 2012, www.nytimes.com/2012/02/19/magazine/shopping-habits.html.
7. Andrew Pole, "How Target Gets the Most Out of Its Guest Data," [Video] *Predictive Analytics World*, October 19-20, 2010, rmportal.performedia.com/node/1373.
8. Robert Reiss, "The Age of Mass Intimacy: CEOs Share Secrets of Connecting with Customers in a Digital World," *Forbes.com*, September 21, 2012, www.forbes.com/sites/robertreiss/2012/09/21/the-age-of-mass-intimacy-ceos-share-secrets-of-connecting-with-customers-in-a-digital-world-like-performing-personalized-songs-to-respond-to-tweets/.

9. John Ribeiro, "Smart TV Eavesdropping Furor Prompts Senator to Quiz Samsung, LG on Privacy," *PCWorld.com*, February 12, 2015, www.pcworld.com/article/2883532/us-senator-quizzes-samsung-lg-on-smart-tv-privacy.html.

10. Duhigg, "How Companies Learn Your Secret."

11. Maya Kosoff, "Pinterest Accidentally Sent Emails to Single Women Congratulating Them on Getting Married," *Yahoo! Tech*, September 4, 2014, https://www.yahoo.com/tech/pinterest-accidentally-sent-emails-to-single-women-96643879969.html.

12. "Businesses on Social Media-Statistics and Trends [Infographic]," GO-Gulf, September 30, 2014, www.go-gulf.ae/blog/businesses-social-media/.

13. Chanelle Bessette, "Social Media Superstars 2914," *Fortune.com*, January 16, 2014, fortune.com/2014/01/16/social-media-superstars-2014-fortunes-best-companies-to-work-for/.

14. "Mayday: Get Help on Your Fire Tablet," *Amazon.com*, www.amazon.com/gp/help/customer/display.html?nodeId=201349900.

15. Duhigg, "How Companies Learn Your Secret."

16. Pole, "How Target Gets the Most."

17. Duhigg, "How Companies Learn Your Secret."

18. Joe Weinman, "4 Ways to Win at Business by Playing Games All Day Long," *Forbes.com*, October 15, 2013, www.forbes.com/sites/joeweinman/2013/10/15/4-ways-to-win-at-business-by-playing-games-all-day-long/.

19. Pole, "How Target Gets the Most."

20. "Audience," *Nielsen*, www.nielsen.com/us/en/nielsen-solutions/nielsen-measurement/nielsen-audience-measurement.html.

21. "Consumer Neuroscience," *Nielsen*, www.nielsen.com/us/en/nielsen-solutions/nielsen-measurement/consumer-neuroscience.html.

22. Gary Loveman, "Diamonds in the Data Mine," *Harvard Business Review* (May 2003): 111.

23. Marc de Swaan Arons, Frank van den Driest, and Keith Weed, "The Ultimate Marketing Machine," *Harvard Business Review* (July–August 2014): 54–63.

24. Tom Simonite, "Software That Augments Human Thinking," *MIT Technology Review* (January 22, 2014), www.technologyreview.com/news/523666/software-that-augments-human-thinking/.

25. Hartosh Singh Bal, "Chessmate," *New York Times*, June 5, 2012, latitude.blogs.nytimes.com/2012/06/05/the-case-for-computers-at-top-chess-tournaments/.

26. Simonite.

27. Tim Wu, "Netflix's Secret Special Algorithm Is a Human," *The New Yorker*, January 27, 2015, www.newyorker.com/business/currency/hollywoods-big-data-big-deal.

28. "Personalized Medicine," Mayo Clinic, mayoresearch.mayo.edu/center-for-individualized-medicine/personalized-medicine.asp.

29. Ibid.

30. Ibid.
31. "Transforming the Way Utilities Relate to Their Customers," *Opower*, opower.com/platform/computer-science.
32. Guillermo Cecchi, "The Quantification of Behavioral Analytics in Psychiatry," IBM *A Smarter Planet* blog, July 3, 2014, asmarterplanet.com/blog/2014/07/quantification-behavioral-analytics-psychiatry.html.
33. Joab Jackson, "Cognitive Computing Could Improve the Ability to Spot Melanoma Early On," *Computerworld.com*, December 17, 2014, www.computerworld.com/article/2860758/ibm-detects-skin-cancer-more-quickly-with-visual-machine-learning.html.

CHAPTER 13

Netflix—Entertaining Disruption

N etflix is a global company with over 60 million subscribers as of March, 2015. It is primarily in the business of distributing feature-length motion pictures, documentaries, television series, animations, and the like. Netflix originally rented physical DVDs that were ordered online but delivered by mail, then added Blu-ray discs, and then offered video streaming over the Internet. In addition to distribution, it creates content as well, and has been nominated for and won major industry awards for some of its popular series such as *House of Cards* and *Orange Is the New Black*.

Netflix has had a major impact in the markets in which it operates, to put it mildly. In North America, Netflix dominates downstream Internet traffic during prime time; it's now responsible for over a third of that traffic. In Australia, even prior to official availability Netflix accounted for 4 percent of bandwidth utilization.[1]

At the turn of the millennium, VHS and DVD rentals required a trip to the local video store to return existing rentals, look for the titles you wanted, ask if they were perhaps in a different section of the store under a different genre, realize they were out of stock, talk to a store clerk, ask if anyone had recently returned any of them, wait while the clerk flipped through the recent return pile, tell your kids to behave and stop playing with the candy for sale, select different titles, hand over your membership card and pay for the rental, candy, and late fees, and then drive home.

Netflix disrupted that model in four major ways.

First, from its founding in 1997, Netflix introduced physical distribution of DVDs by mail rather than a visit to the video store, eliminating multiple road trips: One or more to see if the title you wanted was in stock and then actually get it, and one to return it. Instead of coming up empty handed since blockbuster titles were in high demand and limited quantity, Netflix customers could experience a moment of delight upon finding the bright red Netflix envelope in their mailbox.

Second, prior to Netflix, high-demand titles such as recent releases generally were available only on overnight rentals at premium prices, which meant the following cycle for many people: Get home from work, make and eat dinner, then race to watch the movie they had rented the night before so that they could get to the store before it closed, to avoid paying an extra day in late fees. Netflix replaced this irritating daily fee structure—where arriving at the store one minute after closing meant you had to pay for an extra day—with a flat-rate subscription enabling you to keep DVDs as long as you wanted. The subscription model supposedly occurred to founder Reed Hastings after he was hit with $40 in late fees.

Third, it replaced the walk up and down the aisles of the local video store with online browsing, and the task of remembering what you and your spouse and your kids wanted to see with a cloud-based wish list, your personal queue. Not only did this queue help you remember what you wanted to see and help Netflix get it to you, it also helped Netflix know how many copies of titles to stock.

Fourth, there was the Netflix movie recommendation engine, which suggested titles to you. The video store clerk might make a valiant try, saying that he or she really liked a particular movie, or that most people did, but Netflix has continuously improved its sophisticated personalized recommendation engine, which turns out to be critical to revenue, profitability, customer retention, and customer lifetime value.

Netflix then acted as a disruptor again, this time to itself. Once home broadband networks became capable of supporting streaming video, Netflix began to offer those services.

The prior leader in home video rental, Blockbuster, which had had all the premier storefront locations and name-brand recognition, eventually attempted to match Netflix's pricing model and online ordering and recommendation service, but never did catch up, and has since ceased retail and DVD-by-mail operations. Fast forward to 2014, and even Verizon, with annual revenue of $125 billion, shuttered its joint effort with RedBox—Redbox Instant—after only 19 months.

What makes Netflix such a deadly competitor? It excels in virtually all of the digital disciplines, although in this chapter we will primarily focus on collective intimacy.

Netflix has a high degree of operational and information excellence, both in website operations, back-end big data analytics, digital transcoding and streaming operations as well as in distributing and managing millions of outgoing and incoming DVDs every day. In fact, it's delivered billions of DVDs and over a billion hours each month of streamed content, and now operates in dozens of countries with plans to continue expanding.

It offers solution leadership in conjunction with partners, since home streaming requires an endpoint device, a quality network connection, cloud-based content delivery, and skill in content creation, acquisition, management, and distribution. For example, viewers can watch Netflix streaming on smart televisions with built-in apps or set-top boxes, tablets, smartphones, game consoles and other special purpose devices such as Microsoft Xboxes, Apple TV units, TiVo digital video recorders, or Roku TVs, streaming sticks, or players—cigarette-pack sized devices that connect to Wi-Fi and a TV.

And, it is a role model of accelerated innovation, using a mix of approaches including cloud-based experimentation and open challenges to improve elements of its business such as its movie recommendation algorithms and its cloud-based entertainment service delivery operations.

Finally, Netflix is a paragon of collective intimacy, using data points on the watching habits and preferences of tens of millions of customers to deliver personalized recommendations to each customer.

Information Excellence

Setting aside some components of Netflix's business, such as producing original content, Netflix has two very different types of operations: a physical distribution business and a virtual online entertainment business. For physical operations, it's critical to balance timely delivery of millions of physical DVD and Blu-ray discs with cost-effective management of their shipping and return through a third party—the US Postal Service—whose operations are *not* within Netflix's control. For Internet-based delivery, service operations are no less critical, and again Netflix ultimately must rely on third parties as well: for example, Internet Service Providers (ISPs) such as cable and telephone companies and colocation companies who host Netflix content delivery appliances. Here as well, cost must be optimized while assuring service availability and end-to-end performance all the way through to the user's display device, across various backbone network providers, cloud providers, colocation facilities, mobile carriers, ISPs, and home Wi-Fi networks.

How does Netflix do it?

Within the cloud community, Netflix is known as a leading-edge company. Under the direction of Netflix's chief cloud architect at that time, Adrian Cockcroft, Netflix embraced the public cloud to run key portions of its business well before many companies had even heard of cloud computing, much less begun exploring its capabilities and potential. As one of the largest customers of Amazon Web Services, it managed to accomplish many things. It proved to large enterprises that the cloud was not just a toy, but could be used for mission-critical applications. It pushed AWS to develop needed services, by identifying gaps through real-world deployments. Netflix, through Adrian and his colleagues, shared many lessons learned, regarding architecture, resilience, scalability, operations, cost control, and management of the cloud.

Accelerated Innovation

Netflix uses a multifaceted approach to accelerate innovation, relying on a mix of internal and external talent. Its employees are the cream of the crop, with policies in place to ensure that their talents are aligned to a continuously evolving business. External talent falls into three main categories. One is close-knit relationships with leading partners, such as Amazon Web Services, to co-create innovative solutions. Another is the use of focused challenges: the Netflix Prize which had the goal of improving its Cinematch recommendation engine, and the Netflix Open Source Software (OSS) Cloud Prize, which had the goal of enhancing its IT operations. A third and more subtle source of external talent derives from Netflix's ability to tap into the talents of individual developers in the open source community. These three categories are not unrelated: the OSS Cloud Prize was given in multiple categories for improvements to open source software, most of which was oriented to the Netflix computing and storage running in Amazon's cloud.

Netflix famously hires the best and the brightest, and frees them to do their best by embodying the principles of empowerment to which many other companies only pay lip service. One of Netflix's most distributed content wasn't a Hollywood movie, but a slideshow explaining its HR practices, which contravene those of virtually every other company on the planet. For example, there are no limits to vacation days. As long as employees get their work done, they can take as much or as little vacation as they would like. Employees who don't seem to fit well aren't just let go, they are given generous severance packages. Rather than a formal travel and expense policy dictating *per diem* meal limits, the entire policy is "Act in Netflix's best interests." There are no formal performance reviews, instead, employees get 360-degree reviews with a simple framework of behaviors to start, stop, or continue.[2]

Netflix has run two major open challenges, which generally fit into the standard contest paradigm described in Chapter 15, but with subtle differences based on the nature of the challenge. For the original Netflix Prize, the objective was to improve the Cinematch movie recommendation algorithm. Because movies were rated on a scale of 1 to 5 stars, an improvement in the recommendation algorithm could be expressed mathematically. For example, if customers rated the average recommended movie, say, a 3.97 under the prior algorithm, an improved algorithm might result in an average rating of, say, 4.23, while a perfect—although probably unattainable—algorithm would result in an average of 5.0. Consequently, the challenge had elements such as publishing an anonymized data set on the Netflix Prize website, and having an exact goal for improvement that was explicit and quantitative. However, the Netflix OSS Cloud Prize was oriented to a variety of software tool improvements. Here, improvements were more subjective, and consequently the determination of winners was performed by a small panel of judges, including myself. However, the cloud played a key role in enabling the contest; open-source submissions were made via a cloud-based repository called GitHub, where contestants could register, acquire rules, and submit their entries.

Netflix has also innovated how viewers watch TV. Traditionally, a series such as a sitcom or drama is released at the rate of one episode each week. Netflix, however, has begun to release all episodes of an original series at once, enabling binge-watching, where a customer can watch a new series, say, in a single evening or weekend.

Solution Leadership

Netflix has a powerful solution portfolio based on numerous partner relationships with content owners and developers such as Dreamworks, Sony, and Disney and device manufacturers such as Microsoft, Nintendo, Apple, and Samsung. It has a broad portfolio of titles, and its total solution includes client software that runs on a variety of devices, such as iPads, iPhones, Android phones and tablets, special-purpose devices, (smart, connected) Blu-ray disc players, and smart (connected) TVs. It pays particular attention to the quality of the network, which is obviously a key component in streaming. The Netflix partner ecosystem has had a handful of outages, and Netflix has used them as learning experiences to improve the robustness of the joint Netflix-partner infrastructure.

In addition to relationships with studios, Netflix has also developed its own content. Here, the relationship between collective intimacy, solution leadership, and information excellence is apparent. For example, *House of Cards* is an Emmy-nominated Netflix original series starring Kevin Spacey and directed and executive produced by David Fincher, which was adapted for primarily US audiences from a successful BBC mini-series. It was picked up by Netflix in large part based on an analysis of Netflix customer data by its chief content officer Ted Sarandos. The rights were acquired *immediately* for a cool $100 million for 26 episodes, whereas competitors wanted to see a pilot before bidding. In other words, knowing Netflix's customers (collective intimacy) helped them create a stronger offering (solution leadership) and accelerated their content acquisition process (information excellence).

Sarandos determined that films with Kevin Spacey in them were popular among Netflix's streaming customers, as were movies directed by David Fincher, as were political thrillers. And the original BBC series, which was available on DVD, was also popular.

To be fair, the decision to acquire and produce the series was not just a data-driven analysis, but also based on Sarandos's and Fincher's industry intuition.[3] For example, although Netflix test audiences reacted negatively to an opening scene Fincher ignored the reaction and went on to win an Emmy for Outstanding Directing for a Drama Series for directing that episode.[4]

From Relationships to Intimacy

Netflix never had a purely transactional business; it had ordering and billing relationships since its founding in 1997, and flat-fee subscription relationships since 1999. There are several unique dimensions to these relationships and the way that they focused on intimacy from the very start.

Netflix profiles enable a single relationship with the company to be multidimensional. For example, even though I am the subscriber of record to Netflix, there is one profile for myself, who enjoys movies such as *The Matrix* and *Inception*, and another one for my young daughter, who prefers *Barbie*, *Monster High*, and *The Powerpuff Girls*. Profiles could also be created for the same individual having different personas. Someone could potentially create one profile to help to learn spoken French and one for weekend entertainment, or one for TV series suitable for watching on an iPad and one for sci-fi/action-adventure only suitable for the home theater system.

For both physical discs and streamed entertainment, Netflix can capture a variety of information on customer preferences: which movies were requested (i.e., added to the queue), which were searched for but not found, which ones were offered but not ordered, which genres are of what level of interest. It can conduct a variety of A/B tests for merchandising and how it impacts customer behavior, for example, featuring new movies or old classics first, or seeing whether different-sized icons drive more viewing.

It is clear how the profiles feature helps users and Netflix alike. I would rather not see recommendations for animated cartoons targeted to elementary-school children, and my daughter would rather not see promotions for cerebral sci-fi. Netflix would rather not have to try to determine why the same person likes both *The Matrix* and *The Powerpuff Girls*, especially when that person may not actually exist.[5] Moreover, additional insights can be garnered, for example, that I am the father of a young daughter, and thus we might both enjoy, say, *The Parent Trap* or *Freaky Friday*.

At some level, mere aggregation of even high-level data is useful. Customers want to know the most popular movies, so that they can rent them as well. But, of course, thousands of such data points for each of millions of customers enable a collective intimacy strategy, as we'll describe later.

From Physical to Virtual

Netflix has made the transition from physical to virtual in multiple areas of its business. It was founded on a concept of moving the physical video store online into a virtual video store. One could peruse selections, order, and pay online, rather than in person.

Perhaps more importantly, Netflix CEO and co-founder Reed Hastings knew well before most what the long-term implications would be of the evolution of the Internet. While by 1997 some were aware of the potential of the Internet for ecommerce and thus for online *ordering*, Hastings had foreseen the day when the Internet would be suitable for online *delivery*, which arrived 10 years later when Netflix announced streaming plans, originally for personal computers, and then for an increasing set of partners and devices.

This was part of a long-term strategic plan: As Netflix CEO Reed Hastings quipped in 2005 before video streaming was introduced: "We want to be ready when video-on-demand happens. That's why the company is called Netflix, not DVD-by-Mail."[6]

Moving from physical to virtual ordering has a number of benefits in terms of process improvement and a reduction in assets, such as retail stores and their video clerks. But from a customer intimacy perspective, there are additional benefits. Without dedicated store clerks to write down and tally every customer request, it would have been a challenge to determine the titles that were of interest, yet not found. All of this is easy, of course, over the web, as customers click on video icons or search for unavailable titles.

Moving from physical to virtual delivery has intimacy benefits as well. For the physical DVD business, Netflix has insights into which movies the customer has rented, which ones have been rented multiple times, and for how long they were rented, not unlike a physical store, assuming it implemented data collection systems. Moreover, customers fill out ratings for movies on a scale from 1 to 5, and can rate movies whether or not they were rented from Netflix, which a physical store could also implement.

But for the streaming (virtual) business, the data are even more granular. If a customer rents a DVD and keeps it for a week, there is no way for Netflix to know whether it was ever watched, or if it was, how many times, or which scenes were skipped over or rewatched. But in streaming, Netflix can know everything: the type of device upon which the movie was played, the time of day that it was watched, the geographic region, pauses, the length of the pause, rewinds, fast forwards, and so on. The data collected through streaming is literally thousands of times as great as that collected through rentals.[7]

In other words, moving from physical to virtual dramatically enhances the depth of customer intimacy.

From Virtual to Digical

Netflix is an exemplar of the importance of integrating physical and virtual channels. Although the company originally started as a primarily physical company, with online ordering of physically delivered DVDs, the company was early in offering multichannel integration. A subscriber could receive DVDs by mail, up a simultaneous limit of say, three or four or more based on the level of the account. Most plans allowed unlimited streaming to up to five devices in the home, a device limit in theory due to Netflix's terms and conditions, but in practice probably more due to the quality and bandwidth of a user's Internet connection.

Throughout the book, we've talked about the benefits of digital-physical fusion. Netflix offers not only this, but a cautionary tale for undoing this fusion. On September 18, 2011, Netflix announced that it would split into two companies. One, retaining the Netflix name, would focus on virtual streaming, the other, to be called Qwikster, would offer physical DVD distribution. Three weeks later, Netflix pressed the rewind button and called off the split.

Netflix's original decision was based on the realization that the physical DVD portion of the business was declining as familiarity with streaming services grew, network infrastructure improved, and a variety of devices that could receive streamed content from Netflix, such as Roku and TiVo boxes and smart TVs, became widely available at attractive price points. Netflix's leadership had conducted a strategy review as many companies do, the outcome of which is often to focus on growth businesses and jettison declining ones.

However, there were a number of issues with the planned split. Customers were used to the convenience of a single provider, account, and price for both physical and online services. The Qwikster plan required them to open a new account, pay a higher total price, and have two separate bills to pay. As Hastings commented, "We learned an important lesson: The fact that your company may not be strategically positioned for the next 10 years, [customers] don't care about that."[8]

In other words, having integrated digital-physical operations was important for customer relationships, and trumped financial models of future revenue flows.

Moreover, from an intimacy perspective, Netflix can better meet its customers' needs with deeper insight into entertainment behaviors by integrating all data across both types of channels.

From Company to Community

Reviews are an inherent part of the Netflix service. While customers can simply rate movies on a scale of one star to five, they can also write detailed reviews, and mark reviews from others as helpful, not helpful, or inappropriate. This accomplishes multiple things at once. First, it increases the value of the Netflix service, since one can read reviews and get a sense of whether a particular movie sounds worth watching or would be better to avoid. Second, it provides psychosocial benefits to the reviewers which we'll address further in Chapter 18. They can feel good about making a contribution, and they can stroke their sense of fairness by ranting or praising with abandon, they can stroke their social needs by belonging to a community and by gaining status.

There are also benefits for Netflix. Individuals who generate reviews increase the depth of the bonds they have with Netflix, both psychologically and practically. Someone who generates one or many reviews will feel more invested in the relationship with Netflix. Moreover, it is challenging to move one's reviews to a competing service, creating more stickiness.

It should be noted that there are two kinds of communities at work. The first is the community of Netflix reviewers, and by extension the community of Netflix members who read reviews. The second is the community centered around a member, such as Facebook friends. Netflix customers can opt to connect their Netflix account to their Facebook account, and then viewing history can be shared between friends, and friends can recommend movies to each other.

This enhances the degree of intimacy as well. Knowing what your friends like, what they recommend to you, or conversely, what you liked so much that you went to the effort to recommend it to them, and what was actually watched, provides additional insight into members' preferences.

From People to Algorithms

People are still important at Netflix. Netflix has dozens of freelancers following a 36-page process guide to review content—movies, animated features, TV shows, Netflix original productions, documentaries—in combination with other sources, to generate a variety of data for each piece of content: when it was produced, who it was directed by, who acts in it, where it is set, whether it's a drama or a comedy, and so forth.

Beyond factual data, the taggers provide a wealth of about a thousand micro-tags—such as "quirky," "cerebral," "childish," "surly,"—intended to exactly position each work on a multidimensional scale.[9] These evaluations address not just, say, whether it has a happy ending or not, but on a scale from 1 (sad) to 5 (very happy), *exactly* where does it fall? How romantic is the movie? How morally acceptable is the protagonist?[10]

Then there are additional subtleties: some directors—such as Quentin Tarantino or Tony Scott—largely stay true to a style, others experiment.[11]

Another source of data comes from users: What did they search for, what did they play, what did they pause, what did they never return to? One advantage of such analysis is that it is effortless: Users don't need to spend any time rating movies or writing reviews unless they choose to.

Behavioral data tend to be more important than user ratings. The reason is that what users say or claim or believe is not necessarily true. A user might rate an esoteric foreign film very high, but actually prefer watching *Dumb and Dumber*. Many people claim to enjoy foreign films and documentaries, but actual viewing behavior proves otherwise. Moreover, viewing behavior tends to change due to many contextual factors: the kind of movie watched on the family TV during prime time at home on a weeknight might not be the same as the type of movie watched on a mobile device on a Saturday night while on vacation.[12]

A lot of data comes from Netflix freelance taggers. Even more data comes from Netflix customers, through their ratings, their reviews, and their viewing behavior. But, of course, it is algorithms, designed largely by Netflix engineers and data scientists, that process all of that data to generate not just recommendations, but a customer-intimate user ordering and queuing experience.

These algorithms have names such as singular value decomposition, latent Dirichlet allocation, gradient boosted decision trees, and affinity propagation. The recommendation/personalization engine uses these algorithms, but runs on fuel which is data: billions of ratings, movie popularity, millions of queue additions every day, millions of search terms every day, user interactions with the menu of movie options, preferences and activities of friends, user information such as age, gender, location, and language, and data generated outside of Netflix, such as box office receipts and reviews.[13]

As mentioned earlier, over-reliance on algorithms can produce unexpected results, especially when, as MIT's Kevin Slavin says, there is no adult supervision. To help alleviate this, Netflix provides transparency into the results of these calculations through means such as "Because you watched ... " This builds trust in the system, further enhancing customer retention.

As sophisticated as these algorithms already are, there are still opportunities to make them even better by including even more data. After all, a movie is not a monolithic entity, but is perhaps one of the most complex of all human artifacts, and moreover is designed to create a complex, changing panoply of emotional responses such as joy, anger, sadness, romance, laughter through the interplay of elements including a plot, scenes, characters and their arcs, cinematography and soundtrack. Each of these breaks down further: The soundtrack includes volume, genre, intensity, danceability. Netflix could potentially use data like this to generate even better recommendations.[14]

From Individual to Collective

The importance of recommendations to Netflix and its customers is a bit different from that for Amazon.com or eBay. In eBay's case, the vast majority of items sold are discovered through search. For Amazon.com, recommendations have an upsell benefit: "People who bought this also bought this." For Netflix, though, better recommendations don't generally lead to an upsell, since pricing plans offer unlimited streaming. However, better recommendations lead to higher customer satisfaction which leads to better customer retention and advocacy which leads to higher customer lifetime value and reduced acquisition cost, such as the cost of advertising, sign-up logistics, and free trials. For Netflix, 75 percent of what people watch is based on recommendations, so getting the recommendation engine tuned for the highest possible performance is a critical strategic imperative. It's so important that Netflix has nearly a thousand engineers working on it.[15]

Based on billions, if not trillions, of data points, the integrated insights generated by the advanced algorithms enable a high degree of collective intimacy. Each customer is given a highly personalized set of recommendations, set into a two-dimensional matrix filling the screen of—and scrolling beyond—the personal computer, smart TV, smartphone, or what have you, sorted into a highly personalized set of *micro-genres*, which Netflix calls *altgenres*. Examples might include "critically acclaimed cerebral independent movies," "inspiring children and family movies," or "feel-good romantic movies." Listing them all would be a challenge, because it's been calculated that there are 76,897 altgenres as of January 2, 2014.[16]

But as it turns out, this degree of micro-slicing and personalizing movie preferences creates a strong bond with Netflix customers. Customers tend to view movies more when they are placed on rows higher up on the page, and when they are further left on the row—that is, those that appear first without scrolling when multiple rows of micro-genres with multiple movies appear on the display of recommended movies.[17]

Ultimately, it boils down to business. Collective intimacy through tagging, behavioral analysis, micro-genres, and recommendations means that customers "consume more hours of video and stick with the service longer," according to Todd Yellin, the Netflix vice president of product innovation who devised and manages the approach.[18]

One challenge unique to Netflix is that a customer is not always an individual but is often a household, made up of individuals with differing tastes: Mom, Dad, Grammy, and each kid. Consequently, recommendations are often not just optimized for individual targets, but for diversity.[19] Profiles can help ameliorate this challenge, but are not mandated nor universally used across all households. In fact, even when the household is a single individual, that person may have different moods and interests, so the diversity strategy is effective. Intimacy is not just about fulfilling current customer needs, but also about anticipating future ones, and creating moments of surprise and delight.

A simple metric like overall popularity is useful. After all, most people will probably enjoy what most people enjoy. However, Netflix crisply observes that popularity is the exact reverse of personalization, because overall popularity is the same for each member, whereas personalization should be different for each member.[20] Therefore, Netflix has to balance conflicting criteria such as households versus individuals, popularity versus personalization, meeting expectations and generating moments of delight.

The Netflix collective intimacy strategy directly benefits the bottom line. According to Netflix, members resonate so well with the personalization that drives the selection of rows, the selection of titles in the rows, and the ordering of rows and titles within each row, that they can directly measure an increase in member retention.[21]

■ ■ ■

Netflix has successfully attained market leadership through a combination of a transformational business model—subscription-based physical disc rentals and streaming—and the digital disciplines. Perhaps most critical to its success is the high level of customer satisfaction and retention due to collective intimacy via its advanced recommendation engine, which manages to achieve a finely tuned balance of popularity, user behavior, diversity, novelty, personalization, contextualization, surprise, and delight.

In a statement reminiscent of Steve Jobs's comment that "people don't know what they want until you show it to them,"[22] John Landgraf, president and general manager of FX networks, said, "Data can only tell you what people have liked before, not what they don't know they are going to like in the future."[23] This may occasionally be true, but Netflix has produced a blockbuster hit by applying digital technologies to foster collective intimacy.

Notes

1. "Global Internet Phenomena Report 1H2014," *Sandvine*, 5, https://www.sand vine.com/downloads/general/global-internet-phenomena/2014/1h-2014-global-internet-phenomena-report.pdf.
2. Patty McCord, "How Netflix Reinvented HR," *Harvard Business Review*, January 2014, https://hbr.org/2014/01/how-netflix-reinvented-hr.
3. Brian Stelter, "A Drama's Streaming Premiere," *New York Times*, January 18, 2013, www.nytimes.com/2013/01/20/arts/television/house-of-cards-arrives-as-a-netflix-series.html.
4. David Bloom, "Reed Hastings: Netflix 'Mispredicted' Its Transition to Streaming Service," *Deadline.com*, May 29, 2014, deadline.com/2014/05/reed-hastings-netflix-mispredicted-its-online-transition-737536/.
5. Actually, I do watch *The Powerpuff Girls* with my daughter.
6. Reed Hastings, "How I Did It: Reed Hastings, Netflix," *Inc.*, December 1, 2005, www.inc.com/magazine/20051201/qa-hastings.html.
7. Xavier Amatriain, "Big & Personal: Data and Models behind Netflix Recommendations." In *Proceedings of the 2nd International Workshop on Big Data, Streams and Heterogeneous Source Mining: Algorithms, Systems, Programming Models and Applications* (New York: ACM, 2013), 1–6, xavier.amatriain.net/pubs/BigAndPersonal.pdf.
8. Bloom, "Reed Hastings."
9. Ben Fritz, "Cadre of Film Buffs Helps Netflix Viewers Sort through the Clutter," *Los Angeles Times*, September 3, 2012, articles.latimes.com/2012/sep/03/business/la-fi-0903-ct-netflix-taggers-20120903.
10. Alexis C. Madrigal, "How Netflix Reverse Engineered Hollywood," *The Atlantic*, January 2, 2014, www.theatlantic.com/technology/archive/2014/01/how-netflix-reverse-engineered-hollywood/282679/.
11. Tom Vanderbilt, "The Science Behind the Netflix Algorithms That Decide What You'll Watch Next," *Wired.com*, August 7, 2013, www.wired.com/2013/08/qq_netflix-algorithm/.
12. Ibid.
13. Amatriain, "Big & Personal."
14. Derrick Harris, "Netflix Analyzes *a Lot* of Data about Your Viewing Habits," *Gigaom.com*, June 14, 2012, https://gigaom.com/2012/06/14/netflix-analyzes-a-lot-of-data-about-your-viewing-habits/.
15. Vanderbilt, "The Science Behind."
16. Madrigal, "How Netflix Reverse Engineered Hollywood."
17. Vanderbilt, "The Science Behind."
18. Fritz, "Cadre of Film Buffs."

19. Xavier Amatriain and Justin Basilico, "Netflix Recommendations: Beyond the 5 Stars (Part 1)," *The Netflix Tech Blog*, April 6, 2012, techblog.netflix.com/2012/04/netflix-recommendations-beyond-5-stars.html.

20. Ibid.

21. Ibid.

22. Owen Linzmayer, "Steve Jobs' Best Quotes Ever," *Wired.com*, March 29, 2006, archive.wired.com/gadgets/mac/commentary/cultofmac/2006/03/70512.

23. David Carr, "Giving Viewers What They Want," *New York Times*, February 25, 2013, www.nytimes.com/2013/02/25/business/media/for-house-of-cards-using-big-data-to-guarantee-its-popularity.html.

PART FIVE

Accelerated Innovation

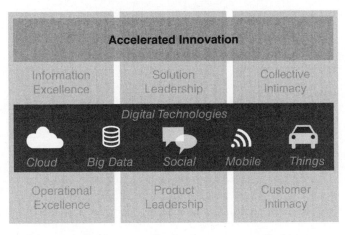

CHAPTER 14

Innovation and Transformation

There is perhaps no topic that perpetually engages leadership as much as innovation. It holds out the promise of renewal, reinvention, and success, yet remains challenging because of complex, nondeterministic relationships between technology, the innovation process, customer behavior, competition, and profitability.

Consultant and author Geoffrey Moore says that since virtually all products and services commoditize over time, failure to innovate equates to a failure to differentiate, and without differentiation, profits deteriorate.[1] As cogent as that argument seems, innovation per se does not equate to profitability. In a study by professor Michael Porter of the Harvard Business School covering 15 years, two industries tied for a close second place for profitability, measured by return on invested capital (ROIC). One was software, which one might reasonably argue is highly innovative. However, the other industry was soft drinks, yet the formulas for the leading soft drinks are a century old, as are key elements of their business model such as outsourcing raw materials production and finished product distribution.[2] There surely has been innovation in the beverage industry, such as incorporating açaí or goji berries, creative packaging and advertising, in-home production such as via Sodastream, and Louis XIV energy drinks, which are made "with real 24-carat gold flakes!"[3] However, the modern formula for Coca-Cola—the one without cocaine—does date back to 1903. For comparison, this is the year that Ford introduced the Model A and the Wright brothers took their first flight, two industries where the "classic" version is notably different from the modern one.

Profitability, then, is not just a function of innovation, but also the impact of Porter's five forces and financial engineering such as moving to an asset-light strategy, where assets are held by suppliers, partners, or distributors.

Another challenge is that great innovations—such as Teflon, X-rays, and microwave ovens—sometimes arrive unexpectedly. This is hardly the kind of process that any CxO would want to count on when projecting earnings. As a result of this unpredictability, a single successful innovation is newsworthy, and a successful track record a seeming impossibility. George Eastman and Kodak invented or licensed most of the key technologies in roll film and then film cartridges, enabling movies and democratizing photography. However, the Kodak electrical engineer who invented digital photography in the 1970s was told by his film-focused management, "That's cute, but don't tell anyone about it."[4] At that time, Kodak held a 90 percent share of U.S. film sales. In January 2012, it filed for Chapter 11.

Clayton Christensen, a professor at the Harvard Business School, describes situations such as these as "The Innovator's Dilemma." He claims that established companies are not usually lacking in vision regarding trends, but are typically unwilling to disrupt their own profitable businesses. Instead they focus on "sustaining"—that is, incremental—innovations and fight for share with existing competitors. As a result, they are at risk from attack by "low-end disruptors" with fewer features but also less costly offers, or new entrants who "compete" against "non-consumption," that is, seduce consumers who don't use the product or "compete" against occasions when the product isn't used.[5]

Gerard Tellis, a professor at USC, argues that is isn't just cold spreadsheets with profit calculations that prevent established firms from cannibalizing their own businesses, but "the incumbent's curse." Winners often exhibit complacency, hubris, and risk aversion: everything seems to be doing just fine, success is proof of brilliance, not luck; and innovations may or may not pay off, and even if they do, that payoff is far in the future.[6]

Perhaps for these reasons, Kodak and Polaroid failed to picture the impact that digital photography would have and Blackberry (formerly Research in Motion) didn't get the message that keyboards, even if they *were* more usable, weren't a match for cool touchscreens and open, app-based extensibility. Technology isn't always the key to innovation and disruption—"fast casual" restaurants such as Chipotle and Shake Shack are focused on healthier, made-to-order foods; Costco, now the second-largest retailer in the world, began life partly as Price Club, which innovated the retail warehouse club.

Even if it were possible to schedule major disruptive innovations, on, say, a quarterly basis, and furthermore have the wherewithal to disrupt one's existing businesses, the market and customers may become the challenge.

Geoffrey Moore extended Everett Rogers's theory of the *diffusion of innovations*, dividing adopters of disruptive technologies into five groups: (1) *innovators*, who are technology enthusiasts (who aren't the actual innovators of the technology but the first to use it), (2) *early adopters*, who are visionaries, (3) the *early majority*, who are pragmatists, (4) the *late majority*, who are conservatives, and (5) *laggards*, who are skeptics.[7,8] Moore's premise is that for discontinuous innovations, there is a challenge in "crossing the chasm" between marketing to visionaries versus pragmatists. Visionaries are contrarian, willing to take risks, and view innovations through the lens of how they might pay off in the future; the pragmatists are the exact reverse.[9] Successfully crossing the chasm can require changes in product positioning, channels, and complementary services. For example, a visionary might accept—or even prefer—working collaboratively in a lab setting to define and refine a product; a pragmatic wants 24-hour support services.

Given the myriad challenges with mastering innovation, rather than being subject to its whims, it is perhaps no surprise that the average lifetime of an S&P 500 corporation, measured as the time between incorporation and either liquidation or acquisition, has steadily dropped from 100 years not that long ago to less than 10 years now.[10] Worse yet, data show that mere survival does not equate to performance: Extensive studies by prestigious management consulting firm McKinsey & Company show that corporations underperform markets because corporations are designed for continuity, whereas markets are designed for discontinuity, in the never-ending battle for the survival of the fittest.[11]

Not only is the lifetime of the typical company decreasing, but the degree of turbulence during its increasingly brief tenure is increasing. Turbulence can be measured by looking at year-over-year or quarter-over-quarter changes in market position. Andrew McAfee, then at Harvard, and Erik Brynjolfsson of MIT determined[12] that not only has turbulence been increasing, but that turbulence is notably higher in high-IT industries—those where IT is an important component of operating expenditures and capital assets. This contagion is spreading, as more verticals become impacted by IT.

In other words, whether they like it or not, today's companies are caught in a cyclone of competitive chaos. IT is a double-edged sword: On the one hand, it enables great flexibility and thus if wielded properly can accelerate competitive advantage or response; on the other hand, competitors have access to the same sword, escalating the bloodiness of the battle.

In such a world, victory belongs not to the contestant with the best battle plan, but with the greatest ability to rapidly improve and adapt, in other words, the one best able to innovate.

Successful Commercial Innovation

Innovation is often used synonymously with *invention*, but is a much broader concept. There are numerous definitions of innovation; but I view successful commercial innovation as having three major components: *invention, commercialization* by the firm, and *adoption* by customers. Each of these phases has what might be considered concept and implementation elements.

Invention of a new product, process, production or operations resource, relationship strategy, or marketing or sales approach consists of *ideation*—the conception of the novel idea—and *reduction to practice*—for example, by building a working prototype. It can be driven by attempting to meet a known customer need, such as a cure for cancer; an unexpressed, previously unidentified or latent need, such as for a portable music player and online music store selling single songs; identifying a problem or opportunity with current practices, such as data center energy use and thus a need for sustainability; exploiting a scientific or technical anomaly or breakthrough, such as the glue in Post-it notes or the use of lasers for printing, surgery, and golf-ball range finding; or addressing social, legal, cultural, or value shifts, such as organically grown food due to environmental and health concerns or data privacy and sovereignty.

Reduction to practice is an important part of invention. Incandescent lighting had existed for decades as a concept, but required the discovery of a practicable filament material and a better vacuum. The principles of heavier-than-air flight had been conceived by 1800, but it wasn't until 1903 that they were realized. The transistor—a solid-state equivalent to the triode vacuum tube—was conceived in 1925, but it wasn't until 1947 that semiconductor materials of sufficient quality were available to reduce the idea to a practical invention. Another electronic component, the memristor, was theorized in 1971, but wasn't reduced to practice until 2008. The first ereader, and arguably, prototype of the World Wide Web, was the memex, conceptualized by Vannevar Bush in 1945, but the Web didn't arrive until 1989 and the Amazon Kindle until 2007. Reduction to practice may need to address efficient algorithms, viable materials, cost-effectiveness, reliability, scale, size, or a viable manufacturing process, as examples.

Commercialization is the process by which the firm takes the invention and builds a business or grows an existing business from it. This requires *business model generation*—the concept, mechanism, business plan, and/or pricing model by which the firm will make money—and successful *execution* of that concept at scale. This in turn may require capital, new process technologies, licensing, and so on.

As reviewed in Chapter 2, Alexander Osterwalder and Yves Pigneur say that there are nine elements to any business model: activities, partners, resources, value proposition, customer relationships, customer segments, and the channels to reach them, coupled with decisions on cost structure and revenue streams.[13] Some strategists such as Osterwalter and Pigneur incorporate the customer value proposition into the business model, but it would seem to make sense to separate how the firm benefits from how the customer benefits. For this reason, author Michael Lewis defines a business model as "how you plan to make money."[14] Others, such as Mark W. Johnson, chairman of Innosight, would call this more limited perspective the "profit formula."[15] A serious business model also needs to characterize the practical realities of the business. One for a grocery store can't just be "buy food and sell it at 20 percent higher," but needs to account for store siting and construction expenditures, spoilage, shrinkage, labor costs, weather-related closings, and so on.

There are numerous business models and within them, pricing models, such as advertiser-supported free-to-use services and the razor-and-razor-blades model, where razors are cheap but blades are profitable, notably found with home printers and ink cartridges. Business models are more expansive than pricing. For example, Netflix's business model includes creating original content, but its pricing model is flat-rate subscription.

Successful execution can require excellence in product or service design and engineering, including user experience; new process technologies for manufacturing or operations (e.g., nuclear power plant control systems); new architectures or technologies to achieve scale, such as deep-tank fermentation for penicillin; and access to capital and markets. Execution is often where things go awry. Inability to scale can invalidate an otherwise terrific business model and invention. Elon Musk, the serial entrepreneur behind PayPal and Tesla, quit his first job at an energy storage company because their technology used ruthenium tantalum oxide, of which only a ton or two was annually mined worldwide.[16] On the other hand, Pets.com successfully executed core operations such as branding, ecommerce, and distribution, but without a profitable business model—it sold below cost.

Adoption by customers—and channels or ecosystem partners—is the final essential element. It requires a *value proposition*—the promised benefit to the customer—and the *realization* of that value proposition—through purchase, deployment, configuration, use, and experiencing benefits from the innovation. A compelling value proposition alone does not guarantee realization, because competitors or substitutes may offer a better value proposition, customers can't acquire every single product and service in the world that offers a value proposition, and existing habits may be hard to break and new ones hard to make. Value realization requires affordability; a fit between the brand and its customers or the power to drive a shift in values, style, and habits; clearly communicated and understood benefits; a trigger to drive to a first purchase decision or trial; the actual experience of the abstract promise of the value proposition, so as to incent repeated use and word of mouth; the ability to motivate users to change age-old habits and overcome inertia; and the ability to reach a "tipping point" or "cross the chasm" from early adopters to mass market by supporting diffusion, actual benefits to real users, network effects, "mavens" that facilitate network effects, and change processes. Adoption can also require the engagement of channels and influencers: to get customers to adopt fluoride toothpastes, P&G invested in repositioning dentists away from filling cavities to managing patients' dental health.

Some companies have achieved excellent customer adoption of their innovations, then realized the importance of a business model. Pets.com has already been mentioned as a failure, but Google is a particularly interesting example of a success. Its founders, Larry Page and Sergey Brin, invented the PageRank algorithm, which offered a great value proposition; it returned more relevant search results and was free to use.[17] However, Google initially had no business model and was "bleeding cash" thanks to the operations required to support exponentially accelerating adoption. Google eventually "borrowed" the pay-per-click paid search advertising business model from Bill Gross's GoTo.com, and now has a market cap of well over a third of a trillion dollars.[18]

It's easy to think of the business model and value proposition as being antagonistic: The net gain to the firm is inversely related to the net value received by the customer. An extra dollar in the customer's pocket is one lost to the firm. But in reality, an innovative business model can help drive adoption and thus both the realization of the value proposition and successful execution, creating a win-win. The Xerox 914 copier was the first plain-paper copier, offering a compelling value proposition relative to the wet chemical processes used prior to its introduction. However, it was a radically different, unfamiliar technology from an unknown company, and too expensive to purchase. In 1959, Xerox introduced the then-radical business model innovation of leasing the machines, including up to 2,000 copies per month in a flat rate. It allowed the customer to cancel the lease on short notice, and bundled in service and support. The copier and its business model were a huge success, creating a global conglomerate out of a company that otherwise would have had a terrific invention with no commercial possibilities.

Another good example of how business model innovation can enable adoption is the Vestergaard LifeStraw. It is basically an oversized straw that can be used to drink contaminated water. Dirty water—filled with bacteria, protozoa, and other contaminants—goes in one end, and a hollow-fiber membrane lets only purified water pass through, helping prevent water-borne illnesses that kill well over a million people annually. While there were no doubt thorny problems in designing and manufacturing the product, a bigger problem was getting customers to pay for it: The largest target market segment is the almost a billion people who don't have access to clean water, but these are the same people who don't have much disposable income. The solution entailed business model innovation. Carbon credits were used to eliminate the cost, since a customer using a LifeStraw doesn't need to burn wood or oil to purify water by boiling it.[19]

The invention can precede the value proposition, as with 3M's Post-its, or the value proposition can precede the invention, when problems or opportunities are identified before they are solved.

It's also easy to miss what made an innovation commercially successful. It wasn't the invention of the automobile or the internal combustion engine that disrupted the preexisting equine transportation market, but the introduction of the Model T. It was the first affordable car (the value proposition) thanks to successfully executed mass production.

There are many businesses that are successful without innovation: Most corner pizzerias do just fine without any breakthroughs. There are also literally millions of inventions that have gone nowhere, as the patent and trademark office can attest. The innovativeness in innovation can arise in the invention, as with the color TV, commercialization, as with an innovative business model, or adoption, as when Post-it notes began to garner interest after free samples were distributed.

Daniel Berns, an author and distinguished professor of neuroeconomics at Emory University, argues that different cognitive and emotional skills are required for different elements. For example, invention requires one to perceive the world differently and then think differently, including being fearless about contradicting established paradigms, whereas successful development of commercial partnerships and fostering adoption require social skills and emotional intelligence.[20]

Berns argues that innovators must have the ability to sell their ideas. Steve Jobs was an obvious master of this skill, with his famous "one more thing." At the other extreme, there is Edwin Howard Armstrong, who invented FM radio as we know it today. However, Berns claims that his inability to sell others on his idea meant that he was not a successful innovator, losing a complex battle of spectrum allocation, patent infringement, and other battles to David Sarnoff and RCA, as well as others. Consequently, it isn't only the ability to interact collaboratively with others during invention that enables successful innovation, but also the ability to influence others during commercialization and adoption.[21]

Various enablers or drivers may be important in different phases and for different markets: inspiration or perspiration; skills, knowledge or creativity; cognitive or emotional skills; being a knowledgeable insider or an outsider unconstrained by existing paradigms; solitude or diverse collaboration; transparency or secrecy; funding or hunger; leadership or empowerment; autocracy or democracy; structure or agility; governance or freedom.

The Innovation Process

Most companies would love to formalize the elements of innovation—invention, commercialization, and adoption—into a repeatable process or "innovation factory." The challenge is that innovation lies somewhere between the extremes of pure serendipity and structured process.

As one example of serendipity, consider the discovery of penicillin. Alexander Fleming noticed that the growth of bacteria in a Petri dish was inhibited by a blue-green mold that had accidentally contaminated the dish. X-rays and radioactivity were each separately discovered due to unexplained fogging of photographic plates. The heating possibilities of microwaves were discovered when a candy bar melted in the pocket of an engineer working on a radar system. Each of these accidents led to multibillion-dollar industries that have had a major impact on our world.

Cyanoacrylates—for example, Super Glue—and solvent-dispersible, solvent-insoluble, elastomeric copolymer microspheres[22]—the essential ingredient in Post-its—were also discovered by accident. Cyanoacrylates were an irritatingly sticky result of experiments that weren't even looking for a glue; the Post-it "low tack" adhesive was a failure to find a strong adhesive. In such cases, rather than ceasing efforts in dismay over what *wasn't* found, the inventor doggedly pursued potential in what *was* found.

On the other hand, Thomas Alva Edison famously said that genius is 1 percent inspiration, and 99 percent perspiration. His invention of the carbon-filament incandescent light bulb was owed to structured, repeated, experiments on numerous possible filament materials, including sewing thread, paper, and ultimately, a species of Japanese bamboo, as well as the realization that the vacuum in the bulb needed to be stronger to prolong filament life.

Rapid experimentation applies not just to invention but also to other elements of innovation, such as business model generation. The "lean startup" movement argues for rapid experimentation, using the customer or early adopters to pivot quickly to new products and business models. Of course, serendipity plays a role here, as well; there is no guarantee that a viable product or business model will arise.

Thorough experimentation and structured processes can only go so far. As 3M CEO George Buckley said after his predecessor had spent several years trying to deploy Six Sigma techniques in 3M's innovation process, with poor results, "Invention is by its very nature a disorderly process. You can't put a Six Sigma process into that area and say, well, I'm getting behind on invention, so I'm going to schedule myself for three good ideas on Wednesday and two on Friday. That's not how creativity works."[23]

The dilemma for leaders, of course, is that one can't just hope that an employee stumbles upon the equivalent of the right blue-green mold or bamboo filament. Even if great ideas can't be scheduled for noon on Fridays, there must be some way to improve the odds.

Innovation leaders such as Procter & Gamble—highlighted in Chapter 16—which implemented an "Innovation Factory," and design firm IDEO have implemented structured approaches, organizations, and culture.

IDEO is the firm that designed iconic products such as the Apple mouse and the Palm PDA, and has since moved on to (re-)design products, services, and experiences associated with everything from mattresses to mammography, for companies ranging from North Face to Steelcase.

According to Tim Brown, CEO of IDEO, its approach to innovation can be described as "design thinking…a discipline that uses the designer's sensibility and methods to match people's needs with what is technologically feasible and what a viable business strategy can convert into customer value and market opportunity."[24]

In other words, invention, commercialization, and adoption.

Brown argues that design has evolved from merely being an aesthetic wrapper put on products at a late stage in their development process to instead become an upfront, critical, and end-to-end consideration.

Tom Kelley, general manager of IDEO and brother of founder David Kelley, says that IDEO's innovation process has five main steps: (1) *understanding* the market, customer needs, and constraints; (2) keenly *observing* the people who are customers and users of the product or service in action; (3) *visualizing* new concepts, including inventing them but also prototyping them; (4) *evaluating* and *refining* these concepts; and finally, (5) *implementing* them (i.e., commercializing the innovations), normally in conjunction with the client firm.[25] It should be noted that the IDEO approach drives invention by clarifying a value proposition, based on identifying a problem or opportunity to be solved. This is more in line with a consultative design firm, than, say, a research lab focused on pure science.

This approach has led IDEO to create solutions for hundreds of client product, service, and marketing challenges in dozens of verticals. To innovate these solutions, Brown says that design thinkers need empathy for client constraints and customer needs and wants, integrative thinking that can tolerate ambiguity and simultaneously comprehend multiple aspects of the problem, optimism that a better solution can and will be found, a willingness to experiment, and the ability to collaborate on a multidisciplinary basis.[26]

Innovation Principles

Other companies besides IDEO have principles, rules, or guidelines for innovation. Google, for example, follows nine innovation principles: "innovation comes from anywhere," "focus on the user," "aim to be 10 times better," "bet on technical insights," "ship and iterate," "give employees 20 percent time," "default to open processes," "fail well," and "have a mission that matters."[27]

Still other companies have other approaches, but the common themes across many innovative companies include: work on important problems, observe closely, think differently, be willing to fail, integrate perspectives, and lead and foster teamwork.

Work on Important Problems. An improvement of even 1 percent can be worth billions of dollars in a large enough problem domain, such as healthcare or transportation. Such improvements are possible through digital technologies—for example, better scheduling and routing algorithms—as well as approaches that have little to do with IT—such as stronger, lighter materials like carbon-fiber composites, used in everything from athletic shoes to airframes.

However, often, much larger gains are possible. The companies that have made such radical, transformational, disruptive impacts tend to use similar approaches: they pick important problems, ask the right questions, and set audacious goals with deadlines.

Radical gains are obviously most beneficial for important problems, those that solve important needs of specific customers, meaningful markets, or society. Examples of the largest problems include desalination, safe cities, malaria prevention, a cure for cancer, driverless cars, electrical energy storage, and cost-effective space flight, but every customer or industry has its own important needs.

To make transformational gains, it's important to ask the right questions. Michael Dell dramatically transformed the manufacturing and distribution of PCs by disassembling computers and asking why "$600 worth of parts were sold for $3,000."[28]

Setting a lofty goal drives bigger improvements than an easily achievable goal does. Designing a car for 1 mile per gallon better performance leads to tinkering with carburetor designs; making it get 100 miles per gallon better performance leads to a hybrid or all-electric.

John F. Kennedy didn't suggest trying to launch an astronaut into orbit *someday*, but committed publicly to landing a person on the moon before the decade was out. He fully recognized that this feat would require things like "new metal alloys, some of which have not yet been invented, capable of standing heat and stresses several times more than have ever been experienced, fitted together with a precision better than the finest watch."[29]

The Google[x] skunkworks asks, "How can we make things not just a little better, but a lot better for a lot of people."[30] The "x" is both a placeholder to avoid pigeonholing the mission of the labs, and the Roman numeral 10, which signifies a tenfold improvement in existing technologies to create disruptive futures: driverless cars, artificial intelligence, augmented reality glasses, and so forth. In keeping with the Kennedy tradition, these projects are called moonshots, and are dedicated to the "idea that incremental improvements are not good enough. The standard for success is whether [Google] can get these into the world and do audacious things."[31]

Observe Closely, Think Differently. Scott Cook, the founder of Intuit, after watching his wife having difficulty managing personal finances, realized that easy-to-use software—Quicken—that would exploit the then-emerging usability of graphical user interfaces could offer important benefits.[32]

According to the Boston Consulting Group, companies considered strong innovators use inputs from key customers 73 percent of the time, almost twice the level at which companies not known for innovation do.[33] For example, leadership at one company believed their customers preferred to fax in their orders rather than use more modern approaches such as, say, email or automated replenishment, because customer feedback to sales personnel did not reach executives.[34]

Professor Berns uses the example of glassmaker Dale Chihuly, who broke with the convention of highly symmetrical blown glass—but only after a horrific car accident where he lost an eye. Of course, perceiving differently doesn't have to be limited to the physical act of perception, but how we interpret the data we amass, which is often based on what psychologists call *framing* (i.e., the context in which the data are received). Berns said, "It typically takes a novel stimulus—either a new piece of information or getting out of the environment in which an individual has become comfortable—to jolt attentional systems awake and reconfigure both perception and imagination."[35]

Instead of changing the perspective of an individual, it may be easier to augment it with that of others who bring a diversity of perspectives. Different people can view the same thing differently. Lou Gerstner, while CEO of IBM, when first presented with a demo of the then-new World Wide Web and IBM website, immediately asked, "Where's the 'buy' button?"[36] Some have said that Xerox executives, after the first graphical user interface including the mouse was created at their Palo Alto Research Center, didn't realize what they had done, only seeing the potential for slight copier improvements; Apple cofounder and CEO Steve Jobs saw the potential to bring computing to the masses, and built the Macintosh.[37]

Be Willing to Fail. Taking *risks* and *experimenting* are essential in testing hypotheses and learning. It's important to treat failure not as grounds for dismissal, but as an essential step on the path to success. One approach is to overcome the fear of failure through suspension of disbelief. There was no shortage of people willing to tell John F. Kennedy that a moon mission was not possible. He reportedly put all of his experts into one room, asked them to suspend disbelief, and even if it *weren't* possible, brainstorm how, theoretically, one *would* get to the moon. Activities might include design, testing, and integration of propulsion systems, spacesuits, lunar landers, control system architectures, and so forth. These elements were then used to generate a step-by-step plan and budget.[38]

It can be dangerous to *not* take such risks and dream the impossible. General Motors and other established car companies let Tesla enter the market with disruptive technology—all-electric automobiles—a threat in itself but also arousing the interest of others, such as Apple. GM's vice-chairman Robert Lutz reportedly said, "All the geniuses here at General Motors kept saying lithium-ion technology is 10 years away, and Toyota agreed with us—and boom, along comes Tesla. So I said, 'How come some tiny little California startup, run by guys who know nothing about the car business, can do this, and we can't?'"[39]

Testing a variety of alternatives to determine which approach is more successful—in terms of profitability, user experience, or performance—is an important element of innovation. Sometimes, such testing can lead to subtle changes; sometimes, to a complete pivot in strategy.

Google applies all of these principles: It "aims to be 10 times better" and is willing to "bet on technical insights," "ship and iterate," and "fail well."[40]

Integrate Perspectives. Finally, all of these elements need to be woven together: *association* of various component perspectives and *integration* into a single, synthesized whole are required to understand how evolving technologies, insights from multiple disciplines, subtle details of customer and user behavior, and results of trials and experiments can be tied together to achieve an innovation outcome. Bruce Nussbaum, the author of *Creative Intelligence*, sums this up with a succinct example: "How do you get ZipCar? Connect the dots of wanting a cheap ride, a value system of sharing, not owning, and new online technology. Very simple. Instagram? Connect the dots of a value system of sharing to new technologies of easy image taking and posting online."[41] Or consider the founder of eBay, Pierre Omidyar, which urban legend holds associated three separate things: An interest in efficient markets, his fiancée's interest in finding collectible PEZ candy dispensers, and the ineffectiveness of newspaper ads in finding them.[42,43]

Lead and Foster Teamwork. None of the above can happen without true leadership. It is up to leaders to create an environment where risks and failure are rewarded rather than ostracized. It is up to leaders to communicate that one day a week spent on a pet project is essential for success, rather than grounds for termination. It's a leadership imperative to balance priorities, ensure that diverse voices are heard in meetings, and to set a tone of listening rather than directing.

In addition to leaders and diversity of technical backgrounds, the active engagement of a variety of individuals is also important. For example, Tom Kelley, the general manager of design consultancy IDEO, suggests that there are 10 "faces" (i.e., roles) in the innovation process.[44] The "anthropologist" is someone who goes out into the field to observe how people behave or use existing products and services and notice fine details that others might have missed. The "experimenter" is willing to take risks and try different things. The "cross-pollinator" associates and synthesizes different unrelated perspectives. The parallels are clear: The anthropologist performs the observing and listening, the experimenter, well, experiments, and the cross-pollinator associates and integrates.

Innovation of Products, Processes, Relationships, and Innovation

Innovation seems often to be interpreted to mean product innovation, such as Edison's carbon-filament light bulb, the telephone, the Xerox 914 copier, the IBM System 360 mainframe, sliced bread, or Pringles stackable chips.

Broadly speaking, the product innovation category can be considered to include service innovation, such as cable television, online tax preparation, automatic car washes, or conveyor-belt sushi. As we have detailed, products and services are increasingly morphing into solutions, and a list of solution innovations would include the first commercial electrical telegraph service, deployed in 1837; the development and deployment of telephony in the late 1870s, which included telephone handsets but also "cloud" telephony services including the first commercial telephone exchanges; and electric lighting in the early 1880s, which included not just light bulbs but also "cloud" electric services such as electrical power generation, transmission, distribution, and metering.

Such solution innovation continues in the modern age, such as when the Amazon Kindle was introduced. It was an innovative product (electronic paper, no backlight, long battery life), with an innovative service (the Kindle Store), with innovative connectivity (Whispernet for free cellular connectivity to download books and magazines), innovative pricing (no consumer wireless contract, Amazon paid), and an innovative ecosystem (Kindle Direct Publishing) to engage authors and other content creators.

But innovation can also apply to processes and thus operational and information excellence or customer relationships and thus customer or collective intimacy.

As examples of process innovation, consider mass production through interchangeable parts, which replaced artisanal hand crafting, or the basic oxygen process for manufacturing steel, which replaced the traditional Bessemer process. The steel mini-mill was a further innovation, replacing the basic oxygen process. Traditionally, steel mills melted iron in blast furnaces—giant ovens that take a lot of money and time to preheat, so don't ever get turned off.

The mini-mill, by contrast, uses electric arc furnaces, which, like a microwave oven, don't require preheating. This changed the economics of steel production, since production could be varied to match demand.

Another example of process innovation: Wal-Mart. Wal-Mart is known as a low-cost retailer, but that begs the question of how it manages to offer such a wide variety of products at low cost. Over the last few decades, Wal-Mart has focused on innovation in its supply chain and logistics. It continuously improved, implementing hub-and-spoke distribution centers, cross-docking (a process by which trailers arrive at warehouses and unload directly onto outbound trailers), use of RFID tags, and point-of-sale terminals with massive amounts of transaction data warehoused and provided to consumer packaged goods suppliers, and so forth.

Not only physical processes can be made better; virtual ones can, too. Google's PageRank algorithm is an example of a better algorithm—a virtual, digital process—for ranking web pages in search results listings. Various financial firms use innovative algorithms for conducting—and hiding—equity trades.

As an example of customer relationship innovation, consider Amazon's one-click ordering and Kindle Fire Mayday button. Or consider the development of software as a service, such as that from Salesforce.com, as a new way to purchase and access software. Commercialization relied on a new pricing model, namely monthly subscription rather than "purchasing" a right-to-use license, and technology model, namely accessing software over the Internet; a value proposition including immediate availability and transparent upgrades, rather than a lengthy project implementation and maintenance cutovers; and adoption by users entailed both enterprise sales and Web self-service. Even a sophisticated collective intimacy strategy can be the subject of innovation: The Netflix Cinematch algorithm was improved through an open innovation challenge.

Often, innovation spans two or more of the other disciplines. The iPhone solution required back-end process changes in content licensing and app onboarding (i.e., information excellence). Netflix's recommenders enabling collective intimacy required back-end process changes in monitoring of user's movie-watching behavior and solution changes for the devices that deliver the service, such as TVs and TiVos.

Innovation can also apply to innovation. Innovation has evolved from the individual inventor, to *shop invention*, as practiced at Edison's Menlo Park lab, the collaborative industrial research laboratory, to open innovation through partnerships, to today's approaches, including platforms, contests and challenges, and idea markets as we'll see in the next chapter. In the future, we will see more and more innovation coming from machines, not just people.

Business Model Innovation and Corporate Transformation

Earlier, innovation was described as spanning invention, commercialization, and adoption, with commercialization including both business model generation and execution. Such innovation, broadly speaking, sometimes complements, enables, or is a byproduct of broader corporate initiatives: quality improvement, reengineering, process improvement, acquisition, divestiture, reorganization, outsourcing, offshoring, automation, retraining, corporate culture shift and transformation, and so on.

Sometimes, innovating a new business model primarily requires a new (to-the-industry) pricing model, such as those highlighted in Chapter 8. Besides a traditional sale resulting in ownership, there are pricing models such as bundling, renting, leasing, subscription, barter, fractional ownership, pay-per-use, nonlinear tariffs including block-increasing and block-declining (volume discounts), razor and razor blades, reverse razor and razor blades, a variety of auctions such as open-outcry, sealed-bid, and reverse, pay-what-you-want, third-party supported (including advertisers, charitable foundations, governments, etc.), freemium, and so forth.[45,46] Freemium models are increasingly found: free-to-play games that are monetized through virtual goods or additional levels; limited free services with the opportunity to upgrade for enhanced services; free usage for the many subsidized by payments by the few; and so on.[47] Pricing models are about more than revenue or payment streams; they include terms and conditions. For example, pay-per-use might eliminate any commitment, thus reducing risk for the customer; inadequate performance might lead to refunds or future credits.

Beyond changes primarily focused on pricing, Karan Girotra and Serguei Netessine, professors at INSEAD in France, argue that there are four general approaches to business model innovation.[48]

Adjusting the product/service mix. This might entail focusing narrowly on a niche product area, such as books or diapers; looking for common components or capabilities, such as for car chassis such as the Chrysler K-car or ecommerce/logistics; or hedging a portfolio, for example, carrying both air cargo and passengers, or perhaps selling cigarettes and cookies, to minimize risk from a downturn in either segment.

Shifting the timing of decisions and process steps. For example, dynamic pricing pushes the timing of pricing decisions such as for airline tickets all the way to the point of purchase as opposed to being set well in advance. Changing the order of process steps can also impact economics, as we'll see shortly with contest economics, which pay for results after activities, rather than paying for activities in advance of results. Splitting up a single large decision into multiple, experimental, iterative ones can also make a difference in risk and outcomes.

Changing the responsibility for decision making. This involves empowering those who are better informed, such as channels or salespeople closer to the customer, or to suppliers who can better manage inventories, or to algorithms, or to ensure incentive alignment with those who stand to gain the most from the decision.

Changing the rationale for decision making. One way is to change the pricing model, say, from activities to results. Another is by managing dichotomies such as short-term competitive bidding with long term supplier performance management.

The business model—including pricing models and the interplay between cost and revenue—can be critical in innovation, especially because the greater the innovation, the more likely it is that customers will need to change their business or personal activities for the innovation to be beneficial, and thus the greater the risk. There are numerous examples throughout business history.

As discussed earlier, the Xerox 914 copier and the Vestergaard Life-Straw are examples of business model innovation facilitating adoption. Instead of outright purchase, the 914 was leased, on a no-commitment basis, and with 2,000 copies per month included. The LifeStraw is "paid for" by carbon credits. Amazon introduced the Kindle, but this required overcoming then-prohibitively expensive cellular telephony subscriber fees by including book download data transfer fees at no additional cost. Netflix introduced DVDs by mail, but paying for a rental by the day would include several days in which the DVD was in the US Postal Service's possession, a factor aligned with a flat-rate monthly rental plan.

In general, companies operating at higher levels of radical disruption require business model innovation as well as product/service, process, and relationship innovation. There are a number of frameworks for thinking through new business models, such as big think strategy,[49] blue ocean strategy,[50] and business model generation.[51] In general, though, these are the relevant control points:

Customers, segments, and requirements. Deciding who the customers are and how they segment—for example, enterprise/SMB, business/consumer, old/young, adult/teen/infant, female/male, early/late adopter, local/regional/global—helps to better delineate their needs and how your offer will benefit them. Canon and Ricoh attacked Xerox's big copier hegemony by pursuing individuals and small and medium businesses.

Channels. Michael Dell had enormous success by bypassing indirect channels and offering PCs via the phone and then over the web; conversely, Apple had success partly by complementing channels with elegantly designed retail stores. Although we often tend to think of channels simply as direct or indirect, bricks and mortar or online, there are many unique variations around the world. For example, in Sri Lanka, trained *infomediaries* explain how mobile phones and services work to other villagers; in India, vendors purchase bicycles preloaded with frozen dairy and juice products.[52]

Products, services, and solutions. The product, service, solution, and support services are the nexus of value generation, so the structure of the solution interlinks with the business model. For example, software running on mobile devices is what enables successful downloads of new apps and games, and thus generates revenue, whether they are paid apps or free-to-play via a freemium price structure or in-app purchases.

Processes, resources, organization, and partnerships. Process changes can create new businesses. Traditionally, cell phone use was metered and a bill arrived at the end of the month. The simple change of paying before receiving service created an entirely new "pre-paid" industry. Moving to an asset-light model can also be useful. The Coca-Cola Company does no bottling, nor does it produce raw ingredients. Li & Fung is a $20 billion apparel manufacturer without any factories.

The value proposition. This is the value that the product promises the customer—the benefit less the cost. For example, investing in weather-proofing foam sealant for doors and windows (the cost) can reduce heating and air conditioning costs by 10 percent (the benefit). Or as Geico proposes, "15 minutes" (the cost) "can save you 15 percent [on insurance]" (the benefit).

Revenues and costs. Technology advances can drive costs to near zero. Creating freemium, loss leader, puppy-dog sale, and razor and razor blade models, where customers can get some products—such as razors, printers, free apps, online storage, online email—at or near zero price can be made up later by selling complements, such as razor blades, upgrades, additional features, or in-app goods.

Competition, Substitutes, and Advantage. Defining competitors (i.e., other firms that the customer can turn to so as to meet the need), substitutes (i.e., other types of products and services or uses of time and money), and their relative advantages and disadvantages can help clarify business model opportunities. For example, a moviegoer can choose to see *Ironman* or *Star Wars*, go to Loews or AMC theaters, stay home and watch TV, spend the money on dining out, or invest it instead.

In short, there are many areas amenable to innovation. All it takes is imagination.

■   ■   ■

Innovation—of processes, products and services, customer relationships, and even innovation itself—is more important than ever before. It can mean the difference between leadership and liquidation.

The key elements found in many successful commercial innovations are invention, through ideation and reduction to practice, commercialization, including business model generation and execution, and adoption, including a customer value proposition and its realization.

Notes

1. Geoffrey Moore, "Darwin and the Demon: Innovating Within Established Enterprises," *Harvard Business Review* (July 2004), https://hbr.org/2004/07/darwin-and-the-demon-innovating-within-established-enterprises.
2. Michael E. Porter, "The Five Competitive Forces That Shape Strategy," *Harvard Business Review* (January 2008), www.exed.hbs.edu/assets/documents/hbr-shape-strategy.pdf.
3. "24 Carat," *Louis XIV*, www.louisxivenergy.com/en/24carat.
4. Claudia H. Deutsch, "At Kodak, Some Old Things Are New Again," *New York Times*, May 2, 2008, www.nytimes.com/2008/05/02/technology/02kodak.html.
5. Clayton Christensen, *The Innovator's Dilemma: When New Technologies Cause Great Firms to Fail* (New York: Harvard Business Review Press, 1997).
6. Gerard Tellis, "PTC'15: Keynote 3.4: Breaking the Incumbents Curse: How to Build a Culture of Relentless Innovation," [Video] *Pacific Telecommunications Council Conference*, January 2015, https://vimeo.com/118317714.
7. Everett Rogers, *Diffusion of Innovations*, 5th ed. (New York: Free Press, 2003).
8. Geoffrey A. Moore, *Crossing the Chasm: Marketing and Selling High-Tech Products to Mainstream Customers* (New York: HarperCollins, 1991); Geoffrey A. Moore, *Inside the Tornado: Marketing Strategies from Silicon Valley's Cutting Edge* (New York: HarperBusiness, 1995).
9. Ibid.
10. Richard Foster and Sarah Kaplan, *Creative Destruction: Why Companies That Are Built to Last Under Perform the Market—And How to Successfully Transform Them* (Strawberry Hills, NSW: Currency Publishers, 2001), quoted in Curtis R. Carlson and William W. Wilmot, *Innovation: The Five Disciplines for Creating What Customers Want* (New York: Crown Business, 2006), 34.
11. Ibid.
12. Andrew McAfee and Erik Brynjolfsson, "Investing in the IT That Makes a Competitive Difference," *Harvard Business Review* (July, 2008), hbr.org/2008/07/investing-in-the-it-that-makes-a-competitive-difference/ar/1.
13. Alexander Osterwalder and Yves Pigneur, *Business Model Generation: A Handbook for Visionaries, Game Changers, and Challengers* (Hoboken, NJ: John Wiley & Sons, 2010).
14. Michael Lewis, *The New, New Thing: A Silicon Valley Story* (New York: W. W. Norton & Company, 1999), quoted in Andrea Ovans, "What Is a Business Model?" *Harvard Business Review* (January 23, 2015), https://hbr.org/2015/01/what-is-a-business-model.

15. Mark W. Johnson, Clayton M. Christensen, and Henning Kagermann, "Reinventing Your Business Model," *Harvard Business Review* (December 2008), https://hbr.org/2008/12/reinventing-your-business-model/ar/1x.

16. Khan Academy, "A Conversation with Elon Musk," *YouTube.com*, April 22, 2013, https://www.youtube.com/watch?v=vDwzmJpI4io.

17. Although U.S. Patent # 6,285,999 lists Lawrence (Larry) Page as sole inventor.

18. Will Oremus, "Google's Big Break," *Slate.com*, October 13, 2013, www.slate.com/articles/business/when_big_businesses_were_small/2013/10/google_s_big_break_how_bill_gross_goto_com_inspired_the_adwords_business.html.

19. Stefan Michel, "Capture More Value," *Harvard Business Review* (October 2014).

20. Gregory Berns, *Iconoclast: A Neuroscientist Reveals How to Think Differently* (New York: Harvard Business Review Press, 2008).

21. Ibid.

22. Spencer Ferguson Silver, "Acrylate Copolymer Microspheres," U.S. Patent 3,691,140. https://www.google.com/patents/US3691140?dq=3,691,140&hl=en&sa=X&ei=ctmyVIPRNcWlgwSYhYH4AQ&ved=0CB0Q6AEwAA.

23. Brian Hindo, "At 3M, a Struggle Between Efficiency and Creativity," *Bloomberg-Business*, June 10, 2007, www.businessweek.com/stories/2007-06-10/at-3m-a-struggle-between-efficiency-and-creativity.

24. Tim Brown, "Design Thinking," *Harvard Business Review*, June 2008, https://hbr.org/2008/06/design-thinking.

25. Tom Kelley with Jonathan Littman, *The Art of Innovation: Lessons in Creativity from IDEO, America's Leading Design Firm* (New York: Crown Business, 2001).

26. Brown, "Design Thinking."

27. Kathy Chin Leong, "Google Reveals Its 9 Principles of Innovation," *Fast Company*, November 20, 2013, www.fastcompany.com/3021956/how-to-be-a-success-at-everything/googles-nine-principles-of-innovation.

28. Jeffrey H. Dyer, Hal Gregersen, and Clayton M. Christensen, "The Innovator's DNA," *Harvard Business Review* (December 2009).

29. John F. Kennedy, "Text of President John Kennedy's Rice Stadium Moon Speech," er.jsc.nasa.gov/seh/ricetalk.htm.

30. "Secret Google Lab 'Rewards Failure," *BBC*, January 24, 2014, www.bbc.co.uk/news/technology-25883016.

31. Brad Stone, "Inside Google's Secret Lab," *BloombergBusiness*, May 22, 2013, www.bloomberg.com/bw/articles/2013-05-22/inside-googles-secret-lab.

32. Dyer, Gregersen, and Christensen, "The Innovator's DNA."

33. "BCG Names 50 Most Innovative Companies," *BCG*, September 26, 2013, www.bcg.com/media/PressReleaseDetails.aspx?id=tcm:12-145313.

34. Lauren Leader-Chivee, "3 Secrets of Innovation That Everyone Misses," *Inc.*, January 31, 2014, www.inc.com/lauren-leader-chivée/3-secrets-of-innovation-that-everyone-misses.html.

35. Berns, *Iconoclast*, 57–58.

36. Gary Hamel, "Waking up IBM: How a Gang of Unlikely Rebels Transformed Big Blue," *Harvard Business Review* (July 2000), https://hbr.org/2000/07/waking-up-ibm-how-a-gang-of-unlikely-rebels-transformed-big-blue.

37. Mitchell York, "How to Get Your Inner Steve Jobs Working," *About.com*, entrepreneurs.about.com/od/becominganentrepreneur/a/How-To-Get-Your-Inner-Steve-Jobs-Working.htm.

38. Barry Schuler, "The One Behavior That Guarantees Failure," *Inc.*, (February 4, 2014, www.inc.com/barry-schuler/the-one-behavior-that-guarantees-failure.html.

39. Bibi van der Zee, "Tesla's Roadster Sport saves the electric car," *The Guardian*, February 3, 2010, www.theguardian.com/environment/green-living-blog/2010/feb/03/tesla-roadster-sport-electric-car.

40. Leong, "Google Reveals."

41. Bruce Nussbaum, "Does Progressive Education = Startup Entrepreneurialism?" blog, January 10, 2014, creativeintelligencebook.com/post/73509462932/does-progressive-education-startup.

42. Dyer, Gregersen, and Christensen, "The Innovator's DNA."

43. The story that eBay was founded partly for Pez dispensers may be an urban legend. cf Scott Berkun, *The Myths of Innovation* (Sebastopol, CA: O'Reilly Media, 2010), 6.

44. Tom Kelley, "The Ten Faces of Innovation," *TenFacesOfInnovation.com*, 2005, www.tenfacesofinnovation.com/tenfaces/index.htm.

45. Joe Weinman, "The Market for 'Melons': Quantity Uncertainty and the Market Mechanism," Working Paper, September 6, 2010, www.JoeWeinman.com/Resources/Joe_Weinman_The_Market_For_Melons.pdf.

46. Andrea Ovans, "What Is a Business Model?" *Harvard Business Review* (January 23, 2015), https://hbr.org/2015/01/what-is-a-business-model.

47. Chris Anderson, *Free: The Future of a Radical Price* (New York: Hyperion, 2009).

48. Karan Girotra and Serguei Netessine, "Four Paths to Business Model Innovation," *Harvard Business Review* (July–August 2014): 96–103.

49. Bernd H. Schmitt, *Big Think Strategy: How to Leverage Bold Ideas and Leave Small Thinking Behind* (Boston: Harvard Business Review Press, 2007).

50. W. Chan Kim and Renée Mauborgne, *Blue Ocean Strategy: How to Create Uncontested Market Space and Make Competition Irrelevant* (Boston: Harvard Business Review Press, 2005).

51. Osterwalder and Pigneur, *Business Model Generation*.

52. Erik Simanis and Duncan Duke, "Profits at the Bottom of the Pyramid," *Harvard Business Review* (October 2014): 90.

CHAPTER 15

The Discipline of Accelerated Innovation

In preceding chapters, we've examined the three digital disciplines that complement and extend Treacy and Wiersema's original value disciplines.

The fourth digital discipline—*accelerated innovation*—creates value for customers by continuously innovating products and services, processes, or relationships using digital technologies. One can make the case that innovation should have been a "value discipline" using Treacy and Wiersema's definition of a value proposition and an aligned value-driven operating model.

The value proposition is clear: Customers don't just value brands with *currently* better products, processes, or engagement approaches, but also value ones that, like Apple, demonstrate a *consistent* ability and willingness to push boundaries, create value, and remain not just relevant, but exciting. In Geoffrey Moore's terms, while there are companies with better processes or products that appeal to *pragmatists*, there are also those who develop bonds with *visionaries*.[1]

Value-driven operating models for innovation align with that proposition. These may include setting up independent units unencumbered by corporate risk-aversion and atherosclerosis, embracing open innovation, rewarding collaboration, fostering a culture that not just accepts but rewards failure, setting corporate-level innovation objectives, and following lean startup and agile development methodologies.

This discipline of accelerated innovation has a focus on speed—but also cost and quality—in the context of turbulent markets, technological complexity, and not just global hyper-competition, but democratization, where anyone with an Internet connection can be an innovator (i.e., dangerous competitor).

Traditionally, the thought was that a company couldn't optimize cost, time, and quality simultaneously: compressing time implied cutting corners on quality, improving quality implied spending more on materials and inspection. Today, however, that thinking has changed.

Today, not only can digital technologies enhance collaboration or enable global challenges to accelerate innovation, but they can also lead to higher quality solutions by incorporating the best insights from the most creative, knowledgeable, and skilled experts globally. They can also reduce cost, through inexpensive digital experiments, crowdsourcing, and exploiting gamification and contest economics (e.g., paying for results), rather than activities and rewarding with recognition, rather than cash.

All of these dimensions are important, but acceleration itself can often provide singular benefits. One benefit is that profits are usually higher in the early stages of the product life cycle, before competitors enter and price competition drives margins down. Reaching higher volumes sooner drives a virtuous cycle of learning curve effects and scale economies. Another benefit is the opportunity for intellectual property protection through patents. Yet another is mindshare and branding. All other things being equal (such as team size), shorter development cycles mean reduced development expenses. Plus, the first to market often gets outsized free publicity.

Also, many markets exhibit network effects, tipping points, and winner-take-all dynamics that benefit first movers. For example, game developers flock to consoles, tablets, and smartphones with the greatest base of customers; conversely, gamers buy devices with the best selection of the best games. In the battle between Blu-ray and HD-DVD, a tipping point was reached when Warner Brothers decided to go exclusively with Blu-ray. Blu-ray won not just incremental share, but all of the market.

As a result of these characteristics, studies have shown that it's better to be overbudget than to be late with commercial innovation. Of course, being first is no guarantee of success. A company can be too early to market, when the ecosystem or complementary products and services are not yet developed. Or, a fast follower can come along with a better product, leveraging lower-cost manufacturing processes, new technologies, greater convenience, or ease of use: Apple's iPod was not the first portable music player, and Google was not the first search engine. However, all other things being equal, it's better to be first.

IT broadly supports accelerated innovation for market leadership. Big data, things, and analytics support paying close attention to customer or user behavior. As an example, a retailer can process video images to determine exactly how shoppers move through a store to improve merchandising, or transaction data to determine which items are purchased together to create new bundles or promotions, or site query data to identify unmet needs. Fostering diverse collaboration can be facilitated through tools such as video or web conferencing, but also through challenges, innovation networks, and idea markets. Experiments can be run in the cloud to innovate purely virtual goods and processes, and on virtual equivalents of real-world objects, such as in accelerating pharmaceutical development by modeling proteins and receptors, or airframe development with airflow across wing designs. Moreover, thanks to intermediaries such as Kaggle.com and Innocentive.com, virtually any company can leverage digital to accelerate innovation, not just technically savvy Silicon Valley firms and their global counterparts.

Innovation has been innovated as well. Originally, the province of solitary inventors, philosophers, and tinkerers, it has become a team sport. It's moved beyond serendipity and random luck to structured experimentation in the context of theory and analysis. It's expanded beyond monolithic industrial labs to collaboration with entities outside the firm. Such collaboration has become more dynamic and ad hoc. Innovation is increasingly data-driven. We are now on the cusp of increasing automation of innovation, as advanced algorithms become increasingly involved in the creative aspects of innovation, such as hypothesis generation and, arguably, creativity.

From Solitary to Collaborative

Thomas Alva Edison, the Wizard of Menlo Park, is one of the greatest inventors—and innovators—of all time, whether measured by sheer quantity, diversity, societal impact, or ultimate commercial value. He is credited with over a thousand patents (although his employees were often instrumental in the research and development leading up to them), including the motion picture camera, the phonograph, the stock ticker, a voting machine, the carbon-filament light bulb and the electric utility to power it, including central power generation through steam-powered dynamos, electric transmission and distribution, and even usage metering.[2]

Edison is often thought of as a brilliant solitary inventor, toiling in great secrecy, and that was true in his early years. However, sale of some of his early inventions, together with his subsequent ability to attract investors, led to what might well be his greatest innovation, the creation of the first meaningful industrial research lab.[3] Edison's lab marked the beginning of a transition from the heroic inventor toiling in solitude to diverse teams, a culture of collaboration versus antagonism, and the fusing of scientific theory with technological practice and experimentation.

Edison's lab was focused not just on ideation but on reduction to practice—prototyping and experimentation through *shop invention*, that is, trial and error in facilities that were a combination of machine shop and R&D lab. Research was inseparable from the rest of the facility, which manufactured and sold products such as telegraph equipment in volume.

Practitioners such as machinists and woodworkers were critical, helping to usher in the transition from lone inventor to team.

Although Edison later co-founded the GE Research Lab, there were substantial differences between that and his lab. At Edison's lab, the influence of Edison was unmistakable, and employees he didn't care for soon departed. At GE, a major thrust was to create a collaborative environment based on mutual respect and cordiality.[4]

Another difference at GE was the integration of scientific research with the legacy of shop invention. Edison had complained about academics, saying they were "content to study the fuzz on a bee,"[5] whereas scientists before the turn of the century held disdain for common tinkerers without strong intellectual foundations, who were merely after money and fame.[6]

The German Model of innovation—based on interlocking relationships between universities, professors, institutes, the government, and industry—resolved the conflict. Companies such as Bayer and BASF would sponsor specific professors, often exclusively, and these professors would then gain access to equipment and materials that they otherwise could not afford.

The approach to innovation that became increasingly adopted at the turn of the last century incorporated these three waves: diverse teams, collaboration, and an integrated approach comprising science and technology. These soon paid off. For example, GE's new research lab developed improved tungsten filaments and the gas-filled bulb that proved superior to Edison's original carbon filament in a vacuum, and Dupont invented the commercially successful nylon and neoprene based on pure research into polymers.[7]

Since then, the world has gotten continuously more complex, and diverse collaboration is necessary for continued progress. This includes diversity of roles and perspectives—firm, channel, customer, partner—and in organizational functions—such as marketing, R&D, and finance—and of formal and experiential skills—such as nanotechnology, information technology, biology, project management, accounting, and advertising—and of participant backgrounds, demographics, and culture. It includes diversity in interaction styles, such as leading versus following, introversion versus extraversion, and interaction versus introspection.

The increasing complexity of technology drives specialization, which, combined with the increasing complexity of solutions, drives collaboration. For example, automobile design and development now requires aerodynamic engineers, electrical engineers, chemists for battery design, and a variety of information technology professionals in areas such as wireless communications, security, artificial intelligence, machine vision, and user interface design.

Collaboration involves more than bringing individuals together. Research shows that brainstorming is overrated; individuals working alone and then consolidating their ideas can generate more and better ideas than when brainstorming as a group. However, the *best* results are achieved when multiple individuals can disagree, discuss, debate, and then achieve a synthesis of perspectives. Moreover, there is a sweet spot for creative success: Individuals need to be able to communicate and understand each other, but too *much* prior experience working together stifles creativity.[8] Structured cloud-mediated collaboration is ideal for such *ad hoc* relationships, and global connectivity enhances the ability of such teams to form and interact even when widely dispersed.

Solutions can't just be partitioned by specialty, because great innovations occur through dynamic, interdisciplinary synthesis, when, as author Matt Ridley says, "ideas have sex," For example, CPS (Ceramics Process Systems), a manufacturer of ceramic composites used in things like uninterruptible power supplies, leveraged insights from a film technology expert from Polaroid to make their composites stronger and from experts in preventing ice crystal growth while freezing sperm to improve its manufacturing process.[9]

Today, even without formally identified *innovators*, the creative powers of rank and file employees can be enlisted. The newest instantiation of the classic suggestion box is gamified, online employee contests. Moreover, enabling employees to "invest" in potential initiatives through prediction markets can help implicitly aggregate the wisdom of those employees, beyond the strategic planning or innovation team.

And, many of today's information technology tools are directly focused on collaboration: web conferencing, audio conferencing, mobile, desktop, and high-definition video conferencing or *telepresence*, enterprise microblogging and social networking tools such as Salesforce.com's Chatter, file-sharing tools, and the like. Instead of commercial tools, some firms have their own implementations to achieve similar goals.

From Internal to External

The great industrial research labs at the dawn of the twentieth century—formal, professionally run organizations such as GE Research or AT&T Bell Laboratories—were one model of innovation, where all research was conducted by employees, with a primary focus on developing proprietary technologies and trade secrets, and fattening patent portfolios. A century later, though, Henry Chesbrough, an adjunct professor at Berkeley's Haas School of Business, argued for a different model: *open innovation*.

Chesbrough contended that numerous factors—increased mobility of talent, increased complexity and knowledge sharing, the emergence of venture capital, and accelerated competition—were driving a paradigm shift, where companies could no longer rely solely on their own employees, their own intellectual property, and their own distribution capabilities and customer relationships.

In Chesbrough's model, companies can take internally developed ideas to market directly, but also through external paths such as intellectual property licensing, spin-offs, and channel development. Conversely, they can take externally developed ideas—from other firms, startups, competitors, academics, independent inventors, or customers—to market by acquiring the rights to them through licensing or outright acquisition and then distributing them through company marketing and sales capabilities. And, they can utilize some combination of the two, where external and internal ideas are brought together and then taken to market using a combination of internal and external channels.

To put it another way, elements of successful commercial innovation—such as invention and commercialization can be accomplished internally, externally, or both.

Open innovation actually has a long history: The Venetian Arsenal, the ship-making arm of the nation-state of Venice, called on Leonardo da Vinci for process engineering help a millennium ago. Over a century ago, P&G acqui-hired chemist Edwin Kayser, because he owned the rights to the patent for hydrogenating oil, the key technology underpinning Crisco shortening. Today, open innovation is increasingly being adopted in a variety of industries. For example, the percentage of drugs under development by the top 10 pharmaceutical firms that were acquired from another company doubled from 2002 to 2012. In the case of Johnson & Johnson, the proportion increased from 20 to 50 percent.[10]

Although Chesbrough refers to innovation external to the firm as "open innovation," there is value in separately denoting innovation which is *external*—that is, beyond the firm's boundaries—from that which is *open*—that is, performed with full transparency and visibility among all stakeholders.

For example, a firm might partner with an external entity under a nondisclosure agreement (which would be closed, yet external); be completely transparent and willing to share internally developed technology (open, yet internal), as when Tesla stated it would not "initiate patent lawsuits against anyone who, in good faith, wants to use our technology;"[11] or fully participate in an open community (open and external), such as those firms that contribute to and benefit from OpenStack, Linux, or the World Wide Web Consortium.

Both internal and external innovation have advantages and disadvantages, as do both closed and open initiatives. Maintaining a center of excellence and patent portfolio in proprietary core technologies can complement the acceptance and nurturing of external sources of innovation through contests, sponsorships, licensing, or acquisitions.

From Closed to Open

Since partners may be bound under nondisclosure agreements and technology can be exclusively licensed, external innovation, by itself, does not equate to "open" innovation. One can identify partners or technologies outside the four walls of the company, then bind them with restrictive nondisclosure agreements, or acquire the technology under an exclusive license. In contrast, an open approach can enable much greater sharing—in both directions—between the company and the outside community, leading to a virtuous cycle of innovation. Wikipedia and Linux are well-known open communities. Perhaps less generally well-known is the shared "repository" GitHub, where anyone can upload, modify, or acquire documents or code fragments or entire applications.

Cost and speed are advantages of open innovation, but the results are available to anyone, thus can be a source of competitive advantage only when combined with additional proprietary insights or a unique capability, say, capital assets, brand, intellectual property, customer relationships, an operations model, or exclusive distribution rights. For example, the Netflix OSS Cloud Prize was an open contest, but one that improved general cloud infrastructure management tools, neither a basis for nor sustainable source of competitive advantage for Netflix. The Facebook-initiated Open Compute initiative is another example of open innovation, lowering the cost of servers by sharing best-practice designs. In a rough parallel to Netflix, because Facebook's competitive strategy is not based on low-cost computing but social networking and advertising, such openness does not sacrifice the crown jewels. In both cases, openness helped with cost and reliability without damaging competitive advantage.

Digital technologies have enabled several new kinds of partly or fully open external accelerated innovation.

In one, the focus of innovation is still that of a given firm and a particular problem. The firm uses digital technologies to extend its reach to a broad variety of select or *ad hoc* participants to solve a particular problem or challenge. Companies like Innocentive, which focuses on areas such as polymer chemistry, genomics, and nanotechnology, and Kaggle, which focuses on data science, address complex technical challenges, such as finding "A Scalable, Cost and Atom-Efficient Synthesis of a Benzothiazepine."[12] Technology can complement human and organizational networks, as when field personnel and their networks help complement or direct digital searches.

Instead of a problem looking for a solution, solutions or other ideas can also be submitted directly to the firm or through intermediaries such as idea markets. Sometimes anyone, within the bounds of corporate intellectual property ownership constraints and submission policies, can submit relevant ideas. Sometimes corporations invite such submissions, as with Procter & Gamble's Connect + Develop program. Other times, they are brokered through sites like Yet2.com or EdisonNation.com, which are marketplaces for buyers and sellers of ideas (i.e., problem owners and problem solvers).

An interesting converse of this approach is to open the firm boundaries not to any *idea* arising externally to be commercialized internally, but rather to any external *commercialization* possibility for ideas already generated. Bill Gross (the Internet entrepreneur, not the bond investor) founded IdeaMarket, where anyone can "submit great ideas, browse through them, vote on them, invest or commit money to them."[13] Other approaches such as Kickstarter enable crowds to fund ideas for projects, often in the creative arts, in return for nonmonetary rewards. In a variation, AngelList enables accredited investors to fund startups.

A variety of intermediaries use different approaches to enlist crowds, in ideation, problem solution, voting, funding, and execution. Innovations need not require multiple PhDs in biophysics; they may involve contributions such as how to structure a modular architecture for a piece of software—one of the things that TopCoder.com does in addition to actual coding—or writing an 800-word blog post on Vitamin C—which a site like Freelancer.com offers.

Several strategies based on open innovation are worth noting. In some, contributions are open to anyone; in others, outputs are available to anyone; in many, both are true. Linux is an open source initiative, started when Linus Torvalds grew frustrated with licensing restrictions of another operating system. Under his licensing, other developers were free to extend it and use it, with those extensions also becoming available to all. It later formed the basis for a commercial offering from companies such as Red Hat, which incorporated and monetized support, and IBM, which could maintain hardware margins while lowering a customer's total cost of ownership. Google offers Android, which is a mobile operating system built on Linux, which itself is offered under an open source license. This software, in turn, is embedded in devices such as connected light bulbs.

In an interesting case of an innovation strategy based on "open," Rackspace found itself competing with Amazon Web Services in cloud computing, but with fewer resources to directly invest. It created the Open-Stack foundation, together with NASA, as a way of engaging a coalition of developers and companies to collaborate to better develop a portfolio of cloud services. OpenStack has since grown to hundreds of members, ranging from AT&T to ZTE.

From Inside-Out to Outside-In

Sometimes the term *outside-in* is used to describe the acquisition of innovations from outside the firm, whereas inside-out means exploiting internally developed innovations through spin-offs or licensing deals. It has also been used to mean adopting the perspective of the customer and her experience, rather than taking an internal process view.[14] Here, we are using the term *inside-out* to mean the model of "pushing" innovations on customers, whereas the reverse model of *outside-in* involves understanding customer needs, wants, behaviors, anomalies, and challenges and using them to guide innovation.

The viewpoint of the inside-out school has been articulated by Henry Ford, who observed that if he "had asked people what they wanted, they would have said faster horses," and by the late Apple CEO Steve Jobs, who said, "A lot of times, people don't know what they want until you show it to them."[15]

After all, prior to the launch of the iPhone on January 9, 2007, it would have been hard to identify someone pining for a lightweight keyboardless touchscreen smartphone with a cloud-based app store that offered multiple apps including one for slicing flying watermelons and another for launching birds on parabolic trajectories. The average consumer wants to relax with friends or needs to shop for groceries, not evaluate price-performance trajectories in OLED displays or ponder whether royalty practices in the music industry can be restructured. As Tom Kelley, the general manager of design firm IDEO says, "Customers mean well—and they're trying to be helpful—but it's not their job to be visionaries."

Moreover, innovation often arises through the development of new technologies, whose application to customer needs may not be immediately evident, say, the blue lasers that enabled Blu-ray discs or the "low-tack" adhesive in Post-it notes.

On the other hand, the outside-in school would argue that solving customer needs is the best approach, by deeply understanding not just what customers say they need, but how they use existing products in practice. As lean startup guru Steve Blank puts it, "There is no way that you're smarter than the collective intelligence of your potential customers."[16]

In a related vein, Forrester Research analyst James McQuivey says that instead of asking, "How can we make a new product that we can successfully sell?" companies should ask, "How can we give people something that they really want?" This simple rephrasing, he argues, can be very potent. Shifting from "make" to "give" implies shifting focus from current capabilities to broad abilities including leveraging new partners. Shifting from "product" to "people" and from "sell" to "want" moves the focus to customers and their needs.[17]

Local market differences can be a driver of innovation as well, as products are formulated to meet conditions such as limited running water or electricity, cultural or flavor preferences, laws and regulations, or dozens of other factors. In a related fashion, attempting to meet or beat competitor capabilities, or work around their patents, can drive innovation.

There is a middle ground between the extremes of launching a product fully formed from out of a skunkworks and designing a product specifically to meet documented requirements. For example, engaging a customer to acquire feedback through test use of early prototypes or advisory boards reduces the risk of investing to scale up production or service delivery operations for an offer no one wants. Customers can be observed as they use current or similar products, even if they themselves don't verbalize or realize issues or anomalous behaviors. They can be brought in to an innovation lab to use or play around with prototypes, which can be changed in real time through agile software development, high resolution visualization, and 3D printing.

Customers don't even need to be physically present. Analyzing customer plaudits and concerns on social media or customer reviews on company or product websites can be another source of insight. In the digital world, A/B testing and betas are commonplace, where different interfaces or marketing campaigns can be evaluated simply by tweaking a few lines of code. It can then be determined which one generates more revenue, has faster response time, generates greater engagement, is more reliable, or scales better.

The use of computer-based analytics to assess customer needs and preferences and design products can perhaps be traced to Howard Moskowitz, a consultant working for the Prego brand of spaghetti sauce owned by Campbell's Soup in the mid-1980s. He trialed 45 different formulations of sauce, garlic, sweeteners, salt, spices, in Los Angeles, Jacksonville, New York, and Chicago and then used computer models to determine that there was a substantial unserved market for chunky tomato sauce. Prego introduced such a sauce and rapidly generated hundreds of millions of dollars in profits.[18]

That was then. Now, the way firms will develop a more intimate relationship with their customers is to get inside their brain. Campbell's Soup contracted with Innerscope Research to conduct *neuromarketing*, examining skin conductance, heart rate, breathing patterns, and posture to redesign condensed soup packaging.[19,20] Nielsen is using EEGs (electroencephalograms) to gauge brain response to different shows.

From Products to Platforms

Creating a platform usable by employees, partners, or third parties can be another powerful means to accelerate innovation.

The Microsoft Windows operating system is perhaps one of the best known such platforms: Numerous companies built software to run on

Windows. For example, Adobe innovated Illustrator and Corel coded Draw. The existence of a platform that already performed many basic functions such as graphics rendering and file management meant that partners could innovate additional value more quickly and inexpensively than if they had to build that functionality from scratch.

Today, platforms include mobile operating systems such as iOS and Android, their app stores, wireless networks, the Internet, cloud computing at the infrastructure, software application, and platform as a service and microservices layers, which enable prebuilt application components to be assembled like Lego blocks. In addition, there are open-source tools and platforms with names like Hadoop and Hive, and tens of thousands more such building blocks for gaining insights from big data, low-cost and low-power chips and sensors, and so forth.

In addition to a platform *upon* which others build innovation, the innovation can be incorporated into the platform through *extension* and *modification*. Linux is an example of all three: Some build applications on top of Linux; some add new features; others modify existing functions or the code enabling them.

CSC Leading Edge Forum analyst Simon Wardley and Mark Thompson, a senior lecturer at Cambridge Judge Business School, describe a process they call "Innovate-Leverage-Commoditize," where firms offer platforms that enable third parties to innovate, then acquire or replicate the third parties' functionality and incorporate it into the platform to unleash another wave of innovation. The challenge is to appropriately manage the balance between growing the platform and ecosystem and scaring off would-be partners.[21]

The widespread availability of such platforms is leading to what blogger and venture capitalist Om Malik calls the "Insta-Company."[22] As he observes, in the 1990s, one needed millions of dollars to build out infrastructure: data centers, servers, storage, and networking gear. "Today," he argues, "all it takes to hang up a shingle is the proverbial dollar and a dream. It's more like a credit card, [an] Amazon [Web Services] account and an idea."

This is how we encounter individuals such as 12-year-old Ethan Duggan, who used his spare time to develop mobile apps,[23] and 14-year-old Lucia Sanchez, who built Crazy Block, an Android game,[24] and companies such as Dropbox.com, valued at billions of dollars, which two MIT dropouts started and based on the Amazon Web Services cloud infrastructure platform.

From Linear to Agile

The traditional approach to innovation management uses a linear process, such as *stage-gate*, where there are multiple stages, such as concept, prototype, proposal, business model review, market assessment, and so forth, and multiple "go"/"no go" gates—say, "Initial Product Team Review"—which can then unlock continued funding or other resources. A portfolio of initiatives traverses this process, with new ones beginning as others complete or drop out. At various gates and milestones, key executive stakeholders from various functions such as R&D or product line management review progress to date, assess the competitive and market environment, review the outlook for the future including financial projections and execution risk, and assess continued alignment with company strategy.

This model is sometimes called a waterfall or pipeline—when everything that goes in the front end makes it through the process—or funnel—when there is winnowing at each stage. This process has been compared to poker, where as the game unfolds, you need to decide whether to bet more or fold your hand.[25] It's an example of a culture oriented toward planning and formality.

However, increasingly, lean startup and agile development techniques are being put to use, even by established multinational conglomerates. Instead of firms having developers perfect the product behind closed doors, customers work closely with engineers, product managers, designers, and others, who rapidly prototype and then bring concepts to market. Instead of full-featured products, the focus is on a *minimum viable product* (i.e., the simplest possible product that does something useful). Instead of formal, structured plans, participants will change course, rethinking business models, features, and priorities.

For example, YouTube was originally supposed to be a video dating service.[26] Twitter initially was Odeo, a podcasting tool, before incorporation of podcasting into iTunes required a complete pivot in the company's mission and product.[27] LoseIt, a weight-loss app, originally built a feature for users to connect with friends. However, it turns out that their users wanted to meet new people, so LoseIt rapidly built a feature that let people find new friends based on shared goals and diet strategies.[28]

Mark Zuckerberg, the founder and CEO of Facebook, calls this kind of approach the "hacker way." It means building the best services over the long term by quickly releasing and learning from smaller iterations rather than trying to get everything right up front.[29] The hacker way is an approach to testing as well, but testing customer acceptance, usability, and overall product concept robustness, rather than, say, reliability or scalability.

Software is particularly amenable to rapid pivots, but increasingly, so is hardware. Initial sketches used to be painstakingly hand-sculpted out of clay, then used to make molds which could be used by the factory to produce a prototype within weeks or months. Now, a 3D printer can do the same thing in minutes, or 3D virtual reality software and goggles can be used to create a virtual equivalent of a "product" or architectural rendering of something as large as a building or even a city, complete with a virtual walkthrough.

Between the extremes of pure agile approaches and pure structured planning there is the possibility of structured flexibility. As mentioned earlier, one of the leading innovation and design firms in the world, IDEO, incorporates flexibility into a five-step process: understand; observe; visualize; evaluate; and implement.[30]

From Employees to Crowds

The history of innovation is replete with employees who have made enormous contributions to their companies. This can include raw technology, as with the invention of the transistor by Bell Labs' employees John Bardeen, Walter Brattain, and William Shockley, or maximizing adoption through design excellence, as with Sir Jonathan (Jony) Ive, the senior vice president of design at Apple, since promoted to chief design officer.

There are many benefits to using employees for innovation: they know the existing product line, are dedicated to the task, can be trusted to keep the work confidential, and have existing working relationships and knowledge of company processes and strategy.

However, employees don't always have the right skill sets, because innovation can take companies far from existing competencies. Moreover, employees are paid salaries for effort and activities, regardless of whether they produce results. It may not be the employees' fault if results don't materialize: A solution to the problem they are addressing may not even exist, or may come from an unexpected discipline.

Moreover, for complex technical challenges, any company is on the losing side of a simple calculation: As P&G observed, in relevant technologies, there were fewer than 10,000 R&D personnel employed by the company, but 1.5 million outside it. Then there are additional practical issues: conflicting work priorities, personal objectives, time and cost to hire and train, recruiting fees, severance costs, and others. Temporary contractors resolve some, but not all, of these challenges.

Thus, there are compelling reasons to enlist expertise beyond employees, or even customers, suppliers, and partners, through crowd-based approaches such as contests, competitions, challenges, innovation networks, open-source initiatives, crowdsourcing, prediction markets, idea markets, crowdfunding, and hackathons. Companies can broadly canvass for suggestions and new product concepts, or attempt to solve extremely focused problems. They can use open-ended solicitations or highly structured contests or challenges with defined rules and time frames. From multiple responses, a single "best" one can be selected, several can be combined to produce an even better one, or they may suggest areas of future research for employees or external solvers.

Challenges can be used in a broad variety of domains and disciplines. For example, at data science competition site Kaggle.com, one contest is intended to determine the population of ocean plankton—a major driver of the health of the world's oceans—through automated analysis of towed underwater images.[31] Another challenge attempts to forecast the usage of city bicycle-sharing systems.[32] Another, run by an insurance company to better price premiums, attempts to classify drivers based on telematics data from vehicle sensors—such as the length of trips taken and how quickly the driver accelerates—rather than traditional demographics.[33]

The details vary, but typically a contest includes the specific goal, timelines, rules and processes for eligibility, entry, submissions, team formation, results validation, prize money distribution, handling ties, and so forth.

Data sets, which may be public, proprietary, or anonymized, may be included. In the case of Netflix, existing anonymized movie ratings were available to contestants. In the case of GE Flight Quest, multi-gigabyte data sets contained information such as daily scheduled and actual arrival times and weather. GE Hospital Quest offered data such as that on hospital utilization from the Centers for Disease Control and Prevention. Often, the data are split into a public set for analysis and algorithm development and a set used to validate or rate submissions. Perhaps most important, intellectual property ownership and openness agreements are well documented: normally, the act of submission transfers IP to the contest sponsor. Sometimes, the submissions are published for anyone to use or build on further.

Some contests are broad, as when companies canvass for new product ideas. Sometimes they are very focused, such as with an Innocentive.com challenge requesting materials for "replacing cellulose acetate fiber filter matrices." Sometimes they are short term, say, a few weeks. Others take longer: the contest(s) to prove Fermat's Last Theorem took 358 years.[34]

Some contests are transparent, with the innovation objective and overall business goal clearly stated, such as with the Netflix Prize. However, companies often don't want to telegraph their intent to competitors. One solution is to ask open-ended, broad questions (e.g., searching for innovations that apply to an entire product line). The other is to search for solutions to a specific technical problem without describing the specific business purpose.

No matter how interesting the challenge, it will fail without solvers. Consequently, enlisting and maintaining participation is an important activity, and may be pursued through an existing community or via public relations and social media. Wikis, FAQs (frequently asked questions), forums, and other social platforms for contestants to ask questions of the sponsors or each other create energy and a spirit of competition. Maintaining momentum by issuing a progress prize, as Netflix did, can be important for long-running contests.

While it's easy to get caught up in viewing innovation challenges through the metaphor of winning a competition, the objective is to solve a problem, not name a winner. Since collaboration between diverse participants usually generates better solutions than individuals operating in solitude, participants are often not only allowed, but encouraged, to team up.

Moreover, the exponentially increasing complexity of today's challenges and base of knowledge have reached a point where few individuals have the knowledge and mental tools to solve them. The Goldcorp Challenge to identify where to drill in Red Lake, Ontario, was won by an Australian team made up of two companies that developed an advanced 3D modeling tool for the mine. The Netflix Prize was won by a partnership of three teams: "KorBell" from AT&T Labs Research, an Austrian team named "Big Chaos," and a Canadian team: "Pragmatic Theory."

A challenge that is open to a crowd can benefit from the size of the crowd in several ways. One is that sometimes (but not always), the crowd knows, on average, the correct answer, better than virtually all individuals, even experts. Another benefit can be that a large group is likely to arrive at an answer more quickly than a small group. The Foldit contest asked people without any special skills in molecular biology to visualize how a three-dimensional object—a model of a protein molecule—might fold. Contestants were able to do better in two weeks than computers and researchers had in 15 years. A third benefit is that when special skills *are*—in hindsight—required, a larger group is more likely to include individuals with those skills. Also, the thrill of competition is likely to be an intrinsic motivator, which tends to drive the best results for knowledge work.

The cloud can help create idea markets and enable competitions. Innocentive, for example, calls out the cloud's role in innovation: "Our global network of millions of problem solvers, proven challenge methodology, and cloud-based innovation management platform combine to help our clients transform their economics of innovation through rapid solution delivery and the development of sustainable open innovation programs."[35]

From Salaries to Prizes

Besides generating more and better ideas more quickly, contests can offer direct financial advantages. Unlike paying for effort and activities regardless of whether the team has the necessary skills or generates any results, as with employees, the contest can be structured to only pay out for results, which can be evaluated quantitatively or qualitatively.

Often, practicality or scalability must be demonstrated, possibly through a proof of concept. In the event no solution is found, in the worst case, the cost of the effort is limited to the cost of running the contest, which can be ameliorated through the use of an efficient intermediary/platform such as Innocentive or Kaggle.

The prize may be cash or nonfinancial: recognition, enhanced reputation, experience development, community participation, or alignment with values—benefits that behavioral economics research shows are often viewed more highly by recipients than cash. If that seems surprising, note that major awards such as the Academy Awards come without any prize money yet are highly desirable. Of course, it may also include both cash and reputation, as with the Nobel Prize.

Beyond the overt benefit of the contest in solving a problem, there are numerous other benefits, such as the public relations value as news of the contest creates positive press or employee candidate interest for the organizer, and increased adoption as contestants are motivated to learn more about the firm's ecosystem. Running a contest for best Android app, say, not only results in a winning app, but thousands of developers who are now motivated to get up to speed on programming for Android.

In addition, solvers with specialized expertise can apply that expertise across multiple intellectually stimulating and rewarding problems across multiple firms. A single company might only occasionally have need for such expertise, leading to boredom.

However, the financial advantages of contest economics to contest organizers can also represent a disadvantage for contestants who put in substantial effort and receive nothing back. A contestant without some sort of reinforcement for participation, either winning occasionally or getting some sort of recognition, learning, or fulfillment of values, may eventually lose interest.

The reality or perception of unfairness in contest rules or problems in execution such as website submission technical issues can cause public relations issues or unforeseen expenses. Salesforce.com ran into trouble running a hackathon oriented toward building a new app because the winner may have reused existing code. Salesforce.com admitted that some of the rules on reuse had been "too vague," and ultimately, decided to respond by paying out an additional million-dollar prize to the second-place finisher (who did not reuse code)—an unexpected cost unlikely to happen with salaried employees.[36]

From Theoretical to Data-Driven

As the complexity of technology increases, so has the number of cloud-based tools to support the process of understanding problem sets and addressing such problems. These vary by industry e.g., circuit simulation tools, 3D modeling tools, molecular dynamics, seismic analysis, finite element analysis tools to assess everything from physical strength to heat transfer characteristics, and so forth.

For example, drug companies need to develop and assess various compounds for efficacy against various diseases. In general, these drugs act something like a key does in a lock. The physical surface of the drug molecule interacts with a receptor in the body or on the bacterium or virus to have some effect. Matching keys to locks is a challenge, because the three-dimensional shapes of the molecules may not be knowable merely from their chemical formulae, such as the sequence of amino acids making up a protein. Therefore, software has been developed to try to create three-dimensional molecular structures based on the constituent atoms and how atomic-level forces act, something like figuring out how to assemble Ikea furniture without the manual.

As a result, computer modeling of the real-world can be used to speed up what otherwise would be a tedious manual process of growing a sufficient quantity of the virus, fabricating a sufficient quantity of the drug being tested, putting them together in a test tube, and waiting to see what, if anything, happens.

Moreover, the late Jim Gray, formerly a Microsoft researcher, argued that science has entered a *fourth paradigm*. The first paradigm of science, he said, was *experimental*, which might also be thought of as observational, for example, dropping two objects of different weights and seeing whether one falls faster. The second paradigm, Gray said, is *theoretical*, devising theories and formulae such as that force equals mass times acceleration. The third paradigm of science, he said, is *computational*: an example being computer-based molecular analysis as above.

But the new fourth paradigm of science, he proposed, is *data-driven*, where incredible amounts of data, such as produced by the Large Hadron Collider, are processed to develop scientific insights.

One of the salient differences in this new approach to science is that theory- or model-building can be abandoned. For example, surprising results from experiments in how radioactive particles interacted with a thin sheet of gold foil led to the creation of the theory of atomic structure that we all know, where atoms have a concentrated nucleus surrounded by a cloud of electrons.

In this fourth paradigm of science, however, it is possible merely to note correlations without creating causal models. Rather than developing a deep understanding of *why* or *how* gold foil reflects particles or what causes cancer, it may be enough to note a positive correlation. For example, genetic analysis has shown that mutations in the BRCA1 and BRCA2 gene are associated with an increased incidence of breast cancer: about half of women with these mutations will develop breast cancer by age 70.[37] Mere knowledge of this correlation can help individuals stay more alert to the possible incidence of the disease, or take preventative measures, without a need for a specific model of how it does so (say, faulty production of tumor suppressor proteins).

Ultimately, though, computing will move from mere correlation to deeper models of the world through what is referred to as semantic computing. As Tony Hey, Microsoft's corporate vice president for research, argues, today's technology is great for basic tasks such as storing and processing data, but needs to get better at things like analysis, interpretation, and inference (i.e., model construction and insights into causal relationships).[38]

From Human to Machine

Machines can help humans analyze enormous amounts of big data, and develop statistical correlations, test algorithms, and conduct simulations. But what about the creative portion of innovation? That magical, out-of-the-box, flash of insight? Digital technologies are beginning to be applied there, as well, through techniques such as *automated hypothesis generation*. For example, computer software was used to analyze the abstracts of almost 200,000 scientific papers to develop theories about which types of proteins—called *kinases*—could activate a specific cancer-preventing protein called p53, and was able to propose nine proteins, of which seven have proved to have the desired property.[39]

Ultimately, the final intersection of innovation with technology will be where computers do all of our innovation for us, at least for as long as the machines are willing to continue to tolerate our presence. This is not just unfounded speculation: for example, cognitive cooking is already a reality and providing a new recipe for innovation.

IBM's Chef Watson uses a database of culinary ingredients and their chemical makeup, together with standard recipes, to gain knowledge about the world. It can then take a semi-random input such as "Tuscan peanut butter and squid paella sandwich" to generate a final recipe that is true to the inputs. It is thus innovating new combinations based on its knowledge base, which is really no different than, say, a jazz musician borrowing beats and riffs from multiple genres and artists. It is clearly not that much of a stretch to use a different knowledge base to respond to inputs such as "bendable touchscreen wearable humidity monitor" and someday soon have a complete design pop out.

Machine acceleration of innovation is not restricted to software. Emerald Therapeutics, in Silicon Valley, offers a multimillion-dollar, highly automated clinical research lab for rent. It can currently run dozens of different types of experiments, using robots and image processing equipment, to do experiments that medical research personnel would otherwise have to conduct laboriously by hand.[40]

From Incremental to Transformational

There is a lot to be said for incremental improvement. As GE points out, even a 1 percent improvement across industries can drive enormous impacts. The key is that 1 percent per se is not a lot, but when multiplied by a multibillion-dollar operating expense stream for a single company, or better yet, a trillion-dollar industry, the numbers add up quickly.

But IT can be used for transformational—not just incremental— innovation of processes, products, and relationships. The mere shift from physical to digital can be transformational. Digital technologies weren't just used to speed up the delivery of physical mail, but to replace it entirely by email. They weren't used to just improve bricks-and-mortar retail locations, but to move them completely online.

But IT isn't limited to mere replacement of physical with digital, or even the fusion of physical with digital. It can be used to completely transform and innovate business processes, product and service concepts, business models, pricing models, and customer relationships.

Uber didn't use IT to print out taxi driver paychecks faster or more inexpensively, it completely rethought the process of matching drivers to passengers using a constellation of digital technologies including mobile and GPS. Nest didn't primarily use digital technologies to put the ordering process for thermostats online, but instead embedded adaptive intelligence and sophisticated algorithms in its devices. The Mayo Clinic didn't use IT to better scan in patient release forms (well, maybe it did), but uses deep analytics against a repository of genomic information to pursue collective intimacy in targeting medicines and treatments.

■　■　■

Innovation applies to products and services, processes, customer relationships, and innovation itself. Digital technologies can be used to accelerate innovation in numerous ways: conducting virtual experiments, enabling rapid prototyping, supporting collaboration, contests, challenges, and competitions, idea markets, innovation networks, prediction markets, open communities, computational modeling, and data-driven analysis, and ultimately, not just machine learning but hypothesis generation and machine creativity. These tactics work individually, but can also build off each other, leading to a virtuous cycle of accelerating innovation.

Innovation is, perhaps, more than anything, about achieving the right balance: between structure and serendipity; theory and practice; competition and collaboration; direction and freedom; management and autonomy; internal and external; closed and open; short-term and long-term; strategy and opportunity; and being simultaneously business-oriented, customer-oriented, and technology-oriented.

Notes

1. Geoffrey A. Moore, *Crossing the Chasm: Marketing and Selling High-Tech Products to Mainstream Customers* (New York: HarperCollins, 1991).
2. "A Brief History of Con Edison," *ConEd.com*, www.coned.com/history/electricity.asp.
3. Paul Israel, "Edison's Laboratory," *GilderLehrman.org*, www.gilderlehrman.org/history-by-era/gilded-age/essays/edison%E2%80%99s-laboratory.
4. "General Electric Research Lab," *EdisonTechCenter.org*, www.edisontechcenter.org/GEresearchLab.html.
5. Donald Scott McPartland, "Almost Edison: How William Sawyer and Others Lost the Race to Electrification," Graduate Dissertation, 2006, 362.
6. Henry Chesbrough, *Open Innovation: The New Imperative for Creating and Profiting from Technology* (Boston: Harvard Business School Press, 2003), 22.
7. David A. Hounshell, *Science and Corporate Strategy: Du Pont R and D, 1901–1980* (Cambridge: Cambridge University Press, 1988), 250.
8. Jonah Lehrer, "Groupthink: The Brainstorming Myth," *The New Yorker*, January 30, 2012, www.newyorker.com/reporting/2012/01/30/120130fa_fact_lehrer.
9. Jeffrey H. Dyer, Hal Gregersen, and Clayton M. Christensen, "The Innovator's DNA," *Harvard Business Review* (December 2009).
10. Jonathan D. Rockoff, "Drug Scouts Chase Hot Prospects," *Wall Street Journal*, March 10, 2014, A1.
11. Elon Musk, "All Our Patent Are Belong to You," Tesla Blog, June 12, 2014, www.teslamotors.com/blog/all-our-patent-are-belong-you.
12. "A Scalable, Cost and Atom-Efficient Synthesis of a Benzothiazepine," *Innocentive.com*, September 17, 2014, https://www.innocentive.com/ar/challenge/9933600.
13. Robert Hof, "With IdeaMarket, Idealab's Bill Gross Wants to Create 1 Million Startups," *Forbes.com*, September 8, 2014, www.forbes.com/sites/roberthof/2014/09/08/with-ideamarket-idealabs-bill-gross-wants-to-create-1-million-startups/.
14. Harley Manning and Kerry Bodine, *Outside In: The Power of Putting Customers at the Center of Your Business* (New York: Houghton Mifflin Harcourt: 2012).

15. Owen Linzmayer, "Steve Jobs' Best Quotes Ever," *Wired.com*, March 29, 2006, archive.wired.com/gadgets/mac/commentary/cultofmac/2006/03/70512.

16. Steve Blank, "BIF9: Steve Blank—The Repeatable Path to Startup Success," [Video], *BusinessInnovationFactory.com*, businessinnovationfactory.com/iss/video/bif9-Steve-Blank.

17. James McQuivey, *Digital Disruption: Unleashing the Next Wave of Innovation* (Las Vegas, NV: Amazon Publishing, 2013), 26.

18. Malcolm Gladwell, "The Ketchup Conundrum," *The New Yorker*, September 6, 2004, www.newyorker.com/archive/2004/09/06/040906fa_fact_gladwell.

19. Ilan Brat, "The Emotional Quotient of Soup Shopping," *Wall Street Journal*, February 17, 2010, online.wsj.com/news/articles/SB10001424052748704804204575069562743700340.

20. "Neuroscience Completes Our Understanding of Consumers," *Innerscope Research.com*, innerscoperesearch.com/approach/.

21. Simon Wardley, "Understanding Ecosystems," *Bits or Pieces?* blog, March 3, 2014, http://blog.gardeviance.org/2014/03/understanding-ecosystems-part-i-of-ii.html; Private communication with the author, March 2, 2015.

22. Om Malik, "New Startup Economics: Why Amazon (Web Services) and Dropbox Need Each Other," *Gigaom.com*, November 16, 2013, gigaom.com/2013/11/16/new-startup-economics-why-amazon-web-services-and-dropbox-need-each-other/.

23. John Koetsier, "This 12-Year-Old Kid Learned to Code on Codecademy, Built 5 Apps, and Is Speaking at SXSW," *VentureBeat.com*, August 14, 2013, venturebeat.com/2013/08/14/this-12-year-old-kid-learned-to-code-on-codecademy-built-5-apps-and-is-speaking-at-sxsw/.

24. Jeff Grubb, "How This 14-Year-Old Girl Designed, Developed, and Released Her Own Mobile Game," *VentureBeat.com*, GamesBeat, March 16, 2015, venturebeat.com/2015/03/16/how-this-14-year-old-girl-designed-developed-and-released-her-own-mobile-game/.

25. Chesbrough, *Open Innovation*, 14.

26. Amy-Mae Elliott, "10 Fascinating YouTube Facts That May Surprise You," *Mashable.com*, February 19, 2011, mashable.com/2011/02/19/youtube-facts/.

27. Nicholas Carlson, "The Real History Of Twitter," *BusinessInsider.com*, April 13, 2011, www.businessinsider.com/how-twitter-was-founded-2011-4.

28. McQuivey, *Digital Disruption*, 47.

29. Epicenter Staff, "Mark Zuckerberg's Letter to Investors: 'The Hacker Way,'" *Wired.com*, February 1, 2012, www.wired.com/2012/02/zuck-letter/.

30. Tom Kelley with Jonathan Littman, *The Art of Innovation: Lessons in Creativity from IDEO*, America's Leading Design Firm (New York: Crown Business, 2001).

31. "Predict Ocean Health, One Plankton at a Time," *Kaggle.com*, December 15, 2014, www.kaggle.com/c/datasciencebowl.

32. "Forecast Use of a City Bikeshare System," *Kaggle.com*, May 28, 2014, www .kaggle.com/c/bike-sharing-demand.

33. "Use Telematics Data to Identify a Driver Signature," *Kaggle.com*, December 15, 2014, www.kaggle.com/c/axa-driver-telematics-analysis.

34. Gina Kolata, "At Last, Shout of 'Eureka' in Age-Old Math Mystery," *New York Times*, June 24, 1993, www.nytimes.com/1993/06/24/us/at-last-shout-of-eureka-in-age-old-math-mystery.html.

35. "What We Do," *Innocentive.com*, www.innocentive.com/about-innocentive.

36. Katharine Fong, "Salesforce Hackathon Fallout: Now Contest Has Two Winners," KQED News, December 3, 2013, http://blogs.kqed.org/newsfix/2013/11/25/salesforce-hack-scandal/.

37. "BRCA1 and BRCA2: Cancer Risk and Genetic Testing," National Cancer Institute, www.cancer.gov/cancertopics/factsheet/Risk/BRCA.

38. Tony Hey, "eScience and the Fourth Paradigm: Data-Intensive Scientific Discovery and Digital Preservation," *Alliance for Permanent Access*, 2011, www .alliancepermanentaccess.org/wp-content/uploads/2011/12/apa2011/15_(Nov11) TonyHey-APA%20Meeting.pdf.

39. "Computer Says 'Try This'," *The Economist*, October 4, 2014, www.economist .com/news/science-and-technology/21621704-new-type-software-helps-researchers-decide-what-they-should-be-looking.

40. Evelyn M. Rusli, "Research Labs Jump to Cloud," *Wall Street Journal*, July 1, 2014, B4.

CHAPTER 16

Procter & Gamble Cleans Up

On March 7, 2000, just when the Dow had finally cleared 10,000, it plummeted 375 points, or almost 4 percent, its fourth-worst point loss in history at the time, destroying $300 billion in market capitalization. The cause? A surprise earnings miss from Procter & Gamble, which ended down 31 percent for the day and 50 percent for the year to date. Three months later, in the midst of continuing financial turmoil, then-CEO Durk Jager resigned, and was replaced by A. G. Lafley.[1,2] Under Lafley's leadership, the stock has turned the tide and tripled, in large part by P&G rethinking its approach to innovation.

Procter & Gamble's logic was straightforward: The need for top-line growth drives a requirement for continued successful innovation, but the need for bottom-line growth means that funds allocated to innovation need to remain relatively constant. Thus, *innovation productivity* needs to increase, a simple principle made difficult in a world with increasingly arcane technologies, global competition, and the complexities of interdisciplinary connections, often ameliorated only through serendipity.

The Procter & Gamble story begins in 1837, when William Procter, who made candles, and James Gamble, who made soap, accepted their (mutual) father-in-law's suggestion to go into business together, partly to better negotiate for raw materials. Since then, Procter & Gamble has become the world's largest consumer packaged goods company thanks in large part to a long history of successful innovation.

One of the first US patents ever awarded, "Apparatus for Molding Candles," was issued to James Gamble and Joseph Hill on December 30, 1841.[3] Gamble's innovation was to use a water bath to cool newly molded candles, thus enabling hundreds of candles to be simultaneously and uniformly produced without the use of ice, an early example of operational excellence: enhanced labor productivity, quality, and sustainability.

Ivory Soap, first offered in 1879, was the first soap whipped with air during production and thus able to float on water, thereby not getting lost at the bottom of the wash tub. Crisco, introduced in 1911, was the first shortening made from vegetable oil, using the newly invented technique of hydrogenation. Tide, in 1946, was the first heavy-duty synthetic detergent (originally intended for clothes *and* dishes—times have changed), based on developments in surfactants. Crest, in 1955, was the first toothpaste to successfully contain fluoride. Pampers, birthed in 1961, was the first affordable disposable diaper. Pringles, in 1967, was the first stackable potato chip, thanks to its hyperbolic paraboloid shape, innovative ingredients, and an innovative baking process.

P&G has also been a pioneer in human resources innovation—introducing profit sharing, half-day Saturdays, employee stock ownership, and employee disability benefits—and in advertising innovation—newspaper, radio, and television, including the first "soap" operas.[4]

It has been a leader in management and organizational innovation, creating *brand* management, where a single manager is responsible for profit and loss for a product, and then *category* management, to ensure that optimized trade-offs are made between related P&G brands within a category, rather than there being all-out internal warfare. It also was an early leader in quality control and business ethics, with guarantees such as "Highest Grade, Honest Weight" and "99$^{44}/_{100}$% Pure," backed by independent certification.

Today, Procter & Gamble employs over 100,000 employees, serves 5 billion consumers globally, operates in 180 countries and has two dozen billion-dollar brands, leading to global annual revenues of over $80 billion, and a market cap of a quarter of a trillion dollars at this writing. It has since divested Crisco and Pringles, but owns numerous name brands such as Always, Bounty, Charmin, Dawn, Downy, Febreze, Gain, Gillette, Head & Shoulders, Nyquil, Olay, Oral B, Pantene, and Tampax. This list may change: On February 19, 2015, P&G announced that it would divest itself of brands representing about 14 percent of revenues to better focus on ones that "played to its strengths."[5]

Like a washing machine, P&G's business environment is under constant agitation: Consumer tastes change, established competitors and new entrants are always ready to pounce. While having nearly two dozen billion-dollar brands is an amazing accomplishment, a company the size of P&G needs to grow by several billion dollars each year, equivalent to adding a few new billion-dollar brands. In 2000, when the stock lost half its value due to a slowdown in growth, unimpressive new product launches, and earnings misses, P&G assessed that was in large part due to a vast majority of new products not hitting their financial targets (i.e., deep problems in the product innovation process).

That's when P&G realized that attempting to generate all of its hits internally would be a potentially insurmountable challenge, and refocused itself on a comprehensive corporatewide open innovation program called "Connect + Develop." In a way, this was not a radical departure from its legacy, since P&G has a century-old tradition of collaborating externally to generate hits.

Internal R&D, beginning with US Patent 2,405, the candle molding patent, does not necessarily represent the balance of P&G's innovation history; the (external) acquisitions of hydrogenation technology to create Crisco and alkyl sulfate technology to create Tide were probably more in line with tradition.

But the old approach—acquiring a company after it had a strong market presence and market cap reflecting that, or accidentally stumbling upon an active area of research—needed to be improved, and a more formal way of collaborating beyond the company's four walls was required.

The innovation turnaround at P&G did not happen by luck, but through planning. P&G recognized the importance of internal alignment, the right culture, the right organization structure, and support from the top. A new technology will not magically make its way to market. It needs support, commitment, funding, and cooperation from a broad array of functions such as manufacturing and legal. One of P&G's learnings, therefore, has been the importance of CEO visibility and commitment to new product concepts. Culture is also critical: employees need to be and feel just as or more rewarded for acquiring external ideas and collaborating with internal colleagues, not always easy in any research culture in academia or in industry, which, after all, traditionally prizes brilliance and invention over collaboration.

A well-thought-out organization structure at P&G has a VP for innovation, with direct reports, such as legal resources and personnel that liaise with external supplier and technology networks, and indirect reports that are responsible for Connect + Develop in the business units. These activities are monitored, improved, coordinated, and aligned with overall business and technology strategy, which prioritizes investments in core technologies in light of corporate strategy and competitive assessment.

P&G's approach can sometimes include setting up a wholly owned subsidiary or joint venture. P&G developed technologies such as tear-resistance and adhesives while researching diapers that were applicable to trash bags and food wrap. These were put into a joint venture with Clorox's Glad brand, reaching over a billion dollars in sales.[6]

From Solitary to Collaborative

In 1859, P&G hired James Norris Gamble, the co-founder's eldest son, as its first researcher, leading R&D. He began to systematically improve the product and production process for soap and candles.

One of the first fruits of P&G's research was the development of Ivory Soap, which matched the quality of imported European soaps, but at a substantially lower price-point. In addition, it was gentle enough to use on skin, but strong enough to use to clean floors. And if that weren't enough, it floated on water, so wouldn't get lost in a cleaning tub.

In addition to technology innovation, Ivory also exemplified marketing innovation. It was P&G's first branded product, was advertised heavily, and James's cousin Harley Procter, who led sales and marketing, engaged third parties to verify the claims about the product. If there ever had been any questions as to the ROI of innovation, Ivory dispelled them as it rapidly became P&G's bestselling product.

Although Ivory is still well-known, the second-bestselling product of that era was Lenox Soap. It had a slightly different formulation making it better suited to washing clothes, but also had a user interface improvement: a shape better suited for holding while using a washboard.

In 1890, P&G opened one of the first R&D labs anywhere, at its Ivorydale production facility. This lab focused on analytical chemistry and grew to become an entire division that fed research insights to a manufacturing process design organization that eventually deployed improved methods in P&G's factories.[7]

There are numerous other discoveries, inventions, and innovations attributed to P&G scientists. For example, pyrithione zinc, an ingredient that reduces dandruff, was discovered after 10 years of research, and commercialized as Head & Shoulders shampoo. Always Maxi-Pads were developed based on a proprietary "top sheet" technology called Dri-Weave, and then further improved to create Always Infinity, through a technology called Infinicel that could absorb up to 10 times its weight in liquids. Liquid Tide was based on research into surfactants. Pert Plus was the first combined shampoo and conditioner.

Besides profitable brands, P&G has also made major breakthroughs in sustainability. Tide Coldwater was formulated to clean most effectively at low temperatures, because most of the energy use of a washing machine is for heating water. Various "compaction technologies," where the same amount of, say, cleaning power uses less volume of product and thus lowers transportation costs and carbon footprint, have also been developed across many categories.

From Internal to External

Rather than relying solely on creative employees, P&G uses a variety of networks maintained by the company as well as available through idea and technology marketplaces. External sources include customers, suppliers, venture capital firms, start-ups, established firms, universities, research institutions, the government, and competitors.

Yes, competitors. In some cases, competitors can create the compelling need, as when P&G's CoverGirl had to create new mascara applicators to work around L'Oréal's patents. In other cases, competitors can become partners, as when the Swiffer Duster arose through a P&G partnership with Japanese competitor Unicharm. Unicharm had the product; P&G had the global distribution muscle.[8]

In an early example of innovation outside the four walls of the company, a new technology, *hydrogenation*, which transforms oils into fats, was acquired by P&G from chemist Edwin Kayser in the early 1900s. P&G then created the first all-vegetable shortening, soon called Crisco, by hydrogenating cottonseed oil. As a lower-cost substitute for butter, it rapidly caught on.[9]

In 1932, P&G licensed alkyl sulfates for use as synthetic detergents. This led to the introduction of Dreft the next year as the first household synthetic detergent, and then Drene shampoo. But this technology really came to fruition in 1946, when Tide was introduced. It was much more effective as a detergent than anything else on the market, and rapidly catapulted to number one. Seventy years later, it still is the market share leader, and commands a premium price.

Crest toothpaste is another important example of successful commercial innovation based on external technology. Indiana University had a research project underway to determine which fluoride compound would be most useful for dental care. P&G researchers collaborated to jointly develop and test various compounds and how to incorporate them into a paste. Within a few years, they had formulated and introduced Crest, which was the first toothpaste shown to prevent cavities and tooth decay.

Fewer cavities, of course, are bad for business if you're a dentist. Crest realized that and created a collaborative relationship with dentists, refocusing them on prevention, rather than just diagnosis and cure. A focus on adoption, not just invention, is, as discussed earlier, key to successful commercial innovation.

A new monofilament-screen-based papermaking process originally developed in Japan was modified by P&G engineers to be softer, bulkier, and more absorbent. This new technology—Confidential Process F—ended up in tissues, disposable diapers, toilet paper, and paper towels, and helped create three billion-dollar brands: Pampers, Charmin, and Bounty.

There are seemingly endless examples. Bounce was developed using dryer-sheet fabric softener technology that was licensed. Ariel, a detergent better known outside the United States, was based on an enzyme cleaner already on the market, used for cleaning blood from butcher's aprons, which was combined with encapsulated bleach, an active area of research at P&G.

P&G's Oral B division collaborated with Braun to develop the world's first powered toothbrush that was clinically proven to work better than a regular manual one.

P&G's Regenerist exploited new peptide technology developed by the French company Sederma to become the top selling product line in the multi-billion dollar Olay product line.[10,11]

P&G's Mr. Clean Magic Eraser began life as a technology called Basotec invented at BASF, which was commercialized in Japan, discovered in a grocery store in Osaka by a P&G "technology entrepreneur," one of dozens of senior personnel located in hubs around the world who prioritize needs, write technology briefs, maintain relationships with global researchers, and keep their eyes and ears open for everything from new patents to products appearing on store shelves, such as this. In addition to product ideas, they also look for process improvements.

This internal entrepreneur then sent an analysis including local market penetration and strategic fit to P&G headquarters, which led to posting on an internal collaboration tool called the "eureka catalog," which, in turn, led to an evaluation of market opportunity, which supported an initial licensing agreement with BASF, which evolved into an agreement for further collaboration.

BASF and P&G then continued to work together in shared labs to improve the product and the underlying technology. This partnership led to a variety of product extensions, such as one targeted at cleaning wheels and tires.

P&G acquired not just technologies, but businesses as well: Vicks VapoRub, a salve invented in 1894 that leveraged menthol, a then-exotic ingredient from Japan;[12] King Gillette's patented safety razor and "razor and razor blades" business model, created in 1901; and Max Factor's "Color Harmony" cosmetics in a palette of matching shades, to name a few.

It would be a mistake to characterize P&G as simply transitioning from internal to external; P&G has a hybrid model. When a need for a technology arises, P&G first looks inside for existing relevant work, *then* looks outside if nothing is found. Only if there are apparently no useful existing technologies does P&G consider attempting to invent an answer internally, create one externally, or both.

Besides outside independent experts, academics, or specialty firms, P&G's top suppliers have tens of thousands of researchers, so P&G often partners with them. Often this involves presenting technology briefs or strategic directions to suppliers under nondisclosure, and then, should circumstances warrant, fostering collaboration between P&G and supplier researchers in each other's labs.

From Closed to Open

There is a spectrum of innovation strategies—from skunkworks to crowdsourcing—that can drive a spectrum of outputs—from proprietary products to fully open products and technologies that are shared. Procter & Gamble uses virtually all of these approaches to acquire various technologies or companies, or to commercialize various capabilities externally.

It is known for evolving from and complementing internal R&D with open innovation, or, as P&G would put it, moving from Research + Development to Connect+Develop. Pringles Prints is a perfect example.

In 2002, P&G held a brainstorming exercise around how to differentiate their snack foods and make them more fun. Someone had the idea of printing pictures, trivia questions, or jokes on to Pringles, the potato-based stackable snack. Simple in concept, it wasn't clear that it could be executed. After all, a potato chip is hardly an Apple Retina display. Moreover, it's not as if production costs and volumes would allow for artists to hand paint each chip; it needed to be done in volumes of millions of chips as they flew out of the cooking machine.

P&G also realized that the words would need to print on a chip measuring just a few square inches, just after it was fried, with sufficient resolution to be readable, in multiple colors, using dyes that were edible.

There are three ways that this challenge could have been solved. A pure internal innovation approach would have assembled a team of P&G's best and brightest, hoping that they could solve problems ranging from cooking and dye ingredients to production processes. A focused external innovation approach would have selected a partner or supplier, perhaps a printing company or dye company, after issuing an RFP, perhaps, or entering into negotiations to license technology or create a joint venture.

But that's not what P&G did. Instead, it created a *technology brief* that explained what it was trying to do, without revealing any product details. P&G then distributed the brief to its network—consultants, universities, partner firms, and so on—and found a university professor in Bologna who had figured out how to print images on baked goods. This professor not only ran a bakery but also had built and refined the baking equipment that printed the images.[13] Partly thanks to an innovative product idea that was then realized through externally developed technology, Pringles continued substantial growth in sales. Moreover, by sourcing technology externally, product development costs and intervals were cut dramatically.

This approach, not only external but also open, was a result of the re-imagination of P&G's approach to innovation initiated by Lafley shortly after being named at the turn of the millennium. Lafley set a goal that half of P&G's innovations arise externally. P&G had about 7,500 researchers internally, and its estimate was that there were 1.5 million researchers outside the company with relevant skill sets.

Utilizing these skills, according to Larry Huston, then vice president for innovation and knowledge, and Nabil Sakkab, then senior vice president for corporate R&D, would require wholesale changes: a change in culture away from "not invented here" syndrome; a change in the self-conception of the organization to include external scientists and engineers; a change in operational processes; and of course, a change in supporting information technology to enable the distribution of and response to "briefs" like the one for Pringles.

Open innovation comprises not only acquiring external technologies but also monetizing internally developed intellectual property through external routes. For example, P&G licensed CoverGirl, a brand of cosmetics, to an eyewear manufacturer. Trademarks and products sometimes go hand in hand: P&G licensed Febreze to Honeywell, which created the Honeywell® Febreze® Freshness™ Cool & Refresh Fan, which comprises Honeywell hardware and Febreze air freshening scent cartridges. P&G has also used Yet2.com, which is something like an eBay for companies looking to buy or sell technologies. Any company, university, research institution, or government lab can act as buyer or seller. Through Yet2.com, P&G was able to acquire several relevant technologies, and also sell off an innovative low-cost "microneedle" technology to a medical company.

From Inside-Out to Outside-In

CEO Lafley defines the scope of innovation very broadly and from the perspective of the consumer. While product and technology are relevant, he says it includes "the brand, in addition to the product; it's the design of the shopping and the usage experience, in addition to the functional attributes or benefits; it is the business model; it is the way we go to market and the supply chain; it is the way we create a cost structure so we can deliver delightful new products at affordable costs."[14] In other words, innovation needs to address end-to-end processes, the total product, and customer relationships and experience.

P&G uses several mechanisms to work outside-in, incorporating customers' needs into their innovation process. Each year, P&G spends $400 million to run 20,000 studies in 100 countries involving 5 million consumers to understand customer needs and wants in detail. For example, it sent a team to India to determine what would be required to create a low-cost razor that would meet the unique characteristics of that market, such as using a cup of water to shave rather than running water at a faucet or a shower.[15]

P&G also determines and prioritizes needs at the corporate and business unit level. For laundry detergent, say, the needs might be lower weight, longer shelf life, or better performance removing oily food stains. At the corporate level, it might include increasing the absorbency of paper products, which would benefit Bounty, Pampers, and Charmin. These needs then drive the creation of technology briefs that feed the open innovation process described earlier.

According to Lafley, P&G is focused on ensuring that the consumer is involved extremely early in the innovation process, so that P&G can co-create and co-design the new product with target consumers. As he puts it, "We want the consumer engaged at the front end ... right after we have an idea, right after we have the kernel of a technology, right after we have the most primitive of prototypes."[16]

Moreover, P&G does this within an envelope of focus and adjacency. It is probably not going to spend a lot of time looking at whether it should enter the commercial spaceflight business, but looks to meet needs adjacent to existing customer's needs or current products and technologies.

For example, Crest, originally a toothpaste, now is also used to brand whitening strips. In some cases, a technology, product or business acquisition might be new to P&G, as with Gillette razors; in other cases it might meet a similar need, as with the acquisition of Tampax even though P&G offered Always; in other cases the fit might be with some P&G distinctive competency or capability, such as technology, brand, or distribution.

From Employees to Crowds

P&G maintains a standing set of networks, for example, through its technology entrepreneurs, and through executive and working relationships with its top suppliers.

But often, that is not enough. New challenges arise for which existing networks are insufficient: P&G doesn't have the solution; outside researchers already in the network don't have the solution; it may not even be clear that there *is* a solution. Therefore, P&G uses its own website, as well as talent, idea, and intellectual property markets such as NineSigma, Innocentive, Yet2.com, and YourEncore to support open innovation through crowdsourcing.

At pgconnectdevelop.com, P&G pursues suggestions in product areas, such as personal care, beauty, and household care; process areas, such as manufacturing and packaging; and customer engagement, such as digital and retail. For example, one brief looks for technologies that can offer a smoother shave by improving the lubricating strip on razors. Requirements are quite specific, ranging from product performance—"maintain the integrity of the film under high shear rates of $>10^4 s^{-1}$"—to usage conditions—"15–45°C water temperature" and "linear velocities up to 0.5 m/s"—to commercialization—such as providing competitive advantage through scalability, and proven technical feasibility.[17]

YourEncore is something like a temp agency for veteran research expertise. Its almost 10,000 researchers are typically retired from long careers, have an average of 25 years of experience, and have in-depth theoretical and practical knowledge. They can work for a few days or over a year, and can work on site or virtually. The value proposition is clear: short-term access to world-class expertise, without the costs and commitment of hiring an employee. Moreover, YourEncore researchers are likely to have had experience across many firms acting as employers or contractors, bringing multiple perspectives and cross-industry insights.

An on-demand base of expert contractors can complement existing R&D employees to meet specialized needs. The time associated with acquiring a contractor is less than that associated with recruiting, onboarding, and training an employee, and the cost is less than recruiting fees, signing bonuses, and ongoing salaries, stock ownership, health benefits, severance, and so forth. However, no matter how good the contractor, payment is *activity-based*, on a time and perhaps travel and living basis without any guarantee of results.

This is one of the reasons that P&G also uses alternative *results-based* approaches from companies such as Innocentive, NineSigma, and Yet2.com. They act as intermediaries, matching companies that have problems with individuals that have the expertise to solve them. While terminology varies, the problems/challenges/technology briefs lay out the problem, and then experts/solution providers/solvers can submit an answer. Rather than a closed, proprietary network of relationships, there is no bound to the number of potential solvers that may have expertise to address the challenge. If the solution solves the challenge, or appears promising, the intermediary connects the solver with P&G—or whoever posed the challenge—and things proceed from there.

P&G has given focused problems to tens of thousands of scientists through Innocentive, and broader problems to hundreds of thousands of people through NineSigma, with a substantial fraction of problems being solved and driving further collaboration between the solver and P&G.

It is in such talent and innovation markets that information technology shines. The fact that there were well over a million more researchers in relevant technologies outside of P&G than inside has always been the case. But, as Jeff Weedman, former VP of external business at P&G said, prior to the Internet and the emergence of cloud services, technologies didn't exist to reach all those scientists, and therefore, "the [sudden] interconnectedness with all the new communication systems meant that we had a much broader sourcing and we could reach all the people that had capabilities."[18]

From Incremental to Transformational

As a final step in its transformation, P&G realized that while incremental innovations were helpful to its growth objectives, it needed to have a few big hits on a predictable basis, not just a field where a thousand flowers bloomed.

It embraced Clayton Christensen's theory of disruptive innovation and focused on creating a "new-growth factory," with the idea that the factory could churn out transformational innovations and business models on a regular basis by focusing on offers that were less expensive, more convenient, more accessible, or easier to use. To maximize growth, this factory focused on "transformational-sustaining" innovations, ones that created maximum disruptive opportunities in existing product lines. This is as opposed to incremental sustaining innovations (i.e., tweaking existing products); commercial promotions or campaigns such as coupons or advertising; or radical "disruptive" innovations (i.e., a total blue ocean approach to innovation).

The transformational-sustaining focus could multiply the benefits of existing market presence with the benefits of compelling differential value. For example, Crest, a strong brand that had been overtaken by Colgate, regained its prominence through Whitestrips and 3D White products, which disrupted the market for dental office whitening, and Pro-Health, which combined numerous benefits such as whitening, fresh breath, and tartar control.[19]

Organizationally, these are supported by groups that focus on inter-BU (business unit) and new white-space opportunities that are kept separate from the core business. These include a New Business Creation group and the P&G Corporate Innovation Fund, which acts as an internal VC (venture capitalist).

In 2015, P&G took things to a new level, when it announced a refocusing of the company on core brands and the sale of scores of brands that were profitable, but didn't fit within its future strategic areas of focus.

■   ■   ■

P&G's results have been impressive. Under Lafley, the stock not only recovered after its precipitous drop at the end of the millennium but has tripled. A large fraction of products that have been launched or are under development have key technologies and components that were brought in from external sources. The success rate of innovation increased even as its costs dropped, dramatically: R&D as a percentage of sales dropped by 25 percent.

Notes

1. Jake Ulick, "Dow Falls Nearly 400 Points," *CNNMoney.com*, March 7, 2000, money.cnn.com/2000/03/07/markets/markets_newyork/.
2. "P&G CEO Quits Amid Woes," *CNNMoney.com*, June 8, 2000, money.cnn.com/2000/06/08/companies/procter/.
3. James Gamble and Joseph S. Hill, "Apparatus for Molding Candles," *U.S. Patent 2,405*, December 30, 1841.
4. "P&G Story of Innovation," *PG.com*, www.pg.com/en_US/company/heritage.shtml.

5. Alexander Coolidge, "P&G: Expect Most Deals to Sell Brands by Summer," *Cincinnati.com*, February 19, 2015, www.cincinnati.com/story/money/business/2015/02/19/pg-execs-hope-to-sell-off-100-brands-by-mid-2016/23666633/.

6. "Glad ForceFlex® and Glad Pressn'Seal®," *PG.com*, October 10, 2012, www.pgconnectdevelop.com/home/stories/jvs-joint-ventures/20121010-glad-forceflex-and-glad-pressnseal.html.

7. "Technology," *PG.com*. www.pg.com/Heritage/technology.php.

8. Azure Corporation and Rotman Information Solutions, "Swiffer Duster—Competitors Collaborating to Win Together," *EnablingIdeas.com*, www.enablingideas.com/how-did-they-do-it/2011/12/swiffer-duster-competitors-collaborating-to-win-together/.

9. Robert Smith, "Who Killed Lard?" *NPR Planet Money*, February 3, 2012, www.npr.org/blogs/money/2012/02/03/146356117/who-killed-lard.

10. Alexander Coolidge, "P&G Reboots Its Olay Regenerist Line," *USA Today*, March 1, 2013, www.usatoday.com/story/money/business/2013/03/01/pg-reboots-olay-regenerist-line/1958085/.

11. Procter & Gamble, "P&G Innovation Story: Olay Regenerist," *YouTube.com*, January 26, 2011, www.youtube.com/watch?v=TCKZl9VWa-Y.

12. "How a Simple Case of Croup Led to a 'Truly Unique Product,'" *PG.com*, April 26, 2012, news.pg.com/blog/vicks/how-simple-case-croup-led-truly-unique-product.

13. Larry Huston and Nabil Sakkab, "Connect and Develop: Inside Procter & Gamble's New Model for Innovation," *Harvard Business Review* (March, 2006), https://hbr.org/2006/03/connect-and-develop-inside-procter-gambles-new-model-for-innovation.

14. TC Haldi, "Innovation at Procter & Gamble," [Video] *Harvard Business Review* (June 24, 2008), https://hbr.org/2008/06/innovation-at-procter-gamble.

15. Bruce Brown and Scott Anthony, "How P&G Tripled Its Innovation Success Rate," *Harvard Business Review* (June 2011), https://hbr.org/2011/06/how-pg-tripled-its-innovation-success-rate/ar/1.

16. Haldi, "Innovation at Procter & Gamble."

17. P&G, "Solid Lubricant for Blades and Razors," pgconnectdevelop.inovasuite.com/pg/ext/downloadFile?idDoc=143115&idObject=4401.

18. Dwayne Matthews, "An Open Innovation Discussion with Jeff Weedman of P&G," *Canadian Business Journal*, August 10, 2010, www.cbj.ca/features/features_august_10/an_open_innovation_discussion_with_jeff_weedman_of_p_g.html.

19. Brown and Anthony, "How P&G Tripled."

PART SIX

Successful Execution

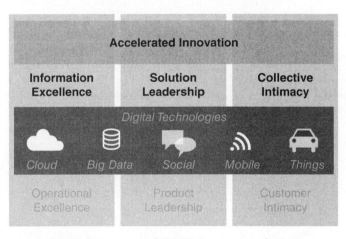

CHAPTER 17

General Electric— Flying High

O ver the preceding chapters, we've looked in depth at each of the four digital disciplines, as well as reviewed an exemplar for each. General Electric, it can be argued, has been successful not just in a single discipline, but in all four.

General Electric is one of the world's largest and longest-lived companies; a paragon of industry. It recently ranked fourth on the *Forbes* Global 2000, based on annual revenues of close to $150 billion, with over 300,000 employees, including 45,000 engineers, and an average R&D investment of over $4 billion per year. GE has also received accolades such as *Fortune's* World's Most Admired Companies, *MIT Technology Review's* 50 Smartest Companies, and *Barron's* Most Respected Companies.

While the average consumer might think of microwave ovens or light bulbs when they think of GE, it's a diversified conglomerate offering nuclear reactors, wind turbines, manufacturing automation systems, medical imaging systems, locomotives, jet engines, mining equipment, and commercial and personal financial services, such as leases and credit cards, although in April, 2015, it announced plans to divest most of these financial services and assets.

Founded in 1892, largely from several of Thomas Alva Edison's lighting and electrical equipment companies, GE was an inaugural member of the Dow Jones Industrial Average in 1896, and is considered to be the only one remaining of that initial group. It is evident that such longevity can only occur through continuous transformation and reinvention. Although GE's legacy is in electricity and "things that rotate," it has come to embrace a variety of digital technologies including software, analytics, and services. It is applying these across the board, becoming a rare example of a company applying all four digital disciplines.

GE recognized the value of IT before just about anyone. In 1954, it became the first company in the United States to deploy a computer for commercial purposes, spending over a million dollars for a UNIVAC.

GE had the prescience to see that this purchase might "eventually be recorded by historians as the foundation of the second industrial revolution."[1] Although the UNIVAC was initially used for mundane "data processing" tasks such as payroll and accounting, it was also used for early information excellence: optimization of material scheduling and inventory control, with plans to expand as quickly as possible into planning and forecasting and enhanced production and logistics optimization.[2]

GE has evolved substantially since then, recognizing the importance of software and digital technologies to its core business, and creating a center of excellence—GE Software—headed by vice president Bill Ruh.[3] Ruh has an academic background in mathematics, and he's held executive leadership positions at Cisco and Software AG and worked for companies such as IBM and MITRE. Ruh drives the strategy for GE's software solutions portfolio, under the moniker of the "Industrial Internet." He describes the Industrial Internet as the place where digital and physical worlds collide and thus where operational technology meets information technology, and he is the GE executive at the epicenter of this strategic initiative.

As Ruh puts it, the four digital disciplines are not separate, but integrated capabilities all focused on customers' needs for business outcomes, such as lower operating costs and higher availability. This shifts the orientation of a company like GE from merely selling a product to helping customers to run their business, for example, optimizing operations and offering algorithms for predictive maintenance. He also observes that software is the cornerstone of all four disciplines, and dramatically changes the nature of competition: Software shortens the development cycle, leading to constant learning and innovation. This, in turn, requires major shifts in skills, culture, and organization, ranging from software development talent to a shift to cross-functional teams, rapid prototyping with customer feedback, and a focus on speed.

To understand this sea change, consider jet engines. Traditionally, product leadership meant things like new physical engine designs, such as a reduction in the number of turbofan blades, and materials, such as ceramic-matrix composites. Operational excellence meant quality control in manufacturing those engines. Customer intimacy meant frequent face-to-face meetings with aircraft manufacturers and airlines to understand their requirements, say, for reliability and fuel efficiency. And innovation meant GE Research PhDs working in their labs on advanced materials and aerodynamics.

All of those are still important. However, now, according to Ruh and Darin DiTommaso, the general manager of digital services and solutions engineering at GE Aviation, for those same jet engines, operational excellence has expanded to embrace information excellence, with GE expanding its focus into service operations, applying sophisticated algorithms, and partnering with airlines to achieve business outcomes: improved processes, enhanced passenger satisfaction through optimized routing, reduced operating costs including fuel consumption, and enhanced availability through predictive maintenance to maximize "time on wing." Product leadership has become solution leadership, by connecting physical jet engines to cloud-based *virtual* jet engines modeled in software, collaboration tools, analytics and even social media through a common aviation analytics platform that enables field engineers to collaborate with central R&D and customers. Customer intimacy has become collective intimacy, with GE gathering data from all customers about their engines' performance, and using that data to tailor individual recommendations to each (airline) customer and engine. Finally, GE has accelerated innovation, through internal R&D process and platform improvements, co-creation and prototyping with customers, and open contests to better predict and improve flight arrival times. The digital disciplines are being applied not just for jet engines, but across GE's multiple divisions.

In GE's vision for the Industrial Internet, tens of billions of machines become connected, machine operations become remote and virtual, data analytics become predictive, the machines become self-healing and fully automated, monitoring and maintenance leverage mobile technologies, and employee productivity increases. GE claims that there are trillions of dollars of opportunity over the next 15 years. These numbers are not pulled out of a hat, but based on a bottoms-up analysis of a variety of sectors. For example, a 1 percent reduction in aviation fuel equates to $US2 billion a year. A similar saving in healthcare operations equates to US$4 billion a year. A 1 percent improvement in oil and gas asset utilization and operational expenses is worth US$6 billion a year. As Senator Everett Dirksen allegedly said, a billion here and a billion there, and pretty soon you're talking real money.

Digital Disciplines at GE

GE's strategy encompasses information excellence, solution leadership, collective intimacy, and accelerated innovation.

Information Excellence. GE is a heavy user of the latest technologies, such as supply chain management and robotics and 3D printing for manufacturing and prototyping. GE has a robust program of internal process improvement and information excellence called "GE Advantage," addressing cost reduction and price optimization, time compression for product introduction and service responsiveness, and product and service quality and availability improvements. These initiatives permeate virtually all of GE's divisions. GE Advantage has 1,000 employees working on 40 process improvement projects, with a goal of generating nearly a billion US dollars in benefits annually. In addition, GE has a number of digitally enabled process optimization systems and services that it extends to customers in various verticals, to optimize flights, intermodal transport, hospital operations, railway operations, and so on. These digital capabilities include offers such as "Movement Planner," a kind of traffic cop for railways that routes trains and directs them to speed up or slow down. In one recent storm-related situation, the software counterintuitively recommended that high-priority cargo be sidelined and low priority be sent through. Because the low-priority cargo tended to be local, this cleared congestion points rapidly, enabling the high-priority cargo to rapidly get to its destination.

Solution Leadership. Although GE traditionally manufactured "products" such as dynamos and locomotives, today those products are merely the visible portion of complex solution ecosystems that include sophisticated software and comprehensive services. Locomotives and Movement Planner are an example; another is GE DoseWatch, which monitors radiation doses from medical diagnostic equipment such as CT scanners and x-ray machines to provide a patient-centric view that helps to balance image quality with radiation exposure. DoseWatch is surrounded by services such as project planning, training, and integration with devices and other hospital information systems. GE Healthcare Asset Management maintains medical diagnostic images in the cloud. This improves medical worker productivity, enables diagnostic image sharing across physicians, and also increases the validity of diagnostic insights.[4] Wind turbines are connected to cloud-based software, jet engines to analytics, and so forth.

Collective Intimacy. Netflix monitors data from *all* of its *consumer* customers, including data points such as movie watching behavior, time of day, device context, and so forth, to deliver recommendations to *each* customer to help optimize his or her entertainment experience. Similarly, GE Aviation acquires flight data from *all* of its *airline* customers. The data span details, including oil pressure and turbine rotation speed, are used to deliver recommendations to *each* customer to help optimize each airplane's fuel consumption and performance experience. GE MultiOmyx uses comprehensive data from human tissue samples from many patients to deliver patient-specific diagnosis and therapy (i.e., optimize each patient's health experience).

Accelerated Innovation. GE has several initiatives for reducing cycle time in its new product introduction process as well as exploiting open innovation through challenges such as Flight Quest and Hospital Quest. FastWorks is a major GE initiative oriented to adopting *lean startup* and *agile* principles. Over a thousand executives have gone through lean training, and over 100 projects have already been launched globally.[5] GE has run two Flight Quest contests. Flight Quest Phase 1 had the goal of better predicting flight arrival times; Phase 2 was intended to optimize flight paths to reduce costs and time while avoiding patches of bad weather. To get a sense of the intellectual firepower that the challenges unleashed, the winners—who are from around the world—used obscure techniques with names such as gradient boosting, random forest models, generalized linear models, ridge regressions, and machine learning based on over 1,000 variables.

Software at GE

GE is a terrific example of an old-line manufacturing conglomerate (with financial services, as well, which are being deemphasized). GE manufactures small appliances, but mostly seems to build multi-ton products like jet engines and nuclear reactors. However, to make progress in all four disciplines as just described, GE has realized that software, processors, big data, mobile networks, sensors, security, and related digital technologies and methodologies are critical to its future.

According to Bill Ruh, by using a combination of lean startup, agile methodologies, and extreme programming, GE's software release cycle was reduced by an order of magnitude: from 2 to 3 years down to $12 1/2$ weeks. The idea behind this combination is to rapidly develop a "minimum viable product," with just enough features and functions to illustrate and deliver to customers how the solution would work and then iterate rapidly. Moreover, rather than software developers waiting for systems engineers to huddle and try to guess what a useful product would be, the methodology emphasizes close collaboration between design engineers, developers, and customers. This rapidly leads to software products or features that customers actually want and find useful, rather than GE gambling an enormous amount of time and money on a "Spruce Goose" that no one wants.

In addition, average software development team size was reduced from 50 down to 9, under the theory that in small teams everyone knows what's going on and work can proceed rapidly; in large ones, accountability issues and communication and coordination complexity slow things down. GE has built a software development center in Silicon Valley and is considering building additional ones globally, complementing experienced developers with the talents of young digital natives who grew up immersed in smartphones and video games. These teams work in settings that look more like a startup than the offices of a century-old multinational conglomerate.

GE has created centers of excellence in data science and analytics, user experience design, and security. Security is particularly important in an industrial setting: It's one thing to lose your photos due to a computer virus, it's quite another to lose control of a nuclear reactor to a hacker. GE's architecture seamlessly melds sensors, controllers, networks, cloud services including virtual "machines" (such as computer models of jet engines), hybrid cloud computing infrastructure and platforms, and machine learning, statistics, and analytics.

Besides specific products and supporting software, such as DoseWatch, GE is refining and extending a horizontal platform and suite of software tools and solutions with broadly applicable capabilities such as analyzing large data sets, with names like Predix, Proficy, and Predictivity that will be useful across various divisions. They address resources and processes: asset optimization—maximizing the utilization and performance of facilities, equipment, devices, or human resources—and operations optimization—for example, shorter and more fuel-efficient flight paths.

In addition to the skills of GE's direct software employees, GE invested over $100 million in Pivotal, a company formed to exploit big data and predictive analytics, and also partners with companies such as Intel, AT&T, systems integrator Accenture, and cloud-computing provider Amazon Web Services (AWS). All these parts fit together. Jet engines, for example, might be monitored with data locally aggregated by Intel processors and uploaded over AT&T's wireless networks, with the resulting massive quantities of data stored at AWS and analyzed with GE software tools.

To accomplish this type of corporate transformation requires ongoing financial commitment, based on the strategic intent of the CEO and the leadership team. CEO Jeffrey Immelt proclaims that "industrial companies need to be in the software business."[6] He said, "We want to make the analytics around our products, real-time data, and operating solutions a GE core competency."

Let's delve more deeply into GE's strategy and achievements in each of the digital disciplines.

Information Excellence

There are multiple dimensions to information excellence: seamlessly fusing digital and physical operations, using information to tune physical processes, using information to achieve long-term process improvement, and using information to improve customer, partner, supplier, or supply-chain processes. Such improvements, as we've discussed, can address cost, quality, time, reliability, sustainability, and more, and can be focused on both asset performance and effectiveness and process optimization.

GE uses a variety of techniques within its process improvement efforts. Perhaps the most well-known is "Lean Six Sigma," which is intended to reduce process problems (defects) and variability and has been used at GE for two decades. At its core, Six Sigma leverages information excellence: accurate data and statistical analysis. "Lean" adds in notions of simplification and streamlining. Design for Six Sigma is also used, which, rather than fixing processes, is intended to ensure that they are optimally designed up front. Six Sigma is not universally viewed as the best approach to process improvement, particularly for unstructured activities such as transformational innovation, but there is little argument that it can add value when used in areas to which it is well suited. Another GE process improvement approach is Work-Out, devised at GE in the 1980's and since spread to other companies. It enables diverse cross-functional teams to brainstorm improvements. Change Acceleration Process (CAP) is both a proprietary methodology and set of tools to help ensure successful implementation of process improvements.

More broadly, GE has embraced a change in culture. In a recent annual report, CEO Jeffrey Immelt called out two books that had a substantial impact: *The Lean Startup* and *The Startup Playbook*. He observed that GE had become too complicated, and had too many "checkers," and not enough "doers." As a result, he decided to engage in a cultural transformation to make GE more entrepreneurial, specifically focusing on simplifying complexity, driving accountability, and investing actions with purpose.

GE is not just focused on improving its own operations, but those of its customers, customers' customers, and customers' customers' customers. Consider jet engines. Sure, it can use Six Sigma to improve the manufacturing process for casting turbine blades. But it views its scope as extending not just to, say Boeing and Airbus and other airframe manufacturers, but individual airlines such as United and Delta and helping them improve their processes. Actually, these benefits, such as on-time arrivals, even extend to passengers (the customers' customers' customers). The same for medical diagnostic equipment, where GE doesn't just make CT scanners, it helps hospitals (its direct customer), doctors, patients, and even their families (part of Hospital Quest was focused on improving the "health care system experience for patient and family").[7]

In the case of transportation, GE doesn't just try to manufacture better locomotives, it also helps railways optimize individual train movement, railway system logistics, and even intermodal (truck/rail/ship) transportation network logistics. GE's Movement Planner is an advanced software solution that provides real-time traffic planning and optimization, minimizing costs. The software takes into consideration the many variables within the rail network—speed limits on tracks, congestion, outages, derailments, track obstructions, potential meet/pass conflicts, ongoing maintenance, and overrides from dispatchers.

At Norfolk Southern, the system has resulted in a 10 percent increase in network velocity—the speed at which trains move through the network—and a significant improvement in on-time performance in key Georgia division corridors. Norfolk Southern has estimated that each mile-per-hour improvement is worth about US$200 million to the railway company annually.

Information excellence can blend seamlessly into solution leadership. Algorithmic process improvement for a railroad system is clearly information excellence, and intelligent products that are self-optimizing are good examples of solution leadership. As an example of the latter, GE's Trip Optimizer System optimizes fuel consumption based on a specific train's makeup and the route traveled. Using the train's trip profile, Trip Optimizer System automatically controls the throttle to maintain a planned speed and eliminate driver-to-driver fluctuations in fuel use. It also minimizes braking and keeps the train on schedule. An advanced energy-management system in the software calculates the most efficient operation by considering such factors as train length, weight, grade, track conditions, weather, and locomotive performance. The trip's profile is updated continuously through a complex network of on-board computers, GPS systems, and advanced algorithms that make adjustments, enabling the train to use less fuel while maintaining a smooth ride.

Solution Leadership

GE has applied exemplary solution leadership discipline across multiple business units: aviation, healthcare, power and water, and transportation. As described in Chapter 9, intelligent, digitalized products (and services) connected to cloud services, together with APIs and ecosystem development, a services wrapper, and a focus on customer outcomes illustrate solution leadership. GE calls intelligent products Brilliant Machines, implying that the machines embed sensors, controllers, and intelligence. The intelligence is administered via GE's Software-Defined Machine infrastructure. The idea behind this is that machine functionality increasingly depends on software—software that can be remotely monitored, revised, and upgraded. Moreover, a "twin" virtual machine such as a model of a jet engine exists in simulated fashion in the cloud, and engineers and software developers can thus understand complex behaviors, upgrade functionality, and rapidly deploy it across the embedded base.

According to Software VP Ruh, there has been a transformational shift in GE's core business, creating both opportunities and challenges. Traditionally, GE collected *average* data from engines during takeoff, cruise, and landing, and these data were deleted unless there was some sort of problem. Averages can be helpful, but disguise a lot of information. It's somewhat helpful to know that the average temperature in New York City is, say, 55 degrees Fahrenheit, but that disguises extremes such as freak subzero deep freezes and 100-degree-plus heat waves.

General Electric's latest production aircraft engine is the GEnx; this is the engine that powers Boeing's 787 Dreamliner, for example. In the GEnx, thanks to multiple sensors, engines provide scores of data streams, such as cooling valve positions, fuel manifold pressure, and turbine frame vibration. *Each* of the 20,000 engines in service has about 20 sensors, which each generate about 5,000 data points per second—360 million data points per hour of flight. The data are compressed to 10 to 50 megabytes, which are then uploaded, decoded, and fused with external data from other sources, such as weather and air particulate data.

Taleris, a joint venture between Accenture and GE Aviation, takes this one step further. It collects data from other sensors on the plane—not just the engines—to help improve maintenance and in-flight performance. According to DiTommaso, the objective is to reduce operational issues, increase efficiency, optimize fuel contingency loads, and implement additional performance improvements such as single engine taxiing. Ruh sums it up as maximizing GE's focus on the customer's business outcomes.

5,000 data points per sensor per second is a lot, but GE's wind turbines generate more than twice that. In the case of the jets, data are currently saved and uploaded for processing and tuning. When inflight bandwidth increases, this may happen in real time. In the case of the wind turbines, local systems can process the data to optimize turbine performance, and turbines can learn from nearby turbines in the same wind farm that are better performing under certain conditions—in effect, like asking a friend for advice.

To clarify the power of this style of solution leadership, it should be noted that GE acquired its wind-turbine business from Enron during its bankruptcy, and in seven years, took the business from also-ran to industry leader by creating "brilliant," adaptive wind-turbine solutions that connect wind farms and the turbines within them to electric utility grids, batteries, and remote monitoring systems. Simply put, migrating from a standalone product to a connected solution helped attain market leadership.

Collective Intimacy

It is natural to think of machines as separate from people. Yet in GE's vision of the Industrial Internet, machines can collaborate with people, even across social networks.

Here's the idea in the context of jet engines: The engine generates a stream of data from a score of sensors, not unlike tweets. Various communities of interest—such as GE engineers, customer engineers, and operations personnel—"follow" the data stream via an aviation collaboration platform. In this way, relationships of a sort are formed between things and people.

In addition, however, there is collective intimacy at work. In the case of Amazon.com or Netflix, data from millions of customer relationships are processed to generate personalized recommendations for each customer: people who bought this also bought that, or people who watched this also watched that.

Something similar happens with GE aircraft engines. Since each engine can upload tens of megabytes of data per flying day, it can all be analyzed. Moreover, there are 20,000 engines in service, each generating data under a variety of conditions: altitude, humidity, air speed, time since last maintenance, oil pressure, and so on. By examining data from each engine, *and* analyzing data from each engine in the context of data from all of the other engines and in the context of weather and particulate data, important conclusions can be drawn and predictions made. Such analysis can be used to conduct predictive maintenance, determining, say, when an engine needs to have parts replaced. It can also be used to tailor specific control actions to each engine, say, when flying at this altitude with this air pressure, temperature, and humidity, a particular configuration of settings will offer the greatest distance per gallon of jet fuel. Such collective intimacy for airlines and their jets is not that much different from personalized medicine offering collective intimacy for people: Maintenance corresponds to targeted therapies; operations optimization corresponds to lifestyle changes.

This same generic approach is relevant to GE's other businesses. Learnings from each wind turbine in a wind farm can be used to tune each of them. Insights from CT scanners on image clarity relative to radiation levels can be used to optimize their balance.

Another example of collective intimacy is GE Healthcare's MultiOmyx system. MultiOmyx is a tissue analysis platform used for pathology—such as cancer diagnosis—and ultimately treatment. It begins with imaging a particular tumor biopsy sample repeatedly under up to 60 different stains, enabling examination of more than 175 proteins, each of which highlights different characteristics. This, in itself, was a breakthrough, because the stains are applied and deactivated without damaging or modifying the tissue sample, unlike prior equipment. Pathologists can then view the tissue via a web-based application, dynamically changing perspectives of the sample under the different stains.

Where it gets really interesting is that software then identifies individual cells, and quantifies and statistically characterizes them. This information is then used to create a unique *bio-signature*, which can then be used to predict a patient outcome, or to develop a personalized recommendation for treatment, often called personalized medicine or patient-specific therapy. These kinds of approaches could be expanded in the future to include, for example, genomic or microbiomic information to better target therapy. In other words, information from all end-customers (i.e., patients) can be used by customers (i.e., hospitals and physicians), in conjunction with big data analytics to derive recommendations (i.e., therapeutic treatment) for each patient: collective intimacy in the service of human well-being.

Accelerated Innovation

GE is no stranger to innovation. After all, it began with one of the most important innovations in human history: affordable, usable, ubiquitous electricity.

Beyond investments totaling $4 billion per year in skilled engineers and supporting resources such as laboratories and test facilities, there are 5 GE Advantage process improvement initiatives directed at new product introduction, such as improved design and validation processes and supporting tools for aviation, integrated solutions for digital energy, and cutting LED time to market by more than half. Others focus on innovation in customer intimacy, such as by using a technique called *differential value proposition*, which measures the incremental operating profit a customer will receive by buying from GE rather than a competitor.

GE's innovation approach is weighted toward internal R&D, innovation through acquisitions, such as Clarient, which extended GE Healthcare's Global Research Center innovation of MultiOmyx to diagnostic image analytics, and joint ventures, such as Taleris, the aircraft monitoring company that GE owns with Accenture. However, GE has complemented these approaches with open innovation via several challenges, and plans to run more.

One, called GE Hospital Quest, was focused on hospital operations. GE has estimated that $100 billion is wasted each year in healthcare due to simple operational issues such as long wait times for procedures or hospital discharge, lost equipment, and repetitive paperwork. GE published several data sets as part of the Hospital Quest challenge, such as hospital utilization, inpatient admission and discharge, and patient experience surveys. GE awarded $100,000 to a set of winning teams which had solutions such as an app to help patients find post-hospitalization care and one to optimize the logistics of hospital porters, the people who move medical equipment or transport patients in wheelchairs or on stretchers.

GE Flight Quest has been run twice. The first Flight Quest challenge—run in conjunction with Alaska Airlines—had the objective of helping airlines and pilots better predict arrival times, for both runway touchdown and gate arrival. Greater accuracy is of value because it means better gate assignments, better rebooking of passengers impacted by delays, greater aircraft utilization, and higher passenger satisfaction.

The second one was even more ambitious. Rather than *predicting* arrival times, it aimed to *better* them. This objective can be quantified: a GE study showed that reducing travel time by just 3 minutes at just under 50 midsize airports such as Salt Lake City could result in dramatic annual savings: 12.9 million gallons of aviation fuel, $65.6 million in operational costs, 274.6 million pounds of carbon dioxide, and 17,900 hours.[8]

Generally, challenges require a few things. A clear objective, a means of alerting the relevant community about the challenge and distributing necessary information to them, an evaluation process—such as a scoring algorithm or prize judges—to determine the winner, and some means of motivation, which is typically monetary.

GE uses Kaggle, a platform focused on enabling data science competitions for a variety of commercial and academic purposes. Kaggle challenges include ones for Wal-Mart, who was interested in using past data on price reductions to predict sales; Aetna, who wanted to predict customer insurance purchases based on past transactions; and a Chinese technical conference, which sponsored a brain science challenge attempting to model physical connections between neurons based on snapshots of brain activity. Among other things, Kaggle offers a leaderboard, which has the effect of motivating participants and adding excitement to a competition.

Through Kaggle, data sets were provided by GE for download, with information such as estimated arrival times, historical weather information, and redirected or diverted flights. The evaluation process was mathematical, based on a calculated difference between actual and projected arrival times at both the gate and the runway.

Rules included such things as how to form teams, who was eligible to enter the contest, how to officially submit contest entries, timelines and deadlines, and the like. Perhaps most important, the rules clearly laid out that entries must consist only of code that GE would be legally able to commercially utilize.

Finally, in terms of motivation, first prize was US$100,000, with a total prize pool of US$250,000.

GE is also partnering with Quirky. Quirky enables anyone to submit ideas such as an ice scraper, power strip, grill accessories, or beach totes, vote on submitted ideas, or solve remaining engineering challenges. Quirky then periodically reviews this data to determine the next wave of products to be introduced.[9] In the case of connected home products such as light switches, Wi-Fi controlled power strips, connected bulbs, or remote home sensors, GE collaborates and engineering and development, and also may manufacture the item.

■ ■ ■

Most people probably don't realize how much GE is doing across multiple industry verticals in each of the four digital disciplines. Thanks to big ideas such as the Industrial Internet, Brilliant Machines, and Software-Defined Machines, GE is successfully implementing information excellence, solution leadership, collective intimacy, and accelerated innovation across its multiple divisions, such as aviation, healthcare, power and water, oil and gas, and rail transportation.

To accomplish this has required a focus on a broad range of digital technologies such as machine sensors and controllers, networks, data and software, hybrid cloud services, machine learning, statistical analysis, and predictive analytics, agile development, and security.

It has also required addressing a variety of non-technical factors, such as workforce demographics and motivation, culture and working environment, lean startup and agile development methodologies, customer engagement and collaboration, partner selection, venture investments, and leadership and governance.

GE is an interesting case demonstrating that not only can a single company apply more than one digital discipline, but that it can apply it across multiple units, and that each unit can apply multiple digital disciplines. Moreover, GE has demonstrated that such approaches pay off, for example, helping to transform its wind turbine business from a near-bankrupt acquisition into a market leader.

Notes

1. Jeffrey R. Immelt, "The CEO of General Electric on Sparking an American Manufacturing Renewal," *Harvard Business Review* (March 2012), https://hbr.org/2012/03/the-ceo-of-general-electric-on-sparking-an-american-manufacturing-renewal/ar.

2. Paul E. Ceruzzi, *History of Modern Computing* (Cambridge, MA: MIT Press, 2003), 32–33.

3. Bill Ruh, multiple conversations with the author 2014–2015; Darin DiTommaso, conversation with the author, September 30, 2014.

4. "2013 Annual Report: Progress," *GE*, www.ge.com/ar2013/pdf/GE_AR13.pdf.

5. Brad Power, "How GE Applies Lean Startup Practices," *Harvard Business Review* (April 23, 2014), https://hbr.org/2014/04/how-ge-applies-lean-startup-practices/.

6. "2012 Annual Report: GE Works," *GE*, www.ge.com/ar2012/pdf/GE_AR12.pdf.

7. "Think It's Possible to Make Hospital Visits Hassle-Free? GE Does," *GE Quest*, www.gequest.com/c/hospital.

8. GE Aviation, "Highways in the Sky: Gauging the Impact of New Flight Paths on the U.S. Economy, Environment and the Everyday Traveler," *GE*, www.geaviation.com/press/pdf/GE_study.pdf.

9. "How It Works," *Quirky.com*, https://www.quirky.com/how-it-works.

CHAPTER 18

Human Behavior and Gamification

We have discussed the four digital disciplines at length, but even the best strategies are meaningless without successful execution, which is impossible without motivated, engaged people: employees, partners, customers, end users, and communities. But the conventional wisdom regarding human behavior, cognition, and motivation—which espouses concepts such as rational decision making, pay for performance, and providing negative feedback through areas for development—turns out often to be incorrect and counterproductive.

Behavioral anomalies, cognitive biases, and motivational drivers have different impacts on each digital discipline. For example, accelerated innovation through contests benefits from competition among solvers, due to people's need for status and their innate enjoyment from solving puzzles; solution leadership benefits from extending the product to a community, due to a need for social connection.

The management techniques that dominated the twentieth century were largely mechanistic, simplistic, and often, antagonistic. Employees were viewed as machines, which could be subject to *scientific management*. Time and motion studies could be used to analyze an exact sequence of motions (e.g., those involved in assembling an automobile transmission). This analysis could be used to define a new sequence, perhaps shaving a second or two off of the procedure. Relationships were fundamentally antagonistic: companies would like the most work for the least pay; employees were assumed to like the most pay for the least work. And employee motivation was based on simplistic carrot-and-stick approaches. To encourage timely arrival for work, pay would be docked for tardiness. Customer relationships were not much different: To encourage greater sales, offer a 10 percent off coupon.

Unfortunately, humans—and many animals, for that matter—behave in complex, contradictory, irrational ways. Psychologists, economists, and neuroscientists have different terms for this: predictable irrationality, behavioral economics, cognitive biases. I simply call the range of behaviors "Lazy, Hazy, and Crazy."[1]

People are *lazy*, or to put a positive spin on it, "efficient," taking mental, emotional, and physical shortcuts where possible. This conferred evolutionary advantages. In times of famine, inefficient physical processes would lead to an early death.

They are *hazy*, using heuristics (i.e., approximation methods) to derive answers. Many problems just can't be solved exactly in "reasonable" time, even with computers, and often there are limited marginal benefits to additional precision. If you stopped to calculate the exact probability that a lion would eat you, you'd be lunch before your first multiplication.

But perhaps the most fascinating characteristic of sophisticated creatures such as humans is that we are simultaneously rational and irrational, sane and *crazy*. We are not just calculating machines, but complex beings that mix cold, rational calculation with habit, emotion, miscalculation, poor or no logic, values, hot buttons, inner drives, and fears.

As a parable for human behavior, in one scientific study, researchers sometimes offered tufted Capuchin monkeys one piece of apple, and then half the time, another. The researchers also sometimes offered them two pieces, and then half the time, took one away. As you might suppose, they (the monkeys) greatly preferred the first scenario, even though in either case, each monkey received, on average, one and a half apple pieces, so *rationally* they should have been indifferent. But of course they weren't, any more than we would be, due to two biases: *reference dependence* and *loss aversion*.[2] In other words, from the frame of reference where you think you'll be receiving two pieces of apple, getting one is a loss, which is unpleasant. We like getting tax refunds, but not mailing in checks, even if our annual tax including withholding is identical. We'd rather have the IRS refund us the apple piece than take it away.

Studies conducted in the fields of behavioral psychology, behavioral economics, neuroscience, and neuroeconomics are fascinating because they tell us about ourselves and what makes us tick, down to the function of regions of the brain such as the anterior cingulate cortex and specific neurotransmitters such as dopamine. However, the main point here is that these "predictably irrational" behaviors—which have been utilized to make video, desktop, and mobile games so addictive—can also be exploited through *gamification* in the service of operational and information excellence, solution leadership, collective intimacy, and accelerated innovation. Gamification uses the tactics and mechanisms that games do, but in, say, innovation, processes, products and services, or customer engagement processes.

In a way, this is not new. Processes were gamified in old-line factories, with a scoreboard showing the number of days that the facility was accident-free and a special parking spot conferring status on the "employee of the month." Products were gamified, with each box of CrackerJacks having an unpredictable prize inside. And relationships were gamified, like the McDonald's Monopoly game that kept you ordering Big Macs to get game pieces or the Publishers Clearing House Sweepstakes that incented you to order magazines. Innovation was gamified, too; examples include the Nobel Prize and the Longitude Prize. What *is* new is the sophistication and impact of gamification thanks to digitalization.

Definitions of gamification tend to cluster around a view that gamification is the application of game mechanisms *outside* of "games." There are many definitions of gamification, and perhaps even more critiques of those definitions. For our purposes, however, the point is not the exact definition, but the concept that processes, products and services, relationships, and innovation can be more successful if they account for human behavior, behavioral anomalies, and motivation. Gamification can be built into products from asthma medical devices to automobiles, can improve business processes, and can accelerate innovation. It's an approach that applies to all the digital disciplines.

Human Behavior

It would be audacious to attempt to boil down to a few paragraphs the entirety of function and capability of the almost 100 billion neurons in the human brain across the diversity of 7 billion people, but that's exactly what we're going to do in this section.

A number of models seem to capture different facets of essential human needs and drives. Daniel Kahneman and Amos Tversky's prospect theory and loss aversion, the intellectual foundation of behavioral economics, focus on human decision making in the context of risk and asymmetries between losses and gains. Their key insight is that losses (whether actual or lost opportunities) are more painful than gains are pleasant.[3] This has implications in many domains, and explains why equity investors find it difficult to sell stocks that have lost value and turn a paper loss into a real one.[4] This fundamental insight led to a comprehensive and growing body of research, and several Nobel prizes.

Author David Rock, the founder of the NeuroLeadership Institute, has proposed the SCARF model: Status, Certainty, Autonomy, Relatedness, and Fairness.[5] People enjoy having or gaining status, fear uncertainty, have a need for control and independent action, relate to groups, and almost universally value fairness, as various elegantly designed experiments show.

The list of models, theories, and frameworks goes on: Self-determination theory focuses on competence, relatedness, and autonomy, and suggests that people who are intrinsically motivated will generate dramatically better results than those whose motivation is external. Author Dan Pink expands on this theme, focusing on autonomy, mastery and purpose, "an approach built much more around intrinsic motivation … the desire to do things because they matter, because we like it, because they're interesting, because they are part of something important."[6] The fundamental research-based insight here is that rewards such as money *can* sometimes improve performance in noncreative tasks, but, counterintuitively, typically *hinder* performance in knowledge work. Moreover, such rewards tend to extinguish any remaining spark of internal motivation, so removing them leads to worse performance than before they were initiated.

Many people are familiar with Maslow's hierarchy of needs, which includes physiological needs like food and shelter, but then expand into self-actualization, esteem, love, and belonging. Harvard Business School professor Rosabeth Moss Kanter talks about Mastery, Membership, and Meaning.[7] Gartner, Inc. research vice president Brian Burke has a somewhat different three Ms in mind: Motivation, Momentum (the trajectory through increasing levels of challenge), and Meaning.[8] Steve Sims, former VP of the Behavior Lab and now chief design officer at Badgeville, which focuses on enterprise gamification, offers a 4S model: people want to feel successful, socially valued, smart, and oriented within a structure.[9] Harvard Business School professors Paul Lawrence and Nitin Nohria argue that people have four drives: to *acquire* things like possessions and status, to *bond* with each other, to *comprehend* (and control), and to *defend* against threats.[10,11]

Besides the observation that it is evidently important to fashion insights into memorable acronyms, there is deep insight and experimental evidence behind all of these models. In summary, they suggest that the following are our key drivers, needs, and *intrinsic motivators* (as opposed to external forces such as monetary rewards, parole officers, parents, or spouses):

Status, ego, competition, esteem, and **recognition** are important drives, which makes sense given that people are the latest in a long line of social animals. As a result, they exhibit a need for status. Social hierarchy is even found in chickens, where hens express dominance through a "pecking order" and roosters through a "clawing order." Creatures ranging from chimpanzees and silverback gorillas[12] to musk oxen to ants exhibit dominance hierarchies, so it's no surprise that we do as well. Presumably, there is evolutionary survival value in groups that have a leader rather than those that display anarchy.

In humans, low status causes a cortisol response, leading to stress, sleep deprivation, and anxiety. Conversely, high status correlates with health and longevity, and not just for nuanced reasons such as correlation with higher income and thus better healthcare. David Rock says that the "neural circuitry that assesses status is similar to that which processes numbers; the circuitry operates even when the stakes are meaningless, which is why winning a board game or being the first off the mark at a green light feels so satisfying. Competing against ourselves in games like Solitaire triggers the same circuitry."[13]

Social connection, collaboration, and being *socially valued* are perhaps our most important defining characteristics. Matt Lieberman, a professor and director of the Social Cognitive Neuroscience Lab at UCLA and the author of the book *Social: Why Our Brains Are Wired to Connect,* argues that we are so social because we are mammals. Infants must bond with their mothers so that they don't run off; mothers must bond with their infants so that they invest the time, energy, and love needed to ensure their healthy development to reproductive age, for obvious evolutionary reasons supporting the propagation of the species. Lieberman argues—with scientific neuro-imaging studies to back him up—that the emotional pain of social loss—a friend, spouse, or relative—is indistinguishable from physical pain in terms of the brain's reaction. Not only do we need to be connected, but those connections must value us and the relationship that they have with us.

Belonging, social norms, relatedness, and *membership* take social to the next level, from pairwise bonds to an entire community. People exhibit biases: positive within the group; negative outside the group. It's not just humans; ants, for example, exhibit a high degree of cooperation *within* a colony, but otherwise can exhibit "intercolony" aggression. Humans have made great progress thanks to their ability to collaborate, rather than always acting selfishly, according to Edward O. Wilson, professor emeritus at Harvard University and the author of *The Social Conquest of Earth.*

Meaning, purpose, goals, and *values,* whether to get promoted to CEO, learn piano, save the whales, quit smoking, or altruistically save someone from a burning house, are the passions that drive us. According to self-determination theory, internal goals are much more powerful drivers than external ones; practicing piano hours a day because you want to play in Carnegie Hall is a much stronger driver than because your parent tells you to. Goals that are aligned with values are extremely strong drivers.

Autonomy, self-expression, and *control* are not just human traits. Species that evolution has selected and individuals who remain alive do so because they exert control over prey and their environment. Lack of control (i.e., helplessness) is debilitating and disease-causing. In a famous experiment, nursing-home patients who were otherwise helpless but who had just a bit of control—determining when to water a houseplant—lived measurably longer than those who didn't.[14]

Certainty is related to control. Certainty does not require control, since the sun rising tomorrow is certain but not controllable, but uncertainty underscores lack of control. Because loss aversion suggests that negative outcomes outweigh positive ones, people generally fear uncertainty, avoid risk, and fear change, such as reorganizations.

Surprise, novelty, variety, and *delight* are different than negative uncertainty, and generally trigger pleasurable response. This is why we watch the news or check our Twitter feed. Psychologists have concluded that intermittent variable rewards—such as those received when gambling—provide stronger reinforcement and are thus more addictive than predictable ones that are identically sized and arrive periodically—such as a weekly paycheck. The neurotransmitter dopamine and the *nucleus accumbens* within the brain are deeply involved with these preferences.

Fairness is almost universal across cultures. In the "ultimatum game," one person gets to determine how to split a prize—say, $100—with another. If the other accepts the proposed split, portions are so awarded, but if the other does not, neither receives anything. If the proposed split is 50–50 or something close, the deal is usually accepted. However, when it is 80–20, say, it usually is not. Notice that this decision is economically irrational, since the second participant is preferring no payment to, say, $20.

Achievement, success, learning and *mastery, smarts* and *competence,* and *pattern formation, narrative development,* and *problem* and *puzzle solving* are also needs and drives. Professor Mikhail Cziksentmihalyi has argued that we don't like tasks that are too easy or too hard.[15] Too easy and we lose interest; too hard and we become demotivated. A Sudoku puzzle with only one square left open wouldn't be much fun; neither would one in 27 dimensions. Dan Pink calls these "Goldilocks tasks."[16] In the fairytale, one of each of the three bears' porridge, chairs, and beds is too large, one too small, and one is just right. Similarly, some tasks are too hard, some are too easy, and some are just right. Other primates are also intrinsically motivated to solve puzzles. Researchers in the late 1940s were surprised to find that even rhesus monkeys enjoy solving puzzles without any extrinsic rewards such as, say, bananas.[17]

Not only do we like problem solving, we like being successful; we exhibit a need for competence. For this reason, games—especially "free to play" games that make their money only through in-app purchases—are easy in the early stages, otherwise disheartened users would never last long enough to become revenue-generating. Even when revenue is not the goal, engagement is, so having users abandon the product or application would be counterproductive. Badgeville's Sims points out that the successful completion of challenges plays to our need for competence, and social validation or social proof does as well.

Positive feedback and a sense of *progress* within a *structure* or *narrative* are important for attaining competence. Imagine how ineffective education might be without any sense of what you had already learned versus not. Progress is motivational, and contrary to the popular belief that negative feedback can help individuals develop, negative feedback is demotivating.[18] Research shows that positive reinforcement is more powerful than negative, because it drives intrinsic motivation—that is, a strong desire to continue, which, in turn, achieves results. As much as we hear about how tough bosses get results, fear and questioning our competence hinders cognitive performance. As Timothy Pychyl, author of *The Procrastinator's Digest*, puts it, "We experience the strongest positive emotional response when we make progress on our most difficult goals."[19] Another way to put it is that we have a need for achievement.

While money is also perhaps an obvious motivator, it is relatively weak compared to those on the list above, and is often counterproductive. Research shows that not only do monetary rewards often *negatively impact* performance on tasks requiring cognitive skill,[20] but monetary penalties often *fail to disincent* bad behavior. One example: A day care center was trying to reduce tardy pickups by parents. When it instituted fines, tardy pickups *increased*, because parents figured that they were paying for the privilege of a later pickup time.[21]

Importantly, the successful implementation of a digital discipline can be dramatically enhanced by literally playing to these needs.

Gamification

With the prior section on human needs and drivers as context, the various elements that we come to expect from games and that are essential to gamification for digital disciplines become clearer. Although some elements support multiple needs—for example, points support status and progress—here's how to think about how gamification elements tie to behavioral drivers.

Leaderboards, rankings, ratings, recognition, and rewards support our need for status. A good example is the seemingly insatiable desire to increase one's follower count on Twitter, but so is the drive to be rated as a top community contributor or reviewer.

Connections such as Facebook friends, Twitter followers, and LinkedIn connections play to our need to be social and socially valued, as do mechanisms within product ecosystems such as Nike+.

Communities, teams, and groups such as LinkedIn groups or even being part of a comment thread support our need for relatedness, membership, interaction, and collaboration. Innovation competitions create communities out of competitors, whether they decide to team up or not.

Various objectives such as getting to the top level, finding a treasure, or saving a princess, or more importantly, supporting Kickstarter or Kiva, which crowdfunds microloans with charitable intent, provide meaning and purpose.

Objective challenges such as collecting the most bananas as well as various combinations of skill and luck align with our need for fairness. Every player has an equal opportunity to win. In the case of online competitions such as Foldit, which used a variety of gamification techniques including an objectively computed score, the structure of an AIDS-like virus that had defied scientific resolution for 15 years was determined in 10 days of game play.[22,23]

Defined game rules support our need for certainty, whereas Easter eggs—functions that are intentional but undocumented and unexpected—and other chance elements and delightful surprises provide the neural hit of an intermittent variable reward.

Challenges support our need for achievement and for demonstrating our competence and smarts. They also fit with our intrinsic motivation to solve puzzles. Rewards can help, but many people play Solitaire or solve crosswords for no other reward than the pleasure of a mental challenge and the satisfaction that comes from success, as was also the case with Foldit.

Levels, maps, badges, trophies, awards, and points provide positive feedback and information on progress within a predefined structure, helping to motivate us to continue. Training, which has been gamified by companies such as Deloitte, is well-suited to such mechanisms.

Each of these, in turn, has subtle variations. For example, lifetime points can designate status in the community; available points may represent virtual goods that can be traded in for actual products and services. Points can expire to generate a sense of urgency or to cap liabilities, or can last forever. Leaderboards can be universal, restricted to an immediate social circle, or based on an interval of time—today, this week, or this month.[24]

Gamifying Information Excellence

While we often think of processes as industrial and highly automated, there are many processes that are the domain of knowledge workers: legal, innovation, product engineering, customer tech support, and of course software development. The application of game principles to processes varies based on the process and the industry. To give a sense of the breadth of applicability, consider a few examples.

Citrix, a large software company perhaps most widely known for its GoToMeeting web conferencing service, is a good example of using gamification in the software development process. They gamified software quality assurance, rewarding the process of discovering software "bugs" and fixing them. The result: a 40 percent improvement in timely code reviews, resulting in more overall software projects being delivered on time.[25]

Rydges, a hotel chain primarily servicing Australia and New Zealand, used software to gamify the sales process. Rather than promote sales of room reservations by offering a discount, it used an approach called "buy to win." The idea was that a customer who makes a purchase has a one-in-five chance of getting it for free. This is mathematically equivalent to a 20 percent discount, but has an outsized impact, due to the same human behavioral impact of intermittent rewards that makes gambling so addictive. The campaign resulted in more than double the number of bookings.[26]

Education is another area of application for gamification. Even decades ago, flash cards gamified the process of learning things like the alphabet and multiplication tables. Today, web-based training often includes in-course quizzes as part of every lesson module. But in terms of large-scale process improvement, an interesting example is the Race to the Top, a "game" with a multibillion-dollar prize, where the customers are states competing for federal educational grants.[27]

Gamification is also being used to make training more fun, for everything from welding to becoming a better salesperson or business consultant; enhancing employee collaboration, and improving employee engagement.

Gamifying Solution Leadership

Products, services, and solutions are perhaps the main province of gamification. After all, games themselves are products, and social games, for example, are solutions, leveraging connectivity and cloud services. But it isn't just Candy Crush and FarmVille that can be gamified.

The Alvio breathing trainer is a medical solution designed to help kids with asthma, the third leading cause of hospitalization through age 15. It turns out that breathing exercises can reduce the severity of symptoms, the need for medication, and sick days lost from school. The challenge is that making a kid take a break from playing to do breathing exercises is more of a workout for the parent than the child. But if the exercises *are* the play, it's a completely different story. The Alvio looks something like the offspring of a rescue inhaler and a Fisher-Price toy, but it's a high-tech cloud-connected device. Sensors within the product detect inhalation and exhalation, and a dial enables varying degrees of resistance. By using the Alvio as a game controller, the kid can play tablet games, moving a fish up and down the screen to catch other fish by blowing in and out, or in a modern variation on the "High Striker" carnival game, kids have to exhale as hard as they can to gain points. Alvio is much more than a game: It is a solution focused on patient outcomes. The software can help parents and doctors track the severity of symptoms and track progress in lung capacity improvement. Such tracking can also provide early warning of impending issues.[28]

Gamified solutions don't just help ill people get better, they help healthy people get better as well. Nike+ products are a good example of gamification. FuelBand and various Nike+ ecosystem components enable users to get NikeFuel points through activities. Customers can compete against themselves (i.e., personal best), progress toward their goals, and gain status relative to their friends or a broader community.

Such solutions can also help meet societal goals. The Ford SmartGauge display, initially offered on the Ford Fusion Hybrid and since deployed in other models, provides drivers with real-time feedback on fuel economy through the "EcoGuide" program; a virtual plant grows green leaves when drivers accelerate more gently and thus achieve high levels of fuel economy. Not only did Ford patent this interface, but it also won "Car of the Year" from *Motor Trend*. The Fusion Hybrid helped Ford dramatically increase its sales and profits.

Gamifying Collective Intimacy

Strong engagement is a cornerstone of customer and collective intimacy. One way to enhance such engagement is to gamify it. Foursquare was an early innovator here, offering points and rewards such as "badges" for each check-in at a venue such as a bar, restaurant, store, or airport. One immediately receives the "Newbie" badge on the first check-in, the "Adventurer" badge for the tenth check-in, the "Explorer" for the twenty-fifth, and so forth. In addition, there are badges for being somewhere with lots of other Foursquare users ("Swarm"), playing to social needs; for checking in at a venue more than anyone else ("Mayor"), multiple airport check-ins ("JetSetter"), and just about any random activity you can imagine, playing to need for status.

Or consider Yelp, which has been successful at engaging customers by crowdsourcing reviews of restaurants and other venues. Yelp encourages reviews, and offers status badges to some contributors via a profile stamp that marks them as creating top content. Why—from the perspective of gamification—do contributors spend time creating reviews? Presumably, for the social connection and even a sense of fairness: Bad venues shouldn't sucker in the uninformed. Yelp is also gentle with guidance on writing reviews. Rather than trying to control length, quality, and format (i.e., micromanaging), it provides a nudge in the right direction and avoids negative feedback by proffering that "This review is shorter than most."[29] Yelp also plays to social and status drivers through a focus on the actual identity of reviewers, supported by name and photograph. As Yelp VP Eric Singley puts it, "Having your real identity associated with your content leads people to put their best foot forward."

Yelp and Foursquare are online services, but real-world product and service companies such as consumer goods manufacturers or airlines use loyalty programs and online communities to maintain contact with customers. A truly loyal customer will not hesitate to provide negative feedback—tough love—to help a brand improve. Such online communities can provide extremely valuable insights; more so than, say, a focus group of prospects who may have never used the product under real-world conditions. Moreover, customers who identify with a brand are more likely to repurchase the product and recommend it, expanding the firm's market share and revenues.

However, clicking "yes" on "Would you like to be on our mailing list?" or joining the "Brand X Club" does not equate to actual participation in a community. A large global consumer electronics company gamified its website, transforming it from one used only for product registration and support data to one that helped build status and reputation with points for product knowledge and generating reviews. This was coupled with financial benefits such as product giveaways, thus tickling the receptors for intermittent variable rewards. According to Steve Sims of Badgeville, this dramatically increased the number of customers who were advocates, and thus increased revenues for the company through greater share of wallet with existing customers as well as increased market share.

One example of how gamification and digitalization are together disrupting traditional business models is the weight loss industry. Weight Watchers employs tens of thousands of people to support 1 million customers at in-person meetings, whereas a digital fitness tracker like MyFitnessPal supports 50 times as many users with only a few dozen employees.[30]

Gamifying Accelerated Innovation

We've discussed open challenges as one strategy for accelerated innovation. The prize money can be an incentive, but in addition, such challenges play to a need for status, puzzle solving, and social connection through the enhancement of reputation and demonstration of competence. For proof that nonfinancial rewards are valued, one need look no further than open source initiatives, such as Wikipedia or Linux, whose contributors are unpaid volunteers. Contributors can enhance their reputation, become a member in one or more communities, and demonstrate competence as well as exercise their skills as developers or encyclopedia entry writers in particular fields.

The prize money awarded for each GE Flight Quest competition was a quarter of a million dollars, and that for the Netflix Prize was a million dollars, so one might question how much of the participation was based on cold, hard financial rewards and how much was for reputation, status, and intrinsic enjoyment. The Netflix OSS Cloud Prize offered awards of only $10,000. Not that most people would turn down the cash, but it can be argued that reputation enhancement was worth much more. There are many people with $10,000, but only a handful that have won the Netflix OSS Cloud Prize.

The Netflix Prize used many of the key gamification principles. Due to the quantitative nature of the challenge and the algorithm, it was easy to evaluate any entrant's *exact* progress and success in real time, and the structure of progress was clear: a Progress Prize for the most improvement in the first round, and a final prize only if the prior algorithm was beat by exactly 10 percent. Netflix communicated a leaderboard, clearly displaying each contestant's progress and social status relative to each other. And, unlike a random drawing open to all contestants or all who bought a raffle ticket, the challenge was highly technical, allowing contestants to scratch their "smart" itch.

Often in innovation, a stage-gate process is used, where a large set of initial ideas is winnowed down over time. One way to do this is for some sort of executive budgeting authority to determine investments. A different way to do it is to crowdsource funding priorities through prediction markets, where employees, customers, or crowds are asked to spend virtual but limited money on one or more investments. Their desire for status and reputation then aligns with the company's need to focus on innovation investments with a high likelihood of payoff, thus gamifying the stage-gate process.

Quirky has made the stage-gate process for manufactured products its core business, and gamified and crowdsourced the entire process. A community of inventors submits ideas, prioritizes them, develops them, names them, prices them, and finally even buys them. Throughout the process, Quirky uses badges, points, and related recognition mechanisms to reward participants, together with a portion of actual product profits to reward the inventor.[31]

A somewhat different approach is used by Kickstarter, which tends to focus more on creative projects such as books and movies than manufactured products, although it's funded thousands of technology projects at a total level of a quarter of a billion dollars in pledges. Here, the "creator" comes up with the idea, but the community doesn't just vote, it votes with its credit cards, funding the project. Rewards can leave the digital world: in the Kickstarter approach, they include the results of the project, say a DVD of the movie, special experiences, such as dinner with the cast or a visit to the movie set, or perhaps being mentioned in the movie credits. Because, as mentioned earlier, people have a fear of uncertainty, Kickstarter recommends that project creators perform status updates to keep their funders informed as well.[32]

Gamification across Disciplines

EMC is one of the largest global technology firms, with a leadership position in enterprise storage systems that store data for virtually every major enterprise on the planet. It gamified its EMC Community Network, which brings together EMC employees and their customers, as well as various technology partners. Community partners earned points and rewards for engagement in the virtual community, as well as for real-world contact.[33]

As might be surmised, such contact between employees, customers, and partners was important in many ways. First, as customers provided ideas or complaints, there was an increase in new product ideas: 40 percent over the pre-gamification baseline. Also, as there was more content created, there was more consumption of that content, leading to greater engagement, and therefore the creation of even more content. What discipline should this be filed under? Perhaps all of them. After all, the product development process was improved, so it's an example of information excellence. Better solutions were created, helping with solution leadership. There was a substantial increase in customer engagement, so if not collective intimacy, at least customer intimacy. And, with a 40 percent increase in new product ideas driven by customers and partners, it's a great example of accelerated innovation.

In the next chapter, we'll look at Opower, an intermediary and enabler positioned at the intersection of electric utilities and their customers. Opower gamifies energy use in the home and small businesses. In other words, it gamifies a solution and process that most of us use: electricity services. It provides feedback on levels of energy use and efficiency, showing how well residential and small business customers are doing relative to the "competition" (i.e., the neighbor).

■   ■   ■

It's been argued that gamification has its limits, and can even be counterproductive. Some have argued that it's best suited for jobs that are not intrinsically motivating, and that it can appear to be manipulative to self-motivated employees or customers.[34] However, surely it's the case that any implementation that carefully considers and then proactively responds to and leverages human behavioral anomalies is more likely to be successful. And while it's been suggested that the attractiveness of gamification may wear off, somehow fans continue to watch sports even after thousands of years since the first Olympics, and people continue to socialize, even hundreds of thousands of years after the first campfire.

Notes

1. Joe Weinman, *Cloudonomics: The Business Value of Cloud Computing* (Hoboken, NJ: John Wiley & Sons, 2012).
2. M. Keith Chen, Venkat Lakshminarayanan, and Laurie R. Santos, "How Basic Are Behavioral Biases? Evidence from Capuchin Monkey Trading Behavior," *Journal of Political Economy* 114, no. 3 (2006): 517–537.

3. Daniel Kahneman and Amos Tversky, "Prospect Theory: An Analysis of Decision under Risk," *Econometrica: Journal of the Econometric Society* (1979): 263–291.

4. Jonah Lehrer, "Loss Aversion and the Stock Market," *The Frontal Cortex* blog, September 30, 2008, scienceblogs.com/cortex/2008/09/30/loss-aversion-and-the-stock-ma/.

5. David Rock, "Managing with the Brain in Mind," *Strategy+Business* (Autumn 2009), www.strategy-business.com/article/09306.

6. Dan Pink, "The Puzzle of Motivation," [Video] *TED.com*, August, 2009, www.ted.com/talks/dan_pink_on_motivation/transcript.

7. Rosabeth Moss Kanter, "Three Things That Actually Motivate Employees," *Harvard Business Review* (October, 2013), https://hbr.org/2013/10/three-things-that-actually-motivate-employees/.

8. "Gartner Predicts Over 70 Percent of Global 2000 Organisations Will Have at Least One Gamified Application by 2014," *Gartner.com*, November 9, 2011, www.gartner.com/newsroom/id/1844115.

9. Joe Weinman, "4 Ways to Win at Business by Playing Games All Day Long," *Forbes.com*, October 15, 2013, www.forbes.com/sites/joeweinman/2013/10/15/4-ways-to-win-at-business-by-playing-games-all-day-long/.

10. Paul Lawrence and Nitin Nohria, "Driven: How Human Nature Shapes Organizations," *Harvard Business School Working Knowledge* (October 9, 2001), hbswk.hbs.edu/item/2543.html.

11. Nohria, Nitin, Boris Groysberg, and Linda-Eling Lee, "Employee Motivation: A Powerful New Model," *HBS Centennial Issue Harvard Business Review* (July–August 2008): 78–84, https://hbr.org/2008/07/employee-motivation-a-powerful-new-model.

12. "Gorilla," *Primate Info Net*, October 4, 2005, pin.primate.wisc.edu/factsheets/entry/gorilla/behave.

13. Rock, "Managing with the Brain in Mind."

14. Ellen J. Langer and Judith Rodin, "The Effects of Choice and Enhanced Personal Responsibility for the Aged: A Field Experiment in an Institutional Setting," *Journal of Personality and Social Psychology* 34 (1976): 191–198.

15. Mikhail Cziksentmihalyi, *Flow: The Psychology of Optimal Experience* (New York: Harper & Row, 1990).

16. Dan Pink, *Drive: The Surprising Truth about What Motivates Us* (New York: Riverhead Books, 2011).

17. Daniel H. Pink, "'Drive,'" *Wall Street Journal*, December 31, 2009, www.wsj.com/articles/SB10001424052748703483604574630034192655434.

18. Robert J. Vallerand and Greg Reid, "On the Relative Effects of Positive and Negative Verbal Feedback on Males' and Females' Intrinsic Motivation," *Canadian Journal of Behavioural Science/Revue canadienne des sciences du comportement* 20, no. 3 (July 1988): 239–250.

19. Timothy Pychyl, "Goal Progress and Happiness," *Psychology Today*, June 7, 2008, www.psychologytoday.com/blog/dont-delay/200806/goal-progress-and-happiness/.
20. Pink, "The Puzzle of Motivation."
21. Dan Ariely, *Predictably Irrational: The Hidden Forces That Shape Our Experiences* (New York: HarperCollins, 2008).
22. John Markoff, "In a Video Game, Tackling the Complexities of Protein Folding," *New York Times*, August 4, 2010, www.nytimes.com/2010/08/05/science/05protein.html.
23. Dean Praetorius, "Gamers Decode AIDS Protein That Stumped Researchers for 15 Years In Just 3 Weeks (VIDEO)," *The Huffington Post*, November 19, 2011, www.huffingtonpost.com/2011/09/19/aids-protein-decoded-gamers_n_970113.html.
24. "Winning with Gamification: Tips from the Expert's Playbook," Bunchball, September 2012, bunchball.com/resources.
25. Weinman, *op. cit.*
26. Ben Hurley, "Everyone Loves Winning: How Rydges Used Gamification to Double Sales," *BRW*, May 16, 2013, www.brw.com.au/p/entrepreneurs/everyone_loves_winning_how_rydges_ky3lAs92n4NvdxAZqNLGuI.
27. "Race to the Top Fund," U.S. Department of Education, March 25, 2014, www2.ed.gov/programs/racetothetop/index.html.
28. "Alvio | The Mobile-Connected Breathing Trainer," Alvio, Inc., alv.io.
29. Eric Singley, as told to Drake Baer, "How Yelp Encourages Users to Write More Thoughtful Reviews (Even On Mobile)," *Fast Company*, March 10, 2014, www.fastcompany.com/3027249/lessons-learned/how-yelp-encourages-users-to-write-more-thoughtful-reviews-even-on-mobile.
30. Brian Burke, "How Gamification Motivates the Masses," *Forbes.com*, April 10, 2014, www.forbes.com/sites/gartnergroup/2014/04/10/how-gamification-motivates-the-masses/.
31. "How It Works," *Quirky.com*, https://www.quirky.com/how-it-works.
32. "Start Your Project—Kickstarter," *Kickstarter.com*, https://www.kickstarter.com/learn.
33. Weinman, *op. cit.*
34. Galen Gruman, "Gamification: The Buzzword That Can Ruin Your Apps and Business," *InfoWorld.com*, January 27, 2012, www.infoworld.com/d/consumerization-of-it/gamification-the-buzzword-can-ruin-your-apps-and-business-183461-0.

CHAPTER 19

Opower—The Power of the Human Mind

n the last chapter, we examined human behavior and gamification. In this chapter, we'll look at Opower—"the global leader in cloud-based software for the utility industry"[1]—a company that is applying gamification to do well by doing good. It has made a business out of helping tens of millions of residential customers and over a million small and medium business customers *reduce* their electricity consumption, a goal of both customers and, it turns out, the utilities themselves.

To do this, it's perhaps no surprise that they use a combination of the cloud, big data, social, mobile, and things—together with gamification elements such as status, competition, and social elements to successfully motivate customers. Opower and its utility partners exhibit information excellence, solution leadership, and collective intimacy, supported by gamification.

Information excellence includes process and resource optimization, in terms of multiple dimensions including cost, time, and sustainability. In the end-to-end process of electric power generation, transmission, distribution, and use, reducing total consumption by feeding information to both utilities and customers helps reduce the cycle time for "demand response"—whereby customers reduce their energy use during peak periods—as well as improving the cost-effectiveness and sustainability of energy resources.

Opower and its partners link things such as smart electricity meters and Wi-Fi thermostats to cloud applications and big data repositories containing usage data from tens of millions of customers. These solutions are definitely focused on customer outcomes, namely reduced energy consumption for their end-user customers and improved compliance and asset utilization for their utility customers.

Opower and its utility partners also provide a high degree of customer and collective intimacy. Opower research conducted around the world shows that most utilities fall well short of meeting customer expectations. Part of the issue is that the relationship between the customer and the utility is transactional, rather than intimate, and focused on sales, rather than outcomes. Opower sums it up as "a customer signs up for service, pays bills, deals with outages, and eventually terminates services."[2] While some might view electric utilities as uncaring monopolies, customer satisfaction is important as never before. Customers have choices, due to increasing structural separation of power generation and distribution, as well as substitutes, namely "distributed power generation" (e.g., solar cells at home).

Moreover, most customers feel that they are paying too much, yet, interestingly, there is no relationship between how much they pay and how dissatisfied they are. In other words, even in regions where electricity is attractively priced, customers can still be highly dissatisfied. The reason for this state of affairs is that qualitative relationship factors are influencing perceptions of quantitative value.[3] This is due to the "affect heuristic:" When we feel good about something, we perceive lower risk and higher benefits.[4] This insight applies to other fields: The likelihood of a physician being sued for malpractice is not generally related to the quality of medical care delivered, but the quality of the doctor-patient relationship, including factors such as how much time the doctor spent communicating with the patient.[5]

Similarly, Opower research shows that multiple dimensions of communication—the quality of the information received from the utility, the degree to which it was personalized, and the convenience of the means of communication—all influence the perception of the quality of the relationship. Text messages, emails, and alerts, for example, require little extra cognitive or physical effort compared to logging in to a website to view data. Opower fosters not just better relationships through better communications but collective intimacy, generating personalized, gamified recommendations for each end-user customer based on calculations performed on data from all customers.

SMBs are responsible for about half of commercial power usage. They're smaller than large enterprises, obviously, but there are a lot more of them. Given that half of new businesses fail within their first five years, one might think that anything that can reduce their operating expenses and improve their cash flow would immediately be attractive to them. However, time and attention are an even scarcer resource than cash for such business owners, so ease of visibility into consumption and the ease of execution of usage reduction initiatives are extremely important.

Opower has managed to crack the code on how to do this. They enable electric power utilities to help their customers to reduce electricity consumption and customer bills. You might think that, as profit-seeking businesses, utilities would want customers to *increase* consumption, but that turns out not to be the case. They want customers to reduce consumption so as to meet governmental and societal sustainability targets. Many utilities—especially in the United States and other progressive regions—are mandated by regulators to reduce energy consumption through mechanisms such as an Energy Efficiency Resource Standard. Additional stakeholders such as environmental organizations, consumer groups, and other nongovernmental organizations share these goals.

In addition, it is in utilities' interest for customers to reduce *peak* consumption. Not only does Opower have a substantial impact on customer power consumption, but it can do so at peak demand periods—such as heat waves—through its Behavioral Demand Response solution, which alerts customers to help alter their behavior during such times. This is important, because it reduces the risk of brown-outs and black-outs, improves sustainability, and improves facilities utilization and thus business economics.

Opower drives significant reductions in electricity consumption, ranging from 1.5 to 3.5 percent, and up to 5 percent during peak usage periods. This may not sound like a lot, but think of it this way: *All* of the data centers in the United States put together—including those for Amazon, Apple, Facebook, Google, Microsoft, Yahoo!, and also corporate data centers such as General Electric's and General Motors' and General Instruments' and colocation space for small companies—account for only about 2.5 percent of U.S. energy consumption.[6] In other words, if everyone used Opower, *all* the other computing applications and services and data centers could come along for a free ride, and there would *still* be a net reduction in domestic energy use and its resulting environmental impact.

As of May, 2015, Opower has saved over 6 billion kilowatt-hours, reduced carbon dioxide emissions by over 9 billion pounds, and saved customers more than US$700 million. Opower co-founder Alex Laskey says that it takes a wheelbarrow full of coal to power one light bulb for a year.[7] Therefore, even small percentage reductions in consumption can have an enormous impact when multiplied by all the light bulbs and other electric appliances on the planet. Alex estimates that in the United States alone, $40 billion worth of electricity—about $30 per month per home—is wasted annually, in simple acts like leaving the lights on when we are not in a room, or running the air conditioning when we aren't home.

Human Behavior and Energy Consumption

I spoke with Alex Kinnier, a senior vice president of product management at Opower, to better understand Opower's strategy.[8] He has a diverse background, with a Harvard MBA and a bachelor's degree in chemical engineering, as a venture capital partner, and as a product management executive at Google. He leads not just product management but the end-to-end chain of capabilities that makes Opower tick: smart-meter and mobile devices, real-time services, and the user experience.

Opower exploits insights derived from behavioral science to help influence customers to become *intrinsically* motivated to reduce power usage. You might think that rational customers would want to reduce their power bills and impact on the environment, but behavior change is not so simple. Opower uses sophisticated technology, but the core insight of the company dates back to a surprising experiment run in San Marcos, California, just after the turn of the millennium, during a hot summer. Electric fans use much less electricity than whole-home air conditioning (A/C), so graduate students hung notes on doorknobs with one of several messages to see if they could get home-owners to use fans instead of A/C, and tracked the results.[9]

One message was focused around a financial incentive, and suggested that by switching from air conditioning to fans, the homeowner could save $54 over the course of the summer. Others were focused on morals or altruism, suggesting that a homeowner could help save the planet by reducing carbon emissions or could be a good neighbor by reducing the likelihood of blackouts.

These messages had a limited impact, reducing average consumption only by 2 to 3 percent. The most powerful message, which reduced consumption by 6 percent, was based on an appeal to social norms. That note said: "Join your neighbors in conserving energy … by using fans instead of A/C." The message also highlighted that "77 percent of San Marcos residents said that they often use fans instead of air conditioning to keep cool in the summer." In other words, behavior could be impacted more via social norms—that is, fitting in—than through the wallet.[10,11]

Opower has taken this insight and created a rich set of interlinked capabilities, designing software to exploit behavioral insights such as this as well as operations automation and information systems integration: connected meters, utilities, and means of messaging consumers through email, text messaging, and mobile devices.

One of the models Opower uses is the "Fogg" model, which posits that behavior is a function of motivation and ability, as well as the strength of a behavioral trigger.[12] According to this model, even if individuals are motivated to do something, they might not have the skills, and even if they have the skills, they might not have the motivation. If they have both ability and motivation, they still need some sort of trigger to set the activity in motion. Behavioral dynamics can create motivation, tools such as easy-to-use apps can provide the ability, and the right messaging can serve as the trigger.

Opower has observed that motivation to engage in digital activity can be predicted based on prior digital activity such as emails, online bill payment, or website activity. Some customers, for example, open most emails and participate in online billing. Others—believe it or not—have no email address, nor do they spend time on the web. Kinnier points out that mismatching messaging to segments creates a poor customer experience and is a waste of marketing and communications dollars, underscoring the importance of segmentation and fine-grained understanding of customer behaviors and preferences.

Opower, Information, and Intimacy

Opower sits in the information flow between utilities and customers. It maintains data on over 50 million homes, and processes over 100 billion meter reads each year. It takes in data from electric utilities, such as smart-meter data from each home as well as load factors. The data can be very granular, for example, how much energy is being used for heating, for cooling, for base loads such as the refrigerator, and for infrequently used appliances. Although someday each appliance in the connected home will no doubt report on its status, for now such insights can be derived from aggregate smart meter data.

Opower then combines data from the home with third-party data—for example the age of a home, heating type, and weather data—to create accurate profiles of each individual customer. This kind of analysis is important: A customer might be using less energy because the family is better at behaving in ways that conserve energy, or because the customer's home was built more recently and therefore is better insulated. A year-over-year or day-to-day improvement could be due to behavioral response; or due to a warmer winter or cooler summer. Customers can also provide information such as preferences for receiving energy usage information: email, text, physical mail, tablet app, and so on.

All of the data are plugged into a big data engine, which then generates messages to customers, phrased in a behavior-impacting way. For example, rather than merely saying, "You used 22 kilowatt-hours," Opower might report that most other homes in the neighborhood of similar size and construction date used an average of only 17 kilowatt-hours, thus incenting you to reduce energy consumption.

Because of the granularity of disaggregated data collection, customers are able to see not just that they use more or less energy than others, but the root causes, say, that their heating energy consumption is higher, whereas their air conditioning energy usage is lower. This provides enough insight to facilitate behavioral change.

And, Opower doesn't just provide information, but the "things" and data that enable monitoring and control. For example, Opower enables utilities to distribute Wi-Fi thermostats, and provides information to customers that enables them to select heating and cooling settings that can lead to reductions in their utility bills. Control is then provided to customers in real-time:

for example, during heat waves, customers can opt out of higher temperature settings or decide to maintain them and enjoy utility bill savings.

In addition to closing the loop on energy usage and providing such information in real time, Opower can also identify a "best" rate plan for each customer—that is, one that minimizes cost while meeting the customer's needs.

Opower doesn't just provide information to customers about their utility usage; it provides information to utilities about their customers. Such customer intelligence analyzes information from multiple utility company applications as well as information that Opower collects regarding customer use of its digital portals. Insights derived in this way can be used to see, for example, how often customers review their messages from Opower and whether they take action as a result. This, in turn, can be used to support A/B testing to see which messages, graphics, or formats are most effective. Directive or suggestive? Financial or social? Text or email? Opower then considers this information in the context of the utility's market segmentation strategy, determining whether, say, certain customers in a given neighborhood or cohort respond better to financial or social messages during the summer months.

To help perform this kind of optimization, Opower helps its utility customers segment their residential customers. For example, one utility, Hydro One, segments its consumers into four groups: "Sensible Seniors," with average education; "Flourishing Families," typically with higher education and income, living in the suburbs, typically with kids; "Heartland Homeowners," typically rural, with average education and income; and "Empty-nest Enthusiasts," typically suburban and rural families with average education.[13]

Segmentation is important, because it leads to greater success with campaigns that utilities, supported by Opower, can run, such as enrollment in budget billing or preauthorized payment plans. Targeted messaging based on segmentation has led to campaign results that were three times more effective.

A subtle balance in leveraging various cognitive biases is required for Opower to be able to incent appropriate behaviors. While people are influenced by social norms, they also typically exhibit another bias: the *fallacy of uniqueness*—the belief that we are more unique and special than we actually are. Such a bias could lead to rationalizing higher energy consumption.

To combat this, Opower uses sophisticated algorithms for comparison. For residences it includes the age of the home and square footage; for businesses, it includes the industry that the business is in—say, dry cleaning or food service, how many hours it is open each day, and its square footage. It can thus provide relevant messaging to customers, indicating that their use is exactly this much higher or lower than, say, comparable dry cleaners or Thai restaurants within a 20-mile radius.

Through the capabilities available through Opower's platform, the unimaginable occurs: better energy efficiency and more engaged and satisfied customers. According to Val Jensen, a senior vice president at ComEd (Commonwealth Edison), "the satisfaction level of customers who've taken advantage of these programs is so much higher than the average customer."[14]

■ ■ ■

Opower is an interesting example of complementing advanced computing technology with gamification and behavioral approaches. It offers an interesting alternative to a strictly automated approach such as a fully connected "smart" home with adaptive components, smart grids, and a fully automated demand response system. Presumably, such an end-to-end system will gain meaningful traction someday, but to date, penetration has been limited due to things like cost and incompatible standards. Moreover, in terms of adoption and participation rates, one of the benefits of the Opower approach is that customers retain control, an important behavioral advantage.

Notes

1. "Company Overview | Opower," Opower, www.opower.com/company.
2. Opower, "Five Universal Truths about Energy Consumers," 2013, www.opower.com/fivetruths/.
3. Ibid.
4. M. L. Finucane, A. Alhakami, P. Slovic, and S. M. Johnson, "The Affect Heuristic in Judgments of Risks and Benefits," *Journal of Behavioral Decision Making* 13, no. 1 (January 2000): 1–17, www-abc.mpib-berlin.mpg.de/users/r20/finucane00_the _affect_heuristic.pdf.
5. W. Levinson, D. L. Roter, J. P. Mullooly, V. T. Dull, and R. M. Frankel, "Physician-Patient Communication: The Relationship with Malpractice Claims among Primary Care Physicians and Surgeons," *Journal of the American Medical Association* 277, no. 7 (February 19, 1997): 553–559, www.ncbi.nlm.nih.gov /pubmed/9032162.
6. Jonathan G. Koomey, "My New Study of Data Center Electricity Use in 2010," blog, July 31, 2011, www.koomey.com/post/8323374335.
7. Alex Laskey, "How Behavioral Science Can Lower Your Energy Bill," [Video] *TED 2013*, February 2013, www.ted.com/talks/alex_laskey_how_behavioral_science _can_lower_your_energy_bill.
8. Alex Kinnier, conversation with the author, April 29, 2014.
9. Robert Cialdini and Wesley Schultz, "Understanding and Motivating Energy Conservation via Social Norms," Final Report, 2004, https://opower.com/uploads

/library/file/2/understanding_and_motivating_energy_conservation_via_social_norms.pdf.

10. Ibid.

11. P. Wesley Schultz, "The Constructive, Destructive, and Reconstructive Power or [sic] Social Norms," 2008 Behavior, Energy, and Climate Change (BECC) Conference, 2008, web.stanford.edu/group/peec/cgi-bin/docs/events/2008/becc /presentations/17-1C-01%20The%20Constructive%20Destructive%20and %20Reconstructive%20Power%20of%20Social%20Norms.pdf.

12. BJ Fogg, "A Behavior Model for Persuasive Design," *Persuasive '09*, Claremont, California, April 26–29, 2009, bjfogg.com/fbm_files/page4_1.pdf.

13. Catherine Pearson, "How to become Truly Data-Centric," *Environics Analytics*, 62, mria-arim.ca/sites/default/uploads/files/Environics%20Analytics_MRIA_Oct% 2029.pdf.

14. Opower, "ComEd, Val Jensen (Senior Vice President, Customer Operations)," *Vimeo.com*, vimeo.com/53340604.

CHAPTER 20

Digital Disasters

Instead of attaining market leadership through the application of one or more digital disciplines, some firms seem to attain a drop in revenues, profitability, market capitalization, brand equity, or customer satisfaction and loyalty, through poor, misguided, or no application of information technology. Forewarned is forearmed: Knowledge of where others have run into problems with information technology may help you avoid repeating their mistakes.

Some digital disasters unfold quickly, as with BATS' (Better Alternative Trading System) IPO, which was halted within a half-hour due to its own trading system failure, with all trades subsequently cancelled.

Others happen in slow motion, as incumbents fail to notice challengers until it's too late. Being a challenger is no assurance of success, either. Although there are different ways to measure survival—for example, a business may close due to shifting life priorities of the founder rather than bankruptcy—it appears that only about half of new businesses last more than 5 years.[1,2] This survival rate hasn't changed very much in 20 years, even with changing macroeconomic conditions, tax policies, or anything else. Moreover, the lifetime of businesses is decreasing, and turbulence, measured as the relative change in market position, is increasing.

Even for businesses that *do* manage to survive—or even grow to multibillion-dollar market caps and revenue streams—product launches are by no means a sure bet. For every successful new product—say, the Amazon Kindle—there are ones that at least at first seem to be swept into the back pages of the history books—say, the Amazon Kindle Fire Phone.[3]

Technology is not necessarily the issue, nor competition. After seeing its market lead go flat, in 1985 The Coca-Cola Company introduced "New Coke" and discontinued the classic formulation with a lot of fanfare and substantial market research showing that consumers preferred the sweeter reformulation. After a backlash from loyal, vocal consumers, it brought back "Coke Classic" within a few months.

Then there are the cases of brand extension gone awry, such as Colgate Kitchen Entrees, Frito-Lay Lemonade, Coors Rocky Mountain Spring Water,

Harley-Davidson Perfume, and Cosmopolitan Yogurt.[4] But these are mere failed products; sometimes the magnitude of the disaster is much greater.

In *Billion Dollar Lessons*, authors Paul B. Carroll and Chunka Mui look at massive failures among large companies and analyze their root causes.[5] They identify several major categories of mistakes, such as "illusions of synergy," for which the poster child is AOL-Time Warner; "faulty financial engineering," such as mail-order catalog retailer Spiegel's bankruptcy, caused by goosing sales by extending credit to customers with no ability to pay; and "staying the course," for which a good example is Kodak's inability to focus beyond film through the end of the twentieth century, and the negative results that developed when it missed the digital photography revolution.

Another good way to make a billion-dollar mistake, they say, is by "fumbling technology." This can be through poor execution, but it can also be based on a poor strategy, possibly due to poor understanding of technology trajectories.

Strategic Errors

Carroll and Mui detail the case of Motorola's Iridium, which was intended to be a mobile voice communications network using a constellation of 77 low-earth orbiting satellites. It was originally conceived in the mid-1980s, when cellular coverage was mostly spotty or nonexistent. These satellites would orbit at an altitude of 420 miles rather than the earlier geostationary satellites, which orbited at 22,300 miles, reducing annoying transmission delays and thus periods of silence during normal conversation. Among its advantages: the ability to make a call from exotic locations such as a rocky beachfront on a remote South Pacific Island or a clearing in the heart of the jungle.

Unfortunately, those were about the *only* locations that worked, because one couldn't make calls from cars, offices, homes, or on city streets where buildings interfered with line of sight to the satellite. Carroll and Mui delineate the issues: The handsets were huge, even for that time, the cost to own one and make a call was prohibitive, the inter-satellite call hand-off software and mobile handsets were buggy, and they were either mostly unusable for the general populace or their usefulness was rapidly being subsumed by cellular phones by the time the system became operational in 1998. Faulty market research focused on the positives, rather than the negatives of the system, leading to overly rosy forecasts.

Iridium ceased operations in less than a year, its billions of dollars of assets auctioned off for a mere $25 million. Motorola and Iridium LLC together lost billions from high capital investments and operating expenses offset by paltry revenues, due to what Carroll and Mui might call a flawed technology strategy that didn't account for competing technology advantages, trends, and performance trajectories, questionable execution of the satellite call routing software, a poor user experience, and misleading market research, according to Carroll and Mui. Iridium may not have been a success in terms of its original market objectives or overall financials, but it did eventually receive a second lease on life thanks to its acquirers, and is still operational, serving unique segments such as the U.S. Department of Defense, with obvious applications for such customers.

In recent times, there have been a number of examples of products and services based on information technology where some would say that the strategy could be questioned. In 2005, eBay acquired Skype, the Internet calling service, for $2.5 billion, with the idea being that buyers and sellers would want to talk as they discussed potential purchases. Evidently they didn't, so eBay sold a large stake to investors. The company was eventually picked up by Microsoft, and eBay made money on the deal. As an investment, it worked. As part of an integrated strategy, some would argue that it sure didn't seem to.

Another example is PayPal, also acquired by eBay in 2002. The idea was that as an online payments processor, which facilitated eBay's transactions, somehow there was a strategic fit. However, here again, some would say that the strategic rationale appeared to be faulty, and eBay announced spin-off plans in 2012.

This is not to pick on eBay: Apple dabbled in the enterprise computing business, Microsoft never got much traction in Zune, Netflix temporarily planned to spin off its physical DVD rental business into a unit called Qwikster. Google has discontinued dozens of products and services in the last few years, including Google Answers, Dodgeball, Google Health, Google Buzz, Google Power Meter, Real Estate, Knol, Jaiku, and Orkut.

It could be argued that while the individual efforts were not strategic, taken as a whole the idea of experimenting, pivoting, and either discontinuing or investing *is* strategic. It's the lean, agile, risk-embracing enterprise approach to innovation and renewal.

However, some would say that Google Health would appear to be highly strategic, given ever-increasing spending on healthcare, an aging population, and ripe opportunities for disruptive innovation by a company skilled in software, big data, and search.

Another about-face: Google acquired Motorola Mobility in May 2012 for $12.5 billion, partly with a synergy argument that "Google is great at software; Motorola Mobility is great at devices. The combination of the two makes sense and will enable faster innovation."[6] Google also wanted Motorola Mobility's patent portfolio to protect the Android ecosystem, given the accelerating importance of mobile to Google's core business and increasing intellectual property lawsuits against which Google needed to defend itself and its licensees.

In October 2014, Google sold the unit including some patents to Lenovo for only $2.91 billion in cash and stock, not including a prior sale of the cable modem and set-top box business to ARRIS. Some might say that acquiring Motorola's patents for a net investment of less than $10 billion was a bargain; others might argue that some of the difference between acquisition and selling price was a misstep. Still others might say that it was smart to try to make a go of it and then reevaluate one's strategy rather than staying the course.

The point of this discussion is that even global leaders with world-class information technology expertise apparently can make strategic choices that may not unfold as planned, and that just because something is digital or cloud does not mean it will be a successful product, service, or business.

Even with the right strategy, execution can be a challenge due to problems in software development, IT operations, project management, security, and more.

Cyberattacks

Not a day goes by, it seems, without one firm or another announcing that it is investigating a breach, sometimes due to a third party that had a vulnerability. LinkedIn had millions of passwords stolen, a third-party Snapchat-related application let email addresses and phone numbers be taken, Target and The Home Depot both had breaches affecting tens of millions of customers.

Security is a challenge for many firms, for multiple reasons. First, due to similar logic to open innovation, no matter how large your security and software teams and how strong their motivation, there are more people outside the firm, with time on their hands, motivated by reputation, a challenge, or financial gain. Second, software projects need to be delivered on time, whereas the search for vulnerabilities can be open ended. Third, the increasing complexity of software means that just getting it to work properly is a challenge, much less bulletproofing it against all conceivable threats. Fourth, there is a cycle—which is nonvirtuous but self-reinforcing—where vulnerabilities lead to exploits, which lead to the increasing importance of security, which leads to difficulty in hiring and retaining security experts, which leads to insecure applications and environments, which lead to more exploits. Fifth, breaking in from overseas locations reduces hackers' fear of prosecution or extradition. Sixth, nation-state actors are sometimes involved in bad deeds. Seventh—well, the list goes on and on.

The scope of threats and vulnerabilities is increasing every day. It takes just a few examples to help illustrate this.

Digital threats used to only impact the digital world. A computer virus, for example, might lead to the loss of digital photos. As technology fuses the digital and physical domains, a virtual attack can have real consequences. Sometime in 2014, hackers attacked the control systems of a steel mill in Germany and gained control of its blast furnace, which led to "massive damage."[7] This wasn't the first such attack: Sources rumored to include the US government created the Stuxnet virus, which caused Iranian uranium centrifuges to spin too fast, causing their destruction.[8]

The link between digital technologies and physical threats doesn't need to be that direct: Although 3D printers can be used, say, for manufacturing replacement parts for your vacuum cleaner, they can also be used to print working guns. Worse yet, these guns can be made mostly out of plastic, instantly compromising the usefulness of metal detectors at schools, courthouses, and airports. Moreover, 3D printers aren't restricted to plastic: Some printers use laser beams to melt powdered metal to print 3D metal objects. This can be used for medical prosthetics or auto body design prototyping, but also for metal guns or other weapons, such as improvised explosive devices. How does one protect against someone printing a weapon on a portable 3D printer in an airline lavatory at 30,000 feet?

There are other examples of new technologies being repurposed. In January 2015, a "toy" drone was found on the grounds of the White House.[9] Such drones could be used for surveillance, but also could potentially be weaponized by carrying payloads such as explosives or being outfitted with guns. Even basic technologies can be used for malicious purposes. For example, the Internet can and has been used to recruit terrorists, or share designs for explosives.

But let's restrict ourselves to cyberattacks, whose business impact can be huge.

Consider the case of Target. It was already wrestling with "a website which badly [lagged] behind competitors,"[10] when it suffered from a data breach that may have impacted over 100 million customers during the 2013 holiday shopping season. Information regarding customer names, mailing and email addresses, and phone numbers, as well as credit and debit card numbers and related information were taken.

The impact to Target, its leadership, and its customers was significant. Earnings were dramatically reduced—profit for the quarter fell by almost half—and reduced revenue guidance and actuals. There is no question as to cause and effect. Sales were stronger than expected before the data breach disclosure, and have been "meaningfully weaker" since.[11] Due to the breach, "Costs may include liabilities to payment card networks for reimbursements of credit card fraud and card reissuance costs, liabilities related to REDcard fraud and card re-issuance, liabilities from civil litigation, governmental investigations and enforcement proceedings, expenses for legal, investigative and consulting fees, and incremental expenses and capital investments for reme-diation activities."[12]

One estimate of losses just to the company is nearly $150 million, although other estimates range as high as a billion.[13,14] Besides the lower-than-expected revenues, there were the costs of crisis management, forensic investigations, management attention, and the opportunity costs of marketing and public relations dollars that were spent managing the crisis rather than on revenue-generating activities. Because the breach happened during the busy holiday shopping season, and many banks limited withdrawals or reissued cards because of the breach, there were untold customer issues and costs associated with the breach, such as inability to make purchases and time spent entering new information in to online accounts. And all of this doesn't include any losses due to thefts such as withdrawals or fraudulent purchases, and the costs to card issuers in customer inquiries and card reissue. Two additional losses: CEO Gregg Steinhafel and CIO Beth Jacob.[15] A chief information security officer position has since been created.

There is no shortage of examples where vulnerabilities in IT infrastruc-ture are exploited by those attempting to make a political statement, those who enjoy making trouble, or traditional crimes of robbery and extortion, updated for the Information Age. There was the hack of Apple's iCloud, where private photos of celebrities' privates were leaked.[16] There was the Sony Pictures Entertainment hack, where numerous embarrassing emails and private employee data were leaked, which may have been extortion, a disgruntled employee, or based on state action due to the then-pending release of the movie *The Interview*.[17] A few days later, during Christmas 2014, there was a Sony Playstation and Microsoft Xbox distributed denial of service attack. In addition to viruses, which merely cause trouble, a new category of revenue-generating malware called ransomware encrypts a user's files until a payment is made.[18] In the future, ransomware will lead to more than just the loss of wedding and prom photos: One can expect that someone will want tens of thousands to return control of a speeding driverless car, which will pale in comparison to the tens of millions to put the control rods back into the reactor core to prevent a nuclear meltdown, turn electricity back on to the country, or unscramble the air traffic control system.

Software Design and Development Challenges

If malfeasance is not involved, misfeasance often is. Projects of all kinds are viewed as successful when they are on time or early, at or under budget, at or above quality expectations, and meet or exceed the desired scope and features. Unfortunately, in the real world, most projects fail to meet all four criteria, and information technology projects are no exception.

According to a Gartner study, about three quarters of IT projects fail. For large IT projects, roughly a quarter fail due to cost issues, another quarter are late, and another quarter have issues with functionality. Of the remainder, half were of unacceptable quality.[19] Of course, a bigger challenge is that the IT project may be viewed as successful, but the overarching business objective may be misguided or misaligned.

A study conducted by McKinsey & Company in conjunction with the University of Oxford of over 5,000 IT projects has somewhat different numbers, but ones that are no less damning. According to that study, large IT projects are 45 percent over budget and 7 percent late, yet deliver less than half the value expected. Cost and time are not necessarily trade-offs as is typically thought: Large, long projects are likely to be late, with each additional year increasing the cost overrun by 15 percent.[20]

A project that is late or costs more than projected is bad, but McKinsey also found that one-sixth of IT projects go so wrong that they *threaten the very survival of the firm*. In one example, a retailer spent $2 billion to modernize various systems and applications. When those efforts failed, it filed for bankruptcy.

The list of issues with IT projects is basically the list of issues with any project: poor or fantastic (not wonderful, but imaginary) business cases or project schedules, poor alignment with business goals, conflicting stakeholder objectives, bad planning, poor or no risk management, poor management interpersonal skills, insufficient or inappropriate technical skills, issues with scope creep, changing priorities, poor tracking, reporting, and issue management, lack of collaboration, perverse incentives, personnel pulled off or added apparently at random, and so on.

The dark, flip side of the power and flexibility of IT is its complexity.

Consider the troubled roll-out of Healthcare.gov, the embodiment of what was intended to be the signature achievement of the Obama administration. This led to the resignation of Health and Human Services Secretary Kathleen Sebelius, after five years of service "marred by the disastrous roll-out" of Obamacare.[21] This likely makes her the most senior global administrator to be sacked over IT project management and software issues.

A simple coding error led to the loss of NASA's $125 million Mars Climate Orbiter, and untold millions more in operating expenses and lost time. Some software, written by Lockheed Martin Astronautics, provided data in the English measurement system of inches and pounds, whereas other software, written at the Jet Propulsion Laboratory, used the metric system of meters and kilograms. As a result, the trajectory was miscalculated, leading the spacecraft to burn up in the Martian atmosphere rather than orbit the red planet.[22]

In addition to software problems, hardware problems are not unheard of. In 1995, Intel took a charge of almost half a billion dollars for a Pentium chip recall due to a bug in processing floating-point division, for example, calculating .0037 / .011.

Scalability can be another issue. An application may work fine for a few users, but perform poorly or not at all for many users. This was one of the issues with the Healthcare.gov site. There are many potential drivers for scalability issues, ranging from how the application is designed to insufficient resources during real-world operation or operation under peak loads, such as health insurance signups or busy ecommerce days such as Cyber Monday.

Operational Issues

Even if the software is well written and architected to scale, the realities of real-world operations mean that outages and disasters can and do happen. The first general-purpose computer, the ENIAC, was built from almost 20,000 vacuum tubes. No tube itself was very reliable, so having this many tubes meant that a tube would burn out on average every few hours, leaving the overall computer usable only about half the time. While there were no doubt software bugs in the very first programs, the first computer "hardware" bug was, literally, a bug—a moth—trapped in the electromagnetic relays of the Harvard Mark II computer, built for the US Navy. Although hardware has gotten more reliable, the scale and complexity of computer applications has also increased, so software-based and hardware-based outages do still occur. Add in human error, data center outages, natural disasters, and operational complexity including management and upgrade processes, and it's a wonder that anything ever works. Half a century ago, bugs and glitches might require the recomputation of a ballistic trajectory or payroll. But now, because the cloud is connected to billions of people and things in real time, outages have immediate, real-world impact.

The Netflix outage on Christmas Eve 2012, due to a software problem at Amazon Web Services, meant that reportedly as many as 27 million people might have been unable to watch movies that night.[23] Even though Netflix is known in the technology community for using numerous innovative techniques to maximize software reliability and availability, this outage was operational: An AWS employee accidentally deleted some data, which led to a cascade of increasingly serious impacts.[24]

Netflix and AWS learned from this experience. AWS refined its change management techniques and Netflix further refined its architecture and mechanisms for serving users out of other AWS regions in the event of a failure in one.

Cloud-connected things mean that it's not just gamers and movie viewers that are impacted: Future outages will impact entire systems, such as the electric grid or air traffic control system.

Actually, we don't need to wait for the future. On September 26, 2014, all air traffic for the Chicago area, and much of it beyond, was brought to a halt due to a fire at an air traffic control center allegedly set by a disgruntled employee.[25] And, the root cause of the August 14, 2003, Northeast blackout, which impacted tens of millions of people in the United States and Canada, was *not* excess demand due to sweltering heat, but faulty software in the monitoring system at First Energy. An alarm application failed, which then cascaded into the failure of other energy management applications. A tree that downed a power line during the loss of those systems, which otherwise would have been locally contained, then cascaded into an enormous problem as various utilities and their electricity generation, transmission, and distribution systems went off line.[26]

Unintended Consequences

The cloud, big data, mobile, social, and the Internet of Things offer exciting combinations that are multiplicative in their power. These combinations also have unintended consequences, such as vulnerabilities to new types of attack vectors and larger attack surfaces, not to mention sometimes erratic behaviors.

There are a variety of nefarious cyberattacks exploiting these complex intersections. In one, Wi-Fi light bulbs use an insecure password-sharing protocol, enabling third parties to determine the encryption key to the local network.[27] In another, a baby monitor can be repurposed to be a bugging device, with eavesdroppers able to listen in from anywhere in the world.[28] Default passwords are perhaps the greatest vulnerability of such devices: One Russian site displayed live feeds from over 73,000 webcams and video monitors around the world simply because their owners never changed the default password.[29]

Besides gaining access to things, there are other vulnerabilities in our digital era. Three quarters of convicted burglars surveyed admitted to using social media to determine who to rob. Family vacation status updates indicate that no one is home. GPS data embedded in some posted photographs or collected by some apps can indicate where someone lives and where they are—and aren't—at any given time.[30] Publicly available information can be used to hack into an account, as when Paris Hilton's T-Mobile account was broken into using the publicly known name of her dog, Tinkerbell, revealing contact information and photos.[31] Increasingly, garage doors, door locks, home security systems, and the like can be controlled through the Internet and by your phone, increasing the opportunities for and severity of attacks.

There are also unintended consequences in the sense that some argue that the ease of innovation in the digital domain and the possibilities of wealth creation are distracting us from more noble goals.

The model of ubiquitous, democratic, global innovation and entrepreneurship leveraging platforms such as those for developing mobile apps has benefits in unleashing innovation. After all, any village may well have the next Mark Zuckerberg. However, it is also not without its detractors. Walter Frick, an associate editor at the *Harvard Business Review*, observes that today's startups are smaller, have less seed capital, and are often more focused on immediately monetizable incremental benefits and "rarely push the boundaries of basic or even applied science."[32] A good example is Yo, an app that was developed in eight hours that sends the voice and text message "Yo" to a recipient. It had millions of downloads and a valuation of millions of dollars shortly after launch. On the one hand, millions of dollars for eight hours of work demonstrates the ability of information technology to create wealth by leveraging platforms and network effects. On the other hand, as the venture capital firm Founders Fund wryly laments regarding how the future has turned out: "We wanted flying cars, instead we got 140 characters."[33]

Edward Jung, Microsoft's former chief architect and now chief technology officer and co-founder at Intellectual Ventures, a global patent licensing and intellectual property development firm, supports Frick's contention. He argues that many of the problems we face as a civilization are too big for any company to handle, and the laissez-faire, rapidly monetizable approach won't work. For monumental initiatives like Kennedy's moonshot, Jung says "The mechanism you *don't* use is to say: 'Oh, well, let's just assume a whole bunch of startups will show up and one of them will build the command module, and one of them will build the rocket, and one of them will build this or that'—and imagine they will all magically integrate."[34]

Erratic Algorithms

In Mary Shelley's classic novel *Frankenstein; or, The Modern Prometheus*, a scientist named Victor Frankenstein harnesses electricity and other secret techniques to bring inert matter to life, thus creating a monster, now commonly (if incorrectly) referred to as Frankenstein. Shortly after, the creator loses control of his creation, as the monster matures and interacts with others, leading to death and destruction.

While that particular story may be science fiction, it serves as a great metaphor for something that isn't: rogue algorithms. Developers harness electricity and other secret techniques to create working programs, thus bringing inert matter to life, and can sometimes lose control of their creation. As the algorithms interact with people and others, unpredictable results can arise. The problem is that these results are not necessarily flaws in the behavior of the algorithm per se, but issues that emerge only under certain conditions due to how the algorithms interact, generally referred to as *emergence* or *system dynamics*.

To understand how this can happen, consider a bidding strategy intended to win an important work of art at auction. A bidder might wait until the auctioneer begins to say "going, going, gone," and then jump in with a bid that is $10 higher than the highest bid. This would be a smart strategy, because by not bidding earlier, the bidder wouldn't raise the penultimate price, and by waiting until the "end" of the auction process, could acquire the artwork for a trivial amount more.

Of course, the strategy can go awry if two bidders were to use the same strategy, as the potential sale price would increase by $10 every few seconds, without limit. Such a situation may seem unrealistic, but it happens all the time.

For example, speaking of creating creatures, *The Making of a Fly: The Genetics of Animal Design*, is a fairly well regarded paperback by Peter Lawrence, a developmental biologist at the University of Cambridge, which was published in 1992 by Wiley-Blackwell, a sister division of Wiley CIO. New copies are currently available for about $60.

However, in April 2011, in something like the hypothetical art auction example, two used book sellers were using algorithms to set the price for their copies of the book, each using a simple algorithm: one priced it at 1.27059 times the other's price, perhaps hoping to gain a little extra profit; the other seller priced it at .9983 times the other's price, giving up a little bit of money but appealing to the value conscious, and showing up earlier in the list of potential purveyors.[35]

The end result is that these two straightforward algorithms made the offered price of the book spiral out of control, peaking at $23,698,655.93, although it's worth noting that Amazon Prime members were eligible for free shipping.

Kevin Slavin, an assistant professor at the famed MIT Media Lab, has researched this and similar examples of behavior in algorithms as they learn and evolve, as they interact with other algorithms, and as they interact with people. His TED talk on the topic has been viewed over 3 million times.[36]

While it is unlikely that anyone would have bought a $60 book for $24 million, massive real-world impacts can and do happen, for example, in the financial markets.

One example is the "Crash of 2:45," which occurred on May 6, 2010, at, well, 2:45 p.m. The Dow Jones Industrial Average, which was already down several hundred points, suddenly dropped another 600 points in 5 minutes for a total of 998.5 points, which represented a loss of a trillion dollars for the day to that point, and then regained the lost 600 points in the next 15 minutes. During this period, companies such as Accenture and P&G traded either as low as a penny or as high as $100,000 per share.

What some say happened is that all of the high-frequency, algorithmic, black-box trading algorithms were triggered by a single large sale by a mutual fund, and a set of cascading and escalating events were then set into motion, not unlike the book price escalation. Like more and more people causing a stampede during a movie-theater fire, the individual algorithms caused a stampede as well as they executed rapid-fire trades. At least that's one theory; there are multiple theories as to exactly who did what and when under which conditions, even after deep analysis of the trading data from that day. These include everything from "toxic order imbalance" to a particular London-based trader. The lack of a clear answer after years of investigation and scholarly research is evidence in itself of the difficulty of understanding such complex systems operating at warp speed.

There are other examples of flash crashes, such as one in Singapore in August 2014, the BATS Global Markets mini-crash of Apple, and, Slavin says, another *18,000* over a period of five years. High frequency and other algorithms can behave and interact of their own volition, like Frankenstein's monster, without any human wisdom or control, or, as Slavin quips, "adult supervision."[37]

It isn't just simple pricing of stocks of books or books of stocks: Slavin points out that companies like Epagogix are using sophisticated algorithms to evaluate and correct movie scripts for new movies, which are then recommended to audiences through different algorithms, such as the Netflix recommenders discussed in Chapter 13. In other words, the Netflix algorithm is the customer of the Epagogix algorithm, and vice versa, potentially leading to unexpected results.

The point of this line of thought is that interactions between algorithms can result in emergent, chaotic, unpredictable behavior. Consequently, an algorithm running on a home heating system to reduce energy consumption might interact in strange ways with the one on the thermostat and the one on the washing machine and the one at the electric utility. There might be a flash crash in the home temperature, or not, and like the Crash of 2:45, it might be difficult to determine a root cause. Restarting the rinse cycle on the washing machine is easy; having a flash crash on a highway full of driverless cars or a fully automated air traffic control system might not be.

Politics and Pushback

The digital disciplines can drive digital disruption. This may be good for the disruptor, but unfortunately, the disrupted may not approve. Uber is disrupting traditional taxi and limousine services in many locations around the world, and they are fighting back using methods such as strikes and lobbying. Ostensibly, the incumbents are concerned about ensuring passenger safety, an equal playing field, and ensuring that drivers are licensed, insured, and have undergone background checks. Some would no doubt argue that the real reason is that Uber and its online rivals have seriously dented the revenue stream of the incumbents.

Tesla is offering not only disruptive technology, but a disruptive business model, bypassing automobile dealers and selling directly to customers, thus impacting those dealer's revenues. In some states, the dealers have dealt Tesla reverses, whereas in others Tesla has charged ahead and set up its own dealerships and maintenance facilities.

Yet another example is laws and regulations in some countries regarding data sovereignty and cross-border data flows. As with Tesla and Uber, there may be legitimate concerns, or these moves may cover an ulterior motive, such as trying to foster a local industry in the face of strong overseas competition.

Niccolò Machiavelli figured this out five centuries ago, when he wrote, "There is nothing more difficult to take in hand, more perilous to conduct, or more uncertain in its success, than to take the lead in the introduction of a new order of things. Because the innovator has for enemies all those who have done well under the old conditions, and lukewarm defenders in those who may do well under the new."[38]

Digital Disappointments

Instead of attaining market leadership through digital disciplines, all too often companies seem to offer only digital disappointments.

Information Incompetence. Instead of pursuing information excellence, some companies seem to offer information incompetence. Consider an expedited package logistics service provider that shows tracking information indicating that the package has arrived at a distribution center nearby and is on target for "on-time delivery." That would seem to be old news in today's modern age. Yet a dirty little secret that one generally wouldn't know except through personal experience, such as my own, is that much of that detailed tracking information represents a *logical scan*—that is, a best guess as to where the package is, which may not necessarily correspond to reality.

Or consider an etailer that offers expedited shipping, for a premium. The two-day shipping is guaranteed—once the package leaves the etailers shipping dock, which may take several days. Or interactive voice response systems that keep asking you for your account number or the last four digits of your social security number. Or companies that can't find your account by something useful, such as your phone number or last name, only by a 15-character alphanumeric identifier. Or companies whose search function can't find items on their own website that a general purpose engine like Google or Bing can.

These types of problems are often compounded by other business issues, such as unempathetic, uninformed customer service representatives who are unable to explain root causes or take corrective action; an inability or lack of interest in offering to credit premiums paid for service level objectives that were missed; no front-line knowledge of offers and commitments made through digital channels. In other words, little information was available, the information that was available was incorrect, and there was no ability to take action based on the information. And, it was not worth their time or energy and/or beyond their ability to turn information into action.

J.Crew lost millions of dollars due to issues with their website and supporting systems such as inventory management, ordering, and billing. As one example of the failure, an adult customer was sent three children's shirts instead of men's shirts, and billed \$9,208.50 for shipping.[39,40] Unless the shirts were delivered by a courier flying first class, that does seem a bit excessive.

Solution Laggardliness. Solution leadership sounds easy, but in practice there are many subtleties. Differentiating product-service systems by leveraging sensors, actuators, and local smarts networked to cloud services isn't always easy for product managers to do, and even with such a strategy, execution can be a challenge.

The Wii U was the latest entry from Nintendo in the game console wars being fought against Microsoft and Sony. It had a one-year head start on new console introductions from rivals. Unfortunately for Nintendo, though, it appears to have had difficulty in successfully implementing a solution leadership strategy.

According to an anonymous game developer telling a behind-the-scenes story about the console launch, there were allegedly a host of problems across product, connection, service, platform, and ecosystem, some representing necessary engineering trade-offs, some illustrating poor execution, if the story is accurate.[41] One trade-off was in the product itself. For the console to be suited for living room use, it needed a quieter fan, implying that there would be less cooling, therefore a lower-power CPU that would have difficulty in delivering the kind of graphics experience gamers crave. To actually build games for the new console required "development kits," basically prototypes with essentially the same functionality, just not fresh off the final production line. These were reportedly cumbersome for game developers to work with. Even small delays, when occurring in frequently used tasks, added days and weeks to a constrained schedule which required getting the game out for the console launch date.

Game developers, of course, are part of the console solution ecosystem, leveraging the development platform to enliven that ecosystem. Reportedly,[42] as questions arose during development, however, what should have been a quick phone call turned into week-long turnaround times, as questions were translated to and from Japanese. Today's games require networks to connect to software updates, as well as to make gaming a social experience by teaming up with or competing against other players. Here too, Nintendo allegedly had difficulty in setting up network infrastructure to enable these kinds of functions.

Finally, according to this insider,[43] these challenges led to limited titles being released at game launch, limiting early sales. This in turn led other developers to switch sides, focusing their game development resources on the upcoming consoles from Sony and Microsoft. And, it isn't consoles that compete against consoles, it's game solution ecosystems that compete against game solution ecosystems: the consoles, the services, and the game titles. The result of a troubled solution leadership strategy? Microsoft's entrant, the Xbox One, sold as many units in one week in the United Kingdom as the Wii U had sold in the preceding year.[44]

Collective Ignorance. Instead of collective intimacy, companies sometimes seem to develop collective ignorance. They ignore their customers' needs and offer one-size-fits-all products, services, and processes instead of segmenting their customers, understanding each one's requirements and personal preferences, and using weak signals embedded in collective data to generate solutions that are of value to each individual customer.

Numerous systems exist today that are intended to digitalize various aspects of the customer relationship: customer relationship management systems, sales force automation systems, marketing automation systems, social media management, customer experience management, and so forth. Statistics vary widely and wildly on how successful these implementations (including purely cloud-based solutions) are, with some studies suggesting below a 1.5 percent failure rate[45] and others suggesting failure rates closer to 30 percent.[46] In some cases, there are implementation issues due to salespeople's general unwillingness to spend any time on activities that are not immediately revenue producing.

Companies can also go too far, beyond intimacy and into intrusiveness. Some companies seem to continue to push the envelope on privacy, occasionally retreating in the face of public outcry. Facebook and Google have perhaps received the most attention. Facebook unilaterally removed privacy settings on its timeline feature, and had the dubious distinction of having *Consumer Reports* break out a separate report focusing on Facebook as part of its annual report on Internet privacy and security. For example, if you visit a site with a Facebook Like button, Facebook receives a report even if you don't click the button or aren't logged in to Facebook. And friends can unwittingly leak information: information about you can be transferred to third parties without your knowledge if your friend is using certain Facebook apps, allegedly.[47]

Arrested Innovation. Instead of accelerated innovation, some companies seem to have decelerated, or no, innovation. Sometimes this involves cumbersome processes that remain because "that's how we've always done things." Sometimes it involves unimaginative, me-too products. Sometimes it involves static, simplistic relationships with customers, where complaints or issues are unresolved and opportunities to innovate by resolving them remain dormant.

One lesson to be learned from observing otherwise successful companies is that there is more to winning in a market than extending a successful brand from an adjacent, much less nonadjacent market. Microsoft's Bing has only slowly been making progress against Google; Google+ has been slow to capture share from Facebook; the Facebook phone (the HTC First) didn't make much headway against other Google Android phones or the Apple iPhone; and to complete the circle, Apple's applications such as Pages and Numbers don't have the market traction of Microsoft Word and Excel. Some might argue that the strategy was off, some might question the overall execution, whereas others could point to the challenges of customer adoption. In any case, it shows that even innovative companies can face challenges in innovation.

Over-intimate relationships can lead to intrusiveness, but privacy is also an issue in innovation. Accelerated innovation and customer intimacy—collective or not—together can create unexpected vulnerabilities. It takes surprisingly little information to identify people: 87 percent of US citizens can be identified based on only three basic facts: date of birth, gender, and zip code.[48] Usually, these are easily available through social networks such as Facebook. Customer intimacy strategies generally like to collect much more data than that, making anonymity difficult, thus creating privacy concerns, even without massive data breaches.

What has this got to do with accelerated innovation? The curtain fell on the second Netflix Prize contest before it could premiere, due to concerns that unscrupulous contestants could de-anonymize the data to determine individuals' movie-watching preferences. To put it another way, inferences drawn from even minimal data on gender, age, and demographics meant that an accelerated innovation approach to collective intimacy needed to be halted.

■ ■ ■

Software coding issues, operational issues, IT project management issues, unpredictable algorithms, and strategic errors can all lead to minor headaches or massive problems. So can privacy issues, politics and incumbent pushback, and cybersecurity. In the never-ending arms war, defenders become savvier and defenses become more sophisticated, yet attackers become wilier.

The bottom line? To pursue the digital disciplines takes digital discipline.

Notes

1. Glenn Kessler, "Do Nine out of 10 New Businesses Fail, as Rand Paul Claims?" *The Washington Post*, January 27, 2014, www.washingtonpost.com/blogs/fact-checker/wp/2014/01/27/do-9-out-of-10-new-businesses-fail-as-rand-paul-claims/.
2. "Survival of Private Sector Establishments by Opening Year," U.S. Bureau of Labor Statistics, 2014, www.bls.gov/bdm/us_age_naics_00_table7.txt.
3. Jared Newman, "Fire Phone: Our First 5 Days with Amazon's Smartphone," *PCWorld.com*, July 23, 2014, www.pcworld.com/article/2456152/kindle-fire-phone-our-first-5-days-with-amazons-smartphone.html.
4. "Top 25 Biggest Product Flops of All Time," *DailyFinance.com*, www.dailyfinance.com/photos/top-25-biggest-product-flops-of-all-time/.
5. Paul B. Carroll and Chunka Mui, *Billion Dollar Lessons: What You Can Learn from the Most Inexcusable Business Failures of the Last 25 Years* (New York: Portfolio, 2009).
6. "Facts about Google's Acquisition of Motorola," Google, August 15, 2011, www.google.com/press/motorola/.
7. R. A. Becker, "Cyber Attack on German Steel Mill Leads to 'Massive' Real World Damage," *NovaNext*, January 8, 2015, www.pbs.org/wgbh/nova/next/tech/cyber-attack-german-steel-mill-leads-massive-real-world-damage/.
8. David E. Sanger, "Obama Order Sped Up Wave of Cyberattacks against Iran," *New York Times*, June 1, 2012, www.nytimes.com/2012/06/01/world/middleeast/obama-ordered-wave-of-cyberattacks-against-iran.html.
9. Michael S. Schmidt and Michael D. Shear, "A Drone, Too Small for Radar to Detect, Rattles the White House," *New York Times*, January 26, 2015, www.nytimes.com/2015/01/27/us/white-house-drone.html.
10. Paul Ziobro and Joann S. Lublin, "Target's Data Breach Adds to CEO's Sack of Woe," *Wall Street Journal*, January 23, 2014, www.wsj.com/articles/SB10001424052702304856504579339194050181258.

11. "Target Provides Update on Data Breach and Financial Performance," Target press release, January 10, 2014, pressroom.target.com/news/target-provides -update-on-data-breach-and-financial-performance.

12. Ibid.

13. "Target Hackers Broke in Via HVAC Company," *KrebsOnSecurity.com*, February 14, 2014, krebsonsecurity.com/2014/02/target-hackers-broke-in-via-hvac -company/.

14. Rachel Abrams, "Target Puts Data Breach Costs at $148 Million, and Forecasts Profit Drop," *New York Times*, August 5, 2014, www.nytimes.com/2014/08/06 /business/target-puts-data-breach-costs-at-148-million.html.

15. Anne D'Innocenzio, "Target CIO Resigns Following Massive Data Breach," *The HuffingtonPost.com*, March 5, 2014, www.huffingtonpost.com/2014/03/05/target -cto-resigns_n_4903659.html.

16. Alan Duke, "5 Things to Know about the Celebrity Nude Photo Hacking Scandal," *CNN.com*, October 12, 2014, www.cnn.com/2014/09/02/showbiz/hacked -nude-photos-five-things/.

17. Vlad Savov, "Sony Pictures Hacked: The Full Story," *TheVerge.com*, December 8, 2014, www.theverge.com/2014/12/8/7352581/sony-pictures-hacked -storystream.

18. Alina Simone, "How My Mom Got Hacked," *New York Times*, January 2, 2015, www.nytimes.com/2015/01/04/opinion/sunday/how-my-mom-got-hacked .html.

19. Marianna Semenova, "Why Projects Fail?" *SlideShare.net*, July 26, 2014, 19, www .slideshare.net/MariannaAlmakaieva/10-reasons-why-projects-fail-or-common -mistakes-to-avoid.

20. Michael Bloch, Sven Blumberg, and Jürgen Laartz, "Delivering Large-Scale IT Projects on Time, on Budget, and on Value," *McKinsey Insights* (October 2012), www.mckinsey.com/insights/business_technology/delivering_large-scale_it _projects_on_time_on_budget_and_on_value.

21. Michael D. Shear, "Sebelius Resigns after Troubles over Health Site," *New York Times*, April 10, 2014, www.nytimes.com/2014/04/11/us/politics/sebelius -resigning-as-health-secretary.html.

22. Robert Lee Hotz, "Mars Probe Lost Due to Simple Math Error," *Los Angeles Times*, October 1, 1999, articles.latimes.com/1999/oct/01/news/mn-17288.

23. "Netflix Blames Amazon for Christmas Eve outage (Update)," *Phys.org*, December 26, 2012, phys.org/news/2012-12-netflix-blames-amazon-christmas-eve.html.

24. "Summary of the December 24, 2012, Amazon ELB Service Event in the US-East Region," *Amazon Web Services*, aws.amazon.com/message/680587/.

25. "Chicago Air Traffic Halted Over Fire at FAA Facility," *CBS News*, September 26, 2014, www.cbsnews.com/news/chicago-air-traffic-halted-over-fire-at-faa -facility/.

26. NERC Steering Group, "Technical Analysis of the August 14, 2003, Blackout: What Happened, Why, and What Did We Learn?" North American Electric Reliability Council, July 13, 2004, 26–27, www.nerc.com/docs/docs/blackout/NERC_Final_Blackout_Report_07_13_04.pdf.

27. Dan Goodin, "Crypto Weakness in Smart LED Light Bulbs Exposes Wi-Fi Passwords," *ArsTechnica.com*, July 7, 2014, arstechnica.com/security/2014/07/crypto-weakness-in-smart-led-lightbulbs-exposes-wi-fi-passwords/.

28. Dan Goodin, "Hack Turns Belkin Baby Monitor into iPhone-Controlled Bugging Device," *ArsTechnica.com*, October 23, 2013, arstechnica.com/security/2013/10/hack-turns-belkin-baby-monitor-into-iphone-controlled-bugging-device/.

29. Ms. Smith, "Peeping into 73,000 Unsecured Security Cameras Thanks to Default Passwords," *NetworkWorld.com*, November 6, 2014, www.networkworld.com/article/2844283/microsoft-subnet/peeping-into-73-000-unsecured-security-cameras-thanks-to-default-passwords.html.

30. Kim Komando, "4 Ways Burglars Use Social Media to Target You," *Komando.com*, December 19, 2014, www.komando.com/tips/12469/4-ways-burglars-use-social-media-to-target-you/all.

31. Mike Masnick, "How Paris Hilton Got Hacked? Bad Password Protection," *TechDirt.com*, February 22, 2005, https://www.techdirt.com/articles/20050222/2026239.shtml.

32. Walter Frick, "Innovation, Then and Now," *Harvard Business Review* (October 2014): 119.

33. Founders Fund, www.foundersfund.com/.

34. Jason Pontin, "Q&A: Edward Jung," *MIT Technology Review* (December 22, 2011), www.technologyreview.com/news/426466/qa-edward-jung/.

35. John D. Sutter, "Amazon Seller Lists Book at $23,698,655.93—Plus Shipping," *CNN.com*, April 25, 2011, www.cnn.com/2011/TECH/web/04/25/amazon.price.algorithm/.

36. Kevin Slavin, "How Algorithms Shape Our World," [Video] TEDGlobal 2011, July 2011, www.ted.com/talks/kevin_slavin_how_algorithms_shape_our_world.

37. Kevin Slavin, "Keynote—Kevin Slavin—Telx MarketplaceLIVE West 2013," *Vimeo.com*, December 2013, https://vimeo.com/82145661.

38. Niccolò Machiavelli, *The Prince*.

39. Michael Krigsman, "J.Crew: Failed Upgrade Hits Financial Performance," *ZDnet.com*, September 16, 2008, www.zdnet.com/article/j-crew-failed-upgrade-hits-financial-performance/.

40. J Crew Customer, "Invoiced $9,208.50 for Shipping; Baby Sized Clothing Shipped; JSP_EXECUTION_FAILED When Attempting to Sign into Website," *JCrew-Customer.Blogspot.com*, August 2, 2008, jcrew-customer.blogspot.com/2008/08/invoiced-920850-for-shipping-baby-sized.html.

41. The Secret Developers, "The Secret Developers: Wii U—The Inside Story," *Eurogamer.net*, November 1, 2014, www.eurogamer.net/articles/digitalfoundry -2014-secret-developers-wii-u-the-inside-story.

42. Ibid.

43. Ibid.

44. Tero Kuittinen, "Stellar Xbox One Sales Highlight What a Disaster the Wii U Has Been," *BGR.com*, November 26, 2013, bgr.com/2013/11/26/xbox-one-wii-u-sales -comparison/.

45. Stewart Rogers, "'70 Percent of CRM Installs Fail' and Other Crappy Stats You Should Ignore," *VentureBeat.com*, January 23, 2015, venturebeat.com/2015/01/23 /70-percent-of-crm-installs-fail-and-other-crap-stats-you-should-ignore/.

46. C5 Insight, "C5 Insight Reveals New Study, Reports Top Factors in CRM Failure," *GlobeNewsWire.com*, September 24, 2014, globenewswire.com/news-release /2014/09/24/668258/10099930/en/C5-Insight-Reveals-New-Study-Reports-Top -Factors-in-CRM-Failure.html.

47. "Facebook & Your Privacy: Who Sees the Data You Share on the Biggest Social Network?" *Consumer Reports*, June 2012, www.consumerreports.org/cro /magazine/2012/06/facebook-your-privacy/index.htm.

48. Latanya Sweeney, "Simple Demographics Often Identify People Uniquely," Data Privacy Working Paper 3, 2000, dataprivacylab.org/projects/identifiability /paper1.pdf.

PART SEVEN

What's Next?

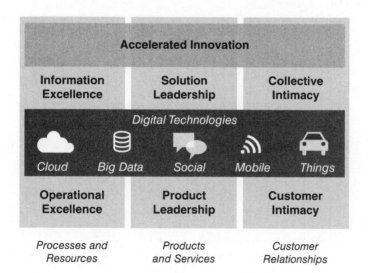

CHAPTER 21
Looking Forward

I n 1798, Thomas Robert Malthus presented arguments that human population could and would grow faster than the food supply, even accounting for human ability to increase production. He concluded that if such growth were left unchecked, a substantial portion of humanity would be doomed to misery, poverty, and starvation.

But Peter Diamandis, author, philanthropist, serial entrepreneur, and founder and CEO of the X PRIZE Foundation, and his co-author, journalist, and entrepreneur Steven Kotler, argue in *Abundance*[1] that technology can transform scarcity into plenty. They say that we live in an age of abundance, where by virtually any metric—life span, child mortality, caloric intake—the world is improving. They use the example of aluminum—once considered a rare and thus prohibitively expensive precious metal, worth more than gold—which became affordable and ubiquitous through extraction technologies such as electrolysis. Now, of course, we wrap tuna sandwiches in it, then throw it away.

Diamandis and Kotler credit four major drivers: "the rising billion," who are emerging from poverty and "joining the global conversation" thanks to technologies such as smartphones and increased penetration of Internet connectivity; "technophilanthropists," for example, billionaire technologists such as Bill Gates who are using their wealth for noble causes such as fighting malaria; "do-it-yourself innovators," who are applying new broadly available technologies; and at the heart of all of these, "exponential technologies," such as communications, computing, biotech, nanotech, robotics, and artificial intelligence.[2]

The Exponential Economy

These exponential technologies are driving what has been called—not surprisingly—the *exponential economy*. Nathan Myhrvold, former chief technology officer at Microsoft, founder of Microsoft Research, and co-founder of Intellectual Ventures, agrees that these technologies are exhibiting exponential improvements in price-performance. These improvements feed off of each other, in what has been referred to as *colliding exponentials*,[3] leading to a virtuous cycle of improvements in performance, functionality, and productivity: lower cost enables broader scale which achieves scale economies and learning curve effects that reduce cost further, and so on and so on.

Numerous general purpose computing technologies are plummeting in cost, riding "laws" similar to Moore's law, which posits exponential growth in the number of transistors on a chip. Kryder's law argues the same for disk storage density; Nielsen's law, for home access network bandwidth; Butters' law, for fiber optic capacity, and so on. Although these laws are not laws in the same vein as Newton's Laws of Physics or Einstein's relativistic reformulations of those laws, they do seem to reflect an apparently inexorable march of technology.

In addition to this virtuous cycle, the fundamental economics of many businesses are shifting. The Internet is a platform, the cloud is a platform, wireless connectivity is a platform, and HTML and app stores and tablets and smartphones and their operating systems are platforms. The economics of these platforms are being driven by more than exponential improvements in price-performance, they are also being shaken by fundamental changes in how they are created and paid for.

On the supply side, the cost structure of these platforms has been revolutionized. For example, the open-source movement has changed the business model of software from a traditional upfront capital investment leading to a forward revenue stream—as with railroads and steel mills—to one based on sharing, contribution, and reputation.

The business model for software traditionally was based on hiring developers, who were paid in dollars (or the appropriate hard currency) and maybe some equity. The firm owned the intellectual property including copyrights for the software. These costs were then recovered by selling the software product, say, Microsoft Windows or Adobe Illustrator or IBM MVS for so many dollars per copy, or perhaps via an Enterprise License Agreement.

But no one hired developers—at least initially—to write Linux; it was a collaborative effort from a global community of volunteers. And it's not just software, the same approach is being used to develop and share best practices for hardware, through projects such as Open Compute.

In the new world, multiple business models coexist. Rather than being employees, developers may stay independent or work for a variety of firms that may or may not have anything to do with the initiative. Rather than being paid in dollars, euros, or renminbi, they may be paid in the joy of contributing to an interesting technical challenge, the ability to develop connections with peers, or through the enhancement of status and reputation by playing key roles, finding bugs, or solving thorny technical problems. The software isn't owned by anyone, but is available for anyone to use. The resulting product, rather than being sold, is available for free. For service platforms such as the Internet, even if access isn't free it is often priced under flat-rate or *unlimited* plans—that is, is available to users or subscribers at zero marginal cost.

In these new economics, the classical economic concept of price elasticity of demand still holds; but when goods are free or available at zero marginal cost, demand expands to be, for all intents and purposes, near-infinite. As a result, such platforms and derivative platforms such as the Android smartphone operating system, or the Arduino open-source microcontroller for helping to build the Internet of Things, are being adopted at high rates, and then being leveraged to create new innovations.

This is not to say that there isn't money to be made in "free." As Amr Awadallah, the CTO and co-founder of big data firm Cloudera, points out, even if someone gave you a car for free, you would still need to pay for gas, insurance, and maintenance.[4] Free cars—or free software—lead to what Awadallah calls *viral consumption*—budget-constrained engineers in enterprises can adopt the technology and prove its value without needing five levels of approval taking six months to get. If you are in the car-maintenance business, free cars for everyone on the planet sound much better than only a few cars owned by billionaires.

Another model is represented by Facebook, which published its best practice computer server designs and offered open access as well to useful big data software such as Hive and Cassandra. This is not because Facebook is thinking about entering complementary businesses such as the computer maintenance business or electric power generation, but partly because enhancements to its designs can be fed back into the company and because driving cost reductions or enhancing sustainability benefit its bottom line without in any way impacting the unique value proposition of its core business.

Overall, computing costs ultimately are based on cost drivers such as processing, storage, and networking hardware, software such as virtualization, operating systems, data management systems, and applications, services such as networking, electric power, and labor and operations costs. To the extent that all of these costs are driven down, it expands the range of uses of digital technologies, and their ability to enable the application of digital disciplines. To put it another way, there is price elasticity of demand.

One implication is that digital technologies can be applied in areas where they haven't been used before: ebooks rather than printed books, connected cars, Wi-Fi door locks and light bulbs. The other is in what might be called discretionary IT. If costs drop precipitously, it can become cost-effective to do an additional "what-if" analysis or calculate results to a few more degrees of accuracy for seismic analysis or portfolio risk assessment.

Moreover, if growth due to elasticity of demand exceeds the drop in unit prices, the overall industry expands. This effect—Jevons paradox—was first noted with coal, where the size of the coal industry grew even as the price dropped.

Although the formal value disciplines approach has been around for only two decades, the underlying practices arguably span millennia, and digital technologies just enable their latest incarnation as digital disciplines.

In ancient times, operations benefitted from simple tooling: ox-drawn plows for agriculture, ropes for pulling stone to build structures such as the pyramids, and molds to make bricks in the heat of the desert sun. From there, process technology evolved to encompass interchangeable parts and mass production. Now, we are entering an era of driverless cars, computer-guided drones, and mobile robots such as those from Kiva Systems in use at Amazon warehouses, together with sophisticated algorithms leveraging real-time information to optimize decision making, the movement of assets, financial hedging strategies, and many different other types of information excellence.

Product leadership perhaps began with the first artisanal products, such as bone and flint arrowheads, tens of thousands of years ago. Most recently, such products have evolved from analog and mechanical standalone entities such as printed books, pendulum clocks and horse-drawn carriages to digital products such as digital watches and microprocessor-infused automobiles to cloud-connected digital solutions ranging from jet engines, planes, and wind turbines to devices such as the Apple Watch.

Customer intimacy has evolved from the days of the first barter of a flint arrowhead for a bite of food and early bazaars and markets where individual merchants could understand what buyers were looking for and maintain personal relationships with regular customers, to organizational constructs such as dedicated account teams, to virtual relationships maintained in cyberspace via social media technologies, to collective intimacy, where big data and sophisticated algorithms are used to tease out insights into latent customer preferences and needs.

The process of innovation has evolved as well, from the first solitary inventors and tinkerers, who discovered or created new processes such as fire and new products such as spears, glue, and paint. It continued through the era of corporate sponsorship of academic research, the first industrial labs and staff scientists that were part of nascent vertically integrated firms, and the modern era of open innovation. As we've seen, the newest version of open, external innovation includes innovation networks, idea markets, execution markets, prediction markets, challenges, crowdfunding and crowdsourcing, open collaborative initiatives, and the dawn of an era of not just machine learning, but machine innovation through hypothesis generation and creative combination, just as in biological mutation and evolution.

There is no reason to think that incremental and disruptive transformation of operational and information excellence, product and solution leadership, customer and collective intimacy, or innovation will end soon.

Future Technologies

If today's IT can be vital to success, what about in the future? The lay perspective is that the future will be more or less like the present. Informed experts often expect linear extrapolation of price-performance trajectories, but reality tends to surprise. Improvements tend to be exponential in the long term, but often exhibit "punctuated equilibrium," where periods of relative stasis succumb to bursts of dramatic improvement.

A good recent example is the *memristor*. This device was hypothesized to exist by Leon Chua in 1971, but was first actually built in 2008 at HP Labs. It promises a thousandfold improvement in price/performance. A device one-tenth the size of a transistor can store 10 times as much data at one-tenth the cost.

The memristor and other approaches may enable neuromorphic computing, where computer systems behave more like human brains in processing complex tasks, such as computer vision and speech recognition, learning, problem solving, and perhaps someday, emotion. Rather than the essentially sequential approach that a traditional CPU uses, such chips could be used to build neural networks and thus mimic not only the brain's parallel processing, but also the brain's ability to learn, adapt, and manage fuzzy and ambiguous concepts. For example, IBM has built a chip with over 5 billion transistors it calls "SyNAPSE," which is modeled after neural networks such as those found in the human brain.[5]

Such physical devices and architectures may further accelerate artificial intelligence, and its placement in autonomous devices and contexts ranging across voice queries on mobile devices, driverless cars, battlefield robots, autopilots, drones, vacuum cleaners, shop floor robots, and "pets." Such intelligence has many dimensions: machine learning, machine translation, perception, such as computer vision, speech analysis, and handwriting recognition, and inference engines, i.e., the ability to make logical deductions from a set of facts or observations.

Another recent breakthrough is *homomorphic encryption*. It is a means of processing encrypted data without decrypting it first, something like a tax accountant correctly processing your annual return while blindfolded. First hypothesized in 1978, it was finally reduced to practice using arcane mathematics—ideal lattices—over 30 years later, in 2009, by Craig Gentry at IBM Research. Although not yet efficient enough to use for real-world calculations, it means that private data might someday be safely given to third parties for processing without the risk of accidental disclosure or breaches.

Quantum computing is another potential breakthrough technology. Although not applicable for all problems, it may be able to dramatically reduce the time it takes to solve many kinds of problems, which often have the characteristic that they have exponentially many possible solutions due to large numbers of possible combinations of even a small number of elements. One such problem is the *traveling salesman problem*, which tries to find the shortest route to visit a multiplicity of cities, as UPS does with ORION. Quantum computing holds out the promise to generate those routes within short enough intervals to, say, route delivery trucks optimally, leading to even greater information excellence.

Future *digital* technologies may not even be digital: The memristor is at its heart an analog device; and quantum computers use *qubits*, which are in two states at the same time.

3D scanning and printing is already impacting manufacturing, at industrial research labs, prototyping facilities, and factories, and in homes. This largely eliminates the traditional dichotomy between information goods and physical goods. Physical goods are becoming essentially indistinguishable from information goods in a format compatible with your home 3D printer.

Image capture and audio capture originally were focused on quality and resolution. Now they are focused on moving from mere data to information, not just recording an audio stream but being able to process it as spoken words, and being able to conduct semantic analysis: understanding what the spoken words are saying. Image and video capture is no longer just about faithful reproduction but about being able to detect objects and their relationships, and not just in one frame but over time and across cameras. These are evolving still further, with sentiment analysis of audio streams and written text as well as facial expressions becoming increasingly able to detect the emotional state of the individual. For example, Beyond Verbal assesses the pitch, timing, volume, pauses, and intensity of speech to determine how the speaker is feeling, based on a comparison with other voiceprints.[6]

For now, virtual reality and a related area, augmented reality, which typically overlays virtual elements onto the real world, is a bit unwieldy, but the most important element, the VR goggles, is becoming lighter, faster, and higher resolution. This is an active area, with Microsoft's HoloLens, (Facebook's) Oculus Rift, and Magic Leap making headlines and driving funding rounds and acquisitions. Computer-driven electro-holographic displays and wireless contact lens displays are also under active development.

Beyond visual and auditory technologies, touch, smell, and even taste are also making substantial progress.

Rather than external devices, the connection between man and machine will eventually occur within the skull. Brain-computer interfaces are no longer merely just fictional fodder for movies such as *The Matrix*; today's technology already enables a bundle of wires to directly stimulate the visual cortex, enabling the blind to see by bypassing such antiquated technology as an actual biological eye. Scientists, engineers, and physicians are tying brains directly to each other and directly to computing fabrics, eliminating unnecessary intermediate components such as speakers and ears, and displays and eyes. They can scan live brain function through technologies such as functional Magnetic Resonance Imaging (fMRI). It's anyone's guess how that will shape social networking and customer intimacy. What will happen when marketers won't need to interpret a tweet to determine your sentiment—they'll actually be able to reach into the emotive regions of your brain to find out directly?

There are plenty more technologies where those came from, including the enabling technologies to make them work. For example, digital brain implants will need power, and plugging them in to charge by the nightstand won't be practical. But "energy scavenging" technologies, which will scavenge energy from the environment, already exist. For example, piezoelectric approaches will use microscopic vibrations to recharge batteries; when you go out for a morning run, it literally may be to reenergize yourself.

Besides all of these, there are the technologies and discoveries that we can't even anticipate, or are currently dismissed as impractical, dead-ends, impossible, or bad science—say, cold fusion or faster-than-light neutrinos. Before dismissing those possibilities, note that many other things that we now accept to be true were originally dismissed, such as the heliocentric view of the solar system, the idea that bacteria could cause ulcers, and the entirety of quantum physics, which no less an intellect than Albert Einstein derided. More recently, the Nobel Prize in Chemistry was awarded in 2011 to Dan Schectman, for quasicrystals, which were long thought to be impossible. As Nancy Jackson, the president of the American Chemical Society said, "When he first discovered these materials, nobody thought they could exist. It was one of these great scientific stories that his fellow scientists thought was impossible, but through time, people came to realize he was right."[7]

Many farfetched scenarios are conceivable. Someday, telepathy between humans will be possible, with thoughts being read through electroencephalograms, carried over the Internet, and injected into the receiver's brain through transcranial magnetic stimulation. Someday, physical objects such as wrenches will be teleported to the farthest reaches of space that humans inhabit. Someday, robots will use neural networks taken from animals or insects such as worms as their nervous system. Someday, computers will generate mathematical proofs that humans can't even understand. Someday, corporations will be governed not just by people but by artificial intelligence, which will help determine where to invest. Someday, robot journalists will be the first to get news scoops for major publications. Someday, people will become cyborgs, with thought-controlled prosthetic limbs. And maybe someday, robots will land on and explore distant planets. Actually, all of these breakthroughs have already happened.[8]

The point is that technology continues to march forward, linearly or exponentially, predictably or unexpectedly, incrementally and disruptively. New technologies can and will enable new approaches to exploit digital disciplines for market leadership.

Opportunities

Yet, as amazing as some the latest technologies are—quantum computing, brain-to-brain communication, self-driving cars, *Jeopardy!*-winning software—most organizations seem to be back in the stone ages. Or as author William Gibson said, "The future is already here—it's just not evenly distributed."

Why is it that an email of millions of bytes can arrive in a few seconds, yet an interbank funds transfer of a few dozen bytes—with not much more data than amount, currency, and routing and account numbers—can take several days to clear?

Why is it that something as complex as a tax return can be filed electronically, and HDTV can be streamed over the Internet into everyone's home, but a United States Postal Service "Authorization to Hold Mail" needs to be filled out by hand and left in the mailbox or dropped off at the post office?

Why can cattle be uniquely identified by an RFID tag, but cars are still identified by pieces of painted, embossed metal affixed to them?

Why does a DVD or Blu-ray purchase often come with an included digital copy such as Ultraviolet, a CD confer rights in iTunes, but a physical book isn't conjoined with a digital copy, causing you to have to choose between a printed edition or a Kindle edition?

Why are drivers' licenses little bits of paper and plastic and passports paper booklets prone to loss or theft, rather than unique identifiers linked to biometrics such as fingerprints, DNA, or retinal scans maintained in a secure repository?

How can a Malaysia Airlines jumbo jet be lost without a trace, with an apparently interminable search for wreckage and black-box recorders, when even five-year olds these days have cell phones and can stay in constant contact?

At this point—where information technology seems to offer limitless possibilities, in a world with billions of connected users, heading towards tens of billions of connected devices, where for all intents and purposes processing, storage, and bandwidth are free, as are many of the tools that one can use—there is no excuse for not fixing issues and filling gaps, enhancing operations, products, and relationships.

Moreover, this can boost profitability. According to one recent analysis, net margins for software companies are almost three times those of companies in other sectors. The lesson for companies looking to improve their financials may be as simple as increasing the value-adding software content of their products and services.[9]

Critical Success Factors

What's required to make it happen? Looking across scores of firms, one sees repeated themes. Successfully achieving competitive advantage based on one or more of the digital disciplines is about more than merely deploying technology, although that's important. There are a number of critical success factors.

Leadership and *Governance*. It really does start at the top, with leaders focused on achieving a winning position and driving unparalleled customer value. All the companies profiled for their application of digital disciplines in the previous pages have had world-class leaders: A. G. Lafley at P&G, Reed Hastings at Netflix, Jeff Immelt at GE, Angela Ahrendts and Christopher Bailey at Burberry, Mark Parker at Nike. The same is surely true for most if not all of the other companies highlighted, such as Dan Yates at Opower. They understand innovation and differentiation, and are willing to invest, take risks, and embrace change.

Middle Management. VPs and SVPs often seem to be the fulcrum providing the leverage to make things happen. They are high enough to command resources and lead their organizations, close enough to the action to make a difference: Bill Ruh at GE, Stefan Olander at Nike, Todd Yellin at Netflix, Alex Kinnier at Opower. They seem to all have a synergetic mix of technical skills, customer insight, ability to execute, and long-term strategic vision.

Organization. Google recognizes that good ideas can come from anywhere. In most companies, the medical department is where employees go when they don't feel well at work. At Google, a medical doctor was the champion of an initiative to ensure that the National Suicide Prevention Hotline appeared as the top result for anyone searching on the term *suicide*. P&G has highly structured organizations to address opportunities including understanding customer needs, enabling open and external innovation, and addressing white-space opportunities between and beyond categories.

Skills and Talent. For a digitally enabled strategy, there must be skilled resources to either directly produce IT solutions, or at least to select and manage the outtasking of such solutions. IT needs to be mixed with math, engineering, user design, statistical analysis, and sometimes physics, law, and other disciplines. Lacking key skills can lead to disaster, as the US rollout of the Affordable Care Act ("Obamacare") showed. The Healthcare.gov site was close to nonfunctional for many weeks after its official launch date.

An analysis of 400 companies found that organizations successfully using IT were significantly more aggressive in vetting new hires: They considered more applicants; scrutinized each one more intensively; involved senior management early and often in the interview process; spent more time and money on training and education; gave employees more discretion; and used more detailed metrics.[10]

Netflix is known for its unconventional approach to HR. It thinks of itself as a pro sports team, trying to ensure that its team members work well together, but also that they are each stars in their own right for the positions that they play. In Netflix's view, each position should belong to a star, who the manager would fight hard to retain, otherwise the employee should be given a generous severance packages to open the position up to a future star.[11] Burberry deliberately hires to ensure that at least 70 percent of its employees—across the entire company—are under age 30, to be more in touch with always-on digital natives and their values and preferences.

Culture. Because of the importance of innovation, insight, intelligence, and diversity, teams composed of trusted, responsible employees representing different perspectives are required. Netflix doesn't have a fixed number of vacation days, instead trusting its employees to be responsible enough to accomplish their work objectives. Zappos is famous for its customer-centric culture. Such a culture doesn't require that a company be a newfangled web company: before Google and its 20 percent off time became famous, in fact, before Google was even founded, 3M was encouraging its employees to spend time in an unstructured way to foster innovation.

Empathy. Companies that expect to focus on customer outcomes and pursue customer intimacy need to employ people who can have empathy with customers. Empathy is about more than attitude. It's also about organizational power and priorities. If a social media response to a customer complaint requires legal approval, it will be neither timely nor empathetic. If front-line sales personnel aren't empowered to resolve customer issues, the customer will be long gone before the approval comes through.

Risk-Taking. Failure needs to be viewed not as cause for termination, but cause for promotion. Leading companies view an appropriate level of failure as a sign that employees are taking an appropriate level of risk. In investment, the highest returns over time come from the equity market, not from

FDIC-insured savings and checking accounts. In business, the highest returns accrue to firms who open up new markets, introduce new products and services, and introduce radical new processes and business models.

Metrics. Companies need to measure revenue and profitability or else end up like Pets.com. But beyond that, there are useful nontraditional metrics. James Slavet, a partner at Greylock Partners—a VC firm that has invested in companies such as Facebook, LinkedIn, and Pandora, suggests five. One is flow state, the percentage of time spent in deep concentration, because multitasking and constant task-switching reduce productivity. A related metric is the balance between anxiety and boredom. When tasks are too difficult, they are frustrating and cause either abandonment or anxiety. When they are too easy, they cause boredom. At the right level of challenge, they help us enter the flow state. To these he adds metrics such as meeting usefulness, wryly observing that employees who can't order a box of paperclips without approval are able to call useless meetings that waste thousands of dollars of loaded salary; "compound learning rate" (i.e., continuous learning); and the ratio of positive feedback to negative, creating a productive work environment.[12]

Corporate Boundaries. Companies are moving away from a traditional vertically integrated structure to a dynamic, networked enterprise. In such an organization, the company is heavily engaged with partners to accomplish noncore tasks. Asset-light organizations generate better returns on invested capital, they are more agile, take less risk, and can not just focus better on core activities, but can collaborate with others who lead in their own area of expertise. Moreover, this type of networked organization can adapt its configuration continuously. This is sometimes called the Hollywood organization model, after the way in which stars, screenwriters, directors, and producers are configured on a one-time basis to shoot a movie.

IT Architecture. The digital disciplines require digital technologies, which must exist within a rational architecture. Firms need to pay attention to their enterprise architecture and the development of platforms and community enablers, tactical necessities such as Application Programming Interfaces, Software Development Kits, and Integrated Development Environments, and their use of pay-per-use, on-demand, prebuilt capabilities such as cloud computing infrastructure, applications, platforms, and microservices. This is how companies can get to market in time, and can also enable ecosystems and network effects to arise.

Creativity. The key technologies are often ubiquitous. Consequently, competitive advantage accrues to those who can creatively employ them in the context of a disruptive strategic vision with alignment and balance between the drivers of competitive advantage and technology enablers.

Security. All of this is for naught if the company suffers cyberattacks or data breaches, as we discussed in Chapter 20.

Reliability. Even in the absence of cyberattacks, issues with reliability or safety can damage the brand and rapidly end the pursuit of the digital disciplines. Leading companies invest heavily in reliability. For example, Netflix uses an approach called Chaos Monkey to harden its IT infrastructure, testing its progress by deliberately taking down key subsystems and pulling cables.

Next Steps

Over the past 339 pages, we've argued that Treacy and Wiersema's value disciplines approach is as valid as ever, but that digital technologies offer new opportunities to develop unique advantages via the digital disciplines.

A number of common themes permeate the disciplines: the need to fuse digital with physical; a focus on customer outcomes; the promise and potential of real-time; the wealth of opportunities for differentiation.

Gaining insights from a book is helpful, but applying them is what drives customer value, can create a competitive edge, and can help attain market leadership. It's worth asking a few key questions to determine next steps.

What is your current business strategy? How effective is it? Does it need to be rethought from the ground up, invigorated, or does it still drive competitive advantage? Will discontinuities such as evolving customer needs and wants, fads, shifting demographics, industry consolidation, or emerging enabling technologies impact your strategy and positioning? What about untapped global markets, or blue ocean opportunities for value innovation?

What are competitors doing? Are there network effects or winner-take-all dynamics that will impact the evolution of your industry? How can APIs, developer ecosystems, and partnering strategies tip the balance in your favor?

Which value discipline is best aligned with your current or desired positioning, differentiators, and competencies? Are the rules of the industry inviolate, or can they be bent or broken to offer new possibilities for value creation? How does information technology transform, enable, and invigorate this and lead to a compelling digital discipline?

Is information excellence an opportunity? Is there the possibility to differentiate based on *better*—such as faster, cheaper, higher quality, more standard, more flexible, more reliable—processes that leverage real-time data-based optimization as GE has done with Movement Planner or that seamlessly fuse digital and physical touchpoints and channels, as Burberry has done? Or, to completely rethink processes and assets as Uber has?

Is solution leadership a possibility? Can your current products or services be made smarter and connect to an infinitely extensible cloud of services, partners, and social media, that offer an experience or a personal or business transformation, in a similar way to how Nike took what used to be a sneaker and made it into a connected device that helped its customers become better athletes? Can your services become embodied in a product? Can your product become a service? Can both products and services seamlessly integrate and be enabled with a new pricing models to create a market-leading product-service system solution? Can your offer develop competitive advantage based not just on feature differentiation, but on outcome differentiation and on social bonds, ecosystems, and communities?

What about collective intimacy? Can your customer relationships be radically improved, and transactions evolve to relationships and then on to intimacy? Can data collected from all customers provide the basis for new insights and a better relationship with each customer, as Mayo Clinic does with genomic data and Netflix with movie recommendations?

Is your approach to innovation innovative? Does it leverage the best of internal and external, proprietary and open, and data plus insight? Do your data scientists—or any employee for that matter—have the technical and organizational opportunity to mine rich fields of data? Are you enlisting the insights of crowds and the expertise of a global, ad hoc community? Are you blocking external innovation with an impenetrable wall of legalese?

How about the human dimension? Are principles of behavioral psychology, cognitive science, self-determination theory, and gamification embedded in your products, services, processes and relationships with customers, partners, employees, and other stakeholders?

Do you have the leadership, governance, skills, organization, and culture to pursue your selected discipline(s), and if not, can you fill gaps through training, hiring, outsourcing, or consulting? What about the financial resources and intangibles such as brand positioning? Are you willing to embrace multiple failures to get closer to success? Can you mitigate or eliminate the issues that have bedeviled many others: poor strategies, leadership and stakeholder issues, self-deception, lousy project management, issues in software development and implementation, security and privacy?

Are you embracing the common themes that span the digital disciplines: real time, dynamic, actionable, customer-focused, outcome-oriented, intelligent, collective, open, social, connected, and fused digital and physical worlds?

The fundamental current running through this book is that IT—and its key elements such as the cloud, big data, social, mobile and things—can do much more than help shave costs or capex; it's strategically important as never before and offers unparalleled opportunities, but leaders need to ensure that IT is aligned with business imperatives.

These technologies are a double-edged sword, and the race for customers and market share will be won by those who can employ them the best. Our great-grandparents lived in small communities and neighborhoods, with one butcher, one saloon, and one general store. Changing butchers required moving to another town.

Today, dozens if not thousands of vendors from around the world can compete for anyone's business. Each vendor is just one search query, email, tweet, like, or click away. Switching costs are rapidly plummeting to zero. That's the bad news.

The good news is that barriers to entry have never been lower, and opportunities are arising to create immense wealth with nothing more than an idea, leveraging platforms and ecosystems that others have built. Consider YouTube, Tumblr, or Instagram. The Apple App Store or Google Play. Open software, hardware, and microcontrollers. These platforms are everywhere: Amanda Hocking—a "Kindle millionaire"—has sold over a million copies of her books, originally writing for the Amazon Kindle platform (although her books are now available on other platforms, in physical form, and have been optioned for movies). The entire investment needed to become a millionaire? Some creativity and a laptop or smartphone.[13]

As long as there are spheres of commerce, society, and government, there will be the need for better processes, products and services, relationships, innovation, and transformation. Information technology can be the key to unlock such value, and the digital disciplines described here offer generic, practical blueprints that can be tailored to your specific competitive or societal objective. They have been and can be applied now.

If there is one thing you should take away from this book, it is that cloud computing, big data, things, and related technologies can help reduce costs, increase asset utilization, and streamline processes, but the real value of digital technologies is in creating strategic advantage, accelerating profitable revenue growth, and attaining market leadership.

One last question: What are you waiting for?

Notes

1. Peter H. Diamandis and Steven Kotler, *Abundance: The Future Is Better Than You Think* (New York: Free Press, 2012).
2. Sam Harris, "The World Is Getting Better, Argues New Book, 'Abundance,'" *TheDailyBeast.com*, February 21, 2012, www.thedailybeast.com/articles/2012/02/21/the-world-is-getting-better-argues-new-book-abundance.html.
3. Curtis R. Carlson and William W. Wilmot, *Innovation: The Five Disciplines for Creating What Customers Want* (New York: Crown Business, 2006), 28.
4. Amr Awadallah, "Introducing Apache Hadoop: The Modern Data Operating System," *YouTube.com*, September 4, 2012, https://www.youtube.com/watch?v=d2xeNpfzsYI.

5. IBM Research, "Brain Power," *IBM.com*, research.ibm.com/cognitive-computing/neurosynaptic-chips.shtml.
6. Amir Mizroch, "App Tells You How You Feel," *Wall Street Journal*, March 11, 2014, B6.
7. Kenneth Chang, "Israeli Scientist Wins Nobel Prize for Chemistry," *New York Times*, June 10, 2011, www.nytimes.com/2011/10/06/science/06nobel.html.
8. George Dvorsky, "The Most Futuristic Predictions That Came True in 2014," *IO9.com*, December 29, 2014, io9.com/the-most-futuristic-predictions-that-came-true-in-2014-1674887659.
9. Sinclair Schuller, "What Do Tobacco and Software Have in Common?" *Gigaom.com*, October 27, 2013, https://gigaom.com/2013/10/27/what-do-tobacco-and-software-have-in-common/.
10. Andrew McAfee and Erik Brynjolfsson, "Investing in the IT That Makes a Competitive Difference," *Harvard Business Review* (July 2008), hbr.org/2008/07/investing-in-the-it-that-makes-a-competitive-difference/ar/1.
11. Patty McCord, "How Netflix Reinvented HR," *Harvard Business Review* (January 2014), https://hbr.org/2014/01/how-netflix-reinvented-hr.
12. James Slavet, "Five New Management Metrics You Need to Know," *Forbes.com*, December 13, 2011, www.forbes.com/sites/bruceupbin/2011/12/13/five-new-management-metrics-you-need-to-know/.
13. Kiri Blakeley, "Who Wants to Be a (Kindle) Millionaire?" *Forbes.com*, March 6, 2011, www.forbes.com/sites/kiriblakeley/2011/03/06/who-wants-to-be-a-kindle-millionaire/.

ABOUT THE AUTHOR

Joe Weinman is an experienced senior executive with a career spanning R&D, corporate strategy, operations and engineering, and marketing and sales at companies such as Bell Labs, AT&T, Hewlett-Packard, and Telx. He also serves on a variety of industry advisory boards.

He is considered one of the leading global authorities on cloud economics, and is the author of *Cloudonomics: The Business Value of Cloud Computing* (John Wiley & Sons, 2012), which has been translated into Chinese (PTPress, 2014). He is the cloud economics editor for *IEEE Cloud Computing* magazine, and a contributor to *Regulating the Cloud: Policy for Computing Infrastructure* (MIT Press, 2015). His work has also appeared in the print and/or online editions of the *New York Times, Bloomberg Businessweek, Entrepreneur, Forbes, Wired, CNN Money, InformationWeek, GigaOm, Business Communications Review,* and *CIO* magazine, as well as a variety of academic publications and conference proceedings.

He has keynoted and presented at well over 100 conferences globally, including for the United Nations, and the business, engineering, or law schools of academic institutions such as NYU, Boston University, the University of Southern California, the University of Pennsylvania, Ohio State University, the University of Arizona, the New Jersey Institute of Technology, University of Rennes, Hong Kong Polytechnic, Technology Institute of Monterrey, Nanyang Technological University, and the Institute for Advanced Studies in Princeton. He has also spoken at dozens of events for companies such as Akamai, Alcatel-Lucent, AT&T, Autodesk, Cisco, EMC, Hitachi Data Systems, HP, IBM, Parallels/Odin, SAP, and Symantec, and financial services and investor conferences such as for the Milken Institute, Credit Suisse, Oppenheimer & Co., SWIFT SIBOS, Buy-Side Technology, and the American Institute of CPA's Annual CFO Conference. Weinman has also keynoted and presented at numerous industry, analyst, and publisher events such as South by Southwest, Mobile World Congress, International Telecoms Week, Gigaom Structure, Dublin Web Summit, The Green Grid, Argyle Executive Forum, the Churchill Club, the Industrial Research Institute, Forbes Telecosm, Gartner ITxpo, 451 Group, Tier 1 Research, numerous IEEE conferences, Cloud Connect, Cloudscape, Cloud Expo, Interop, TM Forum, the Pacific Telecommunications Council, VentureBeat CloudBeat, Light Reading/Heavy Reading, Yankee Group, HMG Strategy, UBM, IDG, CDM, and Capacity Media, in dozens of countries on six continents. He has also appeared on broadcast television in the United States, Europe, and Asia, and in dozens of web videos including the *New York Times* Timescast and TheStreet.com, and is frequently quoted in the press.

Weinman received a Bachelor of Science and Master of Science in Computer Science from Cornell University and the University of Wisconsin-Madison respectively, and completed Executive Education at the International Institute for Management Development in Lausanne, Switzerland. He has been awarded 21 U.S. and international patents in a variety of technologies including distributed and cloud computing, data networking, mobile communications, encryption, and search algorithms.

He has three wonderful daughters, one wonderful mom, and lives in New Jersey. He can be found on Twitter as @joeweinman, via his website, joeweinman.com, or on a United flight heading somewhere or other.

INDEX